Practically Profound

A sign-post is in order if, under normal circumstances, it fulfills its purpose.

—Ludwig Wittgenstein, *Philosophical Investigations*

Practically Profound

Putting Philosophy to Work in Everyday Life

James Hall

ROWMAN & LITTLEFIELD PUBLISHERS, INC.
Lanham • Boulder • New York • Toronto • Oxford

ROWMAN & LITTLEFIELD PUBLISHERS, INC.

Published in the United States of America
by Rowman & Littlefield Publishers, Inc.
A wholly owned subsidary of The Rowman & Littlefield Publishing Group, Inc.
4501 Forbes Boulevard, Suite 200, Lanham, Maryland 20706
www.rowmanlittlefield.com

PO Box 317
Oxford
OX2 9RU, UK

British Library Cataloguing in Publication Information Available

Library of Congress Cataloging-in-Publication Data

Hall, James, 1933–
  Practically profound : putting philosophy to work in everyday life / James Hall.
      p. cm.
  Includes bibliographical references and index.
  ISBN 0-7425-4326-9 (cloth : alk. paper) — ISBN 0-7425-4327-7 (pbk. : alk. paper)
  1. Philosophy.   I. Title.
  B74.H35 2005
  100—dc22   2004019121

Printed in the United States of America

♾™ The paper used in this publication meets the minimum requirements of
American National Standard for Information Sciences—Permanence of Paper
for Printed Library Materials, ANSI/NISO Z39.48-1992.

*This book is for my sons, Christopher, Jonathan, and Trevor
and for my partner and best friend, Myfanwy.*

*It could not have been written without the generous support of
The University of Richmond and of the benefactors of
The James Thomas Chair in Philosophy.*

*I am indebted to The University of Warwick and
The University of Virginia for their hospitality
during various stages of the manuscript's preparation.*

—Richmond, 2005

Contents

Preface

Philosophy: The Profound and the Pedestrian

For many people the very mention of philosophy conjures up an image of graybeards endlessly arguing about obscure topics in words that ordinary folk can't understand. Fortunately, that image is wrongheaded. As I will try to show in this book, philosophy is practical, however profound some of its parts may be; and, with work, even the deepest parts can be made clear.

The variety of things that are called "philosophy" is remarkable. But labels don't always mean what we think they mean. So to avoid confusion later, I will take time to sort out the labels up front—*mis*conceptions first.

1. Misconceptions of Philosophy

A. How we feel about things. People say things like "What is your philosophy of X?" when they really mean "How do you feel about X?"

Eve: "What's your philosophy of education?"

Adam: "Oh, I think education is a great thing."

Using the word "philosophy" this way trivializes the enterprise. In serious contexts, philosophy amounts to a great deal more than this.

B. Worldviews and the meaning of life. Many see philosophy as a quest to find the meaning of life and lay it out in a "big picture" or worldview. "Who are we?" and "Where are we going?" and "Is there any point to it all?" are important questions. But while these questions can be raised philosophically, they can be raised in other ways too—religiously, morally, politically, and scientifically, at least. So we cannot safely assume, simply because someone asks, "What is life all about?" that he is doing *philosophy*.

A Story. A pilgrim decided to give away everything and go into the high mountains to find out what life is. After forty years of wandering, he returned home old and bent. The whole village, on hearing the story of his travail, insisted, "Tell us the answer! What is life?" "Life is a deep, deep well," the pilgrim replied. But one villager retorted, "That's silly. Life isn't a deep, deep well!" And, after a moment of head scratching, the traveler allowed, "Come to think of it, I believe you're right."

C. Skepticism. When philosophers do their work, they are cautious about what they assume and how they reason. As a result, they frequently arrive at skeptical positions. This skepticism can encourage people to think that philosophy is essentially corrosive and belief destroying and that philosophers "don't believe in anything." But philosophers do take positive positions, too, as we shall see.

D. Reflective beliefs about this and that. Philosophy is sometimes identified with the reflective beliefs held about some (usually important) slice of the world. But this is misleading, too. Why call religious beliefs, scientific beliefs, or historical beliefs *philosophy*? Why not call them *religion, science,* and *history*?

E. Inquiry in general. In the ninth or tenth century, "What is philosophy?" would have been easier to answer than it is today. Back then, "philosophy" as an umbrella term covered all that we now call science, mathematics, logic, ethics, history, and religion. Persons engaged in almost any reflective pursuit were called philosophers. But as the centuries went by, things tightened up. As thinkers had more ideas, found more facts, and organized them better, enough data, technique, and literature accumulated to be more than any individual or group could handle. *Disciplines* began to coalesce and gain standing in their own right.

This process is still going on. One of the more recent disciplines to coalesce is psychology—an enterprise housed within the philosophy department of many a university until the early decades of the twentieth century. So it is not surprising that philosophy and psychology still have interests in common—the phenomena of belief and knowledge, for example. But their approaches are different. Psychology, on the whole, has become empirical. Its primary focus on epistemic matters is on how beliefs come about and how the believing organism functions (and malfunctions). In contrast, philosophy looks at epistemic matters from a very different perspective, as we shall see.

The more data that are assigned to free standing disciplines, the less scope there is for philosophy in this old inclusive sense. So philosophy has narrowed as a result of the historical division, specialization, and distribution of intellectual labor. Indeed, were it not for the fact that philosophy has something to say about a particular *kind* of question that connects with *all* of the spun-off disciplines, we could imagine philosophy narrowing away to nothing.

F. The history of ideas and great thinkers. Many people assume that studying philosophy amounts to examining the ideas of the great thinkers. There is much to be said for such an enterprise. But while the ideas of Plato, Aristotle, Descartes, Kant, Hume, Sartre, Wittgenstein, and others are worth careful study, the value of that study resides more in exploring the *issues* they grappled with, rather than the positions they took on them.

2. Focusing In on a Different Conception of Philosophy

So far, I have suggested some things that philosophy is *not*. But I have not said what philosophy *is*. I will approach this by identifying four different kinds of inquiry. By sorting these out, I will bring the special character of philosophical inquiry into focus.

A. Questions of fact. Finding out, describing, and distributing information about what is and what is not the case are tasks in which everyone is involved. But, since there are a great many facts to be discovered, described, and distributed, there is no way for any one person to do it all. So we share the facts out to the disciplines: one packet to the physicists, another to the chemists, and others to the microeconomists and agronomists, and others. In the end, there are hundreds of such fact packets more or less systematically parceled out to specialists in hundreds of different enterprises. In addition, there are also facts that have no special disciplines to cover them. These are the ordinary facts that concern people in their everyday enterprises. Even success or failure at something as ordinary as crossing the street depends on acquiring facts and taking them into account. Otherwise, we are liable to be run over by a truck.

It is possible that at some imaginary time all facts were of equal concern to everyone. But today the electricians get one set and the brain surgeons another. This is not to say that we can safely ignore the areas that have been parceled out to others. But there *are* specialists to give them special attention; and we can normally confine our own responsibility to taking into account what the experts discover, describe, and make public.

We might also suppose that in the parceling out there would surely have been some special bundle for the philosophers. Philosophy, after all, is one more discipline in the curriculum, one more suite of offices in the faculty building. Like physics and chemistry, it must have its special bag of facts to discover, describe, and publish. But, after the various specialists have preempted the physical structure of things, the causal connections of things, and the history of things, I wouldn't know where to look to find the philosophers' fact domain. Setting up philosophy as another fact-gathering discipline is prevented simply because the facts are being rather well gathered already, without philosophy's help. (That is not to say that people have all the facts in hand. But it is to say that there is a fairly decent distribution of labor in terms of which people are pursuing the facts they don't yet have.)

But that is disturbing. If we visualize the facts like a pie to be sliced up and passed out, must we conclude that by the time any philosophers get to the head of the line, all of the slices are gone? And, if so isn't it incumbent on a philosopher who has any integrity at all to go out and get an honest job? Surely it is not philosophy's task to search intellectual refuse bins for leftovers or to panhandle for scientific spare change.

But inquiry into what is and what is not the case is not the only kind of inquiry there is. When I agonize over what to cook for dinner (shall it be Beef Wellington or a can of chili?), when I try to figure out what topics to include in Philosophy 101 (should I do minds and machines or save that for 102?), and when I try to decide whether to run away with Nicole Kidman (if the opportunity should ever arise), I am dealing with important questions that are not even remote attempts at discovering, describing, or distributing facts. These are not matters of *What is the case?* but of *What shall I make to be the case?*

B. Questions of value. Questions of value are not limited to concerns about what is *morally* good or bad. Values and value judgments include verdicts like *true* and *false*, *coherent* and *incoherent*, *beautiful* and *ugly*, and lots more. Whatever values are talked about, it would take an expert in the area to do for them what the appropriate experts have done for the various facts: get them laid out straight enough that the rest of us can rely on their maps. It is not obvious that such value experts exist, however, especially in the moral realm.

I do not mean to suggest that there are no specialists in *any* value area. There are, for example, literary critics (people who are expert to some extent in making a certain kind of esthetic appraisal), able jurists (people who are experts in the formulation of legal judgments), and others. Philosophy, however, has often been identified with value inquiry in the ethical and esthetic realms. One reason for this may be that there is no group of commonly recognized specialists to whom such enterprises can be definitively assigned. Many religious leaders would gladly accept the mantle; but since there are many religions, and many people who recognize no religion at all, there is no general consensus to let them take it on. Shall it then go to the philosophers by default?

In terms of the semihistorical principle that the label "philosopher" be given to reflective people who think about whatever has not yet been assigned to someone else, there is some cultural inertia favoring such a view. Still, conditions are unfavorable for philosophers to seek recognition as moral or esthetic experts. If philosophers (or theologians, politicians, or any other specialist group for that matter) are set up as moral mapmakers, the door would be opened to the potentially serious exploitation of ordinary people. Establishing anyone to sort out moral values for the masses would be a major step toward ideological tyranny, and totally destructive to the integrity and liberty of conscience that make people *persons*. Values are (and need to be) sufficiently *everybody's* business to exclude the would-be guru.

I do not mean to suggest that philosophy has no contribution to make in this arena. It can significantly help in value explorations because people who are philosophically perceptive are likely to do a better job of sorting things out for themselves than people who are not. In a later chapter, I will show some specific ways that philosophy can contribute to making value judgments coherent and reasonable; but no part of that will encourage (or even permit) the notion of giving philosophers responsibility for mapping values in the way that physicists have been given responsibility for mapping energy events within the atom.

However, even if philosophers don't have an area of the facts that is especially theirs or a special handle on evaluation, maybe they can preempt the "why?" questions. Surely both facts and values need *explaining*.

C. Questions of explanation. Everyone asks "why?" all the time; but if we want to do so fruitfully, we need to recognize that "why" has two distinctly different senses—one cast in terms of detailed theory-driven descriptions, the other in terms of goals, purposes, or "ends."

1) The first sort of "why?" is an important extension of questions of fact. *Explaining*, in this sense, starts with observing and describing events and proceeds to some organization of the results. Eventually, a great deal more than observation, description, and taxonomy is involved. It is only when inquiry goes beyond making lists and sorting data, and attempts to fashion abstract and theoretical explanations, that we see the beginnings of science, with all its astounding integrative scope.

Its abstract and theoretical features can be quite startling to anyone fixed on the notion that science is merely "fact collection." It will even include claims that are not apparently about *anything* observable. When physicists say the energy of a physical system is equal to its mass times a constant squared, they use no term that denotes anything we can see, taste, smell, feel, or hear. They are talking about observable things (e.g., atom bombs, the sun); but only in a very indirect sense of "about."

Some might think that anyone who constructs an abstract explanatory theory is doing philosophy, but we should guard against any wholesale transfer of the explanatory level of factual inquiry out of the scientists' hands. On the whole, it is best to leave even abstract and theoretical inquiry in the hands of those who are well versed in the data from which the theories were abstracted (or to cover which they were created).

2) The "why?" questions that seek goals, purposes, and ends are problematic. To begin with, in any given case, they may have no answer. To ask "why X?" in the sense of "what is X *for*?" presumes that X is "for" *something*. If X is *not* "for" something, then spending much time and effort trying to find out *what* it is "for" is footless.

For example, if asked why a flame rises, we would do well to accept a descriptive or theoretical account that talks about the diminished weight per volume of an expanded fluid, rather than trying to discover either the fire's intentions or its destiny.

Where there is good reason to think that intentions *are* at work, or ends in play, the "why?" questions are probably best answered by psychologists and historians, or by others who are familiar with the sort of situation under examination. There seems to be little room for philosophers here.

But what of those times when the "why?" question seeks some "ultimate" destiny or goal? To whom should we turn? Well, where does the expertise lie? If we are to call anyone an expert on such matters, they need to show us that they have some leverage on the issues in question. At the very least, they should have access to clear and relevant evidence.

They should also be experienced with questions of the kind and should have a good record of success with them. But, what would give would-be experts-about-the-ultimate the leverage that they need? What sort of evidence *could* count when deciding between alternative ultimate "whys?" How could success be measured here? If there are no straightforward answers to such questions, then there are no

> **A Useful Distinction**
>
> A genealogical analysis seeks the historical ancestry of an act or idea while a logical or semantic one seeks its meaning or grounds. For example, when Socrates was in jail, one could have asked how that came to be (what caused it), or for his reasons for being there—very different matters indeed!

experts, either. Consequently, this kind of "why" can best be left to people in general. There is no reason whatever to turn it over to "professionals" when there are no criteria for professional competence. I do not think that philosophers have any *less* access to these "whys" than other folk. They can talk about the purpose of it all just as well as a chemist or a plumber. But they have no special license to do so.

But, if philosophers are not in charge of facts or values, and can claim no special leverage on either descriptive or purposive explanations, then what do they do? In a nutshell, they analyze and clarify the conceptual foundations and tools of all the various concept-using enterprises in which people pursue facts, values, and explanations. Their work is semantic and logical, not genealogical or historical. It amounts to examining what basic concepts *mean*, what they *presume*, what they *imply*, and how they *relate to other concepts in use*. Now, this is not transparent when stated "in a nutshell," so we need to unpack it and make clear exactly what is going on when philosophers ask what I shall call "metaquestions."

D. Metaquestions. Plumbers use tools. The quality of their work depends in part on the diversity and quality of the tools they use. A very high-class plumber might hire a helper to work with her, take care of her tools for her, and repair them when they need it. (The helper sees to it that the wrenches are in the right slots, that the pipe-breaker chain is well greased, etc.) An ordinary plumber does not need many tools; nor are the needed ones terribly complex and difficult to keep sorted out and in working order. But in the case of the extraordinary plumber, we can clearly distinguish the job that she herself is doing (using the tools) and the job that her helper is doing (keeping the tools sorted out and in good repair).

Physicists use tools, too. As with plumbers, the tools in use depend on the job being done: voltmeters, accelerators, cloud chambers, pulleys, whatever. In addition to such material tools, there is another set in use, too. Though intangible, these tools are no less important, given the sorts of jobs that physicists do. These are the concepts or ideas that physicists use in their work.

For instance, imagine a physicist watching light flashes in a Wilson Cloud Chamber that are said to track certain particle collisions. She is trying to decide whether the π-whoozons that were described in a recent lab report are anything more than the product of the student researcher's imagination and desire for a good grade. She is using the cloud chamber, power sources, and many other devices. But she is also using a tremendous, theory-laden conceptual apparatus about atoms, and their constituent parts, and energy and its transformations. A complex mathematical apparatus comes into play, too. And that is only the beginning. Indeed, the conceptual tools that she is using far exceed, both in number and complexity, the concrete artifacts that she is manipulating with her hands.

When physicists use a conceptual apparatus, as they must, they are not alone. Part of the equipment that all people bring to their tasks is a conceptual apparatus of ideas, theories, and terms. We manipulate this (with our minds rather than our hands) in every area of description, appraisal, and explanation—whether we are doing history, religion, law, art, psychology, or whatever else. Indeed, consider anyone who pursues *any* question of fact, value, or explanation. They all apply some set of concepts to some set of data in order to describe, evaluate, explain, and exploit it.

I will call all such concept-using enterprises *base level* and note that the conceptual apparatus of any base-level enterprise can be taken as the *subject matter* of a very special kind of inquiry in its own right.

For instance, the physicist's notions of space, time, and causation can all be usefully examined. We can sort them out, make them clear, discover their logic, see what they presume and entail, and see how they relate to other concepts in use. Consider the concept of causation, for instance. It is implicit in almost all scientific inquiry. But, as a matter of fact, its precise meaning is far from clear. We may not have practical troubles using it; but, when we try to spell out exactly what is meant by saying, "X causes Y," difficulties appear.

> *Example.* Ann drops an anvil on her foot, breaking her toes. Bill asks, "What's wrong with your foot?" Ann answers, "I broke my toes by dropping an anvil on my foot." But Bill says, "How does dropping an anvil on your foot cause broken toes?"

We can describe much of what happened in terms of what we can observe: an anvil falling toward a location occupied by toes, an anvil passing through the space most proximate to the toes, and (subsequently) a set of broken toes and an anvil at rest. But is that an explanation of how the anvil caused the toes to break? Indeed, is such an explanation possible without leaving what we can *observe* in the dust?

We can observe the anvil, the movement, the toes, the fracture, and the pain signals; but there does not seem to be anything that we can point to and say, "There is the causing." So what do we say?

If pressed, can we get away with explaining the notion of causing in terms of the spatial and temporal correlation of some X and Y, (i.e., events occurring together, or in immediate sequence, at a certain level of regularity)? That avoids an embarrassingly fruitless search for little "cause hooks" sticking out of the anvil or toes, or "cause beams" reaching across space. But will it do?

Is X causing Y *just* a regular correlation of events? That seems weak; for if we try to understand the notion of causation in this way, we are soon embarrassed by the hordes of correlations of this very sort that *occur*, but are not thought to be "causal" in any way at all.

> *Example.* Once upon a time, some people were upset by solar eclipses, believing that a dragon swallows the sun from time to time. So when there was a solar eclipse, they would beat on a special drum in an intricate rhythm to frighten the dragon away. It always worked. That is to say, the eclipse always ended. Every time. There was an absolute correlation. But did beating the drum really cause the eclipse to end? If not, then "cause" does not mean "high-level correlation."

The point here is that the concept of causation we use in saying X caused Y is not as transparent as we might think. Indeed, the concept of causation is a major issue for anyone who would unravel the conceptual underpinnings of science. But physicists use a great many other concepts, too, many of which have their own complexities, problems, and paradoxes.

Because of this, a physicist can become highly interested in the conceptual apparatus of her own enterprise (how the concepts work and what kind of sense they make), perhaps even more than in the direct application of that apparatus to describe and explain events in the world. As her interest focuses on her methodology and tools, she begins to engage in "metalevel" inquiry— sorting out, examining, analyzing, and clarifying the conceptual apparatus that is used in her base-level inquiries.

But, even as a physicist may study as well as use her conceptual apparatus, so too for historians, theologians, jurists, and others. In this way, second-order (metalevel) inquiry into the conceptual underpinnings of most of the areas of human investigation and activity arises.

It is this second-order inquiry that is the essential and central territory with which philosophers are concerned. This is why most philosophers do "philosophy of . . ."—philosophy of history, philosophy of religion, philosophy of mathematics, philosophy of science, philosophy of law, or philosophy of some other base-level enterprise. They are, then, rather like my imaginary assistant plumber who kept the wrenches where they belonged and made sure that they were working properly.

Unfortunately, this metaphor conjures up an image in which philosophers look like conceptual paramedics. Press the metaphor, and we can wonder where the little redbrick building is that houses the philosophical rescue squad. But of course it does not work that way. Many scientists simply do the philosophical work themselves, changing hats rather than calling in helpers. Indeed, much philosophical work is done by persons who are both philosopher and chemist, philosopher and theologian, philosopher and historian, and so forth.

When this is so two areas of inquiry are pursued by the same person:

- the application of theories and concepts to describe and explain events that occur, and
- the exploration of that theoretical and conceptual equipment itself to clarify and elucidate it.

The latter may sound very abstract and remote. What ordinary persons would want to spend their time asking second-order questions about the concepts employed in (say) chemistry? But the formal sciences are not the only base-level enterprises people pursue. Every day, every person is involved in crucial base-level activities: evaluating, describing, and predicting ordinary everyday affairs. In doing so they use indispensable conceptual tools that may not be as complex, quantitative, or abstract as those of the formal sciences, but that are highly problematic nonetheless.

I look at a sculpture and mutter that it is "terrible," using a value concept to make a judgment. My grandchild watches *The Apprentice,* and I wonder what role this fantasy "reality" is playing in her forming self-image. I decide to return to England; and so I reorganize my budget, redescribing and restringing a skein of facts and would-be facts in terms of a remarkably complex network of quantitative and temporal concepts. Or I decide to get married. Or divorced. Scientists are not the only ones who use concepts. Scientific concepts are not the only ones that need probing. If we would carry out *any* task effectively, the meaning and the connections of the concepts employed must be sorted out, clarified, and understood.

The most universal conceptual tool in everyday use is language itself. Though familiar enough, it is still problematic—shaping in ways that cannot easily be detected or controlled what we can say, what we can think, and (consequently) what we can achieve in all the other tasks that we perform through its use. It was there before we arrived. It is the matrix in which everyone must do his work, whatever that work is.

Example. I describe my office wall by saying that it *is green*. In doing so I follow the structure of English that treats objects as passive things to which properties are quietly attached. A Chinese speaker, however, would say that his wall *greens*—seeing (and describing) it in the agent and action structure built into his language. We bring this passive or active "stance" to our walls. We do not find it there.

So even when we have just begun to observe what is happening, ineluctable conceptual structures are already in play. Given a language, descriptions, evaluations, and explanations will all follow its grammar, for good or ill. Consequently, if language (or the use of it) is flawed or unclear, experience (and accounts of it) will be muddled, too.

Example. In English (and Greek), a common muddle occurs when we take the apparent "naming" function of terms in the language too seriously, believing that there must be something that each term names. This can generate whole books about The Nothing, and generations of argument about where to find The Good, The True, and The Beautiful.

It is not just the syntactical and semantic rules of language that generate problems. There are also many specific uses of it that are far from transparent.

Example. Consider the word "duty." Most people can handle "I can't go on the picnic. Duty calls." But there is a difference between asking, "What is my duty?" and asking, in a different tone of voice, "What is Duty?" It is easy to give a list of duties. But once we do, can we say why these items are on the list and others are not, or why some circumstances generate duties but others don't? What, precisely, are people doing when they invoke "duty?"

Our facile use of a language does not guarantee that we understand it. There can be philosophical work to be done, even in areas where least suspected. Thus, for ordinary men and women, there is a need for a "meta" dimension to intellectual life—not to sort out Freud's psychosexual theory of human development or Einstein's general theory of relativity (though they may well need it), but to clarify the assumptions and implications of our own religious, political, cultural, and educational beliefs, actions, and commitments as citizens, parents, workers, and choice makers. The formal sciences are not the only things worth doing wisely and well.

So people should study philosophy. But the point is not to enlist them in the professional enterprise. The point is to get them to give philosophical (metalevel) reflective attention to their own concerns. Doing that, in the same way that philosophical reflection helped Einstein and Freud do physics and psychology, will help them with their own more everyday but no-less-important tasks.

3. What Kinds of Situations Trigger Metalevel Questions?

A. Conflicting frameworks ("meld failure"). Since people are language users, observation and description involve more than passively jotting down facts. "Facts," in fact, are the product of complex interpretive operations. We structure them in the process of experiencing them and structure them again in describing, cataloging, and explaining them. We never go anywhere without taking our neurological, linguistic, and conceptual equipment along. This would not cause problems if people dealt with all their facts in a single framework. But they use different ones for different purposes; and when they conflict metaquestions come up.

> *Example.* Things don't "just happen." They have causes. So if the city library blew up, everyone would agree something caused it to happen. If the fire chief said it had no cause at all, the City Council would question his competence; and common sense says they would be right to do so: there must be a cause, whether the chief is clever enough to identify it or not.

Even unusual things don't "just happen." Spontaneous combustion may sound like "no cause at all;" but it isn't, except, perhaps, for people who allegedly ignite while watching TV. Actually, even for *that* kind of urban myth, causation is presumed: *pyrotrons,* of course. (If this piques your interest, read Joe Nickell's "Incredible Cremations: Investigating Spontaneous Combustion Deaths" and his other articles listed in "Works Mentioned" at the end of this volume.)

On the other hand, under normal circumstances, people are held responsible for the consequences of their actions. If a customer slapped an officious postal clerk, she would be arrested and questioned. Suppose that she is not psychotic, in a hypnotic trance, or suffering compulsions from faulty toilet training, and so forth. Suppose that, instead, she simply decided after reasoned deliberation that the world would be a better place if this petty bureaucrat got his comeuppance and acted on her decision. She would go to trial, and common sense says rightly so. She is responsible for her actions and must face their consequences.

But when we put the commonplace ideas of causation and responsibility *together*, there is a problem.

> Slapping a postal clerk is an event in the world.
> So there were earlier events that caused it.
> But those events had prior causes, too (etc.).
> So the trail of the assault's causes goes all the way back to events that occurred before the slapper was even born.
> But how can she be responsible for an act that was locked in place in 1970 (or, for that matter, 1066)?

Should we, then, abandon the notion that normal humans are responsible for what they do, or should we keep that notion and abandon the notion of universal causation instead?

But who wants to abandon *either* of these notions, thus allowing either a) that some events in the world occur without causes or b) that no one is ever responsible for anything he does?

So reflecting on human events in terms of judicial and moral concepts *and* empirical and scientific ones generates a cramp of tremendous practical importance for which there is no easy or obvious analgesic. The entire Western understanding of human society is at stake here: law, the political system, the nature of education—indeed, the fundamental fabric of argument and evidence on which the commerce of ideas is based. We will not find a way out by collecting forty more events to see if they have causes, or by rounding up forty more human acts to see if they are responsible. We already have all the facts we need. The problem is what to do with the facts we have: how to make sense of them and how to make them cohere and work together. This is the very model of a philosophical issue.

B. Unforeseen implications. There are many presuppositions packed into everyday thinking—things that we simply assume and use. Sometimes they generate difficulties; especially when we discover previously unrealized implications that conflict with observed facts. When this happens, radical upheavals threaten. In science, it can mean a "revolution."

Zeno, the ancient sage, is remembered for his "paradoxes"—conflicts that arise between what some supposedly self-evident mathematical assumptions say and what "any fool can plainly see." One of these paradoxes is his story of Achilles and the tortoise.

> *Example.* Any fool knows that almost any human can outrun any tortoise. Certainly swift Achilles can. Consider a case, however, in which the organizers (who want to be reasonably sporting) give the tortoise (call it Bixby) a small head start. The question to answer is: "How long will it take Achilles to pass Bixby, once he has started running?" Common sense (and our observations, were we to watch them run) tells us *not very long;* but Zeno (following some mathematical reasoning of a very elementary sort) says *forever.* That seems absurd on its face; but it is easy to see how it arises.

Remember that the tortoise has a head start. So at the time Achilles starts to run, Bixby is not where Achilles is (D-0), but at another point, further down the track (D-1).

Achilles may run as fast as he likes. However fast he runs, it will take him some time to get to D-1 (where Bixby was when Achilles started). Equally obvious, however slowly Bixby runs, he will have proceeded to some more distant point (D-2) during the time that it takes Achilles to get from D-0 to D-1. D-2 may not be very far from D-1, but if Bixby moves 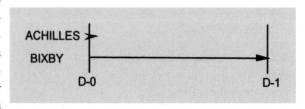 at all, he will have covered *some* distance. So when Achilles gets where Bixby was (D-1), Bixby is no longer there. He is at D-2.

But, of course, however fast Achilles is running, it will take him some further time to get from D-1 to D-2. And (however short that distance is and however

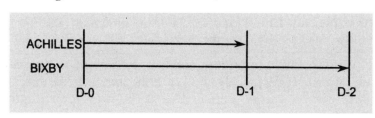

fast Achilles is running), during the time he uses, Bixby will have covered some additional distance. So by the time poor Achilles gets to D-2, Bixby is not there. Indeed, *whenever* Achilles gets where Bixby was, Bixby is gone.

So it is clear that Achilles can never catch Bixby when the latter has a head start. But observation shows that this is wrong, even if it is not obvious just *how* it is wrong. Achilles will be observed to pass Bixby in just a few paces. So either something is wrong with the observations, or with the way the problem is set up. The observations seem hard to dispute; but an adequate reformulation of the problem's setup will force a revision of the entire theoretical conceptualization in terms of which arithmetic is applied to space and time.

The practical outcome is that we are eventually obliged to abandon at least one of the commonplace assumptions about space, time, and arithmetic; perhaps the assumption that units of distance can be infinitely divided, replacing it with the counterassumption (that is not very intuitive) that they cannot—that there is a point at which it is all gone. (Figuring out different analyses of what is wrong here provides pleasant (and important) exercise for logicians and mathematicians. See Adolph Grunbaum, *Modern Science and Zeno's Paradoxes*.)

So discovering a conflict between observation and the basic scientific assumptions of the day (here about space, time, and quantity) forces us to reflect on, sort out, revise, and rework the concepts in use until the whole conception of the world itself is changed—another model of philosophical inquiry.

C. Incoherence. Sometimes, operating (as we must) with a set of assumptions, we discover an inconsistency entailed by them.

Example. The assumption that every description is either true or false (never both and never neither) generates the famous paradox of the liar, and several others. Here is one: the obverse and reverse of a 3 × 5 card read as follows:

A: "B," the sentence on the other side of this card, is false.

B: "A," the sentence on the other side of this card, is true.

Nothing appears wrong about either of those sentences. They are grammatically well formed, and each one attributes an apparently legitimate property to the other. But, taken jointly, something about them is very wrong indeed:

A says that B is false; and A itself is either true or false. What happens if A is true? Then it is true that B is false. But if B is false, then it is *not* the case that A is true. But if it is not the case that A is true, then A must be false. So it follows that if A is true, then it is false. That does not sound promising; and we get similar results if we start by assuming that A is false.

This is distinctly uncomfortable because it conflicts with a notion packed into the foundation of ordinary logic (the law of noncontradiction) that, if abandoned, seems to put set theory, arithmetic and ordinary verbal argumentation under threat.

As before, the problem here is not one that can be solved by looking in odd corners for more facts, building bigger voltmeters, or buying better glassware. When we try to make sense of apparently absurd facts already in hand, philosophy is at work.

D. Misapplied categories. Sometimes a conceptual apparatus works so well in one area that people want to extend it to others. But that can take the apparatus into areas where it simply doesn't fit, and cause puzzles and cramps. Gilbert Ryle, in *The Concept of Mind,* calls such conceptual allocation errors "category mistakes" and gives many examples.

> *Example (adapting a story by Ryle).* A naïve Virginia high school senior has arranged to come up from Narrows to Richmond to see the university. He does not know what it is; but his parents want him to matriculate, and he is curious. We can imagine him roaming from the cloister to the green, scrutinizing the chapel, exploring the tunnels, circling Ryland and Puryear Halls. But he comes away frustrated because, he claims, "I kept asking people to show me the university, and they all looked puzzled and hurried away."

The problem here is that the lad is conceptualizing in an inappropriate way. The concept "university" is a *system* concept, not a *thing* concept. A university is not an object, but a peculiar structure of many objects. So to try to treat a university as though it were a thing—"You will find it just west of the library and north of the commons"—is simply absurd.

"System" or "structure" concepts are common. Still, on trying to deal with new and unfamiliar data, we are much more likely to fall back on "thing" concepts. They are that much more common. People even do it with old data that ought to be familiar. This is why any number of quite sophisticated people have spent years trying to "locate" the mind.

Thus, we can be pushed into philosophical reflection when inept categorization generates odd questions like "Where is the mind?" or "How much does -2 weigh?" or "Does virtue sleep late on Thursdays?" Since virtue neither sleeps late nor rises early, and since -2 does not weigh, trying to apply such predicates to them generates obvious gibberish. Granted, in the case of "mind" the gibberish is not that obvious. It is both subtle and comfortably familiar. All the more reason, in that case, to reflect on your categories before you try to use them—that is, to do some philosophy.

Project for Math Lovers

Look up Nikolai Ivanovich Lobachevski, Farkas Bolyai, and Georg Friedrich Riemann. Bolyai and Lobachevski (perhaps independently) constructed hyperbolic geometries in which an infinite number of parallels could exist. Riemann constructed an elliptical geometry in which no parallels can exist.

Fun for Everyone

Listen to "Lobachevski," Tom Lehrer's tribute to plagiarism. It should be in the record collection of your library. Or look at the score in *Too Many Songs by Tom Lehrer.*

E. Conceptual experimentation.

I have indicated four different situations in which second-order inquiry is forced by circumstance: where two systems of concepts refuse to meld, where traditional assumptions are crippled by refined observation, where logical inconsistency is found buried in a basic way of seeing things, and where concepts are applied in alien territory. There is also a fifth way that conceptual puzzles arise—meddling with concepts that pique our curiosity.

Consider, for instance, Euclidian geometry. One of its foundations is called the "parallel postulate." It says that given a line in a plane and a point in that plane but not on that line, exactly one line can be drawn through the point that is parallel to that line (i.e., does not intersect it, even if infinitely extended). Compared to the other Euclidian postulates, this one is not strongly intuitive. Consequently, it would be cleaner to derive it as a theorem; but we can't do that. So various inventive mathematicians have suggested trying different postulates in its place. One suggestion allows *no* parallels. Another allows as many as we care to construct. While such maneuvers are not very "commonsensical," curiosity urges us to see what happens if we bend the conceptual apparatus a little. In this case, the bending generates two completely new geometries—both coherent, though neither is obviously compatible with the other or with Euclid. Such alternative geometries are interesting as they stand; but they are much more than that. They show (against Descartes) that Euclid's geometry is not an exclusive set of necessarily true descriptions of the world, but one of several alternative systems that fit it (or some part of it) *contingently.* That makes the truth of any particular geometry an empirical matter; and that is a *real* conceptual revolution.

So when people begin to tinker with assumptions, even ancient ones, they may create whole new thought systems that are not only neat, but may apply to and be true of (some part of) the world in which we live.

We have seen five different kinds of situations in which philosophical issues (metaquestions) arise and are worthwhile. Consequently, we have seen that while philosophy is not a rival to science or, necessarily, a compendium of wisdom, neither is it an idle pastime. Indeed, for the professional philosopher and the philosophical lay person alike, it is a crucial means to a practical end: improving the clarity, scope, mesh, and fertility of all our thoughts and beliefs so as to improve the performance of all the tasks in which such thoughts and beliefs are involved.

In the chapters ahead, we shall proceed to do philosophy, raising and answering questions about a variety of important facets of the conceptual world we share: for example, how the concepts of *belief, knowledge, evidence, truth, subjectivity, certainty,* and *error* can be understood in a culture dominated by talk of paradigms and relativity, how *facts* and *values* relate, how *human nature* can be understood, how to make sense of *responsibility,* and how to find an intelligible model for a *good life.* These are profound issues, indeed, but I think that all will agree that they are practical as well.

I

BELIEF

1

Are Some Beliefs Better Than Others?

The present era is marked by an intense struggle between advocates of entrenched political, ethnic, and gender loyalties and others who affirm "multiculturalism and diversity." Though the struggle is contemporary, many of the weapons in play are ancient. It is a new arena for old arguments, as people try to shake off both paralytic skepticism and foolish gullibility to take reasonable stands on issues that count.

Whether to trust *any* of their beliefs is not an issue that vexes most people; but for every belief, however plausible, there is a doubter out there somewhere:

- Skepticism about esthetic appraisals is almost universal.
- Skepticism about religious belief is rampant.
- Many take a very dim view of moral pronouncements.
- Doubts about history and the social sciences are common.
- Few in the mainstream are skeptical about the sciences, but a "new age" minority calls even them into question.
- Fewer still dispute arithmetic.
- Only the dysfunctional worry about what day it is.
- Some philosophers escalate the conflict until it is completely general: can we reliably believe anything at all?

Faced off against each regional skeptic are champions who claim clear and objective justification for each epistemic locality. The conflict between the skeptics and champions is intense and deeply felt, and its resolution is often highly problematic.

How *should* we decide what to believe? Where can we find guiding principles for belief that are tight enough to rule out the tooth fairy and the Easter bunny, but not so tight as to leave us frozen with anxiety over where to catch the bus or how to tie our shoes? Finding some guiding principles is the point of the next several chapters. Then I will turn to *knowledge*.

1. What (If Anything) Should We Believe?

A. What is it to believe "X"? With regard to states of affairs in general (i.e., "matters of fact" or "what happens"), believing "X" amounts to expecting to experience X (or an implication of "X") if and when we are in a position to do so. For instance, believing "there is a sniper in the library tower" amounts to expecting to see a person there with a gun, who is taking shots at those who pass by (if we go and look). Or, saying "Charlottesville is closer to Richmond than Chapel Hill is" amounts to expecting to see that the circle intersecting Charlottesville falls within the circle intersecting Chapel Hill (if we drew two such circles on a map, centered on Richmond), or expecting to get to Charlottesville more quickly than to Chapel Hill (if we drove from Richmond to each of those destinations at a constant speed). Belief about matters of fact is a matter of experiential expectations. All utterances do not express beliefs about matters of fact, but this chapter focuses on the ones that allegedly do. Later, in chapter 10, we will look at those that express appraisals. Many of them merely voice a preference of one state of affairs over others, but some seem to assert the occurrence of "normative facts" (i.e., that certain states of affairs *deserve* to be preferred).

> ### Three Useful Notions
>
> Necessary conditions are ones that have to be met to achieve some result. They should not be confused with sufficient conditions (those which are enough to achieve some result). For instance, U.S. citizenship is a necessary condition for becoming president of the United States. A candidate for president must be a citizen. Being a citizen is not enough, though. If it were, then every U.S. citizen would be president.
>
> The word "epistemic" comes from a Greek term that means "having to do with belief." The "*non*-epistemic" includes obvious things like feelings and attitudes; but it also includes notions (such as attitudes) that *look* like beliefs, but aren't.
>
> The word "cognitive" comes from a Greek root that is common to English words that have to do with <u>kn</u>owing: "re<u>cogn</u>ition" and "a<u>gn</u>ostic" for instance. It means "having to do with knowledge."

B. A necessary condition of belief. One obvious necessary condition of believing X is that the claim "X" must carry some epistemic freight, that is, it must assert the occurrence of some state of affairs that can be expected. But to do that, it has to have some *cognitive* content. That is, in order for it to have content that *can* be believed it must have content that *could* be known. (If there is nothing there to know, then there is nothing there to believe.) Just why this is so will become clear as the injunction is spelled out in practical terms. Indeed, as will be shown, this necessary condition for belief is also the *first* necessary condition for knowledge itself. It is no easier to know than it is to believe that Tuesday sleeps late or P and not-P, no easier *for me* to have knowledge than belief about five-dimensional geometry, and no easier for *anyone* to have knowledge than belief about The Transcendent Other. (Indeed, it is harder. While belief and knowledge share *one* necessary condition, knowledge has at least two more.)

Now, the *practical* point of an injunction is, generally, to avoid snares, pit-falls, and traps. So what are we being told to avoid here?

1) *Simple nonsense.* Suppose someone asks, "Do you believe the square root of Tuesday is prime" But we cannot believe (or disbelieve) the square root of Tuesday is prime, because the sentence "the square root of Tuesday is prime" conveys no information to accept or reject—no experiences to an-ticipate.

2) *Utterances that carry the wrong kind of freight.* A vigorous "Bravo!" at the end of a concert expresses a positive attitude toward the performance (and a hiss would express a different one). Since an attitude can be shared (or not), we can agree (or disagree) with it. But this agreement (or disagreement) is one of attitude, not belief.

3) *Utterances that don't "make a difference."* Utterances with cognitive con-tent make claims that are either true or false; and whether they are true or false makes a difference that can be discerned. That is why these utterances offer us "something to believe," and why there is no point in trying to believe an utter-ance that makes no such offer.

What is at stake when people argue about whether a ring will oxidize is ob-vious. We know what "oxidize" means and its signs are clear-cut, so there is a clear and discernible difference between a (brass) ring that will and a (gold) ring that won't. What is at stake when people argue about whether tobacco is addictive is not *that* obvious, but it is still within reach. The meaning of "ad-dictive" is less settled and the symptoms of addiction are more ambiguous, but the issue is coming clear. So "that ring will oxidize" and "tobacco is ad-dictive" make an offer, can be argued about, and can be believed. Sometimes, however, there is *nothing* at stake in an utterance, even though there *appears* to be. Some utterances make no offer. So they can't really be believed or ar-gued about.

Example. Certain Freudian claims about human sexual development are com-patible with all possible states of affairs. There is no way to confirm or discon-firm either "penis envy" or "castration complex" because there is no distin-guishable difference between evidence affirming and evidence denying these interpretations of behavior. Exactly opposite behaviors are equally predictable, depending on whether the alleged psychosexual stress is overt or repressed.

In the same way, people who subscribe to a "conspiracy theory" or some other idée fixe seem to take *whatever* happens as confirmation of the notion that possesses them. But any notion that is compatible with all possible states of affairs is a very thin candidate for a working belief. Thus, the demand for cognitive content rules out all utterances that are so loose, poorly formed, or obsessively held that there is no recognizable difference between what would be the case if they were so, and what would be the case if they were not.

4) *Claims that are unintelligible.* This has two dimensions:

- First, for an utterance to be a belief candidate for an individual, it must be intelligible to her. This bars anyone from claiming to believe things that are beyond her own comprehension.

    That is why virtue requires us to abjure opinions about things we do not understand. (The best thing to do with things we don't understand is admit that we don't understand them and get on with our work. As Wittgenstein noted in his *Tractatus,* 7, "What we cannot speak about we must consign to silence.")
- For an utterance to be a viable belief candidate *at all*, it must be intelligible to *someone*. Surely, if X can be believed in the human community, there must be someone in that community to whom the statement "X" makes sense.

5) *Self-contradictions.* If an utterance is to be believed by anyone, it must have some content that lasts longer than it takes to make the noises. We *can't* believe P and not-P, because "P and not P" makes a nearly simultaneous offer and withdrawal of the same information, making an offer with one hand while withdrawing it with the other. There is, consequently, no net content there to believe; and this won't do. A belief claim must be consistent, because an inconsistent claim is epistemically freightless taken as a whole.

> *Example.* When I was an undergraduate, I attended a class whose instructor would write material on the board; but, while he chalked with one hand, he erased with the other. There were never more than three or four words on the board at one time. A person who utters contradictions is something like that: writing and erasing, saying and negating, giving and taking back.

I am not dismissing paradoxes (states of affairs that seem to be describable only in contradictory terms) here, only bona fide contradictions (statements that affirm and deny the same thing). If confronted by a paradox, we should continue inquiry, trying to find a way to resolve it. This amounts to taking paradoxes as occasions for effort and ingenuity, rather than as signs of deep mysteries to groove on. There are two reasons for doing so: a) The contradictory utterance that expresses the paradox cancels itself out, leaving us with no content to groove on; and b) insofar as we affirm the possibility of inconsistencies in the world, we deny the possibility of using logic for truth-preserving inference (since it is possible to deduce any conclusion whatever from inconsistent premises).

Summing up, the injunction that in order to be believed at all a statement must have cognitive content amounts to these practical requirements: it must say something, what it says must be intelligible and consistent, and it must convey experiential expectations, the fulfillment or failure of which makes a discernible difference. A statement that fails to do these things simply offers us nothing to believe.

2. A Principle for Preferring One Belief to Another

There are many reasons why we might prefer one belief to another. Unfortunately, not every reason is a good one. So we need to ask, relative to each sort of reason for preferring one belief to another, "Is this a *good* reason for preferring one belief to another?"

By "good," here, all I have in mind is the mundane, practical notion that things that get us where we want to go are good, and things that don't are bad. In this sense of the term, a *good* reason for preferring a belief would be that it is *effective*.

I am tempted to use the word "reliable" here, but saying that something is reliable is not the same as saying that it is effective. An effective procedure delivers what it is intended to deliver. A reliable procedure simply delivers the same thing time after time. Going to Woolco was reliable. They *never* had what I was looking for. It was ineffective *because* it was so reliable. Statements that are reliable in this way are not effective either. Since what they say is not true, they cannot "deliver."

- Caution is required with such a *contextual* notion of what is good or bad because what will be a good reason for preferring a belief, and what will be a bad one, will depend on where we want to go. People with different agendas may well prefer different beliefs accordingly.
- There are also many other senses of the words "good" and "bad" and many settings in which this limited way of using them would be problematic. Sometimes, there are reasons to claim that an effective method, tool, or belief is a *bad* thing.

  Example. There is a real sense in which an incompetent tyrant is better than a competent one.

- This principle certainly works for evaluating tools.

  Example. In target shooting, a rifle with a rigid barrel is good and a rifle with a floppy one is bad. (With the former, people can control where they shoot and can get better at hitting targets. With the latter, a shooter is just as likely to hit his own foot as the target and has no effective means of "getting better.")

- It works equally well for evaluating reasons for believing.

  Example. I watch an installment of *20/20* in which investigative reporters are examining the way analgesics are advertised on television. They point out a number of things, including the therapeutic indistinguishability of all the different brands of U.S.P. aspirin, and the way in which some drug manufacturers take advertising advantage of the major discounts that they give to hospital dispensaries.

What they say is new to me, and it goes against my own home treatment habits with which I have long been comfortable. (I take Bayer aspirin myself, comfortable with the notion that it works "twice as fast." But since I want my children to have acetaminophen, not aspirin, I give them Tylenol, comfortable with the notion that "more hospitals" use it than other brands.)

So although I am trying to economize, I stay with my existing beliefs and practices *because* they are familiar and comfortable, in spite of the fact that, in doing so, I spend considerably more money than necessary to obtain a constant therapeutic result. But this is following an ineffective preference. I could have eased my pain *and* saved my money by being a little more daring.

- These examples highlight a possible complexity that needs to be kept in mind when weighing beliefs on a scale of instrumental effectiveness. Whether a means is effective depends on where we want to go with it. But people often have more than one target before them (as, in the example, I wanted to stick with what was familiar, to obtain pain relief, and to economize). Some multiple targets are quite compatible (as, in the example, relief and economy were—*both* could have been achieved by using generic analgesics). But some multiple targets conflict with each other (as, in the example, staying with familiar products and saving money did). So we need to prioritize targets that conflict, recognizing that effective means to one need not be effective means to both.
- So in this limited, contextual sense, a reason to prefer one belief over another is a *good* reason if it is instrumentally effective in achieving a believer's agenda. A reason to prefer one belief over another that is *generally* effective in achieving a *wide range* of believers' agendas would be a very good reason indeed.

3. Assessing Some Reasons for Preferring One Belief to Another
In this section, I will examine six possible grounds for belief preference to discover whether (and, if so, when) any are *good* reasons:

- preferring a belief just because it is our preference,
- preferring a belief because it is familiar,
- preferring a belief because it is orthodox,

- preferring a belief because it makes us feel good,
- preferring a belief because it is enabling or validating, and
- preferring a belief because it is true (or probably true).

A. Preferring a belief just because it is our preference. In an extremely truncated sense of "good," we might claim that the very fact that a belief is preferred is *itself* a good reason for preferring it. This won't do at all. First of all, it is question begging. Second, and of greater practical importance, whatever value *might* accrue to a belief on these grounds is trivial when compared to the value that *does* accrue to it on *other* grounds.

> *Example*. Fran favors the belief "Mules have no offspring because they copulate so vigorously" over the belief "Mules have no offspring because they are sterile hybrids," and she offers this ground for the preference: "I *like* it!" But, even if Fran's favored belief were a bit better than its disfavored alternative just because Fran likes it, it is catastrophically worse than its alternative because it is *ineffective*. So "liking it" is not a good reason for adopting a belief unless we do not care whether the belief at stake "works."

Indeed, there is generally little or no reason to think that what we prefer is effective *just because we favor it*, since preferences too often fly in the face of the facts. When they do, any value that accrues from the preference itself is negligible.

B. Preferring a belief because it is familiar. If people did not generally prefer familiar beliefs over unfamiliar ones, there would be little point in advertising. For all of their talk about providing useful information, the hucksters' chief raison d'être is to make their spiels so familiar that they become fixed points in the common worldview. They are, in fact, appallingly good at it, as everyone knows from his own experience.

> *Examples*. I recently found myself whistling a tune. When a colleague asked, "What's that?" I recited (actually sang):
>   *There's something about a Muntz TV that makes you sing its praise.*
>   *There's something about a Muntz TV in oh, so many ways.*
>   *They're sold and serviced straight to you and that's the reason why*
>   *—factory way, no dealer to pay—they cost you less to buy!*
>   *For television quality there's something about a Muntz TV!*
>   Too bad that Muntz went under about forty years ago, and I have to make do with a Magnavox. (But my Magnavox is smart, *very* smart!)
>   I also often hum, "You'll wonder where the yellow went, when you brush your teeth with Pepsodent," even while using Crest. (But Crest *is* recommended by the American Dental Association. It contains Fluoristat!)
>   In my generation we learned to organize our self-image in terms of products: fight halitosis (with Listerine), fight dandruff flakes (with Double Danderine), and fight unruly hair (with Wildroot Creme Oil); and many of us are still fighting.

What's in a Name?

People are more likely to vote for a name they know than an unfamiliar one. But, even if advertising can gain name recognition, some names work against a candidate. For various reasons, Chalmondelay Carrington, Bogdan Fleschieu, and Elmer Feeblebunny are unlikely. (The names are real.)

Decades passed before Mitsubishi could sell cars in the United States under its own name and before English parents resumed naming their sons Adolph. Are any male professional wrestlers named Shirley?

Familiarity is rarely the *only* thing at stake in what people favor.

We are not alone, though. There has been little change over the generations on this. Different images and different brand names, no doubt, but all our psyches are cluttered by planted affinities for things that have been made familiar by advertising. What car do *you* drive? What jeans do *you* wear?

Is this habit of "going with the familiar" effective? It *may* be. After all, things that work are more likely to survive long enough to become familiar than things that don't. If Bon Ami *had* scratched, it might not have lasted so long. Nor would anyone be likely to buy BC Headache Powders if they didn't relieve headaches *at all*. But these are cases of "X is familiar because it has been in use for a long time." How about cases of "X is familiar because someone is spending millions to promote it?"

Name recognition wins elections, sells beer and cigarettes, and keeps people loyal to their long-distance telephone providers, even when those we elect are scoundrels, the products we buy are useless or harmful, and our corporate loyalty is to the ripoff artist with the most insidious jingle.

So when we are tempted to favor a belief *just* because it is familiar, it is useful to stop, think about the phrase "as advertised on TV," and go for a better approach. One better approach would be to examine the *accuracy* of the belief itself (especially, but not only, if it is a belief about products and services that cost money).

C. Preferring a belief because it is orthodox. Many people favor beliefs that are normal, orthodox, or conventional over beliefs that are not. These words are not synonyms. *Normal* has a connotation of good health, *orthodox* of righteousness, and *conventional* of keeping your head down. But they are kin. Those who prefer the normal, the orthodox, or the conventional all want to "do what is done." However, comfort and conformity do not always ride together. There are conformists who chafe and heretics who revel. But there is a certain comfort in conformity for most. Enough, indeed, that even those who chose *not* to conform to mass culture often seek a like-minded group to join. Why do all the radicals have beards?

After looking at some of the reasons why this is so, I will ask "is favoring beliefs on this basis effective?"

1) Why might we prefer orthodox beliefs to unorthodox ones?

a) People usually prefer comfort to discomfort, and orthodox beliefs are often more comfortable than deviant ones. So people usually prefer them. A preference for comfort over discomfort is a basic psychological characteristic of normal animals. It takes complex pathology to generate the opposite. Absent such pathology, it takes complex motivations to *put up with* discomfort when comfort is available. Such pathology and such motivations do occur, of course. There are masochists out there; and there are people with the urge to pursue arduous goals, too. But, most of the time, most people prefer cozy beliefs just as strongly as they prefer cozy slippers. Anyone who says to the shoe seller, "I'll take these, they really pinch my toes" has either a problem or an agenda. The same with beliefs.

One reason why people often find comfort in orthodoxy is a combination of simple inertia and a lazy disposition. In the process of socialization that starts in infancy, we acquire a set of conventional beliefs, practices, and inclinations. To become *un*conventional, we would have to displace them; and that would require effort. It is easier just to "go with the flow."

b) Another motivation for conformity is the belief that conforming is an effective way to achieve various highly desired ends. This can be general or specific.

> *General*: A strong motivation to be conventional, regardless of *what* convention is at issue, is provided by the common human desire to be well liked (or at least accepted) by those around us, coupled with the equally common belief that conforming is an effective way to bring that off. Those people who share that belief will work hard to fit into *whatever* conventional pattern is in place.

> *Specific*: A strong motivation to get up and go to church and affirm the creed on Sunday is provided by the common human desire for bliss and fear of pain, coupled with the less common belief that conforming to these received practices will secure the bliss and avert the pain. Those people who share that belief will work hard to fit into *this* conventional pattern of belief and practice.

It is important to notice that in both these cases the motivation for conformity resides in a combination of:

- a disposition—to be liked or to gain bliss and avert pain; and
- an hypothesis—that orthodoxy itself, or some specific orthodox belief or practice, will achieve what we want. But any hypothesis of the general form "X will achieve Y" is a straightforward prediction about matters of fact and might easily be false.

2) Are beliefs preferred for their orthodoxy really "better"?

a) Any motivation to align ourselves with a belief group that rests on rosy predictions about the consequences of doing so is risky. Such motivations are, all too often, exercises in wishful thinking and offer no support to the notion that conformity, as such, is better.

> *Example.* There was a newspaper account, some years ago, of a nerdish young man at the University of Virginia who, finding that he was unpopular and lonely in the general student environment, decided to align himself with a student gay advocacy group. There, he thought, he would be among those who would like and respect him. As it turned out, nerdish young men were no more appealing to gay men than to students in general. He remained lonely and unpopular.

There can be excellent reasons for peer realignment; but they need to take *real* consequences into account.

b) There are situations in which heterodox beliefs are held in such disfavor by the establishment that orthodoxy is necessary for survival. In situations like that, there is plenty of incentive to favor orthodoxy.

> *Example.* The Christian establishment used to torture and even burn people at the stake, for heresy. There was a pretty good incentive, then, for people to affirm the creed.
>
> Even in those days, however, some people didn't find intact survival to be incentive enough and went to the rack or pyre rather than conform. This is, however, a clearly *external* reason for preferring one belief to another; and it could easily be reversed. (Believing the early Mayan creed, for instance, could make death more likely. Their priests didn't sink the heretical children in the *cenotes*, only the orthodox ones.) What made it reasonable to prefer orthodox beliefs in the days when heretics were burned was not that they were orthodox, but that they were enforced by ruthless people. In a society of enforced rebellion, heresy could be advantageous for the same reason. (What I have in mind is the practice of a gang which insists, with sure and ruthless penalties, that its initiates flout the sensibilities of the establishment. "Blooding" as a rite of passage exemplifies this.) So orthodoxy, *as such*, still offers no reasonable incentive for belief.

c) There are situations in which an orthodox belief *is* better than its alternatives, but because of some quality it has besides its orthodoxy.

> *Example.* Farmers who believe that rotating their crops will produce a higher yield share a belief that in the twenty-first century is orthodox. Following it, they rotate their crops and, voilà!, get higher yields. So this is a good belief for farmers to hold; but its value does not derive from its orthodoxy. That is established by the fact that belief in crop rotation was *not* orthodox among farmers in the nineteenth century; but even then those heretics who believed and practiced it got better yields than those conformists who did not. Belief in crop rotation, like so many other beliefs, is good because it is true, not because it is normal.

None of these examples convincingly support the notion that orthodoxy, as such, is a good reason for preferring one belief to another. That should not be a surprise. The notion that orthodox beliefs are better *because* they are orthodox is a simple cart/horse reversal. It is more likely that any orthodox beliefs that are actually better than their deviant alternatives became orthodox because they were better, rather than the reverse. Truth frequently generates clichés. Unfortunately, truth is not the only thing that generates them. So received opinion still has to be confirmed by tests. It might be claimed that it is only if a belief is better than its alternatives that it can become orthodox. If so, there would be a good reason for preferring orthodox beliefs. But that is not the only way orthodoxy happens. Fear and sloth also contribute.

d) The acceptance of orthodox beliefs (and the suppression of those who reject them?) is necessary for the maintenance of social stability, which must be maintained at all costs. Therefore, the general acceptance of orthodox beliefs (and the suppression of those who reject them?) should be cultivated regardless of side effects.

P1 Societies that fail to preserve received opinion encourage dissent.
P2 Societies that encourage dissent cultivate disrespect for their leaders.
P3 Societies that cultivate disrespect for their leaders are prey to revolution.
P4 Revolution disrupts the ordered life and stability of the entire society.
P5 An ordered and stable life should be preferred above all other things.
∴C A society with the correct priorities (i.e., commitment to order and stability) will enforce the preservation of received opinion, at whatever cost.

It is not surprising to hear such a line from the people who are in charge of things. After all, one likely effect of social instability would be their own fall from power. And, though it is rather surprising to hear it from the common folk, it should not be. People regularly internalize the values of the establishment. (When people of color do this, they are called Uncle Toms or Oreos. When women do this, they write books like Marabel Morgan's *The Total Woman*.)

But saying it doesn't make it so, even if it is orthodoxly said. The desirability of preserving received opinion really depends on what that received opinion amounts to; and the desirability of preserving social stability really depends on what kind of society is in place. If a society and its received opinions are dysfunctional and false (respectively), their preservation can easily lead to disasters even more troublesome than dissent and instability. Indeed, history shows that the suppression of dissent is, itself, destabilizing in the long run.

Even when conforming beliefs to some received conventions is an accidentally effective way to insure some immediate good result (acceptance, avoidance of torture, survival, better crops), and even if it (temporarily) helps maintain the status quo, the issue remains: Is the status quo something worth maintaining? The answer depends entirely on the nature of the status quo in question, and on what its received opinions amount to. That a society is stable is no evidence at all that it is worth preserving; and any instability that might be induced by dissent can be worse than the ordinary state of things only if that ordinary state is fairly innocuous. That, unfortunately, is not always the case.

Some groups' standard beliefs are so dysfunctional that trying to maintain their stability by suppressing dissent would be a study in bad judgment.

> *Example.* Consider groups like the one led by the Rev. Jim Jones, whose followers drank their Kool-Ade and were killed by it.

The suppression of dissent in groups like these could eliminate the possibility of healthy and needed change. When change is *needed*, heresy should be *fostered*.

A much more important problem than that of the religious outer fringe (but less obvious, perhaps), occurs in the political exploitation of conformity.

> *Example.* Consider the notion of the normal that some members of American society want to impose on everyone. Their "normal" would exclude gays, philanderers, and other "sexual deviates;" atheists, agnostics, Jews, and other "practitioners of false religions;" undocumented Hispanics, African Americans, Asian Americans, and other "aliens;" and the illiterate, the poor, and (above all) uppity women, from a significant role in the nation's drama.

While Americans are, for good historical reasons, a diverse people, they are now told that anyone who does not conform to the "one true way" is a threat to the stability and good order of the state. The one true way appears to involve being heterosexual, serially monogamous, white, money driven, indoctrinated to the Book, and if not male at least docile.

Such an agenda is rubbish; and what is at stake is far more sweeping than the forcible maintenance of orthodox absurdity within an existing outer-fringe cult. It is an attempt to forcibly impose a *so-called orthodoxy that does not even exist* on the nation as a whole. It is a stalking horse for tyranny.

When orthodoxy, and the stability that it is said to bring, are so vigorously encouraged, it is well to ask "whose orthodoxy?" and "at what price?" For, at the bottom line, orthodoxy is only as good as its content. It is of *no* value in and of itself; and those who prefer a belief just because it is orthodox prefer it for a very poor reason.

D. Preferring a belief because it makes us feel good. Many beliefs, and their attendant practices, appear to generate a strong sense of well being in those who indulge in them. Childhood beliefs and rituals about Santa, the Tooth Fairy, and the Easter Bunny come to mind. What could possibly be wrong with affirming the warm and reassuring beliefs embodied in those myths?

> *Example.* Many people find the beliefs and rituals surrounding Santa, and his elves and reindeer, very appealing: beliefs like "virtue is always rewarded," and rituals like putting out milk and Oreos on Christmas Eve. Children who believe the story and practice the ritual enjoy it to the point that they will cling to it even at an age when little doubts have started to nag.

It may strain even an eight-year-old's credulity to think that a fat man with a big sack of toys and a ten-speed could squeeze through the flue of a gas-fired space heater, even if his or her very own stocking is hanging on the damper handle.

At about that time, believing segues into *pretending to believe.* But, before that, there is a stage at which the innocents just *will* to believe. Who would fault them for believing "the magic of Christmas" when it makes them feel loved and secure? And who could fault their parents for encouraging them in all this, even when *they* know it is all "just pretend" (i.e., a lie)?

I read "The Night before Christmas" annually to *my* three sons; and they all enjoyed it, stretched their believing until they absolutely *had* to give it up, and now say that they will propagate the myth to their own kids when the time comes. Not everyone, of course, shares such a positive view. Many see real trouble lurking behind even such well-intended "feel good" beliefs.

"Virtue is always rewarded" isn't *true*—at least not in this world. So believing it can generate doomed expectations. The Santa story also encourages belief that expensive toys don't have to be paid for and that is a dysfunctional belief if there ever was one. So even warm and reassuring beliefs can have a down side. (See Tom Flynn's *The Trouble with Christmas.*)

Lurking problems may be more obvious in some of the other myths that adults encourage their children to accept "because it will make them happy." Consider, for instance:

- the notion that all things work together for the good of those who love the Lord—that endurance in the face of adversity will insure rich rewards by and by
- the notion that marriages are made in heaven—that there is someone out there who will love us just the way we are, when the time comes
- the notion that if we think positive thoughts, we can conquer mental and physical malfunction—"pull up our socks" and shake off depression, or grab the rabbit ears and make a pledge to the faith healer, and throw away those crutches one fine day.

There is a pattern of epistemic dysfunction here that diverts people from doing constructive things that they could do and encourages them, instead, to wait placidly for good things to happen. Since such beliefs subvert alternative approaches to life's hurdles that *work*, they do harm—even though they make the believer "feel better" right up to the time when they drop dead of their untreated diseases. Consequently, believing them is unwise, even if most of the harm is only to ourself.

The worst kinds of trouble that can lurk behind "feel good" beliefs become obvious when we turn our attention to adult beliefs and rituals about things like manifest destiny, white supremacy, and the raging libido of women who wear Spandex jogging suits. Such beliefs make their believers feel good about *themselves* by demeaning various *others*, encourage fantasies of subordination and exploitation, and when circumstances permit erupt in aggression. Such beliefs also encourage those who are demeaned to seek comfort by internalizing the damning judgments about themselves and accepting their lowly status with servile humility. That is poisonous, too.

> *Example.* Goober believes that women are quivering voids lusting to be filled—fair and willing receptacles for random deposits. (Those who flaunt themselves in public in Spandex jogging suits are only bolder than most.) This fantasy apparently makes him feel knowing, powerful, and irresistible; but it has a dark side. Even though Goober has not, so far, attempted physical aggression, he *talks* sexual violence all the time. His *mind* is so tumescent that, in addition to the danger that he may act out *sometime*, his talk poisons the environment for anyone within earshot *all the time*. No woman hears him without feeling soiled; and every immature, undisciplined, or sexually disordered man who hears him is encouraged to "poke one for her own good" since "she wants it so bad."

> *Example.* Thelma thinks that "black" people were fashioned by God to serve "white" people. She believes that they are childish, superstitious, slow witted, highly sexed, strong, and insensitive to pain. She also believes that they, like the livestock, are the responsibility of "white folks" to supervise, discipline, and protect. So she:
>
> - gives worn-out clothes and furniture to her housemaid,
> - is scared of (but has fantasies about) the trash man,
> - gives $25 dollars a year to the Congo Mission,
> - votes for head-knocking law enforcement and supports the restoration of the chain gang,
> - says that "pickaninnies" are "cute" and "adorable" but yanked Bubba Junior and Crystal Dawn out of public school when they hit puberty, and
> - keeps her two best bedsheets (the ones with eye holes) laundered, ironed, and ready, just in case.

There is no doubt that such beliefs and practices make Thelma "feel good" about her "own kind of folks" and their place in the world; but there is also no doubt that they encourage fear, misunderstanding, economic exploitation, social exclusion, systematic legal discrimination, and violence.

> *Example.* National, cultural, and religious chauvinisms make their *champions* happy but do so at great cost to their *targets*.

Consider without comment:
- the Crusades and various other Christian missions, especially in South and Central America and Africa, the ongoing war in Northern Ireland, and assorted *Jihads;*
- English, Spanish, Dutch, Belgian, German, French, Chinese, and Japanese imperialism all over the globe;
- U.S. imperialism in Canada, Mexico, the Caribbean, the Pacific, Southeast Asia, and the Middle East;
- Russian imperialism in Eastern Europe, the Middle East, and Southeast Asia; and, on smaller stages,
- Iran and Iraq, Israel and Palestine, India and Pakistan, Cyprus, Angola, Nigeria, Sudan, and Zaire.

So even if believing the Santa story because it makes us feel good is innocuous, and believing "it will all work out" stories on such grounds is only problematic for the believer, believing male supremacy, white supremacy, and culture supremacy stories on these grounds is lethal. Even though there is nothing wrong with feeling good in itself, there is a great deal wrong with encouraging sexually, racially, or nationally exploitative behavior (or the internalization of our own allegedly subordinate status and destiny). This can be generalized: whether or not it is OK to prefer a belief because it makes us feel good depends on how all the consequences of the belief work themselves out in concrete cases.

E. Preferring a belief because it enables or validates. Currently, there is a lot of debate about affirming and cultivating beliefs that would enable and validate those who are marginalized and relegated to an inferior status by the dominant scheme of things: women, people of color, children, and gays, for instance. Since the *form* of the argument is the same, whichever target group is selected, I will focus on beliefs that enable and validate women. Whatever is discovered there can be transferred to the other cases. Should we prefer beliefs that enable and validate women over beliefs that don't? If so, why?

A significant amount of ground has been prepared for this issue in the examination of the previous topic. It has already been shown that preferring a belief because it makes us feel good by demeaning others is not desirable. But if beliefs that demean *others* are bad for *me* to hold, then on the general principle that sauce for geese is sauce for ganders it follows that beliefs that demean *me* are bad for *others* to hold. Indeed, a mere respect for consistency will demand generalizing it completely: beliefs that demean *anyone* are bad for *anyone* to hold; and from this general principle, it clearly follows that beliefs that demean women are bad for anyone to hold. So there is an effective argument that it is not desirable to affirm or promote beliefs that demean women.

One obvious reason why demeaning women is undesirable is that it *disables* them. If the demeaning is generally accepted, it will engender an atmosphere in which opportunities will be denied them. If it is internalized by women themselves, it will undermine their self-esteem sufficiently to prevent their pursuit of whatever opportunities there are. Only if it is neither generally accepted nor internalized is there a chance for all women to function in an undiminished way. In American society, however, it is widely accepted and commonly internalized. So: people in that society should avoid affirming and promoting beliefs that demean women.

This seems to be a much more modest conclusion, however, than is generally sought, that is, that people in American society should affirm and promote beliefs that *validate and enable* women. Even scrupulous avoidance of beliefs that demean and disable them might still leave them unvalidated and unenabled. Where is the inference ticket to the positive injunction to validate and enable?

The logical passage from *don't disable* to *enable,* and from *don't demean* to *validate,* would work if *not disabling* equaled *enabling,* and *not demeaning* equaled *validating.* But without these two equations, "beliefs that validate and enable women are good for anyone to hold" does not follow from "beliefs that demean and disable women are bad for anyone to hold." And the equations *don't* hold: not disabling and not demeaning are *not* the same as enabling and validating:

- *Disabling* people involves taking away or rendering ineffective abilities, means, knowledge, and opportunities that (absent intervention) are present and realizable.
- *Enabling* people involves supplying or rendering effective abilities, means, knowledge, and opportunities that (absent intervention) are lacking or unrealizable.
- *Demeaning* people involves debasing the dignity and standing that (absent intervention) they have.
- *Validating* people involves corroborating and affirming the dignity and standing that (absent intervention) they have or would have, or creating and bestowing dignity and standing that (absent intervention) they lack.

Consequently, we could refrain from beliefs that disable women without committing to beliefs that enable them. And we could refrain from beliefs that demean them without committing to beliefs that validate them. This is because refraining from one belief never commits us to replace it with another. We can simply *refrain.*

There might, however, be *independent* grounds for intervening to validate and enable someone who (absent intervention) lacks or is unable to realize dignity, standing, abilities, means, knowledge, or opportunity. It might be good to favor beliefs that do not demean and disable, *and* good to favor beliefs that enable and validate. This is clearly the case when it comes to removing impediments to dignity, standing, and so forth, that are artificially imposed. If we should not impose such impediments, then we should do all we can to remove them.

Caution is called for, however. It is one thing to work at removing an impediment to a real ability or capacity. It is quite another to try to believe into existence an ability or capacity that simply is not there. An individual's inherent abilities and potentials, after all, are not demeaning or disabling. So true descriptions of (and beliefs about) them are not demeaning or disabling either. Reality is what it is, and accurately describing it is just telling the truth. Consequently, negative beliefs about people that are true (absent intervention) don't demean or disable them. Voicing them is simply saying what is so. So there is little reason to refrain when the occasion demands. Similarly, positive beliefs about people that are false (absent intervention) don't validate or enable them. Declining to subscribe to or voice them is simply declining to believe or say what is not so. So there is every reason to avoid voicing them, even when "kindness" tempts.

On the other hand, *dwelling on true negative beliefs about people* may be debilitating in the sense that it disables the targets' ability to actualize other potentials they *do* have. Enough haranguing about what we can't do can have a chilling effect on accomplishments of which we are perfectly capable. So truth may need to be softened by concern. Notice, however, that there is an asymmetry here. Concern may encourage us not to dwell on shortcomings; but it is no good reason to affirm false hopes. For instance, there is a problem with believing "I am Woman, I can do *anything*," Helen Reddy to the contrary. No one can do that; so affirming that someone can just sets him up for inevitable failure. And that is not *effective* enabling, however nobly intended.

> *Example.* Liz has two left feet. In spite of them, she dreams of a career in ballet and her parents have sprung for dancing classes for years (where she dwells in the back line full of determination and ineptitude). Her eye-hand coordination, in contrast, is exceptional. Indeed, her dissections are kept by her biology teacher as models for the other students. So telling her, "Keep buying lessons, kid. One day you'll be a star!" is cruel exploitation even if she replies, straight from a Busby Berkeley script, "Gee, Madame Pollona, that'll be swell."

Somebody needs to suggest that she consider research biology, surgery, or some other career for which she has real potential. Thinking positive thoughts that have no possibility of fulfillment, that is, encouraging doomed hopes, does not enable anyone.

This does not mean, of course, that we have a license to subscribe to and voice *false* negative beliefs about people's talents and abilities. When we do *that*, we *do* disable and demean them.

> *Example.* Lacy is remarkably good at chess. With only a modest amount of watching two of her teachers play, she was able to whip all comers by age eleven. Now itching to enter competitive play, what is she told?

Big Sister: Don't talk about chess so much, boys will think you're a "brain" and won't like you.

Mother: Stop asking to go to chess club. It isn't a suitable place for girls.

Father: Don't concentrate so hard on that game book, baby. You're getting lines around your beautiful eyes.

A Neighbor: Why won't you babysit for us? You could earn money for clothes and makeup, and it will help you get ready to be a mother yourself someday.

Talk like this shows that Lacy's primary role models all have false expectations of her, deny her real abilities, and are hell-bent on disabling her until she fits a "girl pattern" they admire.

It should be apparent by now that while refraining from demeaning and disabling people is vital, and taking pains to validate and enable them when we can is important, the success of such efforts depends in large part, like so much else, on what is the case. This is because what is the case determines what is true, and what is true is an effective limit on the success of good intentions. Refraining from negative beliefs is no panacea when the beliefs themselves are true, and favoring positive ones hasn't a prayer of success when the beliefs themselves are false.

The general preferability of true beliefs over false ones keeps recurring. It is time to turn to it directly. This is the most important criterion for belief preference; but it is also the most complicated.

2

True Belief and Standards of Evidence

There is a tradition that true (or probably true) beliefs are better than false (or probably false) ones. In this chapter, I will examine what "true (or probably true)" and "false (or probably false)" mean, and see whether this is a good tradition to follow.

1. Which Beliefs Are True?

To discover what "true (or probably true)" and "false (or probably false)" mean, we need to locate ourselves on the general map of "truth theories" and "truth criteria."

A. Truth theories and truth criteria. A truth *theory* is a theory about what truth is (or about what "truth" means). Relative to beliefs, then, a truth theory is an account of what *constitutes* the truth of a belief. A truth criterion, on the other hand, is the standard, and the accompanying procedures, in terms of which we can discern whether or not a belief is true.

So as I am using the terms, truth theories and truth criteria are not the same things. This needs to be kept in mind because the three main truth *theories* (which are called the correspondence, coherence, and pragmatic theories) can be mixed, rather than matched, with the three main truth *criteria* (which are, confusingly, called the correspondence, coherence, and pragmatic criteria).

B. What three truth theories share. The three main truth theories differ sharply about what constitutes truth, but they do share some basic presuppositions:

1) Truth (whatever it may be) is, first and foremost, an occasional property of well-formed descriptive sentences. While the word "true" has other uses ("he is a true hero," "be sure that the door hangs true"), these are derivative from, or secondary to, the central one (as in "when he said, 'mules are sterile,' what he said was true").

2) Among well-formed descriptive sentences, those that aren't true are false. This entails that any well-formed sentence that is neither true nor false must not be a *descriptive* sentence. There are, of course, many nondescriptive sentences: imperatives ("Close the door!"), interrogatives ("How would you like your eggs?"), and ceremonials and entreaties as well.

3) The denial of a true well-formed descriptive sentence is a false well-formed descriptive sentence, and vice versa. If "mules are sterile" is true, then "it is not the case that mules are sterile" (or, "mules are fertile") is false. If "P" is a descriptive sentence, then "P" and "not-P" cannot both be true. But if "P" and "not-P" cannot both be true, then their conjunction ("P and not-P") cannot be true, either.

4) Whether a well-formed descriptive sentence is true or false does not depend in any way on its speaker. For example, the sentence "mules are sterile" is either true or false, quite independently of who says it and of what that speaker may believe or feel.

What the truth or falsity of a well-formed descriptive sentence does depend on—hence, what its truth or falsity actually *amounts to*—is the issue on which the three classical truth theories disagree.

C. How three truth theories differ. The three main truth theories differ from each other in significant ways.

1) The *correspondence* theory of truth is that the truth of a well-formed descriptive sentence amounts to its accurate representation of (or correspondence to) the way things actually are "out there" in the nonlinguistic "real" world. In this account, a true sentence accurately represents a real states of affairs; and a false sentence, depending on how you look at it, either represents no state of affairs accurately, or some state of affairs inaccurately. So in this theory, "mules are sterile" is true because this sentence accurately matches the nonlinguistic fact that mules cannot reproduce.

This theory is problematic, however, because what this "matching" amounts to is problematic. Sentences and states of affairs are different sorts of things, so how can one match, picture, reflect, correspond to, or capture the other? Consequently, the appeal of the correspondence theory depends on the merits of some assumptions about the existence of an external, objective, and accessible world, and on complex philosophical and scientific theories about language itself.

2) The *coherence* theory of truth is that the truth of sentences amounts to their logical consistency with other sentences that are true, or to their coherent place in some accepted body of beliefs. In this theory, "mules are sterile" is true because it is consistent with other sentences like "mules are hybrids" and "hybrids are sterile," or because it is a coherent piece of (say) farm lore.

This theory is problematic, however, because:

a) While "mules are sterile" may cohere with *farm* lore, we might also find that "mules have incorporeal offspring" coheres with *other* lore. But if both cohere with a body of accepted beliefs, then both (on this account) are true.

b) "Mules are sterile" and "mules have incorporeal offspring," however, do not appear to be consistent with each other. Indeed, their conjunction looks like a case of "P and not-P."

c) But if the conjunction is both true and a case of "P and not-P," the coherence theory of truth has run afoul of the generally shared assumption that the conjunction of "P" and "not-P" *cannot* be true.

The "paradigm case" theory is a special variety of coherence theory. In it, a claim's truth is a function of whether or not it coheres with a paradigm claim that is stipulated to be true—which claim constitutes the paradigm being a matter of intuition or convention. A paradigm case for arithmetic might be "2 + 2 = 4." A paradigm case for nutrition might be "milk is wholesome." A paradigm case for drivers might be "red means stop." Once a paradigm case is stipulated, this theory functions like any coherence approach: what coheres is true, what doesn't is false.

The appeal of the coherence theories of truth depends on the merits of some assumptions about the coherence of the world itself, on whether more than one system of belief can be genuinely coherent, and (if so) on what sort of decision procedure might be established for choosing between rival coherent systems (or paradigm cases).

3) The *pragmatic* theory of truth is that the truth of sentences amounts to their effectiveness in use, that is, that those who believe them engage in successful practices and avoid unsuccessful ones.

In this theory, "cotton and clover affect the soil in complementary ways" and "mules are sterile" are true because those who believe them rotate their crops and get higher yields and don't waste their time at the stud farm trying to breed mules. Conversely, "soil nutrients are self-rejuvenating" and "mules are sterile because they copulate with extreme vigor" are false because those who believe them try to raise cotton in the same field year after year and have poor crops, or try to base their family planning on the emulation of mule behavior and have too many children.

This theory is problematic because a belief can be effective for a long time before it trips anybody up, and two directly conflicting beliefs can be effective under some circumstances.

Example. For many centuries belief that the Sun revolves around the Earth was common, and a highly successful system of celestial navigation was built on it. Ancients (and moderns) who use that system to sail from Carthage to Crete reach their destination accurately and on time. But, anyone who uses it to shoot a rocket from Cape Kennedy to Mars will miss.

One could try to finesse this anomaly by saying, "If we want to go from Carthage to Crete, the Sun revolves around the Earth; but if we want to go from Cape Kennedy to the Moon, the Earth revolves around the Sun." This, however, comes close to saying that the Sun *does and does not* revolve around the Earth, which would stand in conflict with the generally shared assumption that "P and not-P" cannot be true.

On the other hand, if we say that the truth value of "the Sun revolves around the Earth" is undetermined until a context is specified, then it doesn't seem to have a truth value of its own; and that is problematic.

- It conflicts with the very reasonable view that "the Sun revolves around the Earth" is a complete and well-formed descriptive sentence that, *as such*, has a truth value. If it does *not* have a truth value as it stands, then either it is not a descriptive sentence or it stands in conflict with the generally shared assumption that descriptive sentences are either true or false.
- It seems to allow for a sentence's truth to depend on what we want to do and on when we want to do it; and that kind of subjectivism clearly conflicts with the generally shared assumption that a sentence's truth is independent of its speaker.

This account of what truth amounts to is so problematic that it would lose its appeal altogether if the alleged flaws of the correspondence or coherence theory could be mended. It is a "fall-back" theory for those who think the other two are too problematic to salvage.

D. Truth criteria. A truth *criterion* is a theory about what marks a sentence as true and about the procedures and standards that we can follow in order to find out whether a sentence is true.

1) The *correspondence* criterion of truth says that we can discover whether a sentence is true by laying it up against some piece of the nonlinguistic world and seeing whether it matches. So we would discover whether "mules are sterile" is true by watching mules and seeing whether the sentence and their behaviors "match."

But, as has already been noted, what "match" amounts to here is problematic because sentences and states of affairs are not the same sort of things. As "match" is normally used, we could match two pictures, two sounds, or even two sentences. But how can we even attempt to "match" a sentence with visual or aural observations? Does "Mules are sterile" either look or sound like mule behavior?

There are, however, several more subtle approaches that might explain how a true sentence and an actual state of affairs "match."

a) Whatever truth criterion is used, a working descriptive sentence must express or affirm a proposition that has a semantic connection to the real world. That is how such sentences manage to be "about" something. If alleged descriptive sentences fail to express or affirm propositions with such connections, there would be no *descriptive* point in uttering them.

Perhaps the "match" needed, on this theory, occurs between reality and the proposition that a sentence expresses, rather than between reality and the sentence itself. If so, the fact that sentences and states of affairs are different sorts of things is not a problem.

But sentences and propositions are different sorts of things, too, as are propositions and states of affairs. So not much is gained by interposing this intermediary between sentences and the world. If sentences had to match propositions and propositions, in turn, had to match states of affairs, we would have *two* obscure matches connecting *three* types. This may be subtle, but it is pointless. Intermediaries are about as much help to correspondence talk as "demiurges" were to Greek religion.

b) Whatever truth criterion is used, descriptive sentences occur in the context of conventional language use, in terms of which they are associated with specific experience expectations. This is what provides them with a meaning that can be believed or disbelieved. Absent such associations, they would be (descriptively) empty.

But experience expectations are sufficiently of the same type as experience itself that we *can* tell the difference between times when they are fulfilled and times when they come up craps.

Of course the sentence "Your dog is going to bite me!" does not remotely resemble a dog bite. But believing it involves expecting bite experiences, and the experience of a bite expectation is very close kin to the experience of a bite itself—close enough, indeed, that we can recognize a match: *"Yes, that is just what I expected!"*

As soon as we start moving in this direction, however, there is very little reason to keep on talking about whether the sentence matches the states of affairs. For we are already talking about whether the belief conventionally associated with the sentence succeeds or fails when put to practical experiential tests, which is a *pragmatic* matter if there ever was one. We might as well admit it and abandon the notion that a *working* truth criterion can depend on any sort of language to world correspondence.

In doing so, however, we need not abandon a correspondence theory about what *makes* a sentence true. We can still say that true sentences are the ones that correspond to the way the world is, even though the best way to *see* whether a sentence is true is by putting the belief conventionally associated with it to work, and seeing if the experience expectations that make up that belief are fulfilled. This couples a correspondence *theory* to a pragmatic *criterion*.

2) The *coherence* criterion of truth says that we can discover whether a sentence is true by checking out its logical connections to other true sentences or to a body of accepted beliefs. Consistency is the mark to look for.

In fact, we do something like this every time we make a prediction based on past experience.

I'll get sick if I eat corn dogs and ride the Hurler. I always do.

All we need to be assured of the truth of *many* beliefs is that they test out as consistent with the other beliefs we hold.

It would be nice, however, if we had some reason to believe that those other beliefs were true themselves. If X is consistent with Y, and Y is true, then X is fine; but what is the criterion for Y's truth? When the answer is "more of the same," then this entire gambit vanishes into an infinite regress or collapses into a vicious circle.

For it not to be "more of the same," there has to be some way to ascertain the truth of Y besides its coherence with (say) Z. Falling back on a correspondence test for Y seems forlorn; but pressing an experiential test, of the sort just discussed, seems just the thing. If so, we can use a coherence test to determine the truth of a claim when a *secure* body of beliefs is already in place; but we will turn to a set of experiential (pragmatic) tests when the security of our body of beliefs is, itself, in question.

3) The *pragmatic* criterion of truth has already been laid out in the discussion of why correspondence criteria are so problematic.

> Descriptive sentences occur in the context of conventional language use, in terms of which they are associated with specific experience expectations.
>
> These expectations are sufficiently of the same type as experience itself that we can tell the difference between times when they are fulfilled and times when they come up craps.
>
> The way to see whether a sentence is true is by putting the belief conventionally associated with it to work, and seeing if the expectations that make up that belief are fulfilled.

This is, in fact, the truth criterion on which people ordinarily rely.

E. Conclusions.

1) That a descriptive sentence *is* true (or false) amounts to its capturing (or failing to capture) things the way they are. This is a *correspondence* theory; but in it, what correspond are the experience expectations conventionally associated with a sentence and the experiences that actually occur in the world.

2) That we *find* a descriptive sentence to be true (or false) is the result of putting it to one or the other of two tests:

- an experiential test for success-in-use (a *pragmatic* criterion), or
- a test for consistency with other claims that are already well established (a *coherence* criterion).

When working from a set of well-tested claims, *coherence* is the test we need for an individual claim in play; but when such a secure context is not at hand, or when the context itself is at issue, a *pragmatic* test is called for.

This combination of a correspondence theory and pragmatic and coherence criteria has the added advantage of being consistent with the way in which people ordinarily talk about and weigh their descriptive beliefs. So it is a very promising position from which to start the search for what we ought to believe.

2. True Beliefs Are Better Than False Ones

Not all beliefs about matters of fact are reliable, of course; and whether one is or isn't reliable is not always obvious. Metaphorically speaking, beliefs range from "solid as a rock" through "slippery as ice" to "treacherous as quicksand." Think about these, for instance:

- Swallowed grape seeds will lodge in the appendix until it fills and bursts.
  This is plausible, but unreliable. Although my grandmother told me this when I was four, she was mistaken.
- It is cheaper to fly to Miami from Boston than from Richmond.
  This is implausible, but reliable. Half as far can cost twice as much if you don't start from a hub.
- If you're not on a network, never borrow disks, buy programs and media only in factory-sealed packages, and keep the hardware secure, you need not worry about viruses.
  Surely this sounds safe. But a few years ago a leading word processing program was shipped infected.
- Font size affects memory space—bigger type fills more space on the hard drive. So if you're short of memory, shrink the font.
  This doesn't make any sense if you understand computers; but Dilbert's boss is not the only one who believes it.

True beliefs are composed of experience expectations that are fulfilled when events play out. False beliefs are composed of experience expectations that crap out in use. Probable beliefs are composed of experience expectations that are closely similar to or consistent with those comprising true ones. Improbable beliefs are composed of experience expectations that are closely similar to or consistent with those comprising false ones.

Using the terms this way, true beliefs are more reliable than false ones, probable beliefs than improbable ones, and more probable beliefs than less probable ones. So the operative issue is, simply, whether more reliable beliefs are *better* than less reliable ones.

I cannot imagine a reason for thinking that reliable beliefs aren't better than unreliable ones. Finding some may be problematic; but surely, if there are any to be found, they are the ones to favor. So absent such independently demonstrable pathologies as masochism (where unreliable, or even misery-producing, demeaning, and disabling beliefs are desired): *being true (or probably true), that is, being reliable in use, or being closely similar to, or consistent with other beliefs that are reliable in use, is one way for a belief to be better than another.* This is especially important because, as noted in the previous chapter, all the *other* ways in which a belief might be better than another are affected by whether the belief in question is true.

Vigorous skeptics will reject this position, arguing as follows:

- There are no individual beliefs that are really reliable.
- So there are no sets of beliefs that are really reliable.
- So there is no way to use the suggested criteria.
- So this entire approach is sterile.

But I have not (yet) claimed that any beliefs have been found to be reliable. I have only said that *if* some are found to be reliable, I will:

- call them "true,"
- prefer them, because of their reliability, over beliefs that are found to be unreliable, and
- call the latter "false;" and

if some not-yet-tested beliefs are very much like, or consistent with, true or false beliefs, then I will:

- call them "probable" and "improbable" respectively,
- note that these states come by degrees, and
- prefer the probable ones over the improbable ones, and the more probable ones over the less probable ones.

In the next section, I will focus close attention on *locating* beliefs that are true (or probably true). No matter how much better true (or probably true) ones might be than false (or probably false) ones, they will do us little good if we cannot find them. I will show that even though finding them is problematic, it is not impossible.

3. Are Any True (or Probably True) Beliefs Available?

A. The variety of beliefs. There is (or has been or will be) someone to believe almost any imaginable claim. Here is an expanded list of some things that, with one or two exceptions, various people actually believe. Some of them are true, some probably true, some probably false, and some false. The question is, "How can we tell which ones are which?" The answer is, "Evidence!"

- Swallowed grape seeds will lodge in the appendix until it fills and bursts.
- Peanut butter and bacon sandwiches are fattening.
- It is cheaper to fly to Miami from Boston than from Richmond.
- It is cheaper to drive from Richmond to Washington, D.C., than fly.
- August has more days than February.
- Roosevelt sold out the United States at Yalta.
- J. Edgar Hoover was a transvestite.

- Six hours alone in an elevator during a power outage have more minutes than six hours in Tahiti with your lover.
- The only Paris is in France.
- There is a Richmond in Kentucky.
- The names of only two cities in the United States start with "X."
- If you're not on a network, never borrow disks, buy programs and media in factory-sealed packages, and keep the hardware secure, you need not worry about viruses.
- Bigger type fills more pages. So if you're short of paper, downsize the type.
- Bigger type fills more space on the hard drive. So if you're short of memory, downsize the type.
- Mules have no offspring because they are hybrids.
- Mules have no offspring because they copulate with extreme vigor.
- Mules, being sacred, have incorporeal offspring.

B. Looking for evidence. Solid evidence is the key to sorting out beliefs, but finding it is often more complicated than it looks.

First, evidence can be misleading or unreliable for a variety of reasons. So we need some standards for evaluating it.

Second, people appeal to many *kinds* of alleged evidence:

- what they see, taste, smell, feel, or hear,
- their clear and distinct impressions,
- messages from the suppressed half of the bicameral mind,
- visions and revelations, and so forth.

So we need to identify the likely varieties and see how each one fares in terms of the standards established.

After exploring some standards in the next section, I will use them to weigh eight varieties of alleged evidence in chapter 3.

4. Evidence Standards

What makes Bertrand Russell's pronouncements take precedence over Bishop Russell's? (Bishop Walter Russell, late of Swannanoa, Virginia, claimed contact with Jesus and others by way of "cosmic consciousness." He published the insights he gained in this way, offering them for sale to the general public.)

What is it about Prophet Jones's therapeutic claims that makes them less convincing than those of the Mayo Clinic? (Prophet James Francis Marion Jones, late of Detroit and Chicago, had a reputation as a healer as well as a prophet. Many individuals from his thousands of followers gave him expensive gifts in gratitude for his healing word.)

Obviously enough, *evidence* is what makes the difference in both cases. But just "evidence" is not enough. The crucial thing is the *quality* of the evidence.

But what makes one piece of evidence convincing and another not? What makes one body of evidence clinch a case and another leave it hanging?

There are at least seven common standards for separating evidential wheat and chaff. Though not self-evident, their sheer endurance makes a prima facie case in their favor, putting the burden of proof on anyone who would reject them. Good evidence is:

- relevant to the issue at stake,
- repeatable and public,
- cross-checked,
- controlled for limiting conditions,
- the object of due care,
- controlled for ambiguity, and
- formulated in a viable theoretical framework.

A. Relevant to the issue at stake. As obvious as it is that good evidence must be "connected to" or "have a bearing on" the claim being made, relevance is often ignored. What sort of evidence was offered in Pretoria to support the claim that indigenous South Africans were sufficiently different to be kept "apart"? The same sort of evidence that was offered at the slave markets in Charleston, New York, and other cities, not all that long ago, that some people were sufficiently different to be bought and sold: that they were black. But skin color is the very paradigm of irrelevance when human rights are at stake.

People cannot *reasonably* balk when asked to back up their claims with relevant data; but people are often unreasonable. Even though the absence of relevance in the "evidence" offered in advertising is usually obvious and appalling, people are taken in by it again and again. Still, when they are being reasonable and have their wits about them, they reject such fluff.

No claim could possibly be more relevant to XYZ than the simple assertion, "XYZ." What evidence is there for the soporific power of opium? Its dormative potency, of course. Nothing could be more relevant than that; but nothing could be more sterile, either. If the burden of an argument is to convince someone of XYZ, then saying "XYZ" *cannot* help, even with embroidery. If they already buy XYZ, the statement is redundant; and if they do not, it is no help. So the demand for relevance must be hedged: "Relevant, but not a reiteration of the very thing at issue."

B. Repeatable and public. "Private" and "one-off" evidence makes most people suspicious. They want to know *why* it cannot be repeated or *why* no one else has access to it. Absent a plausible account of "why," people will ordinarily reject "private" or "exclusive" evidence out of hand. This can occur in all sorts of settings.

Example. Some years ago, a student named Greg was walking to his room late at night. As he passed the chapel, its doors crashed open and he heard a voice say, "Come into My house and pray." Greg, frightened, took off down the hill, never looking back.

When he told me about it, I wondered whether I would have heard the voice myself, had I been there. If *not*, one scenario would have followed. It would have begun with some calm inquiry about previous hallucinations, with a possible referral to counseling. If *so* a different scenario would have followed. Looking for an explanation for such extraordinary events, I would have gone into the chapel and checked things out.

Note that in *either* case, there is more than one way to interpret Greg's report: maybe he was just fooling me, maybe he was in contact with the Beyond, maybe his fraternity brothers had a low sense of humor, maybe religious theater was being revived, maybe he was on something. Choosing between rival interpretations raises further issues (e.g., ambiguity and how to resolve it, and theoretical frameworks and how to choose one) that I will deal with later in this chapter.

Other examples of events that are not easily replicable or publicly accessible include Yuri Geller's spoon bending, Shirley MacLaine's access to her prior selves, and the biblical Samuel's one-on-one sessions with God.

My point here is not to deny the putative data in such cases out of hand. There is little to be gained, for instance, by insisting that Geller's spoons don't bend. Still, there is much to be gained by asking *how it happened.* After all, many magicians bend spoons by trickery, and Geller—a magician himself for years—steadfastly refused to bend them with a magician nearby. This may suggest an alternative to his own explanation that he did it by "mind power." (See James Randi's *Flim-Flam.*)

One reason I'm not *totally* suspicious in such cases is that difficulty in getting replicable public confirmation isn't limited to the Shirleys, Yuris, Samuels, and Gregs of the world. And, for that matter, even Geller may have a *good* reason why he won't or can't bend spoons with a magician on stage. Perhaps it isn't that they are uncomfortably alert to his misdirection. Perhaps they really do "disturb his vibrations." So just because someone makes a claim that cannot be backed by public data, we cannot automatically say, "He's a nut" or "He's a fraud" and put him away.

Further, there may be people with modes of experience that ordinary folk don't share. Many people can hear high-pitched notes that others cannot. So can dogs, for that matter. One person I know can infallibly distinguish Burgundy and Bordeaux. Numerous Japanese make good livings sexing chickens. So not everyone who claims unique capacities is a charlatan or fool. On the other hand, some *are.* Distinguishing gifted people from the frauds and fools is never easy; but it is not impossible. And it is important in the New Age.

So before accepting or rejecting Greg's claim to have heard a voice that no one else could hear, we might investigate, under strict controls, just how his auditory equipment compares to our own. Hard inquiry should settle the matter, and good sense insists that we press. Similarly, when provided with a plausible reason why evidence corroboration of one sort or another *is* impossible, we must insist that the alleged private or unrepeatable evidence pass some of the other criteria with flying colors. We rarely insist that a piece of disputed data pass each and every test. Some tests cannot be applied to some phenomena. Since we cannot ask a meteor to fall again, we look for other witnesses. If there are none, by chance, then confirmation has to fall back on still other devices. We do expect disputed data to jump *some* hurdles.

C. Cross-checked. Evidence that is difficult or impossible to confirm on the previous criterion should be checked on more than one channel. As has been shown, we are not always in a position to check data publicly or repetitively. Suppose that I have an experience when alone and am not convinced that it constitutes adequate support for a claim that I want to make. There is no one around to ask, "Did you see that?" And there is no convenient way to make the phenomenon keep happening while I call for help. Sometimes I can verify it anyway, by way of what I call (for lack of a better label) "cross-channel" checking.

> *Example.* Years ago, in southern Indiana, I drove up to a level crossing on the main line of what was then the Pennsylvania Railroad. I looked both ways and saw that the track was clear to the horizon in both directions. Before proceeding, however, I rolled down a window and turned off the radio. With the background noise abated, I quickly discovered that I could hear and feel what I could not see: a ground rumble and a high-pitched whine in the air. Then, in an instant, a freight train thundered by. Had I not heeded a sign that said "Look *and* Listen," I would have been scattered along the tracks from Route 3 to the Wabash. I am alive to write about evidence because there is more than one route open for finding out what's happening.

This criterion also helps you guard against hallucinations, delusions, and fantasies. How would you know, if you saw pink rats running around the ceiling of your room, that you needed a physician? There would be lots of ways; but a main one might be that you *only* saw them—that is, you didn't hear or smell them—and, if you had climbed a ladder and tried to feel them, would have had trouble with that too.

> *A Cautionary Tale.* In my senior college year, I took Attic Greek. Having a knack for languages, I made a B the first term, even though I had rarely attended class. So I decided to try for a second-term C without attending at all. With only days to go, I translated and memorized the texts that the syllabus said the examination would cover, while friends brought me coffee and cigarettes. The examination went smoothly until I noticed a large, iridescent insect sitting on the

left page of my blue book. In a reflex motion, I swept the page with my hand; but my hand passed through the bug. With aplomb that startles me in retrospect, I thought, "I'm hallucinating" and went on writing. *Insects that can be seen but not felt can be ignored.* But, alas, while reliance on the standard tests of evidence is virtually automatic, knowledge of Attic Greek is not. I made a D.

Cross-channel checking is an internal substitute for publicness. Publicness, among its other virtues, helps people distinguish their own systematic delusions from what everyone has access to; cross-channel checking helps them locate more particular, single-track illusions, confusions, and failures. Where possible, we get others to have a look; and, if it is the sort of thing that others can't get at, then we give it another "look" ourselves.

D. Controlled for limiting conditions. The quality of evidence varies as a function of whatever quirks, disabilities, or peculiarities mark either the individuals who gather it or the circumstances in which they work. The best witnesses (and, consequently, the best evidence) will be as free of such limiting conditions as possible. The kinds of limiting conditions that can flaw a particular case are almost innumerable. We must avoid them where possible; and where that is impossible we must at least be aware of them and be ready to compensate for them as they arise.

> *Example.* A beer truck collides with an orphanage bus at the corner of Broad and Malvern streets. The police, trying to figure out how it happened, locate three people who were there when the smash occurred. One of the three sells pencils at that corner every day, wearing dark glasses and accompanied by a guide dog.
>   While Sir Arthur Conan Doyle or Agatha Christie might convince us of a case where the evidence of a blind witness was more reliable than that of sighted rivals, it would be a fantastic case. Since, ordinarily, being blind is a major limiting condition on evidence collection, the police will interview the blind witness last, if at all.

It would be nice if all limiting conditions were as obvious as total blindness, and all impaired data could be controlled for by appealing to conveniently present unhampered observers. But reality intrudes.

> *Example.* Charles had to wait until his Navy physical to find out he was color-blind. Nineteen years of experience had not revealed his perceptual impairment. It took sophisticated tests to do that.

Emotional and psychological hang-ups also intrude; and they can be even more subtle than disabilities like color blindness.

> *Example.* While Harry Truman was president, his daughter aspired to a career as a concert singer and gave a recital at Constitution Hall. Some music critics, as

well as many socialites, attended. Paul Hume, the *Washington Post*'s capable and experienced critic at the time, gave her performance a bluntly negative review. "Give-'Em-Hell-Harry," perhaps the last tenant of the Oval Office before the media managers invaded it, took public umbrage in a letter in which he referred to Mr. Hume as "off his beam" and dismissed his critique as "poppycock." Harry, after all, thought Margaret's performance was first-class. But, however appealing we may find the notion of a president who speaks out (which Truman surely did), we should not be surprised that informed opinion supported the critic rather than the daddy.

Emotional involvement, generally, limits our ability to adjudicate disputes objectively. This is why people scrupulously follow strict rules in court to guard against the infection of evidence by the special involvements of those who give it. When a lawyer confronts an adverse witness, the technique of interrogation changes. In this most-codified area of inquiry, controlling for bias is a serious matter, indeed. Lives depend on it.

In addition, a certain amount of expertise (familiarity with the kinds of things at stake) is a necessity for any opinion to have standing, whether the issues at stake are sophisticated and complex, or quite mundane.

> *Example.* On holiday in Pennsylvania, years ago, I went "deer spotting." One local could identify deer in deep woods, across a valley and three-quarters of a mile away. And, on the three occasions that I "saw" a deer on my own, he had to point out that one was a stump, the second was a cow, and the third was a tractor.

This is why it would be useful to have a magician on stage with Mr. Geller, and why general practitioners often need to consult specialists for second medical opinions.

Blindness, bias, and lack of expertise are only samples of the variety of forms that physical, psychological, and experiential limiting conditions can take. There are "environmental" ones, too, ranging from adverse weather to faulty instrumentation. So prudence, and a proper respect for Murphy's Law, demands that whenever data is collected we must ask, "What could conceivably go wrong here?" and either root it out or control for it.

E. The object of due care. All things being held equal, evidence should be the object of disciplined and painstaking labor and study—not slapdash, careless, or thrown together.

> *Example.* The 1989 "proof" of cold fusion that turned out to be the result of contamination, uncontrolled variables, and no small haste to publish says everything that needs to be said.

On the other hand, all things are hard to hold equal. A snap judgment by an expert may be legitimately preferred to a painstaking appraisal by an unperceptive or unintelligent novice. This is another reason why we cannot insist that *all* the criteria be met *every* time.

F. Controlled for ambiguity. *Ambiguous* evidence can be read this way and that. It may mean one thing or another. Slippery and interpretable in many different ways, what it supports and denies is a function of how it's taken. Taken one way it supports P. Taken another way it supports not-P. Its support, then, is of little use.

Little (if any) evidence is *totally* ambiguity free, however. So the realistic first concern is usually to minimize ambiguity rather than eliminate it. The second concern should be to avoid equivocating over whatever ambiguity does occur. Ambiguous evidence that has been exploited through equivocation is useless.

Example. In the ninth century, those who claimed the earth was round, not flat, would have run against the received wisdom of the day. The establishment, skeptical of heresy, would have insisted on evidence to support the radical "round-world" view. Such evidence was available, however, as Irving Copi illustrated nicely in his essay, "Crucial Experiments," in Edward Madden's *The Structure of Scientific Thought*.

If we stand at the ocean front and watch a ship sail out to sea, we will observe that the hull disappears first, then the superstructure, then the mast and sails, and finally the little pennant on top. As *any* ship sails (as we say) "over the horizon," it disappears "from the bottom up." Of course the progressive intervention of the curved surface of the earth between the eye and the object viewed explains this visual phenomenon in a perfectly straightforward way:

Unfortunately, however, that same observation can just as easily support the claim that the earth is flat. All that we have to do is change one premise that was

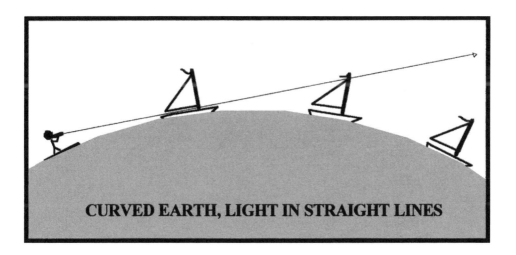

CURVED EARTH, LIGHT IN STRAIGHT LINES

operating in the previous account (which I conveniently did not mention). The premise in question is that light travels in straight lines. Suppose, instead, that light travels in curved lines. Then the hull-first disappearance of departing ships can still be easily explained.

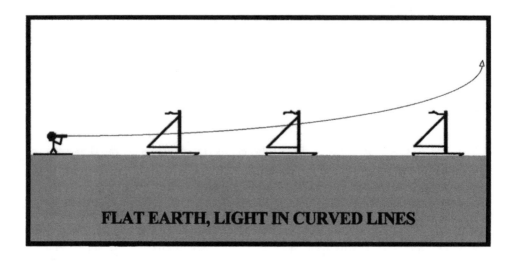

FLAT EARTH, LIGHT IN CURVED LINES

Eyeball evidence is often ambiguous as it stands. Given one set of assumptions, it supports one claim; but given a different set, it supports another—even contradictory—claim. Consequently, by itself, it is not decisive. *It can be read in more than one way.* Most evidence, even of the commonest sorts, is ambiguous in this way.

What to do about that depends on the case. What to do about how ships disappear over the horizon would be to try to establish, on independent grounds, just how light does travel. Of course, people all "know" that light (usually) travels in straight lines; but that can only be established in the context of one or another complex set of assumptions and one or another covering theory. (The fact is, of course, that light does *not* always travel in straight lines according to current theory. It travels in straight lines only when the space it traverses is straight itself, so to speak.)

The availability of alternative theories and assumptions means that choices have to be made even at that level. And where choices have to be made, procedural standards are needed. Without them, there is no effective basis for choosing between:

- curved earth, straight space and light in straight lines,
- flat earth, straight space and light in curved lines, and
- curved earth, curved space and light in geodesics.

Each of these views is logically possible, and has had its advocates at one time or another.

Furthermore, if the "curved space" theory sounds metaphorical, we might wonder whether it is really any better than the flat earth view. It is, but it takes enough showing that not everyone is convinced. It has been only a few years, in fact, since the International Flat Earth Society disbanded. Its members flatly maintained that the orthodox (round) view of the world is a mistake, supported by unexamined assumptions, and incomplete or fraudulent data. (Robot photographs taken from early rockets, for instance, suffered from "lens distortions." First-hand reports from people who had been to the moon, looked back at the earth with their own unaided eyes, and brought back full-color photos that showed the entire earth disc were obvious "fabrications.") Consequently, standards for choosing the assumptions and theories in terms of which evidence will be interpreted are essential.

So evidence requires interpretation, and interpretation depends on the exercise of judgment in selecting the assumptions and theories that frame it. But, even if evidence cannot be ambiguity free, we can at least insist that it be ambiguity minimal and that its interpretation be absolutely *equivocation* free.

G. Formulated in a viable theoretical framework. This has several aspects. At the least, it means that evidence should be construed in terms of a theory that is not *ad hoc*, that is, is not "made to fit."

> *Example.* There was once a man who agreed that the earth is round, but believed that it is a hollow ball with its inhabitants on the inside surface. In his view, as we jump from the surface, we get closer to the earth's center; and, as we tunnel in, we actually proceed outward into its shell. The evidence (taken one way) that supports his view is the same evidence (taken a different way) that backs up the orthodox view.
>
> The success of this hollow ball view depends on adjusting a large number of other basic ideas—in optics and physiology, at least. For instance, the provision is made that the closer an object gets to the middle of the ball, the smaller it becomes.
>
> This is needed in order to cover the visual appearance of what the orthodox would call "elevating" objects. (The size of the sphere is known to be too small to account for the apparent shrinkage of distant objects on purely perspectival grounds.)
>
> So even this theory can "save" at least some of the appearances. Indeed, with *enough* adjustment to everything else we believe, *some* interpretation of eyeball evidence should support *any view at all* about the shape of the earth, what revolves around what, or anything else for that matter.

The degree to which a theory is viable is an inverse function of how much of this sort of ad hoc adjustment is required to make it go. It is also a function of how fertile, coherent, economical, broad in scope, quantifiable, and experientially applicable the theory is.

But as long as the appearances are saved, why not have the world the way we like it? Why are theories with these features thought to be "better" than ad hoc, sterile, incoherent, profligate, narrow, purely qualitative, and experientially inapplicable ones?

"Better" is a verdict, of course. Verdicts are more normative than descriptive, so they have some special problems. They are, however, unavoidable. "True" and "false" are verdicts too; and the whole point of common sense skepticism is to decide when to use which. Only a philosophical nihilist would claim that truth and falsity are irrelevant to choosing what assertions to make, for truth is exactly what we are looking for when making that choice.

We are looking for something very much like truth when choosing what theories and explanations to use. Since the theories we choose will eventually fund our descriptive talk (determining what descriptions will count as true), choosing the right ones is crucially important. I am suggesting that the right ones are the "independently viable" ones.

There are three kinds of reasons for calling theories and explanations "independently viable"—practical, logical, and esthetic.

1) Practical.

a) The aversion to ad hoc theory construction is a matter of productivity. A theory that anticipates events, rather than being trimmed to fit them after the fact, leads in productive directions.

Example. Copernican astronomers know where to look for yet unseen planets rather than waiting for accidental discoveries and cobbling together ad hoc explanations.

b) "Broad" and "parsimonious" theories are favored over "narrow" and "excessive" ones because accepting no more complexity than is minimally required to save *lots* of appearances makes a concrete difference in practice. It simplifies labor, increases efficiency, and reduces the sheer variety of possible errors—all by the simple expedient of rejecting complex theories of narrow scope in favor of simple theories of broad scope.

Example. As noted before, modern astronomers have chosen a modified Copernican view over Ptolemy's scheme, even though the preferred view does not uniquely underwrite accurately finding a planetary location. (Remember that sailors use Ptolemy's apparatus to do that every day.) They choose Copernicus over Ptolemy because his theory is *simpler*. It says that *all* planetary paths are conic sections; and *one* covering model is simpler than separate and different accounts for each planet's path. This simplicity, in turn, means that the theory has great scope (covers a lot of data). Further, conic sections are themselves simpler than the cycle and epicycle paths that the Ptolemaic view requires to keep predictions reliable.

c) Yet another advantage flows from all this. Since a viable theory has broad scope but is not ad hoc, it is fertile. That is, it actually suggests new ways to expand the scope of its own application.

d) The application and manipulation of quantifiable conceptualizations are easier and more precise than purely qualitative ones.

e) Because viable theories are empirically connected, flawed ones either get repaired or weeded out over time. The possibility of such repair, revision, and replacement is their greatest practical virtue. It is in no sense a flaw. Contra "creation science," good conceptualizations are not unchanging. A theory that is not open to correction, like a description that is not open to test, carries no freight, as Daisie and Micahel Radner point out in their *Science and Unreason*. The very *best* theories are genuinely self-correcting: that is, they generate occasions for their own testing and refinement.

A caveat is in order, however. Being empirically connected is not a matter of where a theory comes from, or whether everything it talks about is directly observable. If all scientific ideas had to be derived from experience—that is, were observation statements or generalizations of them—modern science would be dead in the water. Who can see, taste, smell, feel, or hear "mass?"

It is, rather, a matter of what can be done with a theory's output, that is, the empirical success or failure of the descriptions and predictions that it generates and supports, when taken with appropriate auxiliary hypotheses that cannot be generated out of those hypotheses alone.

This is *confirmational* rather than *genetic* empiricism, as was clearly seen by Karl Popper in his *The Logic of Scientific Discovery* and Carl Hempel in his *Philosophy of Natural Science.*

2) Logical. Viable theories are internally coherent and mesh nicely with any others that are in use. This is a matter of simple logical consistency; and consistency is a virtue for theories just as it is for descriptions (and for the same reasons). Further, *independently* viable theories achieve all their other virtues without circularity. This is also a matter of logic; and question-begging theories are just as useless as question-begging descriptions.

3) Esthetic. Conic sections are far more elegant than the Ptolemaic cycles and epicycles that they replaced. The elegance in question here, like much of the elegance of recent science, is mathematical. But elegance is not *just* a mathematical notion. Thermodynamics is more elegant than animism as an account of vulcan activity, the double helix than random chance as an account of genetics, and evolution than piecemeal creationism as an account of biological speciation. In all these cases, it is more a matter of deftness than of numbers. Nor does the notion of elegance apply only to scientific matters. Forcing a mate in three by sacrificing the queen is more elegant than marching massed pawns across the board for multiple promotions, a deft header off a corner than having your opponent score an own goal, and a waltz or merengue than break dancing.

Elegance alone, of course, is not enough to make a theory fly. Nowhere is it written that a clumsy account cannot work. Further, there are philistines who insist that it, like all esthetic matters in their view, is "in the eye of the beholder." So elegance may strike us as a soft virtue, and my examples as unmoving.

If so pragmatic and logical considerations should suffice. Given that people must construe their evidence in terms of some theory or other, there is every reason to do it in terms of broad, fertile, testable, highly quantitative, and parsimonious ones that cohere well and are not ad hoc. Elegance can just be the icing on the cake.

H. Conclusions. Relevant and noncircular evidence, examined with care by seasoned witnesses under circumstances reasonably free of limiting conditions, which can be replicated and is open to public examination (or at least corroborated across the sense modes), is relatively unambiguous, has been checked for defective processing, is free of equivocation, and is formulated in terms of a viable theoretical framework, is highly desirable, but rare. Most evidence has some faults.

So ordinary folk settle for the best they can get and keep their guard up. That is easy to do when arguing with the flakier proponents of Hollow Ball geophysics or those who say life is a deep well. It is harder when assessing orthodox views held by ostensibly intelligent and responsible individuals. But real doubts can arise in the mainstream. Even the most central beliefs and customs of the majority can go awry. So while it may be tiresome to keep our guard up against risks in our own garden, it is still necessary.

3

Two Kinds of Evidence

There are at least six kinds of evidence to which people appeal to support their beliefs: experience, reason, authority, intuition, revelation, and faith. In this chapter, I look at variations on experience and reason.

As obvious as the early points may be, we need to start with them in order to lay a foundation for dealing with the more problematic varieties of evidence (revelation, for instance) and the beliefs that are based on them (that polygamy is evil, for instance). So I will start with very ordinary things about very ordinary matters: looking, tasting, smelling, feeling, and hearing; and sorting out, reflecting on, and inferring from what we see, taste, smell, feel, and hear.

With a clear sense of how ordinary beliefs about "facts" arise out of observation, interpretation, and inference, we will be better equipped to deal with beliefs about religious and political ideology, and so forth, later on. Claims like "today is Monday" and "if I don't eat soon, I'm going to faint" may not sound as profound as "life is a deep well." But if we start close to home and walk carefully, the profound may become transparent—even if some of it turns out to be transparent nonsense.

However, there's a danger that I'm palming an ace here. When we get to "exotic" beliefs, I could say, "This is how I handled ordinary ones, so I must handle these the same way," when in fact I need not. I might do that intentionally, because I have an agenda, or inadvertently because of something I haven't thought through. But decisions about what to believe, and about how reliable our beliefs are, have a practical impact on what we do. So we need to make those decisions on good grounds—not because a writer has hidden an ace or dropped a stitch. So be careful.

1. Experience

For starters, we look, taste, smell, feel, and listen. This is a twenty-first-century Euroculture commonplace. Most of us are "empiricists" to some extent (many *completely*), even if we are aware that there can be problems with particular experiential bits—for instance, that we may, in any given case, be mistaken for a variety of reasons. (We may not have looked the right way; there may be limiting conditions at work on our conceptual and physical evidence gathering apparatus; etc.). This is why we must use tests to see whether a particular piece of experiential evidence will carry freight. Unshared, unrepeatable, ambiguous, carelessly gathered, and equivocally interpreted experience is of little use.

A. What counts as experience? Should we put any limits on what kinds of experience count? Some will have to be imposed when truly "off the wall" experiences are cited—such as Bishop Russell's appeal to conversations with George Washington to support his beliefs about human destiny, or those of the lady I read about in *Parade* when I was about twelve who read *Pravda* with her elbows (really!) to support her claims about current events. But the restrictions should not be arbitrary. We need reasons that are *general, fair,* and *objective* to say "no" to cosmic consciousness and truth-discerning elbows.

The restrictions that look most promising are the very ones examined in the last chapter as *general* evidence criteria and tests. When people fund their beliefs with "experiences" that cannot be confirmed in any way, are not public or cross-checkable, are question begging and ambiguous, and shoot themselves down with contradictions, and so forth, there are good reasons to draw back. Not because we are narrow-minded bigots or epistemological philistines who cannot recognize the wonder of the universe, and so forth, but because such inconsistent, unrepeatable, unconfirmable, not unequivocally interpretable, and unintelligible "experiences" just don't carry freight.

Nevertheless, talk about experience is not necessarily limited to talk about what we see, taste, smell, feel, or hear with our ordinary equipment. It can include *whatever* types of input can be confirmed in the network of testing described above. If someone offers a variety that lies beyond the ordinary but is confirmable in that network, fine. Otherwise, no.

This is exactly how to deal with things like ESP—*not* by ruling them out on the grounds that we cannot effect them ourselves. *That* would be bigotry—like that of a man born blind insisting that because *he* cannot see it, it is unreasonable for anyone to believe the sky is blue. We do not want to close the door in *that* way against *any* possible experiences—including elbow reading. What we do want to do is subject the claims that are made in every venue to rigorous testing, using standard tests. (For the record, using such tests, ESP fares badly. For the reasons why, see Terence Hines's *Pseudoscience and the Paranormal*.)

B. Is experience enough by itself? In whatever forms and whatever circumstances experiences occur, they don't arrive as self-confirming truths or even as working beliefs. They arrive as raw data that needs to be processed before anything can be done with them. Experience must be *worked*.

Consider the following scenario:

- *You are alone.* It is not just that other people have all gone away. There *are* no other people.
- *You are without language.* It is not just that you are in a foreign land and don't speak the local language. You have no language *at all*.
- *You have no memories, nor any capacity to generate them.* It is not just that you tend to forget things from long ago. You have no past because you never remember *anything*.
- *You have no pattern recognition capacity.* It is not just that you get confused. Nothing is *ever* familiar. There are *no* links.
- On the other hand, there are no restrictions whatever on the experiences you might have.

Imagine, then, in this state, sitting on some asteroid, with the whole drama of the ages unrolling in 3-D Technicolor. Every neural receptor you have is being bombarded constantly with sounds and colors, twinges and tweaks, flavors and odors, and so forth.

The only problem is that you can't remember any of them from one moment to the next, recognize any pattern or structure in what occurs, conceptualize or arrange any of it under any kind of syntactical or logical order in terms of any kind of language, or talk about any of it to anyone else or even to yourself.

Finally, still in this context, suppose that:

- Another person appears, not realizing the condition that you are in, who wants you to describe what is going on and report what you believe about it all; and
- You (somehow) acquire, on the spot, both short-term memory and a 100 percent ability to talk colloquial American. (The short-term memory is just so that you can remember your visitor's questions long enough to try to answer them, and the language capacity is just so that you can say *something* more illuminating than "stuff happens.")

Even with these newfound talents, a problem remains: you have nothing to report. This is because experience *alone* (which is the only resource you have had up to the moment) is insufficient to underwrite beliefs (much less *reports* of beliefs) of any kind. For, while experiences have a major role in underwriting beliefs, they are sterile until the one who has them structures, orders, and makes sense of them in terms of:

- a language already in place and remembered;
- previous experiences already in place and remembered;

- patterns of familiarity, unfamiliarity, similarity, dissimilarity, connection, and nonconnection already in place and remembered; and (usually)
- other beliefs, already in place and remembered.

The notion that twinges and tweaks simply fall into your lap as transparent, self-explaining, unambiguous, and lucid deliverances of truth is as absurd as the notion that we can make a ceramic pot without doing anything to the clay; and that just doesn't make sense. We have to impose some structure on raw materials to give them form, or—talking now about sensations rather than clay—to give them meaning. Even if the form (or meaning) is "implicit" in the clay (or sensations), so that it only needs to be "brought out," nothing can happen until the *subject*, using all of the conceptual apparatus at her command, goes to work.

So experience, for all of its importance to what we believe, does not produce insight and understanding by itself. It only does that in the context of the organization that is brought to bear on a situation being observed, in terms of the beliefs, attitudes, outlook, language, memories, prior understandings, theories, wants, and desires, and so forth, that are already in place.

On the other hand, we cannot usefully impose just any pattern on just any material. No matter how excellent a design may be, we still need good material to make a conveyance that will carry what we want carried to the place we want it to go.

- We can't make useful fire-ladders out of tupelo wood. It breaks too easily and it ignites quickly. So we use steel.
- We can't make useful fountain statuary out of soap. It dissolves. So we use stone.

Similarly, no matter how sound the material may be, we also need a good design, good tools, and skill. Good stuff is necessary, but it is not sufficient. Nor can we fashion working beliefs out of any old experiences according to whatever interpretive whimsy strikes. Even as reliable material is necessary but not sufficient for successful products, reliable experiences are necessary but not sufficient for successful beliefs.

These further necessities (good design, good tools, and skill) show why even the most reliable experiences need to be structured within a viable frame of reference and with due care. Only when we have looked at the skill, the care, and the governing model in terms of which experiences are being noted or overlooked, included or dismissed, sorted and emphasized, can we decide whether a particular belief is just some individual's idle fancy or is likely to carry real freight to the right destination.

C. Construal. Observation is a two-place relation. It calls for both an observer and an observed. The observer and the observed both make contributions that are essential to the generation of beliefs. The observer's initial and most basic contribution amounts to construing, that is, categorizing, sorting, making sense of, and interpreting, what the observed supplies. *Observations*, that is, construals of what is observed, are the constituents from which basic beliefs are generated. Basic beliefs, in turn, are the foundation on which more complex beliefs are inferentially built.

The observer's contributions to observation are something *done to* (or *with*) what is observed, that is, part of the observing *subject's* activity rather than of the observed *object itself*. Traditional usage would call such "subject" operations *mental*. Following that line, and broadly dubbing "mental" activity *reasoning*, *all* subject operations could be absorbed under "reason." Three problems, however, suggest that this line is best avoided:

- Using the label "mental activity" tempts us toward mind/body dualism, which as we shall see is highly problematic.
- Using the label "reason" for all mental activities (and "mental activity" for all subject operations) leads to the inclusion of feeling, wanting, willing, and so forth—effectively ignoring needed distinctions between reason, affection, and will.
- It obscures the difference between construing what is observed and inferring from the construed observations.

The subject operations involved in construing, like those involved in inferring, are *epistemic*. Both are ways in which a subject's intentional operations contribute to the formation of beliefs. Inferring is epistemic because belief formation is its point; construing is epistemic because belief formation is its product.

> *Analogy.* On a farm, everything has its season: winter for preparation, summer for harvest. While much of the preparation takes place out of sight, the harvest can be seen from the road. Preparing flats and seedlings in the barn in February is one thing. Harvesting the crop in August on the front forty is another. On "belief farms," construing is the former, inferring the latter.

Historically, philosophers have paid more attention to the harvest (inferring complex beliefs) than to the preparations behind it (construing what is observed). But it is imperative to recognize the contributions that the subject makes to observation itself.

These include categorizing what is observed according to natural or conventional kinds. And that, for humans at least, crucially involves *the imposition of language*: *imaging* (semantic representation), *typing* (sorting into kinds), and *filing* (saving)—all of which are needed to underwrite *recall*. You can't open a file that hasn't been entered, titled, and saved. Nor, without subject contributions, can you correctly believe things such as *"this is like the toothache I had last year"* and proceed appropriately.

There are four essential components in that belief, if it is correct:

- that you *did* have a toothache last year,
- that you *are* having a toothache now,
- that you *recall* having the former, and
- that you *recognize* that this one is like it.

The first two are contributed by the observed. The others are contributed by the observer. With these, and some additional subject-contributed recollections, such as, *I went to the dentist then, she found a bad wisdom tooth and pulled it,* and *I felt lots better afterward,* you are in a position to draw the reasonable conclusion: *I think I will go see the dentist again.*

Although Plato was content (in *Meno)* to label recall a gift of the gods, recent work by cognitive scientists and epistemologists has improved our understanding of it a little. We still do not know *precisely* how it works, but it is quite clear that it does—for people, at any rate. On the other hand, so far as is known, it doesn't work for rocks. That is why they have no beliefs, write no books, and never start wars.

The subject's operations of recall and recognition begin with semantic imaging, that is, the use of representational devices that refer to, or remind us of, things (and characteristics of things) other than themselves. At the simplest level, it employs pictures, models, and onomatopoetic vocalizations. Even simple images are useful. Stories of the hunt are enhanced by wall sketches of mastodons on the run; and such sketches are cheaper, easier, and safer to keep in the cave than mastodons themselves.

More complex images are useful too. The verbalized recounting of the hunt employs one variety of them in profusion: words. Imaging that employs words is more conventionalized than that which relies on pictures, models, and onomatopoetic vocalizations; but they function in much the same way and have several advantages:

- They can be conventionally associated with (and replace in use) non-verbal images that are too difficult for most people to produce easily. For instance, while we may not be sufficiently adept to demonstrate a certain play of light and dark with pigments, with appropriate experience, the word "chiaroscuro" can call it to mind; and with additional experience and vocabulary we can even explain it to others.
- They can be learned by mimicry and reinforcement by people of ordinary abilities.
- They can readily be ordered into structured use, that is, incorporated into a language. This involves both the systematic assignment of specific representational functions to specific words (the semantic specification of vocabulary) and the systematic assignment of specific

representational functions to the ordering and inflection of words (the syntactic specification of grammar). While both are largely the product of social conventions (first learned by mimicry and reinforcement, and then from teachers), they remain open to intentional change.

To make *ordered* use of an *ordered set* of representational devices to refer to things (and characteristics of things) other than themselves is to take up *language*.

Word imaging is the first step in that process. First words are simple markers for sensory patterns recognized. Those words in use constitute further patterns that can also be recognized. This self-nourishing process generates both syntax and an increasingly abstract set of verbal signs. In this way, language grows in scope, complexity, and utility.

A language can be precise and highly developed (consider those of cartography and orchestral scoring), or loose and minimally developed (consider "the language of flowers"). Full blown (consider Mandarin or Swahili), a language makes it possible to sort an infinite variety of observations in fruitful ways and capture them in communicable claims.

Each new person "learns the language" in the process of socialization. No one "makes it up from scratch." It is there first. This is one of the reasons why people in different cultures, marked by different languages, "take" things differently. For good or ill, what we see is a function of the language we have been provided. People develop in different cultures, each of which is marked by (and marks its members with) its own language. Alternate languages provide alternate ways of construing the world.

But the fact that the world can be differently construed in different languages does not mean that it must be construed in just one way within any one language. Our language is socially generated and learned, and our construing is under its constraints, but no single way of taking things is completely determined either socially or linguistically. Language changes in use; and each user can change it.

Over time, a language will come to reflect the sorts of construing that work. The vocabulary and syntax that develop and endure over great stretches of time show not only the "construing inclinations" of their makers and users but also the "construing potentials" of the reality they wrestle with. So reality shapes language, even as language shapes perceived reality. Each language is in a *feedback loop* with reality, stabilizing the way in which those who use it see and represent "the world."

Example. Consider a thermostat. Falling ambient temperature closes the switch, which turns on the furnace, which supplies heat, which raises the ambient temperature until the switch opens, which turns the furnace off, which stops the supply of heat, which allows the ambient temperature to fall . . ., and so forth.

This results (with a good thermostat and a good furnace) in a relatively stable ambient temperature.

Some construals are simple and direct (seeing an animal as food), others complicated and abstract (interpreting a rising employment rate as a harbinger of inflation). Some are nearly universal (seeing every event as *caused*), others local to very specific belief sets (e.g., seeing every event as *intended*). Whatever the level of simplicity, concreteness, and scope, however, construing is ubiquitous. Whatever we see, we see *as*.

- Frugal Tim saw the tree limbs blown down by the storm as fuel and gathered them to burn; but environmental Ann saw them as shelter for animals and left them where they fell.
- Dick and Jane, on their first fishing trip and familiar only with domestic animals, saw the bears as friendly and lovable, and went out of their cabin to pet them.
- Ralph took the new teller's graceless posture and chattiness as come-ons and invited her over for drinks, while Steve saw them as signs of youth and nervousness in a new job and warned her about Ralph's reputation.

We do not always, of course, "make sense of things" successfully. Some construals are better than others. Whether one is better than another depends on many factors, including:

- the flexibility and scope of the language in use,
- the level of the construer's mastery of that language,
- the care exercised,
- the elimination or control of bias and vested interest,
- the absence of distractions, and
- the discovery and control of relevant variables.

Even at its simplest direct level, construing is subject to all the glitches, and appraisable in terms of all the criteria, laid out in chapter 2.

2. Reason
Few today would be startled at the notion that working beliefs begin (or maybe end) in experience; but most *would* be startled at the notion that working beliefs begin in the reflective light of reason—a fortiori in the reflective light of reason *alone*. No one has claimed that sort of thing for years. It is unwise, however, to think that what is (or is not) in vogue at some particular time is the final court of appeal. Unless we are content to be arbitrary and temporally provincial, it would be better to keep reason (even *pure* reason) on the list of possible bases for working beliefs unless and until substantial grounds are found to remove it.

First, we need to look at what "reason" amounts to. Then we can ask, "What is the role of reason, so understood, in establishing beliefs?"

A. What does "reason" amount to? Usually, when we talk about "reason," we are talking about *inferences* of one sort or another. Inference is the activity of drawing conclusions from premises or assumptions—usually by a process of thought on the part of a human subject.

Perhaps it is also something that a less complex organism, or even a device, might do. Chimps solve problems. Computers with very simple programs extract the entailments of data sets. Do such processes involve *inference*? Are they exercises of *thought*? There are nice philosophical problems here. To pursue them, read A. M. Turing's "Computing Machinery and Intelligence" and Daniel Dennett's *Brainstorms* for starters. In a lighter vein, read Isaac Asimov's *I, Robot*.

Inferences come in many forms:

- They can be aimed at strict closure (deduction) or at probable closure (induction).
- They can involve indicative descriptions of contingent matters of fact, or imperative, evaluative, or other modal utterances about matters of either fact or value.
- They can involve applying general principles to particular cases, generalizing principles out of numerous particulars, and extrapolating from observed similarities between cases to probable unobserved similarities between them.

Here are a few examples of simple reasoning, good and bad:

Since everyone who has previously jumped from the Triboro Bridge died as a result, the City Commissioners have refused to allow bungee jumpers to hold any meets there.

The surveyor inferred that the eastern and southern boundaries of this lot meet at an angle of 97 degrees since it is quadrilateral and its other corners have already been measured at 89 degrees, 91 degrees, and 83 degrees.

Mary reasoned that plagiarism would be an honor violation since the code bans cheating, and plagiarism looked like cheating to her.

Bill plans to get "WashBordz" ab implants because he wants babes to chase him the way they do the guys on *Baywatch*.

Inferences are fallible in two distinct ways. Consequently, not everyone who infers succeeds.

First, every inference employs assumptions; and if *they* are flawed the inference itself is flawed. If an inference is to be secure, its assumptions must be secured; and this is something no inference can achieve for itself. The reliability of assumptions will depend, sooner or later, on the quality of the noninferential data that is available, and on the ways in which that data is "taken," sorted, and interpreted. Since inferences can't establish their own assumptions without circularity, an inferential justification would require further assumptions. So absent infinite regress or circularity, some noninferential justification (usually experience of some sort) will be required. The only likely shot for *pure* reason involves inferring from rationally necessary (a priori) assumptions.

Second, each inference processes its assumptions, and that processing can be flawed. Sadly, an inference can no more guarantee its procedures than it can prove its premises. Certain bad procedures—some "informal" and some "formal"—are, however, well known and avoidable.

a) Informal inference failures are usually due to a failure of relevance between the assumptions and what is allegedly inferred from them, or to the exploitation of some ambiguity in the terms employed. Such flawed moves are traditionally called *informal fallacies*.

Post hoc, ergo propter hoc (false cause), question begging (circularity), and accident are a few of the common fallacies of relevance. Equivocation is the most common fallacy that exploits ambiguity. A few real examples will help:

A politician: *New York and California, two-party states, have annual per capita incomes thousands of dollars higher than South Carolina, a one-party state. Don't let party loyalty hold down your paycheck any longer. Vote Republican!*
Such irrelevance is called post hoc, ergo propter hoc.

A student: *I know that God exists because the Bible—which is His Word—says so; and He wouldn't lie.*
Such hyperrelevance is circular—a case of *question begging*.

A teacher: *Clark could understand the readings in Philosophy 101 if he tried. The dean says this year's freshman class is the best we've ever had, so Clark can't be as slow as he seems.*
Even assuming that this year's class is best *on average*, this is irrelevant to Clark's own ability (*accident*). Even oceans have shallows.

A newspaper editorial: *Bennett's educational vision should be implemented. He is America's top educational authority.*
This *equivocates* on an ambiguity in the word "authority" between "one who is expert" and "one who is in charge."

Inferences involving such informal fallacies are fatally flawed. Not meeting even the minimal prerequisites of the argument game, they never really make it onto the playing field.

Once it is known that a particular inference is free from such flaws, a real argument is in play. Whether it will finally succeed will depend on whether it follows reliable procedures for preserving the capital it started with (and, of course, on whether it started with good capital).

b) Many reliable formal procedures have been codified and known for centuries, along with various unreliable ones that look enough like them to be tempting. It is known that (and known why) inferences that involve moves such as *affirming the consequent, denying the antecedent,* and *undistributed middle* squander their capital. A few examples will show why. (For a far more complete treatment of formal arguments, good and bad, see Irving Copi's *Introduction to Logic*):

Affirming the Consequent: *There is irreversible brain damage when the brain's blood supply is blocked for ten minutes. Lothar has irreversible brain damage. So they must have cut off the blood to his brain for ten minutes during his lobotomy.*

Denying the Antecedent: *If you smoke, drink gin, eat pizza, and chase women, you die. So since the Buddha never smoked, drank gin, ate pizza, or chased women, he must be alive today.*

Undistributed Middle: *All Amish adult males have beards. So since Ice T is an adult male and has a beard, he must be Amish.*

It is also known that (and known why) inferences that rely only on moves such as *modus tollens, constructive dilemma,* and *hypothetical syllogism* deliver their capital untarnished.

Modus Tollens: *If this section includes an example of every argument form it will go on forever. So since it obviously does not go on forever, it must not include a complete array.*

Constructive Dilemma: *If the receiver was ahead of the last defender at the time the ball was passed, he was offside and play should be stopped. If the left mid decked the kicker from behind as she passed, a foul was committed and play should be stopped. At least one of those two things occurred, so play should be stopped.*

Hypothetical Syllogism: *If every experience is filtered by a socially determined frame of reference, then every experience description is culturally biased. But if every experience description is culturally biased, no such description can be evaluated from outside the culture in which it occurs. So if every experience is filtered by a socially determined frame of reference, then no experience description can be evaluated from outside the culture in which it occurs.*

Note again that good processing is not enough. With bad assumptions, even the best processing can lead to foolishness—as in the last example.

So reason is, at least in part, the process of inferring conclusions from assumptions, which can be done badly or well in a variety of ways. So understood, it obviously plays an important part in funding beliefs.

B. Is "reason alone" enough? People assert beliefs that they think are about matters of fact and based on reason alone. Some of them are quite familiar and widely shared. For example:

- In base ten arithmetic: *2 + 2 = 4.*
- In two-valued sentential logic: $[(p \supset q) \cdot p] \supset q$
- In Euclidian geometry: *the shortest distance between two points is a straight line.*

Other beliefs that are claimed to be based on reason alone are more startling and are often disputed. For instance:

> According to Alvin Plantinga (because he thinks the ontological argument works): *God exists.*

Reason, however, is *not* capable of generating beliefs about matters of fact by itself. The reasons why are similar to the reasons why experience by itself can't—but turned inside out. An examination of the examples just enumerated will show why, contra appearances, *they are not about matters of fact.*

I have shown that pure experience is incapable of underwriting working beliefs because, although it provides possible *content* for beliefs, that content is chaotic and meaningless without the skillful exercise of a wide variety of human talents. Inversely, pure reason is incapable of underwriting working beliefs because, although it provides *structure* for belief, beliefs need some content to be arranged and reflected on.

Back to the asteroid, in a new situation: It is no longer input but nothing else; now it is everything else but no input.

- *You are aurally, visually, olfactorily, kinesthetically, calorically, and tactilely inert. Any input mode you can think of, you lack.*
  It is not that your receptors have just been turned off or removed, but that you never had any receptors. Consequently, you have never had any input—not even of your own embodiment, much less of any "external" events.
- *Your brain and the rest of your central nervous system, however, are in full working order.*
  Rather like the proverbial potato with "a certain low cunning," you are just *there*, "ticking over."

Under these conditions, if there is a mental life at all it will be limited to local feedback. Nothing *intrudes* or *arises* about anything *else*.

Now, suppose that a device picks up your brain waves, translates them into English, and broadcasts them widely. Suppose further that some people tune in on the broadcast. Which of the following are they likely to hear?

- $E = mc^2$.
- Cogito, ergo sum.
- God is that than which no greater can be conceived.
- A low hum.

Trying to construct beliefs without input is like being sent to the pottery shed again; but this time being told to make a ceramic pot without using any clay, a *pure* ceramic pot that incorporates no raw material at all; and that just doesn't make sense either.

I am obliged to conclude that the exercise of the mind absent any and all experiential input is just as sterile as the exercise of sensation absent any and all interpretation and inference. Pure experience is chaos, and pure reason is structure without content. Working beliefs are not forthcoming from raw experience or pure reason, but only (as far as reason and experience are concerned) from the two working together: *construed experience* furnishing the material used and *inference* using the material furnished. Working beliefs about X rely on experiences of X: ones about China on experiences of China, ones about inner being on experiences of it, and ones about other minds on experiences of them. If China, inner being, or other minds aren't there to experience, you are out of luck.

3. Experience and Reason Working Together

There are many ways in which reason and construed experience can be jointly used to generate beliefs. None is foolproof. Here are two:

- Generalizing from particular experiences to universal claims is common, and sometimes effective. (Note that this is not the only way to reach universal claims, however. Einstein didn't reach $E = mc^2$ by generalizing twinges and tweaks. E, m, and c twinge not, neither do they tweak.)
- Deducing particular claims from general principles that are already in place is also common—equally common and equally chancy.

These two patterns often run in a loop: observing, then generalizing, then deducing consequences from the generalization, then observationally testing to refine the generalization, and so forth

A. Generalization. Having already employed memory and pattern recognition to massage individual experiences into usable data, we can generalize that data to make predictions about the patterns into which future experiences are likely to fall. Even when done with great care, however, this process enables *probable* claims only, never *certain* ones. To generalize is to extrapolate from what *has* been observed to what has *not* been observed; and that relies on the assumption that observed patterns will continue indefinitely (which is only probable at best).

This assumption, called "the principle of the uniformity of nature," is not provable without circularity. *That* is "the problem of induction." In my view, this is a problem only if people expect more from generalization than is healthy. People with excessive expectations should be familiar with disappointment; and expecting certainty when generalizing is surely excessive. Since they start with a probable assumption, generalizations can generate no more than probable results.

The broader the data sample on which a generalization is based, and the more variables that are taken into account, the higher the generalization's level of probability. Under very controlled circumstances, that probability can even be "beyond reasonable doubt." Even then, however, error *is* possible. "Highly probable" ≠ "for sure."

On the other hand, "not for sure" ≠ "arbitrary and capricious" either. So while remembering that even the best generalizations are uncertain, we should forebear going to pieces about it. To panic and say, "Generalizations are never certain, so I will confine myself to deduction and never generalize again," would be as silly as a trucking company executive saying, "The fleet average for Peterbilts is 6 mpg as compared to 117 for Yamahas; so we should replace all our tractors with motorcycles." The probabilistic nature of generalizing is no reason to abandon ship.

> *Example.* Until 1963 I believed all swans were white. When I saw my first black one, I didn't swear off generalizing. I became more cautious by making *more careful* extrapolations on *better* grounds, not by refraining from generalizing altogether.

B. Deduction. We can also generate beliefs by deduction from whatever principles, theories, and construed observations we already have in hand: deducing further beliefs from beliefs in place. This gives tighter closure than generalizing does and even has the reputation of being "certain." But the certainty of deduced conclusions is conditional. For the conclusion of a deduction to be established as *true*, not only must the deduction be validly carried out, the "beliefs in place" must be true themselves. For the conclusion of a deduction to be established as *certain*, the deduction must be valid and the beliefs in place *necessarily* true. If the beliefs in place are only *contingently* true, the output will be contingent too. Sadly, for those who crave necessity, empirically significant beliefs in place are *always* contingent. Necessary truths, such as "either it is raining or it isn't" tell nothing about the world, for they are equally compatible with anything that might occur. We can't get anything out of a deductive inference that is not, in some sense and in some form, already packed into its premises. It is rather like unpacking a suitcase: we shouldn't be startled on unpacking to fail to find a Rolex when all that was packed was a Swatch.

To those with high expectations, it may be a disappointment that deductive inference can *only* preserve the truth we start with. But surely that is not enough to make us give up deduction. After all, it does preserve whatever truth we start with. If we do the logic right, whatever is there at the start will still be there at the finish. On the other hand, if we start out with bad principles and false claims, we should not be startled when dubious claims appear on the bottom line. It is not unlike canning beans. Canning beans does not improve them or make them new, it just keeps them from spoiling. If we start out with moldy beans and a faulty canning kettle, we should not be startled when botulism strikes. Nor should we be discouraged from canning. Properly canned beans are better in December than "fresh" ones that have remained in the field since July.

Deductive inference does have one result that bean canning lacks: by explicitly synthesizing the bits that are implicit, piecemeal, in a set of assumptions, and arranging them so that their relationships are visible, we may bring into focus items that we have not noticed before. Such "elucidation" is unlikely in the bean cannery.

But there still will not be anything in the last line that was not implicit in the combination of the preceding ones. In manipulating premises and deducing conclusions, we do not create new truths. So when looking for new truths, we need to do more than manipulate the content and form of the beliefs that we already have in hand. We need to search out new *input*.

Expanding the scope and variety of our experience is the obvious route to go, but there are at least four different ways to do that:

- get out (or further out) "in the field,"
- increase the diligence and skill with which we observe,
- acquire new (or improve existing) instrumentation, and
- construe what we observe in new ways.

All four are best done with your imagination, creativity, and aggressive commitment to experimentation unchecked.

The wider our orbit the more input we are likely to have. All things held equal, those who live in isolation booths lack the variety of things to observe that are readily available to those more venturesome souls who roam the woods, dive the oceans, and walk the city streets. This is why "closet" science is not credible. Speculation without fieldwork is sterile because it is not anchored to events. Aggressive exploration anchors and connects our attention to *diverse* events. Consider the difference between observing gorillas by going to the zoo and observing them by living with them in the rain forest.

The greater the diligence and skill with which observation is carried out, the richer its harvest will be. Unpracticed physicians are poor diagnosticians. Preoccupied or sleepy sentries are poor guards. Even tall and long-armed goalies make fewer saves if they are hungry, searching the box for four leaf clovers, or daydreaming about the World Cup. This is why "untrained" science is not credible. We need to *learn* how to look and how to control for outside variables. So we check credentials when hiring medical technicians. Have they learned what to look for? Are they sufficiently diligent to spot something they are *not* looking for? Consider the difference between the results when a Cub Scout and Tonto "read trail sign."

The better and more extensive the instrumentation available, the richer the "strikes" will be. This is true of oil exploration, medical research, and everyday affairs. Oil development companies hire geologists rather than dowsers, typically, because successful well placement is more likely using a seismograph than a witching wand. Seeing Neptune waited on lenses. Radio astronomy waited on, well, radio. The mark of twenty-first-century medical practice is instrumentation, too. It may be overkill to do an MRI of an ingrown toenail; but for a life-threatening, soft-tissue disorder it could be indispensable. Good "bedside manner" cannot compensate for the lack of a microscope or x-ray machine. This is why old country doctors are at a disadvantage to even the youngest practitioners who read their journals and catalogs to keep their training and instrumentation current.

C. Hypothesis creation. Between 1880 and 1920 a number of highly creative physicists broke brand-new scientific ground. They invented new ways of looking at facts, constructed new theories, and with those new tools in hand went on to discover new facts. The core of what they did was neither the generalization of observations nor deduction from principles and observations in hand. It amounted to the free creation of new hypotheses; and it turned the world upside down.

Much of what the more pedestrian scientists have done in the last eighty-five years has been to exploit the turf those revolutionaries broke. Eventually, that exploitation complete and the new paradigm well established, stable, and old, another "revolution" will occur—new thinkers breaking new ground once again. Startling things will happen, new questions will be asked, new data will be discovered; and then there will be new turf for the pedestrians of several future generations to plow. This will not happen by people generalizing on what they have observed or drawing deductive inferences from what they already have in hand. It will happen, once again, by free hypothesis creation—by "bold invention."

How that happens is obscure. *That* it happens, however, is clear. It is also clear that most of the world's population contributes very little to it. Most of what most people do, including me, amounts to exploiting the ground that a few others have broken. But, of course, if the insights of the few have no experientially testable output, then they will not be of any use to the rest of us. It may well be that everything deep is obscure, but the converse does not follow.

4

Other Kinds of Evidence

Is there any evidence beyond construed experience used by reason? Authority, intuition, revelation, and faith are four possibilities.

4. Authority

Funding beliefs with appeals to authority is something most people do, necessarily, every day. Having said that, I must explain and qualify it. Why are appeals to authority so common and necessary?

I have previously suggested two bizarre scenarios—one with no input, another with input but no tools to process it. Consider a third—one that allows all the different kinds of input that people generally have and all the processing tools they generally possess, but where second-hand evidence of every kind is strictly barred. In *this* scenario, everything that you believe must be found and processed *on your own*. No one can be an "authority" relied on by others. Life there would be much more complicated and tiresome than in the real world, where much of what anyone believes relies on the testimony of others—sometimes an actual person you know (or know of), but sometimes only what has found its way into the "record." The fact that this is seldom "hands on" is often a good thing.

> *Example.* It is perfectly reasonable to let the question "is potassium cyanide lethal?" be settled by someone else. Indeed, almost everyone who believes that it is lethal has never taken it, never seen anyone take it, and never known anyone who took it; and the belief is not even second hand. It is *third* or *fourth* hand; and, often enough, based on reading Patricia Cornwell or watching *Monk*, with a little reinforcement from the news.
>
> Fiction, reinforced by confessed opinion manipulators! How much of what is believed comes from such sources is a little scary; but it need not be paralyzingly so. People who write for public consumption put their claims into an arena

where testing and refutation are possible. Indeed, academics and scientists are supposed to publish their work for just this reason.

Example. I first visited England many years ago. Upon landing, I went down an escalator and caught the underground. Eventually, I left it, climbed a long flight of stairs, looked up, and saw Big Ben. Before I climbed those stairs, it was perfectly reasonable for me to believe that I was in London and not Bangkok. I had no first-hand grounds; but I did have considerable exposure to novels and histories read, movies and news reports seen, and stories heard from dozens of my more cosmopolitan colleagues. And I made good on that when it cashed out, first hand, on demand.

The reason to be confident in such cases is that the evidence in play is *in the public arena*. Consequently, if it were a hoax, *someone* is likely to notice and pass the word.

There would be little or no intellectual progress in an authority-rejecting world. No one could "stand on Galileo's shoulders." For that matter, no one could rely on his own memory of previous observations either. Why trust yesterday's self any more than a neighbor, a historian, or a news analyst? But in the real world we do not need to invent the internal combustion engine or personally rediscover the principle of the wheel each morning before attempting a trip to the office. What better reasons to believe that the engine will run and the wheels roll than that: you bought the car from a manufacturer's dealer who understands car stuff first hand, does business in public, and can be sued; and you have driven cars hundreds of times and learned how they work. So you don't really have to wonder what will happen when the ignition key is turned each morning (unless, perhaps, you have taken up a sideline business at which the local posse has taken offense).

Of course, we should not think that there are no *risks* involved. There is always the risk of simple mistakes—and the longer the chain of intermediaries, the higher that risk is; there is the danger of intentional deception; and, most important, there is the need to be as sure as can be that the "authorities" we turn to *are* authorities on the matter at issue.

Going to someone as an authority who is *not* an authority on the matter in question is one of the commonest fallacies in reasoning. When listening to the competing claims of various parties who present themselves as authorities, you must decide whom to believe. And that, of course, demands careful attention to a whole network of questions, previously explored: what is confirmable, what can be replicated, what is public, and so forth. So you should accept a claim from some "authority" that X is true only if you have every reason to think that if you ran the appropriate tests yourself you would get the same results the "authority" alleges. That is how a person becomes a *real* authority, after all: issuing claims that pass public tests again and again.

Unfortunately, people use "authority" in two distinct ways:

- to represent a person, group of persons, book, or other source that has tested expertise in a given area (bridge, race car driving, colonial American genealogy, whatever).
- to represent a person, group of persons, book, or other source that has a position of power or prestige in a given community (the clergy, the Council of Deans, the police, whatever).

This double use would be OK if people were never confused by it; but they are. Regularly.

> *Example.* In the middle of the Vietnam War, many citizens clamored for the United States to withdraw its forces. But the president's spokesman, Ron "Zig Zag" Ziegler, told the press that because Nixon was the nation's constituted authority on foreign affairs, he knew what he was doing, and shouldn't be questioned.
>
> Cynics, however, suspected that Nixon was being called an expert by virtue of the power he held; that is, that he was called an authority (expert) just because he was an authority (position holder), in spite of the fact that it is always possible (and sometimes plausible) that a position of great importance is occupied by a dunce or a scoundrel.

The point here is not about Nixon. Rather, it is that *no* office or position invests automatic insight on its occupant. So while appealing to the right kind of authority (i.e., a recognized expert) is fine, appealing to the wrong kind (i.e., a position or power holder) is simply absurd; and that point is timeless and nonpartisan.

> *The best thing to do is what the King says: send another boatload of soldiers to quell the Incas and keep the world safe for monarchy. The last twenty boatloads never came home, but we should never question the King's authority. He is the King. He knows best.*

So while we might think that appeals to authority invoke a new kind of evidence to add to reason and experience, they don't. When we go to a *bona fide* authority, what do we get? *Their* reason and experience second hand. It isn't that there is something *alongside of* thinking and experiencing called "appealing to authority"; it is simply that the thinking and experiencing that we appeal to need not be *our own*.

Further, authority—used as an extension of experience and reason to admit second-hand data—can only be as good as the first-hand experience and reason that fund it (to which we are appealing by way of the expert). Being second hand never makes it *better*.

5. Intuition

Intuition is said to be *immediate*. Alleged cases include a variety of phenomena ranging from special female insight to precognition. Lacking any specific positive force, the word "intuition" operates largely as an *excluder,* that is, its basic function is to rule out the ordinary ways that people arrive at beliefs. Thus, to say that some particular belief is "intuited" is usually to claim no more than that it is *not* deduced, *not* generalized from observations, *not* reached by the senses, and so forth.

Claiming that a belief was *not* arrived at in an ordinary way does not, of course, explain how it *was* achieved; and to think that it does is to commit the "naming fallacy."

The naming fallacy amounts to construing a mere label as an explanation, for example, when people with upper respiratory irritation are impressed by the diagnostic skill of a physician who tells them they have *laryngitis*. It occurs whenever *intuition* is offered as an "explanation" of situations where we simply *do not know* the source or grounds of a belief but hate to say so. Used that way, the term is only a cover for missing information and is no more illuminating than citing *metabolic abatement* as the cause of death on a coroner's certificate. This is, furthermore, an especially dangerous instance of the fallacy because the term "intuition" has acquired heavy connotations of miraculous, occult, and esoteric faculties being in play.

Which Word Wears the Pants?

An excluder is a term that rules out one or another of a variety of properties rather than affirming any specific property in its own right. To explore this useful notion, read Roland Hall's "Excluders." I will use this idea (and explain it more completely) in chapter 10.

People may claim a belief is not arrived at in ordinary ways, even though ordinary procedures *are* in play. This can happen because:

- the uncurious may not bother to look,
- the inattentive may fail to notice,
- the challenged and inexperienced may not have access, and
- the agenda-driven may willfully ignore.

But the establishment of intuition as an independent provenance for belief depends on the occurrence of beliefs that show no ordinary roots even after a *thorough, careful, unbiased,* and *systematic* search. And, under such scrutiny, most alleged "intuitions" yield to more pedestrian explanations:

A. An ordinary belief source may simply go unnoticed. Watson may have thought intuition was the source of Holmes's belief that the one-legged man burned the will and only later, if ever, spotted the peg prints on the hearth that actually turned the trick for him. A judgment may have been made, or an inference drawn, by way of experience and inference routines that are so practiced as to have become second nature, habitual, or automatic. Once learned, internalized, and not forgotten, a path may be so familiar and well worn that walking it requires no self-conscious attention. (It may even go better without it. Thinking about a familiar routine can get in the way of following it.)

> *Examples.* Bruce has been a detective for thirty years and is pretty good at his work. Part of his detecting does consist of clue-generated hypothesis construction and experimental hypothesis testing; but the most important part, he says, amounts to using his "nose" to *smell out* what is going on.
>
> Joe is a well-practiced and successful physicist and engineer. He says that he often relies on *hunches* to find solutions to problems. Like many of his colleagues, he says that he can often just *see* what experimental maneuvers are promising.
>
> Betty and Bill, returning home from a day at the light bulb factory, discern the state of their union without using a magnifying glass or a computer. No need to *figure out* how things are. They can *tell*, especially if things are bad. One spouse's, "How did you know it's been a bad day?" is often best answered with the other's, "I could just feel it in the air."
>
> Tom shows a bunch of bananas and asks, "How many?" Without removing his mittens and counting, Jay sees and says "Five."

Nothing mysterious is involved in any of these cases, only permutations on reason and experience—no occult leaps, only the practiced pursuit of well-worn trails. It is not amazing that Bruce has good hunches at crime scenes or that Joe can image a piece of lab apparatus that will work. It would be amazing if they *couldn't*. It would *really* be occult if, reading about cold fusion attempts, Bruce said, "It would work if they put the cathode in front of the anode," or if, reading a story about a killing, Joe said that the stepmother did it. But, of course, they don't. Bruce has no physicist's intuition, nor has Joe any detective's.

Similarly, since established domestic relationships do have a normal atmosphere, it takes a partner who *can't* tell that it is out of balance to generate perplexity. (How could *anyone* be so thick, preoccupied, or out of touch?) And Jay, like other normal adults, has counted bananas frequently enough before to make the feat an unlikely spot for the late show.

B. Some alleged cases of intuition turn out to be no more than the result of luck, coincidence, or fraud.

> *Examples.* Roy wakes up at midnight and says, "Aunt Bea just died." Dale asks why he thinks so and he replies, "I just feel it in my bones. She's dead, you'll see. Call Andy." So Dale calls Andy and discovers that Aunt Bea *has* just died.

Zorg (available at a 900 number 24-7) tells Barney (trying the free initial consultation), "You often feel misunderstood and rejected, but your deep inner character will win the heart of a loving partner if you will just be yourself." The next day, Barney tells a coworker, "It was like Zorg had known me all my life. You should call yourself."

Pat (at a prayer breakfast in Philadelphia) tells God, "Someone here is suffering with hemorrhoids," and seeks divine healing. Squirming with pain and embarrassment, Lou wonders how Pat could tell and hopes that his divine leverage matches his uncanny perception.

If Aunt Bea was diagnosed with terminal cancer seventeen months ago, and Roy has announced her demise frequently, Dale could discount the present hit by noting that he "had to get it right sooner or later." If Zorg says the same thing when the coworker calls, Barney can discount the alleged insight as a one-size-fits-all cold reading. If Lou reflects on the hemorrhoid rate among people who attend prayer breakfasts, Pat's discernment can be discounted as a safe guess. Only intuition cases that cannot be discounted so easily can legitimately demand a unique place in the epistemic Sun. Are there any? Even the story about Roy, Dale, and Aunt Bea *might* qualify, with a little amendment—Bea was never sick, had no vices, and ran ten K a day; Roy has never made a claim beyond the range of ordinary perceptions until he wakes at midnight and says, "Aunt Bea just died"; and so forth.

C. The hard-core cases of intuition are the ones that involve allegedly irreducible "nonphysical" experiences and "noninferential" insights.

> *Example.* Marty, pregnant wife of an Air Force pilot, clutched her abdomen in response to a sudden sharp pain. Looking at her watch (to time the intervals in case labor had begun), she noted it was 3:14. No more pains occurred, so she resumed her routine. Later that afternoon, Marty got a call from the air base infirmary. Her husband ruptured his diaphragm, making a bad landing, and had been taken to the hospital for surgery. *His injury occurred at 3:14, precisely.*

Is this a mere coincidence, or is it an instance of the "paranormal" intuitive awareness that is said to occur between some couples and twins?

The label "paranormal" is not very tightly defined. It covers at least three different kinds of phenomena, not all of which directly involve unusual *epistemic* dimensions.

1) Beings and their activities such as aliens, Nessie, and Big Foot (on the corporeal side), and demons, souls, and ghosts (on the incorporeal side). While we can believe that such things exist on paranormal grounds, the belief is often based on ordinary experiences that the believer has had (however unorthodoxly construed). They have *seen* Nessie, *talked to* the departed, or *been on* a space ship. "Intuition" may not be necessary here, but it is often called on to back up the construal: *I was directly aware that it was my dead Father's spirit speaking to me at the séance—I didn't have to figure it out.*

2) Enterprises such as alchemy, astrology, and witchcraft, whose practitioners claim access to data, procedures, insights, and predictions that are beyond normal human ken. Intuition is regularly asserted in such contexts as a covering label for otherwise inexplicable epistemic claims. Note, for example, how much astrological predictions are unlike scientific ones.

> *Example.* Compare "According to Mendel, since Olaf and Lori are both true blondes, their children will be also" and "According to Madame Zorg, money matters will be important next week because I am a Libra." The first has a complex and testable experiential basis. Does the second?

An appeal to something like "intuition" is pretty evident here. But there are many problems involved if we take that appeal to explain anything. For instance, even the most highly skilled astrologers can't agree on the rules for their enterprises; and more importantly the accuracy of their predictions—except for those formulated to be compatible with any and all states of affairs—is systematically no better than chance.

3) Claims to obtain information by way of clairvoyance, remote viewing, telepathy, precognition, crystal balls, tarot cards, and the like. Here, *paranormal epistemic access* is clearly asserted. But if this is what "intuition" amounts to, problems abound.

With all the types of allegedly paranormal phenomena in mind (beings, enterprises, and abilities), consider the following embellishment of a tale presented as true by The Rt. Rev. Leslie Weatherhead in his remarkable book *The Christian Agnostic:*

> *A Story.* A young English couple, Nigel and Penelope, lived in Rome where Nigel was an undersecretary at the British Embassy. While there, Penelope gave birth to a golden-haired daughter, Aurora, and hired a young Italian nanny to care for her.
>
> Gina, the nanny, would take Aurora for walks, bathe, and feed her, and (after presenting her to her parents for "good nights"), sing her the lullaby *Caro Mio Ben*.
>
> While on a ski holiday, the family was struck by tragedy (in the form of an Alpine postal bus). Little Aurora was killed, and Nigel and Penelope injured. Later, physical recovery complete but still grieving, the parents returned to England.
>
> Normal life resumed: Nigel was reassigned to Stockholm, and Penelope became pregnant again. But her peace of mind was marred by a recurring dream in which a golden-haired girl would stand at the foot of her bed and say, "I'm coming back," waking her in terror. With counseling, however, the dreams stopped some weeks before a blonde daughter, Felicity, was born.
>
> A young Swedish nanny was hired to care for Felicity; but each afternoon, at teatime, she would return Felicity to her mother and go home. One day at tea, little Felicity—cradling and rocking her doll in her arms—began to sing,

"Caro mio ben . . ."
Aghast, her mother shrieked,
"What are you singing? Who taught you that?"
To which Felicity sweetly replied,
"No one taught it to me, Mummy. I have always
known that song. It is *my* song."

This story may be a myth, an exaggeration, or a lie, of course. If we have good reasons to think it is, it can simply be dismissed. Even if, giving Weatherhead credit for *some* veracity, it is true, however, it can be read in more than one way. How can we best construe it?

The story was originally presented as evidence for belief in reincarnation. But if the reincarnation hypothesis cannot be discounted in any other way, it can certainly be set aside in favor of the idea that Felicity learned the lullaby telepathically from her mother (who, obviously, still nursed memories of Aurora). The general principles of theory formation insist that we favor hypotheses that mesh with the rest of our beliefs with the least disruption and the most harmony, and a little telepathy is vastly easier to assimilate than migrating souls.

Since the story minimally suggests that some human beliefs and performance capacities are not acquired via the standard routes, it is a solid candidate, at least initially, for some paranormal sense of "intuition." But if stories like this tempt us to consider adding *telepathy* (or some other nonsensory path) to the list of routes-to-belief, we should not yield before extensive investigation to confirm the story's reliability, and the review of every possible way to explain it. For, while what is reported *may* amount to the transmission and reception of signals that can be located, identified, mapped, and verified, it may *not*.

In fact, alleged telepathy cases don't fare well in controlled tests. And there are theoretical problems with the idea that they involve not-yet-mapped signals: all known signals attenuate over distance, but these don't. (If the allegedly epistemic neighborhoods of the paranormal are of interest, read *The Skeptical Inquirer* for six months before spending a bundle on "new age" books.)

The bottom line is: *What routes pass muster?* Any route, even telepathy (and the other allegedly paranormal epistemic paths, for that matter), can be added to *look, taste, smell, feel,* and *hear,* if and when it passes the tests they have passed.

So we are left with a dilemma.

On pain of repeating the naming fallacy, we can't take "X intuitively knows what Y knows" to mean "X is *telepathically reading Y's mind*" until that technique is mapped and figured out (until, perhaps, *mind waves* are located and tested). Short of that, all we can take "X intuitively knows what Y knows" to mean is "no one has any idea how X does it."

On the other hand, if we identify and map the telepathy information channel (and verify that it works), it is no longer *paranormal* in any interesting sense. If (say) "reading mind waves" were verified to work under test conditions, then the list of *normal* information channels would immediately become look, taste, smell, feel, hear, *and read mind waves.* And exactly the same thing would happen if any of the other allegedly paranormal epistemic routes proved out. Indeed, many things are rare without being paranormal—talent and intelligence for example. But even when we see evidence of a *very* rare skill (say the spotless first-draft manuscript of Bertrand Russell's *Principia Mathematica*), admiration is in order—not holy awe.

So using "intuition" to label untestable (or failed) "paranormal input" is sterile; and *verified* "paranormal intuitions," should any occur, are neither *paranormal* nor *intuitive.* They are not an alternative to experience reasonably employed, but only one of its less populated neighborhoods—just as appeals to authority are not an alternative to experience reasonably employed, but only its second-hand district.

Consequently, claims of "intuitive" epistemic input provide no reason to reject or make exceptions to the principle that beliefs are best generated by reflection on, and inferences from, construed experience.

6. Revelation

Many people affirm beliefs that, they say, have been "revealed" to them in one way or another. Revelations usually occur in religious settings, with one or another God as their alleged source, but they are not confined to any particular era, region, or ideology. Usually, the allegedly revealed beliefs are not of a sort that could be gained by ordinary experience or inference. Their content runs a gamut of alleged facts, predictions, evaluations, and commands that vary in the scope of their application from the individual and personal to the universal, all made known to man by an "outside" source.

The vehicle can vary from allegedly inspired interpretations of ordinary events to words written in the sky, voices heard in the night, and texts found on hillsides scattered from the Middle East to rural Pennsylvania. "Inspired" interpretations of the "omens and portents" found in natural events are somewhat less spectacular than the receipt of verbalized messages; but all of these phenomena equally presuppose the reality of a "revealer" or "inspirer."

Here are a few examples:

- From Mt. Sinai: *Thou shalt honor thy father and thy mother.*
- From Arabia: *There is no God but Allah.*
- From Nicea: *Jesus Christ is of one being with the Father.*
- From New York: *Exactly 144,000 people will go to paradise.*
- From Pennsylvania: *The world will come to an end in 1899.*
- From California: *Armageddon will occur in 2000.*

A. Such claims occur widely enough that the phenomena cannot be rejected without examination. Some (or all) of them may not make it onto the roster of *reliable* beliefs, and revelation itself may not make it onto the roster of *reliable* belief sources; but neither the beliefs nor their alleged channel can be kept off on a priori grounds.

However, the alleged revelations that occur, and the beliefs based on them, are so divergent in content that there is no way anyone can reasonably believe *all* of them. For instance, there is no room for accommodation between the following two allegedly revealed beliefs:

- *Jesus Christ is of one being with the Father.*
- *There is no God but Allah.*

For that matter, there is often no room for accommodation between two allegedly revealed beliefs that belong to the same tradition and are derived from the same allegedly revealed text.

> *Example.* There is no way that Calvinist and Arminian views on free will can both be true. This is why the Reformed Church in America and the Wesleyan Methodist Church are at some theological odds in spite of the fact that they both claim the label "Christian" and affirm biblical literalism.
>
> While they are more tolerant than their theological ancestors (who killed each other over this issue in the sixteenth century), the logical incompatibility of their views still remains.

Because of this rivalry, it is just as absurd to *affirm* a belief merely because it is said to be revealed as it would be to *reject* one merely because it is said to be revealed. Judgment and a decision procedure are called for in every case for picking which (if any) to affirm and which (if any) to dismiss.

B. An appeal to revelation is, inherently, an appeal to the authority of the revealer, and for most people to the authority of the original recipient of the revelation as well. Consequently, it is wise to ask three questions about alleged revelations:

- "Where is it supposed to have come from?"
- "How was it mediated?" and
- "Are those two sources generally reliable?"

But the only way to answer the last one is by examining the *content* of the full range of revelations that come from a source by way of a mediator, to see how dependable *that* is. The cachet of an alleged authority is derived from the reliability of its output, not *vice versa*.

> *Examples.* Since the world did *not* end in 1899, we should be careful about relying on those (now memorialized at World's End State Park, Pennsylvania) who predicted that it would.

Since the Jehovah's Witnesses raised the revealed paradise population limit of 144,000 when their membership passed that number, there is no reason to trust the sources of either figure indiscriminately.

Since honoring your father and mother is a useful precept for social stability, you might usefully look at other precepts of the same provenance, even if you discount a literal reading of the story about Moses on the mountain and how he acquired them.

C. Direct or immediate revelations are fairly unusual. Most people don't claim to have had any themselves. Most people who hold "revelation-based" beliefs are relying on reports of events in *someone else's* life. When they do so they appeal to authority twice over; and their belief is only as reliable as the weakest link in an authority chain consisting of:

- the revealer,
- the direct recipient(s) of the revelation, and
- however many intermediaries there are between the recipient(s) and the present believer(s).

This opens up more occasions for mistakes and deceptions; but the bottom line is still *how reliable are the "revelations" themselves?*

D. Revelation claims are not confined to faraway places, saintly individuals, or ancient times, but it is tempting to be casually dismissive toward contemporary ones. Prophets are still without honor in their own country. Though this can be unfair, it is not necessarily unreasonable: we are likely to know much more (and more directly) about a contemporary and ordinary seer than about a distant and legendary one. So we are in a much better position to raise the issue of fraud and deception; and raise it we should. While alleged revelations that come in ordinary situations to ordinary people deserve the same respect that we would give to claims by Moses, Jesus, or Mohammed, respect ≠ credulity.

> *Example.* I am recounting this particular story because it was told in my hearing by a man who claimed to have personally had a communication from God (in English) on an ordinary April day in Georgia. If I had ever had a revelation myself, I would tell that story instead. The reporter, an evangelist, was popular on the revival circuit in the 1950s. I heard him at the Walnut Street Baptist Church in Louisville, Kentucky, in 1956.
>
> While a high school senior, Max Morris worked closely as an unofficial "big brother" with a boy in his family's church. The boy, Timmy, liked to play hooky and get into mischief; so Morris tried to help him walk the straight and narrow.
>
> One day, Max was called into the principal's office and told that Timmy had been injured in an accident and was in the hospital, calling for him. Timmy, playing hooky again, had been fooling around with a blowtorch in his dad's garage when it exploded.
>
> Arriving at the hospital, Max was horrified at Timmy's condition: badly burned, only semiconscious, and obviously about to die. Gagging at the sight and smell, Morris fled.

"Later," he said, "overwhelmed with the horror of what the blazing gasoline had done to the little boy, I prayed:
'Oh God, Dear Jesus God,
If that's what fire will do to human flesh,
then please dear God, please Jesus,
don't let Hell be literal Fire.'
But God reached down and put His hand on my shoulder, and said
'I'm sorry Max, but that's the way it is.'"

How should we react to such stories? Morris wanted his hearers to react in a very specific fashion, and a number of them did. As his story progressed, there were groans of anguish from many; and at its end some were shouting, "Spare us, spare us from the flames!" Some, however, squirmed with embarrassment or struggled to suppress laughter.

Many people to whom I replay this story dismiss it, saying, "Consider the source." Others nod gravely, saying, "Sad but true, that's just what the Bible says." If I said (with suitable alterations) that it came from a Himalayan guru who eats nothing but goat cheese and meditates day and night, or from a Persian scroll (carbon dated 385 B.C.), still others would take it as profoundly important. But the way in which we react should be based on reasons better than ad hominem attacks, spurious appeals to authority, and exotica or antiquity indexes. There are standard criteria for working beliefs and effective evidence; and they are worth recapitulating.

We should rule out putative beliefs that are nonsensical, epistemically empty, inconsequential, unintelligible, or contradictory.
We should not favor beliefs solely because they are liked, familiar, or orthodox, make us feel good, or are enabling or validating.
We should favor beliefs that are true (or probably true).
We should link (probable) truth to evidence that is:

- relevant to what is at stake,
- repeatable and public,
- checkable on more than one channel,
- controlled for limiting conditions,
- the object of disciplined and painstaking labor,
- as free of ambiguity as possible,
- not equivocated over, and
- construed in a viable conceptual framework.

A viable conceptual framework is:

- simple and parsimonious,
- fertile,
- not ad hoc,

- broad in scope,
- coherent,
- quantitatively manipulatable,
- empirically connected, and
- meshes with our "take" on *other* experiences.

It should, of course, be remembered that only the rarest bits of construed evidence satisfy every one of these criteria. A representative sample will do. For instance, when dealing with religious or mystical experiences, the "repeatable and public" and "cross-check" tests are often blocked by the nature and circumstances of the event. This alone should not make us excessively nervous. If other people had been in Morris's room when "God spoke," or if such events could be called up on demand, or if the speaker were also visible, the case would be substantially different. But we can't discount such stories just because the reporter was alone at the time, cannot repeat the feat at will, and was only receiving on one channel. People have private, unrepeatable, single-channel (but reliable) experiences all the time. They just have to be validated in other ways. If the circumstances in which information is allegedly revealed block *these* tests, we simply turn to the *other* tests. Of course, if we discover that the report in question is structured in such a way that it blocks out *every* test, we should apply the brakes sharply.

Using the standard criteria will necessarily raise issues about the general coherence and functionality of the life of the person who is making the claim. If we discovered, upon investigation, that Morris had been in an asylum for years, only being let out on work release to preach at revival meetings, we would balk. Morris was not a lunatic, however. His conversations and conduct were normal in every way but one. To claim that he was demented simply because he told stories like this one would involve an extraordinarily arbitrary definition of dementia. For that matter, we are not obliged to dismiss everything a demented person says, just because he is demented. Even crazy people get some things right some times. There is no more necessity that everything a lunatic says is false than there is that everything a sane person says is true.

The next thing we would want to consider is the possibility of fraud. Since people do lie from time to time, we should look at length and with care at the character, background, and general behavior of the person making a revelation claim before making any major donations or lifestyle changes. After all, caveat emptor is still on the books. But Morris was not a fraud either; or at least he was not in the same racket with Marjoe Gortner (whom I heard the same year): no flashy car, no costumes, no miracles for cash, no collections for a new tent—just a simple, straightforward message ("repent or burn in hell") from a simple, straightforward young man. For that matter, it is possible that even the worst sort of charlatan could, in the middle of a scam, have a revelation that shows exactly how things are. (If that happened, but the vision was dismissed because of the charlatan's reputation, that's just the price a scam artist pays. "*Crying wolf*" is still on the books, too.)

If there is no reason to think that a revelation reporter is demented or a charlatan, we turn to the putative experience itself. Indeed, since it is only fair to assume that people are sane and honest until proven otherwise, the main focus will almost always be on the story itself; that is, the reporter's interpretation of the experience: *does it interpret those events in the most useful, illuminating, freight-carrying, and reasonable way available?*

Just because an experience is "religious" or "mystical" doesn't make it any more transparent or free of the need for interpretation than other experiences—whether the religious experience is a Georgia lad talking to God and going out to evangelize Kentucky sinners, or Constantine seeing *In Hoc Signo Vinces* written in the sky and going out to evangelize or kill barbarians. So assuming that Morris had the experience and was sane and honest, we ask whether he found the best way to construe it.

Clearly, his notion that God actually reached down, grabbed his shoulder, and spoke in English is not the *only* interpretation possible. There is a vast range of alternatives. So we should, as best we can, lay them out and look at them. Here are two alternatives for this case:

- Morris was acting out stress anxieties and fixations generated by his childhood conditioning (including such things as his own childhood diet of hellfire sermons),
- Morris had religiously loaded nightmares as a teen and is not able at this time to differentiate his memories of them from his other memories of the same time.

With only modest effort, we could come up with a dozen or more accounts; and, since an option that has been overlooked might be the best one, thoroughness is crucial. Only when the list is reasonably complete can we ask, "Which account is best?"

Morris's own construal of the event is clearly problematic: Is it simple? Is it *ad hoc*? Is it fertile? Does Yahweh's possession of a hand (to put on people's shoulders) mesh with everything else Morris wants to say about Him? So his construal gets no automatic pass. Indeed, it is problematic enough that we should call it the *best* construal only if there were strong reasons for setting aside every less obviously problematic alternative to it.

The point of view or frame of reference from which an experience is construed is equally important, whether the experience is "revealed" or "ordinary"; and the legitimacy of every such point of view must be weighed on the *same* criteria if charges of special pleading are to be avoided.

So like all the other experiences that people have, "revelations" must be accepted or rejected in terms of the best judgments we can make about the actuality of the event, the reasonableness of the way it is construed, and the reliability of the inferences that are drawn from it. "Revelation," then, is *not* another item on the "kinds of evidence" list, but only another neighborhood of the vast and variegated array of experiences that people have that require thought, reflection, and decision before use.

7. Faith

Authority, intuition, and revelation are neighborhoods in the general domain of construed experience within which (or on the basis of which) we reason. Those who properly say that they believe something by authority, intuition, or revelation offer at least implicit evidence for it (even if second hand, habitual and unnoticed, or unlikely). As such, their claims should be weighed on the usual and familiar evidential scales rather than on any specially designed ones. But those who say that their beliefs are rooted in *faith* offer no evidence for them at all. To believe something on faith is to accept it without grounds and without questions.

A. This is a common human phenomenon, not confined to any particular belief neighborhood. Some who ignore or avoid evidence are motivated by nothing better than intellectual sloth. Others, however, claim to have a reason. Two "reasons" are common:

- Some suggest that where faith occurs, evidence is unnecessary: *"My faith is so strong and sincere that there is no way that I could be wrong. I don't need 'evidence.'"*
- Others suggest that evidence *gets in faith's way.* For example, some reject arguments for the existence of God as undermining the very faith they are intended to support.

Both of these notions are wrongheaded. People passionately believe innumerable things, many of which are incompatible with each other. So they *cannot* all be right. So some people, necessarily, are relying on faith to believe things that are not so.

B. On the other hand, if conceivable evidence *is* relevant to whether what we believe is true, it would be catastrophic to ignore it. What if the belief is false? Should we hold on even then? What if looking for evidence would show that it is false? Should we hold on blinkered? How can it be more *virtuous* to believe by faith alone, evidence be hanged, in a world full of scam artists and scoundrels?

- "Should I just shut up and drink the Kool-Ade, or would it be OK to try some on the cat first?"

- "Should I ask about those Concorde flights and walnut desks, or just give money to the United Way on faith?"

Ignoring evidence is even more dangerous when what is "faithed" flies in the face of data that is obvious and readily available. A reasonable temperament would suggest—when we are told to believe X without worrying about evidence, or that worrying about the evidence will interfere with our faith—that there may be some evidence that makes X implausible that someone wants to keep concealed.

C. Weighty situations can arise in which we must believe, decide, and act in spite of the fact that we are without evidence, have no time to look for some, and lack any notion of where to look. An important insight of existentialist philosophy is that declining to act—even when we "can't be sure" of what to do—*is* to act. When belief, decision, and action are demanded, those who dither are said to be guilty of "bad faith." "Faith," here, seems to mean "act of will." Those who will to believe and act must live with the consequences—even when they land in hot water and are tempted to deny responsibility. Whatever you decide is still your own decision, as any good existentialist knows. (On this theme, Marjorie Grene's *Dreadful Freedom* is a good read; and with W. K. Clifford's "The Ethics of Belief" is also a good antidote to William James's *The Will to Believe*).

Lamentably, even with evidence, beliefs can turn out badly. The evidence itself may be irregular in some way, or it may have been misconstrued in one fashion or another. *Just* believing, *just* leaping, is even more hazardous, however. It is foolhardy, consequently, to make such leaps in situations where they are unnecessary.

Those who ignore available evidence or, as sometimes happens, willfully fly in the teeth of negative evidence, bear no resemblance to courageous souls who take "existentially necessary leaps of faith." Absent necessity, their behavior is, in fact, merely irresponsible. Absent evidence, we can all too easily believe what is false; and the passion, commitment, and total involvement with which we believe are not sufficient to make things so.

D. We might try to establish faith as a *kind* of evidence (rather than a substitute for it) with an argument like this:

> Every belief is ultimately based on faith. Wherever the chain of evidence goes, it must terminate with something we *simply accept*. If not, then it doesn't terminate at all, which means it must be infinitely long—which is absurd.
>
> Maybe the chain goes back to confirmable experiences, maybe to what we were taught as children, maybe to the epistemic structure of the mother tongue, whatever; but *simply accepting* has to come into play, sooner or later.
>
> So starting with *whatever* we start with is an act of faith; and since *every* belief can ultimately be traced back to one act of faith or another, there is no way to deny that faith itself is the ultimate evidence for every belief.

To be sure, the particular confirmable experiences that we offer as evidence for a belief (and for the decisions and actions based on it) must have been "accepted." Furthermore, that acceptance, for sensible people, is usually based on the prior acceptance of the principle that confirmable experience is, in general, good (i.e., reliable) stuff to base beliefs on. This could be construed as, "People who offer confirmable evidence in support of their beliefs have *faith* in its reliability."

But there is no act of faith involved in seeing that confirmable evidence is reliable. The act of faith, if there is one, is in the affirmation that reliable starting points are better than unreliable ones. But deciding to go with reliable evidence rather than unreliable evidence (or no evidence at all) is a very peculiar "act of faith." It is *not* arbitrary and idiosyncratic. Indeed, if "better" just means "more reliable," as far as evidence is concerned, it is trivially *necessary*.

I can live with that. Indeed, every sane person does. That is why reasonable people look at bus schedules rather than tea leaves when they want to catch a bus and check the weatherman rather than an astrologer when planning a picnic. So why behave differently when what is at stake is health or eternal destiny, rather than a missed date or a rained-out holiday?

I am not rejecting the notion that chains of evidence have to start somewhere. That is obvious enough. But it is equally obvious that some places to start are better than others:

- Those who start with confirmable experience are working on the *reasonable* principle that the quality of a belief is a function of its reliability. They put evidence in play.
- Those who start with faith are working with the *unreasonable* principle that the quality of a belief is a function of whether it is believed. The principle is unreasonable because the fact that X is believed has no bearing whatever on whether X is true. People believe falsehoods (astrology, for example) all the time.

To rely on faith, in this sense, is simply to opt out of the evidence game altogether. We might as well say, "I accept X without grounds; grounds have nothing to do with it."

E. When those who say things like "the dead will rise again" are asked why they believe that is so, a common answer is that they were told as much by someone in whom they have great faith. In such a case, they may have evidence of a sort for the belief itself (an appeal to authority), and their faith in their "source" may amount to nothing more than trusting its reliability. If so *this* kind of "faith move" is just another instance of relying on second-hand confirmable evidence and is as weak or as strong as the authority relied on. Consequently, we should ask whether the believer's confidence is supported by evidence that the source is reliable, whether the evidence available *to the* *source itself* is reliable, and so forth. The degree of a believer's trust should be a function of the source's demonstrated reliability. Trusting a source does not *make* it reliable.

On the other hand, the more radical sense of faith may come into play when the authority is selected: "I didn't pick my authority because it is reliable or anything like that—the choice was a simple leap of faith"; if so, the move collapses back into believing without grounds.

When remote reliability is hard to assess, especially if the stakes are high, there are strong reasons to back off from authority appeals and check things out first hand. The usual reason for appealing to an authority is to save time and effort. So the move makes little sense if it demands an *increase* in time and effort. So if a particular source is not immediately available for consultation (for clarification) or observation (for a character check), and if there are major problems about the accuracy with which the source's claims and actions were recorded and transmitted, and if the stakes are *very* high, it might be the better part of wisdom to test *the claims themselves*.

There is a tendency on the part of some believers to equivocate. The line between faith alone and what is trustingly believed on second-hand evidence is easily fudged. Even within a single context, faith may vacillate between "trusting a reliable source" (as long as its content is experientially confirmable by *someone*) and groundless "leaping" (when its content is not experientially confirmable by *anyone*). Thus, for example, some treat the Bible as a compendium of testable data for passages where that works (consider those alluding to oil in the Middle East); but simply as a list of things to be "just believed" for those that are incoherent or otherwise unbelievable (consider the creation of the sun after mornings and evenings were already in place).

Such moves can occur in secular as well as religious contexts. If a teen comes home from the mall with a large box of Godiva chocolates and says he bought it with savings from his allowance, his parents may believe what he says because experience has taught them they can trust his general disposition to tell the confirmable truth. Or, if his track record does not encourage such trust, they may disbelieve him, depending on his general disposition to lie. But if they say, "We have faith in Moonbeam and accept everything he says without ever checking," evidence has gone out the window and trouble will soon be knocking at the door.

8. A Reminder and an Interim Conclusion

I have argued that true (or probably true) belief claims are better than false (or probably false) ones in the following way:

- *beliefs* are experiential expectations,
- *belief claims* articulate experiential expectations,
- *true* belief claims articulate reliable beliefs, and
- reliable beliefs are *better* than unreliable ones.

Of course there is the possibility, relative to any belief, that errors of one sort or another have occurred. So it is possible for a belief that *looks* reliable to collapse in hard use. That is why we should take such care to verify the beliefs we rely on with every available evidential test.

I suspect that even radical skeptics will allow that this is adequate for *beliefs*, since even in the best of circumstances belief statements are "hedged." To affirm a belief is to say only that we rely on the expectations it articulates, and most people are realistic enough to realize that even the best vehicles break down from time to time. So we let our beliefs run as far as the evidence will take them but anticipate occasional trouble.

There are situations, though, in which people want to say much more than this; indeed, ones where they want to say they *know*. Knowledge claims are, prima facie, much more aggressive than belief claims. Because of that, they are met by much more aggressive skepticism. While very few people really think that every belief is just as good as any other, many people are convinced that every *knowledge* claim is just as bad as any other.

In the next chapter, I shall turn to this more challenged area: what, if anything, can we rightly claim to *know*?

II

KNOWLEDGE

5

Knowledge, Fraud, Error, and Uncertainty

There is a cycle in academic life. The 1980s and 1990s echoed the conformity of the 1950s; and at the turn of the century the campus seemed ripe for a second Age of Aquarius when the flower children of the 1960s saw universities as tools of the establishment, where professors imposed orthodoxy on the powerless. (Free people, it was said, should reject such intellectual tyranny, and free universities should become places for open-ended talk—arenas without lions.)

Not every aspect of the 1960s has reappeared. But a deep mistrust of the canon has, along with a widely shared idea that the intellect should not be hobbled by such notions as *objective truth* and *facts-to-be-known*. As a result, editorial Cassandras again wonder if traditional teaching and learning are fatally at risk:

- Have rhetoric, intimidation, and political correctness driven argument, evidence, and truth from the field?
- Will "collaborative learning" genuinely supplant old-style linear and adversarial thinking, or will the ancient canon and its lions simply be replaced by a new canon with lions of its own?

Such worries, however, are overblown. Postmodern epistemic subjectivism, the unplanned child of Cartesian skepticism run amok, is a pretense that even the postmoderns lay aside when the seminar is over. At day's end, they do *not* wait for the bus in their offices or the faculty lounge—the reason being that *they know it doesn't come there*—in spite of their verbal denials of fixed truths and knowable facts. They don't follow through on those denials because they *can't*. (They could, of course, take over the transit company and *make* the buses stop there. But while that would *change* the facts, there would still *be* facts—just different ones than before.)

In real life, facts are always the thing. To settle on the subjectivist side may be *chic*, but it offers brief survival on the street. There, we either admit that there are facts and try to come to terms with them, or we suffer badly. If we pay attention, our encounters with stubborn facts force two basic epistemological points on us: reality shapes knowledge, not vice versa; and knowledge is power, not vice versa.

> *Example.* A lymphoma patient quits chemotherapy, adopts a diet of unpolished rice, and spends hours each day visualizing his white corpuscles eating his cancer cells. Trusting that this will see him through to old age, he cancels his medical insurance and buys a retirement villa in Costa Rica. Six months later, he dies.
>
> While we can honor the adage "any frying pan in a fire," did he not ignore his most promising skillet when he stopped the meds?

Ordinary people, of course, claim to know *many* things: the day of the week, the square root of sixteen, where the closest bus stop is, and how poison ivy looks, for starters. Particular individuals also claim to know additional things, in areas of their own expertise: the atomic weight of zinc, the difference between A major and A minor, the name of Plato's prize student, and the limitations of sampling techniques in poll taking. How does this work? Can we rely on the process? Are there pitfalls?

1. Knowledge

Traditionally, knowledge is said to amount to "justified, true belief." I shall examine that bit by bit.

A. Belief.

Smith: "The crosstown bus stops at 17th and K."

Jones: "Do you really believe that?"

Smith: "No, I don't *believe* it. I *know* it."

This seems to suggest that "knowing" X is an *alternative* to "believing" it. This is misleading, however. The real force of Smith's second statement is not that he believes *otherwise*. He is not trying to say, absurdly, "I know the crosstown bus stops at 17th and K, but I believe it doesn't." His point, rather, is that he doesn't *merely* believe it. Belief is a *precursor* to knowledge, a necessary (but not sufficient) first step.

As we have seen in the previous chapters, beliefs amount to complex expectations that arise out of construed experience and reason, as captured in statements that have coherent, intelligible, and testable content. While that is all that a claim requires to express a *belief*, it is only the first step toward *knowledge*. Two more conditions must be met for us to "move up"—truth and justification.

B. True belief.
The fact that a claim must be true to be known sets belief and knowledge apart. Nothing prevents us from believing falsehoods. We can be-

lieve that elephants fly. Even though the claim that they do is false, it has intelligible consistent content. We can picture the difference between a world in which they do and a world in which they don't. But we can also readily discern that the real world is of the latter sort. That's why we can't *know* that elephants fly.

Those who believe that elephants fly may even think that they know it, or believe it so passionately and express it so fervently that they persuade others to think they know it. But it is still false; and what is false cannot be known. We cannot know what is not so. And, however hard we believe, believing does not make it so. Believing can *help* make things so, of course. For instance, beliefs can affect athletic performance (the "cheerleaders are watching" effect) or the efficacy of pills (the "placebo" effect). But beliefs in such cases affect our own internal circuits, not what is "out there."

> *Example.* When I was a boy, movie magazines regularly advertised "bust creme" to help preteen girls "develop." Given the sexist imagery of the time, girls who spent their allowance on these products could hardly be blamed for their fantasies; but they could certainly be faulted for their credulity. Even though the testimonial letters in the pulps glowed with hopes fulfilled, the creme didn't work.
>
> Times haven't changed. *Somebody* must be buying the "weapon" enhancement salves now flogged on the web; more fools they.

Whatever truth theory and truth criterion are adopted, a claim to know X when "X" is not the case is a paradigm of a claim gone wrong: "X is known" entails "'X' is true." So "X is known and 'X' is false" is a logical contradiction on its face.

Nevertheless, it is possible to believe a falsehood reasonably—if it *appears* true according to the preponderance of the available evidence. In such circumstances, we may think we know something—and even be justified in saying that we know it—only to discover later that it is not the case at all. This is because the necessary conditions of knowing and the necessary conditions of being entitled to say, "I know," are not the same.

We are entitled to say "I know" when the target of that claim is supported beyond reasonable doubt in the network of well-tested evidence. But that is not enough to guarantee that we do know. If it were, then many ancient people knew that the world was flat. But that won't do. The world isn't flat and never has been.

On the other hand, if we tighten the conditions of entitlement-to-say, to make them as strict as those for really knowing, then we risk the conclusion that no one is *ever* entitled to say they know. But that defeats the purpose of the expression (which is to draw a contrast between what is known and what is merely believed). So that won't do either.

Further, if we find out that something that we thought we knew is not so, we don't say, *I used to know, but I don't know anymore.* Rather, we say, *I thought I knew, but I was wrong. I didn't know at all.* Thus ordinary usage confirms the fact that truth (however defined and marked) is a necessary condition of genuine knowledge.

However, even when a claim is coherent, intelligible, freight carrying, and true, we may still not really know. We may be making a lucky guess. Or we may even be trying, ineptly, to lie. So a third condition for knowledge is necessary.

C. Justified true belief.

Here are five commonplaces of epistemic life:

- People claim to know various things.
- Not all of their knowledge claims are compatible.
- So we must choose which to accept and which to reject.
- Groundless (or badly grounded) choices are dysfunctional.
- So effective choosing requires good grounds.

In everyday situations, when people argue about what is "actual knowledge" and what is "mere opinion," they usually appeal to the same grounds on which they separate more reliable beliefs from less unreliable ones: verifiable experience, consistency, and so forth. But they set the standards higher, because what will justify saying "I *believe* X" with reasonable security is not enough to justify saying "I *know* X."

The difference is like the one between the levels of proof required in court in civil and criminal cases. Civil suits and belief claims require only the preponderance of the evidence. Criminal cases and knowledge claims require evidence that will justify a verdict "beyond reasonable doubt."

Unfortunately, "beyond reasonable doubt" is not very specific. So claims-to-know are open invitations to opposing claims-to-doubt, even when very strong positive evidence is in hand. How much evidence, after all, is "enough?" How much doubt is "reasonable?"

Knowledge claimants need answers to these questions because the burden of proof is on them. This is another difference between asserting a belief and making a knowledge claim. Belief claims are so tentative by their nature that they are typically allowed to stand unless there are pressing grounds for a challenge; and when they are challenged, the burden of proof is on the challenger. We can "believe what we like" until someone shows otherwise. Knowledge claims, on the other hand, are not tentative at all. They flatly assert, "This is the way things are." Consequently, those who make them are expected to be able to back them up.

That is why people hedge their bets when they are unsure, saying "I believe" instead of "I know." It lowers the stakes. To say this is not to diminish the importance of particular beliefs, or of belief in general. But believing should stand on its own merits, without trying to usurp the status of what is *known*.

An analogy. No matter how admirable kick ball may be, it is not soccer. To say that some people are playing kick ball, not soccer, does not denigrate them or the game they are playing. Of course they should not try to pass it off as soccer; but, as long as those who play it recognize what they're doing, it can stand on its own merits. Soccer is not the only game worth playing.

2. Skepticism

A. Local skepticism. For any particular knowledge claim we might make, there is usually someone with doubts. This is one reason why people argue so often and so contentiously. Although these disputes can be annoying, they are normal and healthy. They are the public threshing ground for separating epistemic wheat and chaff.

There are four primary grounds on which skeptics dispute particular knowledge claims: fraud, error, uncertainty, and subjectivity. All four are possible in any given situation, and reminding ourselves of that fact helps us come to terms with the world somewhat less gullibly. This is especially beneficial at the heart of our own ideology, morals, religion, politics, and economics—loyalty to state, clan, and kind. Local skepticism is an effective antidote against chauvinism of every stripe.

B. General skepticism. There are *general* skeptics, too. From their viewpoint, the problem with knowledge claims is not that some are better than others (so that people need to sort them out), but that all of them are equally unreliable (so that people need to give them up altogether). As they see it, there is never enough evidence to justify a knowledge claim: *nothing* can assuage the possibility of reasonable doubt.

There are several grounds for general skepticism, all of them extrapolations of local doubt to the universal level:

- the possibility of universal fraud or deceit,
- the possibility of universal error,
- the universal uncertainty of claims about matters of fact, and
- the universal subjectivity of all human assertions.

I will examine the first three in this chapter, subjectivity in the next.

3. Three Targets for Skepticism

A. Frauds, lies, and deceptions. Being sold a bill of goods is high on the list of things people try to avoid. And we are certainly aware that people are trying to sell us a bill of goods *frequently*.

Example. According to TV, Bayer aspirin, Tylenol acetaminophen, and Advil ibuprofen are *all* more effective than each other for common headaches. But we cannot simultaneously know that A is better than B and that B is better than A for the same thing. *Better than* is an asymmetrical relation. So the television hucksters cannot know what they collectively assert.

Example. The credibility of a story about a tree in Arizona that recites sonnets would be enhanced if it appeared in a venue other than the *National Enquirer*. In the absence of unimpeachable witnesses, such stories are heavily discounted by all reasonable people.

But the fact that people frequently try to sell one another a bill of goods cannot convincingly be extrapolated into the claim that everyone is always trying to sell everyone else a bill of goods. The world has plenty of liars in it, but there is little reason to think that everyone lies all the time.

After all, the expectation of veracity is a precondition of the very possibility of communication. Absent that precondition, *nothing* can be relied on. Indeed, if everyone always lies, anyone who says "everyone always lies" is a liar, and everyone doesn't always lie.

B. Error. Engaged in a program of "systematic doubt" about sensation, René Descartes concluded (in his *Meditations on First Philosophy*) that very few experience-based knowledge claims are beyond doubt, because almost any such claim could be based on an experiential error or on a misconstrual of experience. As he saw it, the only experiential item that we cannot doubt is our own existence.

But, as will be seen, that exception to universal doubt is just as liable to error as the rest. So raising Descartes' ante slightly, the position comes to this: since experiential error is always possible, we can never be sure that a particular experience-based claim has not gone awry. Indeed, since experience can go wrong in *any* case, it could go wrong in *every* case. Consequently, *no* experience-based knowledge is possible.

There are three separate notions at work here:

- experiential error is always possible,
- the possibility of experiential error makes any experience-based claim uncertain, and
- certainty is a necessary condition of knowledge.

I will deal with the second and third in part C. The notion of possibly universal experiential error is my immediate concern.

1) It is true that any specific experience, or description of one, could be a mistake or a misconstrual.

Consider seeing auras or photographing them. Some aura perceivers are epileptics, some are on drugs, and others are highly suggestible. Some who photograph them don't understand the workings of lenses and color emulsions. So whether what is seen or photographed is actually an "aura" is open to doubt. (See the discussion of Kirlian photographs in Terence Hines's *Pseudoscience and the Paranormal*, pages 301ff.)

Consider recognition and identification. We see a friend at a distance who, on a closer look, turns out to be a total stranger; or we see a friend at close range who turns out to be a double. Caution is required; further, if (as in the "Charlottesville Anastasia" case) an inheritance depends on an accurate identification, *great* caution is required. There is always a chance not only of fraud but of well-meant perceptions distorted by diet, disease, attention dysfunction, conditioning, or circumstance.

Consider memory. We can often "remember" experiences (a first birthday, perhaps) which reason suggests we could not possibly remember. Perhaps we remember a picture of it, or what we have been told by others who were there and do remember.

Finally, consider dreams, hallucinations, and delusions.

So we can obviously be wrong about a perception or a remembered perception. So no particular perceptual claim is safe from the possibility of error. We can never be sure about any specific case.

2) Descartes not only rejected the experiential claims that are doubt-*prone*, but any that can be doubted *at all*. He did this to see whether *any* experiential knowledge was doubt-*proof*. Only that could provide the toehold required to scale back up the cliff of error.

He found his own existence as a thinking being beyond coherent doubt because, he argued, the process of doubt itself presupposes the doubter's existence to engage in it:

"I think but am not," he said, is false on its face. Using ~ for "not," · for "but," and ∨ for "unless," we can formalize this as:

> ~ [(I think) · ~ (I am)]

But if "I think but am not" is false, then, by De Morgan's law (the denial of a conjunction equals the disjunction of two denials), "I do not think unless I am" is true. So:

> ~ (I think) ∨ (I am)

But that is equivalent, by the definition of ⊃ ("if, then"), to "If I think, then I am." So:

> (I think) ⊃ (I am)

But that, by the equivalence of "if p then q" and "on the premise p, q follows," can be written "on the premise 'I think,' 'I am' follows;" that is, "I think, therefore I am." So:

> *I think.*
> ∴ *I am.*

Unfortunately, there are three things wrong with this argument:

a) Whether "I think but am not" is a *logical* or a *performative* inconsistency is an interesting issue. (See Jaako Hintika's "Cogito Ergo Sum: Inference or Performance?") Either way, "I think but I am not" is self-defeating in some sense. However, its component "I think" is *not* self-evidently true. The occurrence of doubt may guarantee the occurrence of thought, but it does not guarantee the existence of the substantial ego that "I think" presupposes. Consequently, while something along the line of "thinking occurs, therefore *something* exists" may be indubitable, the jump from "thinking occurs" to "*I* think," and the jump from "something exists" to "*I* exist," both import a dubious component.

This is more obvious in the third person: "Thinking occurs, but Descartes does not exist" is not obviously self-contradictory; it might even be true. And while "Descartes' thinking occurs, but Descartes does not exist" may be obviously self-defeating, it is only so because the antecedent presumes (*not* self-evidently) what the consequent denies. If the antecedent's presumption is, in fact, false (i.e., there is no Descartes to do any thinking), then the antecedent itself is false and the material implication is only *trivially* true.

The enduring personal self is a *construction*. It provides one possible account of how thought might occur, but not the only one. Framing things Bishop Berkeley's way, for instance, there is no need for a local ego, just a cosmic one. Berkeley argued (in *Three Dialogues between Hylas and Philonous)* that both the human thinker-and-experiencer and his thoughts and experiences need have no more ontological status than as occurrent "ideas in the mind of God." Since this provides an alternative to Descartes substantial ego, we need *grounds* to choose one over the other. If Berkeley might be wrong, so might Descartes.

b) Inference mistakes are as easy as sensation mistakes. The truth of Descartes' conclusion depends not only on the truth of his premise but also on the reliability of the logical rules for inference and substitution, and the correctness of his use of them. So although the argument "looks" valid, it could be flawed by the use of a bad rule (like affirming the consequent) or by the misuse of a good rule (like inadvertently dropping a negation sign when applying De Morgan). Consequently, God had to be imported alongside the *Cogito* itself, to warrant both the legitimacy of the rules and the accuracy with which they have been followed.

> *Example.* Any logic instructor knows how easily inference errors can occur. Even practiced logicians have been known to drop a negation sign, misdistribute or forget instantiation restrictions. (I once derived $p \supset (p \cdot q)$ from $p \supset q$, without using absorption, in forty-seven steps with only one error.) All we can do is check and recheck, unless God is available for backup.

c) However, the existence of God is anything but indubitable on its face, and the ontological argument (to prove that such a God does exist) is anything but transparent. Indeed, as I have shown in *Knowledge, Belief, and Transcendence*, it is either question begging or formally invalid. So Descartes' exemption of valid inference and of his own and a beneficent God's existence from the domain of systematic doubt is unjustified.

d) Assume that *some* indubitable premise survives systematic doubt and that a coherent (rationally secure) worldview *can* be built on it. Unfortunately, alternative coherent systems can be constructed on the same premises, and the multiple constructions need not be mutually compatible.

Example. The rules for bridge and the rules for pinochle are both perfectly coherent rule sets for card play. Although they share an archetypical axiom ("follow suit"), they are incompatible: some of their individual elements are mutually exclusive. But that does not mean that either set is inconsistent itself or has "ignored the axiom."

Whether discussing world descriptions or card games, there is no *purely rational* decision procedure to choose one over the other. And, as far as world descriptions go, that means that there is no *purely rational* guarantee that any particular one portrays the world the way it is.

Example. Euclidian geometry is a perfectly coherent system. But, as may be recalled, Riemann's and Lobachevsky's geometries are, too; and all three share a large number of common geometric postulates. Each is true of a different slice of reality, depending on the forces that happen to be at work on space itself in the slice in question. At least two are false of any specific slice; and we cannot decide which two by reason alone. We must decide, instead, by laying the systems up against the observable facts (stellar displacement, for instance) to see which system carries the freight and which ones leak.

This plurality of possible coherent systems means that any attempt to achieve closure in the reconstruction of general knowledge from favored axioms is doomed. No matter how perfectly coherent the rational palace might be when it gets built, it must still be asked whether *this* palace fits *these* facts. That a system has been rationally generated, recognizes an archetypical axiom, and is internally consistent does not answer that question. So Descartes' program of a priori reconstruction is fatally flawed.

Since it fails, drawing a successful line between mere belief and genuine knowledge requires taking a closer look at the alleged possibility of universal experiential error. We need not abandon the epistemic field to the radical skeptics, nor attempt an a priori "reconstruction" of it, if this allegation turns out to be wrongheaded.

3) A closer look at experiential error. Rudimentary guidelines for empirical inquiry have already been laid out, and are familiar:

To base a claim on experiences, we want them to be repeatable, publicly confirmable, cross-sense checkable, unambiguous, and so forth. Further, when we extrapolate the experiences that pass muster into a system, or subsume them into a construction, we want the result to be self-corrective and fertile, that is, to generate crucial experiments, get us somewhere, and generate further inquiry.

By these familiar standards, people write off many experiences and experience accounts as unreliable. This is entirely proper. People know what to do in concrete cases of error; and they do it.

But radical skeptics (such as Peter Unger, in his *Ignorance: A Case for Scepticism*) insist that empirical errors are not just possible and common, they are universal and (sometimes) undetectable. No test is enough and no claim is safe; the rot is pandemic. Further, since even the best reasoning is only truth *preserving*, these possibly universal experiential flaws mean that we cannot reason our way to safety either. There are three things wrong with this:

- it ignores the parasitic status of error;
- it denies essential distinctions; and
- it is self-defeating.

a) General skepticism ignores the parasitic status of error. Some labels can only be intelligibly applied if there are identifiable cases where they do *not* apply. Such terms are said to be "parasitic."

> *Example*. Suppose you take a twenty to the bank for change and the teller rejects it as counterfeit. Embarrassed, you go back with another. Same result. Also, a fifty. Same result. In panic, you take all your cash to the bank, getting the same verdict on every note.
>
> Customer: "Is there a local epidemic of funny-money?"
>
> Teller: "No. All money is counterfeit."
>
> Customer: "Has someone managed to collect all the good stuff and replace it with homemade?"
>
> Teller: "No. All money is counterfeit and always has been."

This is perplexing in a way that "all of the cash *now in circulation* is fake" is not perplexing, for the very notion of "fake" or "counterfeit" notes only works when defined in contrast to stipulated legal tender. The notion of a counterfeit note is parasitic on the paradigm of a proper one. So if we cannot conceive, or offer an example of, what is *not* a counterfeit note, the notion of a note being counterfeit collapses. If we cannot specify a paradigm case of what *is* money, then there is no meaningful way to say of any piece of paper that it is *not that*.

In the same way, useful applications of the words "error" and "mistake" are parasitic on occasionally getting things right. The only way a belief can intelligibly be called an epistemic error is in contrast to others that are recognized as reliable. So skepticism has a cutting edge only when its proponents are willing and able to recognize cases of accuracy. Local skeptics are willing and able to do that. General skeptics aren't. So while the former are often correct, the latter have taken language "off the rails."

b) General skepticism throws away essential distinctions. By defining factual knowledge in such a way that it has no instances, they strip all epistemic force from such words as "mistaken," "misleading," "illusory," and "deluded."

The use of these ordinary words cannot intelligibly survive their erasure of epistemic contrasts.

> *Example.* We can intelligibly differentiate the anxieties of a mental patient who fears being treated by what he sees as a disease-transferring x-ray machine from those of a teacher I know who fears catching the flu from his students:
> - There are clinical diagnostic grounds for distinguishing the "paranoid" from the "normal" and figuring out who is which.
> - On those grounds, the patient and his anxieties are paranoid, but the teacher and his are not.
> - Epidemiology is an area of solid, tested research.
> - Although there are no known disease transferring x-ray machines, the flu is well known to be contagious.

But if the general skeptics were right, we *cannot* draw these contrasts—the anxious teacher is just as likely a victim of systematic error as the mental patient. What is it, then, to be deluded? A working distinction has been lost.

> *Example.* We can intelligibly distinguish a normal person's color perceptions and those of someone who is red/green color-blind. The distinction is there to be drawn, and there are clinical tests to draw it.

But if the general skeptics are right, we *cannot* draw that distinction. Anyone is just as likely to misread a traffic signal as anyone else. What is it, then, to be color-blind? Another working distinction has been lost.

Furthermore, the distinctions which general skepticism erases are not dispensable. If we actually stopped drawing distinctions in these terms between what we know (e.g., that a watch gains four minutes a day) and what we believe (e.g., that Dave Barry will never become president), we would simply have to draw the same distinctions with new terms.

We would be obliged to invent new terms to perform the task, because the task *needs performing*. If all we have are opinions, then, at the very least, we have two very different *kinds* of opinions:

- those by which we can reliably anticipate events, and
- those on which we dare not rely.

Shall we now call them *insight* and *natter*, where we used to call them *knowledge* and *opinion*? Whatever the labels, distinguish them we shall. So there is not much practical point to the general skeptics' threat. The practical distinctions are there to be made, and have to be made, to get things done.

c) The general skeptics' notion that all claims could be mistaken is self-defeating. When they deny the occurrence of paradigm cases to which purported errors could be compared, they pull their own teeth and defuse their own argument. The only way to make doubt significant is to stipulate something in contrast to which a mistake is a mistake. Being unwilling to do that, they deny in practice the significance of what they themselves say. In a nutshell, if all claims are merely opinion, so are theirs.

In a kind of triple somersault, the general skeptics' use of this argument takes them off the end of the epistemic pier:

- by denying the existence of paradigm cases against which error could be defined, they erase the very meaning of "error";
- by calling everything opinion, they obscure practical working distinctions that must be made in order to function; and
- by debilitating all claims to know anything, they debilitate their own claim to know nothing.

On the other hand, the fact that it is incoherent and self-defeating to say that we may *always* be mistaken does not diminish the possibility that we are, in fact, mistaken *in a given case*. It means only that charges of error should be specific and presented on specific grounds.

> *Example*. This very minute, I may not be at my desk typing. I might be having a hallucination, suffering a delusion, or be strapped to a table with a control needle in my brain.
>
> If I have any reason whatever to suspect such things, I will put them to whatever tests I can, in the common arena: I will not *allow* myself the paralytic luxury of general skepticism. I just want to know whether am I projecting "at my desk" images or am actually at my desk—right here and right now.

- My inquiry will have to begin with the specification of something that is sufficiently established to say, *this is not a fantasy*—my paradigm of reliable experience.
- Then I will compare the present experience to it.
- If the present experience does not measure up, then I will conclude that it is probably flawed in some way and start trying to figure out *how* it is flawed.
- But if it does measure up, I will accept it as legitimate and reliable, subject to correction, and get on with my life.

Establishing the paradigm case is crucial. As will be seen, the general skeptics' practical confusions are due, in large part, to their selection of a *wrong* paradigm case—a fatal flaw in their argument.

> *Example*. Suppose that Fred says that any chess player is just as good as any other. "Bobby Fischer is no better than anyone else at chess!" he says, adding,

"Just like the rest of them, he never made a grand slam in a chess game in his life!"

Fred is right about *that*. Try as hard as you will, you simply *cannot* take every trick in a chess game. There aren't any tricks to take. But Fred's inference that since you cannot take every trick, it doesn't matter how you play, is ridiculous. Evidently, the poor fool doesn't know the difference between chess and bridge. After all, there are rules and goals in bridge that don't pertain to chess at all. The fact that you cannot make a grand slam in chess is utterly inconsequential. That isn't the point in chess. The point in chess is checkmating.

Of course, if it turned out that no contemporary chess player was capable of achieving checkmate, it would speak ill of contemporary players; and if checkmates were in principle impossible, but still the only point in playing chess, that would speak ill of chess. But checkmate is not impossible, either in principle or in practice.

General skeptics use a wrongheaded paradigm case for knowledge, in much the same way. Their confusion begins with their demand for *certainty* as an additional necessary condition of knowledge. They say that there is no distinction to be drawn between experiential knowledge claims because no such claims are ever *certain*.

But to claim that the general inability to achieve certainty about experiential claims entails that one such claim is as good as another, is just as wrongheaded as saying that the general inability to make a slam in chess entails that one chess move is as good as another. If certainty were an appropriate standard for experiential inquiry, its lack would be a real criticism of that enterprise. But it is *not* a legitimate standard for such inquiry.

C. Uncertainty. As seen above, the necessary conditions of knowledge are traditionally summed up in the phrase "justified true belief." (I am not talking about *sufficient* conditions here. It has been evident since Edmund Gettier's "Is Justified True Belief Knowledge?" that the fact that a belief is justified and true is not always enough to guarantee its knowledge status.)

General skeptics, however, add *certainty* to the list of *necessary* conditions to make it "justified certain true belief," and then reason:

> *P1. Certainty is a necessary condition of knowledge.*
> *P2. No empirical claim is ever certain.*
> *∴C. No one ever has any empirical knowledge.*

What is wrong with this argument?

1) It invites equivocation because "certain" and "certainty" are deeply ambiguous words. There is nothing wrong with ambiguity, as such. Ambiguous words simply stand ready to perform different roles in different contexts. Indeed, as Max Black points out in *Models and Metaphors*, it may be the fuzzy, ambiguous edges of meaning and use that make human communication

possible at all. The problem is that ambiguous words are treacherously attractive sites for *equivocation*.

If a word is used in one sense in an argument's premises, but in a radically different sense in its conclusion, or in different senses in its several premises, there is no valid reason to think the argument "follows." But, if the equivocation over a word's several senses is subtle, the argument may look as if it "follows" even though it doesn't.

My reservations about the general skeptics' contention, that experiential knowledge is impossible because it requires certainty that cannot be achieved, is not due to the ambiguity of "certainty," but to the fact that their argument subtly and deceptively equivocates over its three senses.

There is a kind of certainty (C_1) that people strive for in all inquiry. Call it "solid evidential support." But the fact that this is a necessary condition of knowledge only makes knowledge *difficult* to obtain, not *impossible*.

There is a second kind of certainty (C_2) that *cannot* be achieved in most inquiries. Call it "logical necessity." It is especially difficult, perhaps impossible, to achieve about empirical matters of fact. So if C_2 were a necessary condition of all knowledge, we could know very little, perhaps nothing.

There is a third kind of certainty (C_3) that is very easy to obtain on virtually any topic. In fact, it frequently occurs without effort (and without justification). Call it "conviction." So if C_3 were a necessary condition of all knowledge, it would impose little or no limit to what we could know.

a) Evidential certainty (C_1). The certainty that people want about matters of fact is *evidential*. It allows them to anticipate the consequences of their actions with justified confidence. It occurs when there is enough good evidence available to (and understood by) them, to make their descriptions and predictions *reliable*. This is not just a matter of being confident in our opinions. (That is C_3.) It is a matter of having evidential grounds for our opinions that justify them and of being sufficiently aware of those grounds to justify asserting what they establish.

This kind of certainty is exactly what people are looking for—and find—when they run public tests, look for repeatability, check out the limiting conditions, and so forth. To be sure, *some* people don't take such pains and, consequently, claim to know things that are not so. But if we exercise ingenuity and effort, we can establish a great deal of C_1 about the claims we make, or—when needed—*change* them.

Consequently, it might be better to avoid "certainty" talk altogether here and simply say that to know, there needs to be a strong link between what is "known" and solid, well-understood evidence. This would sidestep the problems created by the fact that people are easily confused and equivocate readily. If we want to say that grasped secure evidence is a necessary condition of knowing, why not just *say* that, and leave "certainty" out of it?

b) Logical certainty (C_2). Many statements are logically certain. Here is an example:

S1) If P implies Q and is the case, then necessarily Q.

This is ironclad because it is a *tautology*. A truth table shows that it is true regardless of the truth or falsity of its components:

P	Q	[(P	⊃	Q)	·	P]	⊃	Q
T	T			T	T		T	
T	F			F	F		T	
F	T			T	F		T	
F	F			T	F		T	

Logic shows that the negation of any such tautology constitutes a self-contradiction. It is easy to demonstrate that the negation of S1 (and—all things held equal—the negation of any other tautology) is explicitly inconsistent. It need not be formalized, but it can be, as follows:

1. $\sim\{[(P \supset Q) \cdot P] \supset Q\}$ Negation, S1
2. $\sim\{\sim[(P \supset Q) \cdot P] \vee Q\}$ Material Implication, 1
3. $[(P \supset Q) \cdot P] \cdot \sim Q$ De Morgan's Law, 2
4. $(P \supset Q) \cdot (P \cdot \sim Q)$ Association, 3
5. $(P \supset Q) \cdot \sim(\sim P \vee Q)$ De Morgan's Law, 4
6. $(P \supset Q) \cdot \sim(P \supset Q)$ Material Implication, 5

This is an easy device for discovering whether a statement is logically true without running large truth tables: see if its negation can be reduced to the assertion and denial of the same thing.

In this way, we can see that empirical statements are *not* tautologies or contradictions. They are *contingencies*. As such, they are not even *candidates* for C_2. So if C_2 *were* a necessary condition of empirical knowledge, there would be none.

A Caution. There are statements that look like exceptions to the claim that empirical statements are contingencies. We can construct tautologous and contradictory statements that contain descriptive terms, for example, "Either it is raining here and now or it isn't" and "The dog barked all last night but was silent from eleven to midnight." The skeleton of such statements is an analytic skeleton, and their logical truth (or falsity) is a matter of that skeleton alone. So such statements carry no descriptive freight; even though they look as if they do, they ride empty.

It is difficult to see how anyone after Hume's *Inquiry concerning Human Understanding* and Kant's *Critique of Pure Reason* could think that statements about matters of fact should (or *could*) be anything but contingent. It should be a source of neither surprise nor regret that if C_2 *were* a necessary condition of factual knowledge, then people have none—or, if they do have knowledge of matters of fact, then C_2 is *not* a necessary condition of such knowledge at all.

c) Psychological certainty (C_3). Psychological certainty amounts to "feeling sure" (i.e., not having any doubts) about the truth of a claim. It can occur with virtually any claim. Here are a few that have been made with it:

S2) Jesus is alive.
S3) God is dead.
S4) Hospitals use Tylenol because it's better than aspirin.
S5) There'll always be an England.

Unfortunately, psychological certainty is notoriously unreliable, as these sample claims show. It is unreliable because people can feel blissfully confident about claims for which they have no secure evidential basis, indeed, even in the teeth of counterexamples.

C_3 is not the same as C_1. Not having any doubt is not the same thing as grasping a network of present secure evidence. The difference should not be hard to see. Indeed, ordinary language provides a device for highlighting it. Compare the following two sentences:

S6) I am certain that the office door is locked.
S7) It is certain that the office door is locked.

The first is a piece of psychological autobiography and the second is not; the pronouns flag the difference:

- The truth of *S6*, in a given case, may have little to do with whether the door is really locked. Much depends on what it takes to make the speaker free of doubt. Some can feel sure with no evidence for what they feel sure about. Others have the sense to restrain themselves.
- The truth of *S7* depends only on whether there is secure evidence present to the speaker that the door is locked.

The fact that people confuse C_1 and C_3 is *one* of the reasons why they say things such as, "A knowledge claim can be true for one society and false for another" or "True for one individual and false for another." That would work if a proposition's truth were a function of whether (or how strongly) it is *believed*. For, what we are sure of is often a function of social conditioning (or private psychological quirks). But what we grasp secure evidence for is *not*— at least not in the same way or to the same extent.

C_3 is neither a necessary nor a sufficient condition of knowledge.

It is not a necessary condition because we can have doubts or anxiety even as we grasp a network of secure evidence.

- Many teenagers doubt their own normalcy, even after mining the self-help shelves at Barnes and Noble.
- Many a polished actor gets the flutters on opening night, even when the lines have been set in stone by practice.

It is not a sufficient condition of knowledge because we can be overweeningly confident and still be wrong.

- Many confident people tout vinegar therapy.
- Many well-meaning parents impose crackpot theories of child rearing on their hapless offspring without any hesitation at all.

Though it is clearly neither necessary nor sufficient for knowledge, C_3 can be beneficial in some contexts. This is because it lowers the anxiety level with which we operate. Those who have convictions (and a little courage) are likely to cope better than those who are consumed by doubt.

These occasional benefits, however, are mitigated by the fact that C_3 can also feed and raise the fanaticism level in a world that has enough fanaticism already. We would wish that those who pursue religious wars, racists, and sexists had a little *less* C_3. Historically, more than one martyr has beseeched his or her tormentors to realize that they *might* be wrong. Today's world is consistent with that history.

I shall say no more about C_3. Careless people can confuse it with evidential and logical certainty; but the general skeptics are not *that* careless. The potential for equivocation over C_1 and C_2 is where general skepticism usually breaks down.

2) It commits the fallacy of four terms. The argument,

P1. certainty is a necessary condition of knowledge,
P2. no empirical claim is ever certain,
∴C. no one has any empirical knowledge,

can be read in several ways, depending on whether we interpret the two iterations of "certain(ty)" as C_1 or C_2.

Unfortunately:

- *P2* is only true in the C_2 sense of "certain," and in the cognate sense of "certainty," *P1* is false. Logical certainty is not a necessary condition of all knowledge.

- *P1* is true only in the C_1 sense of "certainty," and in the cognate sense of "certain," P2 is false. Many empirical claims are as *evidentially* certain as they need to be.

The only way to make *both* premises true is to read "certainty" in *P1* as C_1, and "certain" in *P2* as C_2. But that is simple equivocation. When general skeptics say that all knowledge requires certainty, but certainty about matters of fact is impossible, they are only noting that all knowledge requires C_1, but that C_2 cannot be achieved in certain contexts.

We should not despair, however, because once we see the equivocation, we can see that nothing is missing from empirical claims about matters of fact that is either possible or required. Why should we despair at being unable to demonstrate what is, by definition, undemonstrable—that contingent, empirical claims are truths of logic? Such claims, by the very meaning of "contingent" and "empirical," cannot be truths of logic. But that does not mean that they are flawed in any way.

The demand that empirical claims be C_2 is simply confused. Saying that an empirical claim should be doubted just because it is not a truth of logic is as confused as saying that watermelons should be thrown out just because they can't be peeled like bananas, or that we should stop admiring the way Bobby Fischer played chess because he never made a slam. Once we realize that looking for logical necessity about matters of fact is as silly as trying to discover the cube root of Beethoven's *Fifth*, we can get on with our work.

3) The certainty that we actually need is available. Empirical claims aren't C_2, but they can still be certain enough. Consider:

S8) The average flea weighs less than one ounce.
S9) Only one person (me) is in my study right now.

Since claims that are logically certain are claims whose denials are self-contradictory, these two claims are *not* C_2. No matter how strongly we believe that they are true, they are not truths of logic.

- It is logically possible that there are enough heavy (and so far undiscovered) fleas to bring the fleet average above the level stated. Weight is a function of density, so just one *very* dense flea might be enough to entail the denial of *S8*. But while that is so unlikely that the odds against it are astronomical, it is not "self-contradictory."
- Similarly, there is no self-contradiction in saying there is more than one person in my study right now. There *might* be a little fellow hiding behind the monitor, watching everything I do. If so, *S9* is not a logical truth.

But these two claims *are* secure in the C_1 sense. We are just as secure in asserting the truth of these two propositions as a rational person could want, inevitably contingent though the two sentences may be.

We can be certain (C_1) about matters of fact in different ways:

- Looking. How can I be certain (C_1) that *Greater Tuna* is a two-man show? Because I have seen it and know just what two people look like. I didn't even need to count.
- Tasting. How can I be certain (C_1) that rattlesnake tastes like chicken? Because I have eaten both, frequently.
- Smelling. How can I be certain (C_1) that the animal I ran over last night was a skunk? Because I smelled it.
- Feeling. How can I be certain (C_1) that "smooth as a baby's bottom" is an apt simile? Because I have raised three babies, know what their bottoms feel like, and know how that compares to the way other things feel.
- Hearing. How can I be certain (C_1) that Beethoven's *Missa Solemnis* is an orchestral mass, not a flute solo? Because I have heard it (and sung it, too).
- All of the above. How can I be certain (C_1) that I am the only person in the faculty building right now? Because I have searched it systematically for someone with a match.
- Generalizing. How can I be certain (C_1) that the average flea weighs less than three hundred pounds? Because I have seen lots (I have a dog), and they are small, as dictated by their feeding habits.
- Counting. How can I be certain (C_1) that at least 500 people legally reside in Rollingwood Precinct? Because I have counted the voters' registration list and understand basic arithmetic well enough to know that $15{,}692 \geq 500$.
- Relying on proper authority. How can I be certain (C_1) that there are left-handed sugars? Because Bill Myers says so, is a respected chemist, and would lose his job if he were wrong.
- Inference from what I already know. How can I be certain (C_1) that if I jump from the 16th Street Bridge onto Rock Creek Parkway, I will die? Because I know that everyone who ever did it died and that I am an ordinary, fragile human being.
- Relying on a network of beliefs. How can I be certain (C_1) that Jefferson was ambivalent about slavery? Because that is the only position attributable to him that is consistent with everything else we know about him—based on the massive written records from his time.

We can be certain (C_1) of all such claims by availing ourselves of the massive amounts of tested (or testable) evidence that is both present and sufficient to take all of them "beyond reasonable doubt," even though it is *logically possible* that any of them *could be* false (but only if there is a true claim to compare it to—remember how "counterfeit" works).

This is *not* to say that such claims cannot be doubted. They can; and the claim about Jefferson is a prime example. History is written by the winning side, after all. Nor is it to say that none of them has any problems other than the mere fact of its contingency. Many do; and the claim about the average weight of fleas is a prime example of that. Generalizing on limited data is always risky. It *is* to say, however, that such claims should not be challenged simply because a justified true belief that they are the case is not C_2. Indeed, the notion that this is a fatal flaw is itself fatally confused.

4) A conclusion and a caveat. This particular argument against the possibility of empirical knowledge about matters of fact does not work. It fails because it equivocates over serious ambiguities. This does not mean that *no* argument against the possibility of empirical knowledge about matters of fact succeeds. There is another yet to be examined.

Further, this is not to deny that skepticism (of a sort) is useful. A healthy dose of *local* skepticism is always useful, that is, we ought to reserve judgment about the alleged knowledge claims that people make until they are carefully checked out. *Be* skeptical. Adopt a good Missouri show-me attitude. There is nothing wrong with *that*.

6

Knowledge and Subjectivity

The failure of any global skepticism that is based on the possibility of universal error or uncertainty does not leave the way clear to assert that bona fide knowledge occurs. Consider this argument:

> *P1. All alleged knowledge is infected, in one way or another, by subjectivity.*
> *P2. Bona fide knowledge must be objective.*
> *∴C. No alleged knowledge is bona fide knowledge.*

This, in several forms, is the topic of this chapter and the next.

1. Subjectivity and Objectivity

A. Subjects and objects. A subject is any *S* to which intentional properties can be accurately attributed. An object is any *O* that is the target rather than the locale of such properties. *Desiring, reading,* and *planning* are three exemplary intentional properties. So for instance, anything that desires, reads, or plans is, to that extent, a *subject*; and anything that is desired, read, or planned is, to that extent, an *object*. An individual may, consequently, be either a subject or an object, depending on circumstances. If Sam desires Myrtle, then to that extent, Sam is an *S* and Myrtle is an *O* (and vice versa). It is better if they desire each other in full knowledge that both of them are subjects in their own right. This does not alter the fact, however, that they are the *objects* of each other's desire.

Things such as rocks, trees, and bowling balls, that are *not* capable of having intentional properties, are never subjects. Such objects can have intentional properties in a *derivative* sense when they are *used* by subjects who have an end in view. When they have intentional uses they may be described with the derivatively intentional term "useful." That does not, however, make them subjects. They still have no intentions of their own, so far as we know. Things that *are* capable of intentional properties are either subjects or objects, or both, in a given situation, depending on which way(s) the intentionality runs.

B. Subjective and objective. "Subjective" and "objective" do not always draw the same contrast. Consider:

Subjective	Objective
Pertaining to a subject	*Pertaining to an object*
Impulsive	*Deliberate*
Private	*Public*
Internal	*External*
Volatile	*Stable*
Idiosyncratic	*Commonplace*

Not everything pertaining to a subject is impulsive, private, internal, volatile, and idiosyncratic; and not everything pertaining to an object is deliberate, public, external, stable, and commonplace. Furthermore, each of the terms on these lists can be used in more than one way, too; for example, "What goes on behind closed doors" is private in the sense that the doors *should* be closed, but public in the sense that it *can* be observed by anyone who happens to be present. Sorting it all out can be very tricky.

Consider: Only subjects are capable of action (intentional behavior). So since "impulsive" and "deliberate" can only be applied to actions, they can only describe what *subjects* do. But one of the things subjects do is make judgments. So while any judgment is subjective in one sense (it is made by a subject), it may be either subjective (impulsive or based on internal phenomena) or objective (deliberate or based on external phenomena) in another.

C. The subjectivity and objectivity of subjects. The acts and properties of subjects may be subjective, objective, or both:

- A subject's properties can be private or public, internal or external, volatile or stable, and idiosyncratic or commonplace, in virtually any combination.
- A subject's acts can be impulsive or deliberate, private or public, internal or external, volatile or stable, and idiosyncratic or commonplace, in virtually any combination.
- Some combinations are improbable. Volatility and impulsiveness, and stability and deliberateness, usually ride together. Volatile deliberateness and impulsive stability are unlikely.

So we cannot assume, just because a property or act of some subject is subjective in the sense that it is, say, *internal,* that it cannot be objective in the sense that it is *deliberate*; or, just because it is objective in the sense that it is, say, *public*, that it cannot be subjective in the sense that it is *impulsive* or *idiosyncratic*.

2. Subjectivity and Knowledge

Consider the following skeptical argument. Experiential phenomena are private. They have no demonstrable connection to "externals." They are also the occasion of "spin" because of the individual or cultural perspective of the subject who has them. Any claim that is about private phenomena, or is subject to such spin, is therefore *subjective* and disqualified as a vehicle for knowledge (which is *objective* by definition). So since no experiential claim is free of such privacy and bias, we are never justified in claiming experiential knowledge.

A. Privacy. Experiential phenomena are private because:

- Experience is no less private than dreaming, for any experience might, in fact, *be* a dream.
- Experience is no less private than an illusion or delusion, for any experience might, in fact, *be* an illusion or delusion.
- Every observer is trapped inside his or her own private stream of phenomena from which there are no bridges to any external reality to substantiate what is going on.

1) Dreaming. People usually determine what is or is not the case by their *perceptions*. But there is no assurance attending an ordinary "waking" perception that cannot occur in a "dreaming" one. Dreaming and waking states are (or at least can be) equally perceptually convincing. So the conviction that attends a waking perception cannot guarantee that its purported objects are any more "real" than those in a dream. There is, indeed, no reliable internal test to reveal dream contents for what they are. Internal inconsistency will work sometimes. But many dreams are nicely coherent. When that is the case, some external test is absolutely necessary. So to say truly that we *know* that experiences are of "real" things, we would have to find an *external* way to differentiate them from dreams. If that is not possible, then experience-based knowledge of externals is not possible.

2) Illusions, delusions, and the like. Many people have never knowingly hallucinated, operated under posthypnotic suggestion, or suffered psychotic delusions. But even such fortunate individuals are aware (or should be, if they read) that such experiences do occur and that they can be thoroughly enveloping. Indeed, they can catch us up so totally that, from inside, we cannot see our way out.

Example. Ben, a paranoid schizophrenic, lives out his hours in a world populated by people and things that we cannot see, playing his part in a dialogue most of which we cannot hear. That his world is radically discontinuous with ours is obvious to us, but unknown and unknowable to him. Unaware (from inside) of what we so quickly spot (from outside), he has, as we say, "lost touch with reality." But how can we be sure that he is the one who is "lost," not us?

"Waking dreams" need not be this inclusive or enduring to cause problems. Even if we can *sometimes* fight our way clear of a simple hallucination, we cannot *always* do so. Even if we can sometimes identify them in hindsight, it is not that easy "in stride."

> *Example.* When I "saw" the insect on my blue book, I realized I was hallucinating because it was *only* visual and I had other tests available. An even slightly more inclusive hallucination would have been much harder, if not impossible, to shrug off, however.

A major *caveat* is called for then, and not just because of systematic psychotic delusions and inclusive hallucinations. The experiential results of chemical recreation, sensory deprivation, exhaustion, fasting, and self-flagellation, and even the theatrics of illusionists, demand the same warning. If we do not know that there is (say) an illusionist at work, we can be as easily misled in a waking state as in a sleeping one by experiences that are—from inside—totally persuasive.

3) Radical privacy: the egocentric predicament and solipsism. What goes on in one person's mind and experience cannot be compared to, or tested against, what goes on in another person's mind and experience, because nobody has access to anybody else's mind and experience.

> *Example.* I wonder whether what I call seeing green is the same as what my wife calls seeing green. At one level, of course, there is an external test: see if our behaviors correlate. Independent observers can hold up color cards and see if we call the same chip by the same name. But even if we do, that only means that our verbal behaviors match. It does *not* show that our sensory contents match. We still know nothing about the character of the experience going on in the two of us. Is *that* the same?

> *Example.* I wonder whether what I see is real or is just an event in my internal light show. A standard way to check it out would be to ask other people if they see it, too. But how do I know that "they," too, are not just events in my light show? All this "test" does is compare *one* possibly spurious projection of my mind with *other* possibly spurious projections of my mind.

As Wittgenstein noted in *Philosophical Investigations* ¶265, looking closer, or asking "other observers" what *they* see, to confirm an experience is like reading a second copy of the same newspaper to corroborate what the first copy says. Just so, if what is at issue is whether our own experiences get at the "real" world correctly, then a larger collection of our own experiences (even if they are experiences of "corroborating witnesses") is question begging. Wherever we turn, we are the only ones there. As Wittgenstein suggests in the *Tractatus* at 5.6 and 5.642, the limits of our experience are the limits of *the* world.

So if experiential evidence is all that backs up a claim and the *only* experiences we can have are our own, there is no way to evade the conclusion that the claim in question is radically subjective (private). So as a result of the radical privacy of our minds and perceptions, whatever we may *think* we know is, in fact, only *opinion*.

The claim that all experience is private is true in at least one sense: our experiences are our own, not somebody else's. There is no way for Joe to have Mary's experiences or for Mary to have Ted's, and so forth. Mary can tell Joe about hers, and if he is empathetic he can respond to them second hand; but the notion of his actually *having* her experiences is confined to fictional scenarios such as that of "The Empath" (*Star Trek*, Episode 63, 1968 [Star Date 5121.0]). In the real world, he not only cannot have her experiences, he cannot even know exactly what they are like. The only way for him to know that would be to *have* some of them, and that he cannot do.

Example. I don't know how it would feel to break my leg (never having broken one), nor do I know how it would feel for Bill Clinton to break his. But these two pains of which I am ignorant are very different. While I might break one of my legs and discover what *that* pain is like, his breaking one of his does nothing for me. Try as I will, I *cannot* feel his pain. It won't even help if he tells me about it in detail and lets me observe the anguish on his face and hear his cries. All of that is wheel spinning for anyone but Clinton himself. His grimacing and describing are just another sequence in *my* light show, another chapter in *my* book.

In fact, no constituents of anyone's experience stream provide any reason to think that *anything* exists outside it. Our privacy is absolute.

4) The futility of piecemeal replies to these arguments. There are cases (such as trying to wake ourselves up to escape a dream hazard) that indicate that, at least sometimes, we *can* find our way out of a dream "from the inside." But skeptics respond that this could be a case of dreaming that we know we are dreaming. A third copy of the newspaper is no more helpful than the second. In fact, skeptics have the same reply available to *any* piecemeal rebuttal. When a rebuttal is offered they can raise the ante, expanding the range of their doubt to include the legitimacy of whatever is the basis of the rebuttal itself. At some point, consequently, while we can make a number of specific moves to blunt the edge of a skeptic's *specific* doubts, what we really need is a *general* rebuttal—one that will put the axe to the root of the whole business.

5) General rebuttals. Many attempts at a general rebuttal have been made. The classic route involves "epistemological dualism." Another attempt appeals to the "transparency" of some experiences. Neither works.

a) Epistemological dualism distinguishes experiential data ("phenomena," or "sense data" such as sounds and color fields) from the things that are said to cause them and argues that while only the former are *directly* known, the latter can be known by *inference*. I can't directly know other people's pains; but I can infer them from their observable behavior. I can't directly know the tree in itself under which I recline; but I can infer it from the shades and textures my senses directly access.

This epistemological two-step comes in many particular shapes and forms, but the essentials are laid out in A. J. Ayer's *The Problem of Knowledge*. It was invented to show how we know objective facts. The trouble is that it doesn't achieve that. All it actually generates is a network of inferences spun out of our sensations, which is just as private as the sensations themselves. Since there is no way to demonstrate that any particular inference is *correct*, and we can infer many *different* ways in which any particular experience might have been caused, how could we establish a *specific* conclusion about the nature of the objective world from the phenomena? We *can't*, as Hume made clear in *An Enquiry concerning Human Understanding* long ago.

To deduce causes from sensible effects is slippery at best. If we had lots of cases where *both* causes and effects were accessible, then we would have a pattern to follow. Then, by inductive and analogical reasoning, we could say that a novel case is (probably) like the ones already seen. But the dualists are not talking about that kind of inference—inferring a perceivable X from a perceivable Y. They are talking, instead, about inferring a substratum of physical reality (which cannot be perceived at all) from phenomena (which are *all* we ever do perceive)—a leap into the void.

For many such reasons, epistemic dualism was under well-deserved attack by the mid-twentieth century in works such as J. L. Austin's *Sense and Sensibilia*. But rejecting it does not entail the general skeptics' triumph. There are at least two more possible rebuttals to consider.

b) *Transparent* experience guarantees its sources. Even if *inferring* knowledge of the external world from the phenomena is dicey, such knowledge might still be salvaged if some experiences are "transparent."

In his "The Claims of Religious Experience," H. J. N. Horsburgh maintains, for instance, that certain human understandings are based on "self-authenticating" experiences. Because these experiences are "transparent," he says, we can accurately see through their phenomenology to the nature of the reality that lies behind them.

Can an experience itself ever directly show us what it is "of?" Must there not be a context of other experiences, inferences, and explanations in which to construe what it means and what, if anything, it denotes?

After all, if the phenomenological content and the ground of an experience are not the same thing, that content cannot guarantee the characteristics of its ground. Experiences that have very similar phenomenological content can have radically different grounds (looking at the Eiger and dreaming of the Matterhorn, for example). Identifying the *actual* ground of an experience presupposes recognizing the difference between our construals and what we construe.

> *Example.* If a stranger told me, "Ahura Mazda descended on clouds of Light and told me to fight Darkness," I might doubt that the alleged event occurred at all. (Perhaps the stranger is a liar or a Zoroastrian televangelist). Suppose, however, that the speaker was not a stranger, but a person I know and trust. Even if I did not deny the occurrence of the experience itself, under these circumstances, I could still dispute the objectification that my friend put on it—that Ahura Mazda was *there to be seen.*

Indeed, since experiences require interpretation, and alternative interpretations are possible, we must *decide* in every case whether each one denotes what it immediately seems to denote. That an experience seems particularly lucid and unambiguous as it occurs is no authentication at all.

> *Example.* In 1953, working as a correspondence checker in a federal bureau, I read a letter from a man who said that he had been locked up in a hotel room for seventeen years. He wanted to be rescued because of what he said the maids and bellmen were doing to him—using a ray machine to infect his body with venereal diseases transferred from the astral body of "Blackjack" Pershing.
>
> Hotel hostage or psychotic? I had no doubt that the writer was locked up somewhere, that he was unhappy, and (even) that there was a machine of some sort that people were using on him. But the forlorn scenario that his letter offered—which *he* found utterly convincing—did not check out in the larger experiential context. (I started with his letter's postmark and checked the city directory. There were no spas, but there was an insane asylum.)

> *Example.* In a large city bus terminal, I went from dock to dock looking for a bus to the University of Richmond. Failing to find one, I asked some drivers; but no one could help. It was so frustrating and tiresome that I gave up and walked.
>
> In retrospect, I know that this was a dream. Although it was internally coherent, the rest of my experiences provided a context that showed this particular one was not veridical. This started with the knowledge that Richmond has no city bus terminal.

Contextual checking is necessary to decide about the authenticity of any construal of experiential events. It is no more self-evident that someone who claims to be bathed in outpourings from the reservoir of grace *is* so bathed, than that my letter writer was actually being infected with germs from 1917. We should respond evenhandedly to whatever experience accounts occur. If *any* must be weighed in context, then *all.*

Consider these further cases, none of them made up, and none of them any more "transparent" that the others.

- A Virginia politician claimed during a presidential campaign in the 1980s that the U.S. government is controlled by a drug cabal run by Elizabeth II and that the media don't report it because they are controlled by the same cabal. (I will not name the politician in order to spare embarrassment to his party.)
- A Manhattan radio station says all that city's blacks are going to be rounded up, sent to a concentration camp, and killed.
- A radio evangelist says we can save our (or a friend's) soul by sending in $5 for a "blessed" handkerchief and also receive an autographed picture of Jesus Christ. (Great stuff can be heard on the radio late at night. I do assume that the picture was autographed by the evangelist and not by Jesus himself.)
- A mystic says, "I saw the holiness of God, and it was blue."

To reject the notion that experience is ever "transparent" is not to say that allegedly transparent ones should be tossed. Any that will bear contextual scrutiny can be kept. The concern of reasonable people is neither to preserve nor reject any particular belief. It is, rather, to weigh competing claims and choose all and only those that will bear scrutiny. The only thing that needs tossing is the notion that scrutiny is not required. The "transparency" ploy just doesn't work.

But admitting this still does not entail skeptical triumph. It simply clears the ground for the possibility of a better argument. Here's one:

c) The radical privacy argument for general skepticism is sterile. Even if the egocentric predicament and the allegedly intractable inaccessibility of the external world were true, the world that we live in, know, and talk about would be absolutely unchanged. Granted, we would need to remind ourselves from time to time that "having a conversation" is just a matter of one neighborhood of our stream of awareness schmoozing with another neighborhood of our stream of awareness, and so forth. But as long as that stream is coherent, the operational-behavioral world is no different from what it would be if we were "really" conversing. The same is true of *all* we do. The truth or falsity of the global skeptics' claims makes no discernible difference about *anything*.

Example. In *Three Dialogues between Hylas and Philonous*, Bishop Berkeley suggested that nothing can be known to exist beyond minds and events in them and framed all phenomena as events in the mind of God, rather than as mentally perceived consequences of physical occurrences. Deriding this view, Samuel Johnson is reputed to have kicked a rock and said, "Thus I refute Berkeley"—contending that the objective reality of the physical world was proved by the toe pain that followed the kicking.

But kicking a rock does not refute Berkeley because, *operationally*, there is nothing at stake here. Berkeley and Johnson surely agreed that anyone who goes through the experiences called *kicking a rock* will find that followed by the experiences called *toe pain*. The only issue between them is how best to explain that sequence. Johnson's option was that it amounts to human mental phenomena caused by the interaction of a physical foot and a physical rock; Berkeley's that the entire affair amounts to impulses in the Divine Mind. Wanting as economical an account as possible, he chose one substance over Johnson's two. Such mental monism is a major simplification. Physical monism, however, is too. Either way, toe pain follows rock kicking. What is important in understanding human affairs is what happens in human lives; and that can be conceptualized physically, mentally, or even spiritually, as we please. *Angst* over the essence of their substance is pointless.

Even if the contents of our awareness are so private that a world populated by independent witnesses can't be reached, the witnesses we *can* reach are enough. It doesn't matter if they are, themselves, our own private phenomena. In terms of their testimony we can still distinguish private experiences that are ephemeral from those that are enduring and stable. So even if the "objective external" world turned out to be, for all we know, only the enduring and stable part of our subjective internal one, it makes no practical difference in anything we might think, say, or do.

Furthermore, if we abandoned the labels we ordinarily use to distinguish between "subjective fantasy" (say, running off to Tahiti with a passionate billionairess) and "objective reality" (say, cleaning the rain gutters) and called them *both* subjective, we would still need a verbal apparatus to make the *same* distinction. You can say that everything is a subjective state of your own mind; but having done that, there is still the practical everyday distinction that must be made between those subjective states of your own mind that are like daydreams, and so forth, and those subjective states of your own mind that are like being run over by a truck. And that is the same distinction that we used to draw between imagination and reality, projections and the real world, inner subjectivity and outer objectivity. But if it is the same distinction, why should we abandon the centuries-old, everyday way of drawing it?

So even if the skeptics' argument for radical privacy is irrefutable, in the sense that we cannot prove it false, it is utterly sterile and blurs distinctions that we need to make, can make, and do make, in order to survive. So it need no longer concern us. In the last few decades, however, global skeptics have put up *another* argument to show that all alleged knowledge is subjective—this time in the sense that it is inexorably *perspectival.*

B. Perspective. Experiential data are irremediably biased because they vary as a function of the "perspective" in which they are gathered. That perspective may be physical or conceptual, individual or social.

1) Visual experiences, for example, are the product of at least two factors: the object itself, and the perspective from which it is observed. Ordinarily, people handle this by agreeing to a set of conventions for gathering visual data (head on, standard temperature and pressure, etc.) to establish a paradigmatic point of view. Similar factors affect smells, sounds, and tastes.

Examples. If you displayed an ordinary pie pan and asked its shape, those who saw it straight on would probably say "round," but those off to the sides might say "oval." Indeed, if the pan is tilted back sharply, even front-and-center observers may call it oval. But tilting a pan does not change its shape, only its angle of observation and the resultant images on the observers' retinas.

For similar reasons, you best hunt bears from downwind, if you're in a canyon you cannot easily locate the source of thunder, and the effect of sticking the tip of your tongue in a glass of wine is unlike that of rolling an ounce of it around in your mouth.

You should be nervous about wines labeled "Serve very cold." It would seem that there is some aspect of the wine's attributes that needs masking by manipulating the circumstances under which it is tasted. But if the perspective needs manipulating to sell the product, that already suggests that the product has some objectively discernible properties—unpleasant ones.

2) The angle from which we look is only a small part of the our "perspective." Other parts are the nature of our primary and supplementary equipment, the condition of that equipment and the way it is used, our prior experience and conditioning, and our relevant dysfunctions.

All of these things can vary from one looker to the next; so all of them must be taken into account when assessing what individuals claim to see. For instance:

- *dogs can't see colors;*
- *frogs see only moving objects;*
- *eyeless people don't see anything;*
- *people with macular degeneration see blank spots;*
- *people with heavy cataracts see only light and dark;*
- *many people cannot discriminate red and green;*
- *one-eyed people have poor depth perception; and*
- *people without microscopes can't see germs.*

Seeing is also a function of the past experience (and the concepts that we have built out of it) that we bring on site. Prior experience and the anticipations that it generates are as important in determining what we see (as opposed to what we look at) as the thing that is "out there to be seen."

Example. The members of a certain rain-forest tribe never experienced large open spaces before their lives were invaded by European explorers. Their visual experience was limited to what is common in rain forests: lots of nearby growing things, all around, underfoot and overhead. They had never seen a vista of the sky or a distant horizon. As a result, on being taken to a savanna for the first time, they described a distant approaching wagon as *growing*. They did not have the experiential background to handle long distances and attendant changes in apparent size.

So a significant part of our visual world varies as a function of the way our eyes are made, how they work, how we use them, what we have learned from their previous use, and what conventions and habits are in place. How then can we say that what we see (hear, smell, feel, taste) is the way things "really are?" How can we separate the part that comes from the *object* from what the *subject* supplies?

3) Recall the "sonnet-reciting tree." To reasonably appraise claims about it, we are obliged to evaluate the interpretation that the reporter (a forest ranger) has put on the events that he experienced, even if he is an individual of unimpeachable probity. Even people who regularly tell the truth can screw up the interpretation of an actual experience from time to time. We need not deny that the ranger had the experience that he called "hearing the tree" to reject the sense he made of it; nor that St. Teresa (founder of the Discalced Carmelite Order and author of *Interior Castle*) had experiences that she called "seeing the holiness of God" to reject the sense she made of them.

All experience accounts (not just unusual ones) are complex affairs. A physiological response of an organism to a stimulus may initiate them; but then comes the filtering, interpreting, sorting, bending, and classifying that it takes to make them "make sense."

Sometimes the interpretive dimension of an experience account is so common that we are unaware that any interpretive moves are going on. But, however automatic or unconscious the process may be, it still occurs. In contrast, the interpretive dimension is obvious in the ranger's and the saint's claims. They are far enough off the beaten path from what "everybody says" to alert even the unwary.

Furthermore, if we alter the circumstances in which an experience occurs and is processed, we construe and report it differently.

Example. The Emerald City of Oz in Lyman Frank Baum's charming book was not an emerald city at all—just an ordinary one; but one where everyone wore green spectacles all the time. If Richmond's City Council provided green glasses and made everyone wear them, few people would think the city itself had changed. Most would realize that the only thing that had changed was the hue produced by the circumstances under which the city was necessarily perceived. But suppose a pill with the same greening effect and weave an ideology and cult where greenness is a focal point of community ritual. After a few generations, people might say how important it is to keep taking the pills so as to see the city "*the way it really is.*"

The universal presence of construal constitutes a "slant" that cannot be eliminated or even, reliably, identified and controlled. Indeed, aggressive skeptics argue that since every bit of experiential data involves construal, every experiential knowledge claim is no more than a spin on events. If they are right, none of the claims that generally pass for knowledge of the external world are secure enough to qualify. Objectivity is inaccessible. What passes for reality is *always* in the eye of the beholder.

4) Carlos Castaneda's stories of a sorcerer who used an umbilical "rope" to swing across ravines invite skepticism. But they also show how skepticism can extrapolate from indicting the highly implausible to impugn even the most familiar accounts of ordinary experiences.

Castaneda's story is so foreign to both the scientific mind-set and ordinary non-Native American cosmology that it is implausible and fantastic to most other people. It is more difficult to dispute accounts that are part of the fabric of our own culture; and the more people who serenely accept them (and the more central they are to that fabric), the greater the difficulty. A wide variety of Christian religious claims, for instance, though no more *scientific* than Castaneda's stories about Yaqui practice, are far more *familiar* to most of us. Indeed, they are so "built in" to the fabric of public life that few people muster the effort to doubt them.

Little Smoke?

Castaneda's accounts may be read in his *The Teachings of Don Juan: A Yaqui Way of Knowledge,* and its many sequels. While there is a strong probability that his stories are complete frauds, I am using them on the assumption that he was telling the truth as he saw it. Some of the evidence that he made it all up is laid out in Richard deMille's *The Don Juan Papers.*

> *Example.* For many people in the Unites States, the authenticity of the shroud of Turin is not as easy to dispute as it should be, the divinity of Jesus is even more difficult to tackle, and the notion that there is a God—to bless America—is beyond doubt.

But sauce for geese is still sauce for ganders. Simple fairness demands that the Yaqui claims and the Christian claims be weighed on the same scales, with the same even hand; but they rarely are.

> *Example.* Virginia law prohibits religious messages on license plates. But I have seen "HELIVES" and "EXALTJC"—even though a man who applied for "ATHEIST" was turned down. It is easier to do what is done, even in the cradle of democracy.

For most of us, those scales include controlled experimentation. So we might think that the lack of public (photographed?) demonstrations of umbilical rope swinging would settle the authenticity of the ravine feat in the same way that the discovery of no premedieval fibers (by way of carbon dating) settled the authenticity of the shroud. Life, however, is more complicated than that:

> *PRO.* A lack of photos does not disconfirm the Yaqui story if belly button ropes don't photograph. If Western methods don't work, why not use the

Yaqui's own? Perhaps those ropes are phenomena that can only be confirmed within their frame of reference (on their turf with their methods).

CON. But, according to them, we can see some parts of the world only with the help of "Little Smoke." Can't we dismiss claims about things that can be seen only with enhancers?

PRO. No. Everyone uses enhancers of some kind. If the necessity of using devices to see them does not entail that bacilli, chromosomes, and sunspots are bogus, it does not entail that belly button ropes are bogus either.

CON. Then can't we dismiss Yaqui visions because of the particular enhancer used? The Yaqui helpers are not at all like microscopes or telescopes. Doesn't blowing smoke alter the organism and render its perceptions unreliable?

PRO. But people who eat carrots to improve their night vision say that they can see things that others can't; and all because of chemically induced self-alteration.

CON. But there is a difference between night fliers and Yaqui ravine swingers. The former can confirm their claims with what the night-blind *can* perceive, independent of chemical inducement, by turning on more lights or waiting for their pupils to accommodate. Smoke-induced evidence, on the other hand, is systematically closed off. The only way to confirm it is to use Little Smoke ourselves. Such a block on independent confirmation means that this view does not just involve altering the organism; it *necessarily* involves altering it, and in a risky way to boot.

PRO. But what does "alteration," risky or not, have to do with whether what is seen is *there*? Orthodox Christians say that we must *die* in order to see some parts of reality clearly; and while that entails that the *living* cannot know whether heaven is real, it does not entail that heaven is a fiction. Further, many Christians believe that, with prayer and fasting, glimmers of paradise may be seen in the haze. Just so the Yaqui say that using Little Smoke allows us a glimmer of parts of reality that are usually hidden. Failing to see, if we are unequipped, proves nothing.

CON. But the fact that we see something doesn't entail that it is *there*. High Yaqui see ropes, fasting Christians see paradise, and drunks see elephants; but there's no reason to think any of them have a better bead on reality than we do. The drunks, surely, are *mistaken*; if not about seeing elephants, at least in thinking that what they see in delirium is part of the real world.

PRO. Maybe. But Little Smoke isn't booze. It heightens our sensations, rather than dulling them. Why should we think, that the objects of those heightened sensations are hallucinatory?

CON. Why should we think that those "heightened" sensations have any external object at all? Chemical friends may simply facilitate their users' *internal* awareness. But, even if they have a better handle on their inner life than square folk do, that won't bridge the gap between a head's head and what is actually "out there." Such "sensitivity" provides no privileged access to facts.

PRO. But if the Yaqui's seeing the ropes doesn't show that they *are* real, then a non-Yaqui's not seeing them doesn't show they *aren't*. We're all in the same boat. We know what we have access to, they know what they have access to, and that's that.

Note that both sides claim knowledge of the real world and appeal to public experience to confirm it. But they appeal to different publics that construe events in different conceptual frameworks that confirm different, apparently incompatible, "knowledges."

This result can be read two ways: as a confirmation of the traditional skeptical contention that there is no real knowledge at all, or as a confirmation of the relativistic skeptical contention that while there is lots of real knowledge, none of it is universal.

The first reading goes this way:

- Experiential confirmation is in the eye of the beholder.
- So it provides no warrant that a claim is accurate.
- But a successful knowledge claim must be accurate.
- So there is no experiential warrant that any knowledge claim is successful.
- So there is no experiential knowledge.

Postmodern relativists, on the other hand, note that experiential confirmation is not in the eye of the *individual* beholder, at any rate. (Leaving it *there* gives insufficient attention to the social character of people, experience, and language.) Rather, they contend, it is in the eye of a language-using *culture*. So they read the result of the dialogue this way:

- Experiential confirmation is always relative to a culture.
- So the truth of experiential claims is always contextual and culture dependent.
- But if knowledge is "justified, true belief," and truth is contextual and culture dependent, then knowledge is contextual and culture dependent itself.
- So all experiential knowledge is contextual and culture dependent.
- So while experiential knowledge does occur, it is always "local" rather than "universal."

This view is called "cultural epistemic relativism." It is the dominant epistemological theory among those committed to "multiculturalism and diversity." It has many sources, embodies numerous illuminating philosophical insights, has more than a few problems, and is the topic of the next chapter.

7

Knowledge and Cultural Relativism

If, as Joseph Butler said in his *Fifteen Sermons,* "Everything is what it is and not another thing," then what is true is always and everywhere true (provided it is stated completely and with clarity of reference).

> *Caution.* There are reasons for the qualifiers. Truth is a function of what occurs; so of two statements that look alike, one can be true and one can be false, depending on the particular events that they actually describe. "It is raining" may be true (and may be known) in Tahiti at a time when "It is raining" is false (and cannot be known) in Kuwait. This looks like a contradiction; but it isn't. Fleshed out, the two iterations of "It is raining" are not the same. They are elliptical for "It is raining at time T in Tahiti," and "It is raining at time T in Kuwait," respectively. And there is nothing inconsistent at all about the possibility that, at time T, it is raining in Tahiti and isn't in Kuwait and that both of these facts might be known, simultaneously, to be the case.

If, on the other hand, truth is a function of time, place, and conceptual circumstance, then knowledge itself is temporally, physically, and conceptually local. For, if so, the same knowledge claim could be both true and false, and two incompatible knowledge claims could both be true, depending on the time, place, and conceptual circumstances in which they are voiced. Thus, it could be true and known in Beijing that acupuncture cures hernias, and true and known in Akron that it does not; and true and known in Peoria that rain drop formation is a function of temperature and humidity, but true and known in Pago Pago that it is a function of whether the gods have been propitiated. One widely held view that this is the case is called "cultural epistemic relativism."

1. Sources of Cultural Epistemic Relativism

The intellectual sources of cultural epistemic relativism include:

- the notion of "cultural *normative* relativism,"
- the notion of "institutional facts,"
- the notion of "the sociology of knowledge,"
- the notion of "language games,"
- the notion of "paradigms," and
- a general antipathy toward logical positivism.

A. Cultural normative relativism. The notion that *values* are culturally determined—*When in Rome, do as the Romans do*—should be familiar. "Taste" is the model: *de gustibus non disputandum est*. But taste can be sharpened. Anyone can differentiate *fino* and *oloroso* sherries; but with practice, we can even distinguish Gallo and Harvey's *olorosos*. Tasting is a two-place relation to which the taster and the tasted both contribute. Nevertheless, by the early-twentieth century, the notion that moral and esthetic values are functions of our time, circumstance, and culture was regarded as a universal truth by virtually all liberals, most social scientists, and many philosophers.

Ironically, if this notion *is* a universal truth, it is one item of nonrelative knowledge and hence a poor foundation for epistemic relativism. However, the value of acts does depend, in part, on the context in which they occur. Giving water to the thirsty is good. Giving water to the drowning is not. Discriminating on the basis of *some* differentia (gender for prospective pilots, e.g.) is bad. Discriminating on the basis of *other* differentia (eye-hand coordination for prospective brain surgeons, e.g.) is good. Value *contextualism* is obvious, upon reflection; but value *relativism* needs showing.

Until recently, the notion that evaluations are culturally (or even privately) determined served as a basis for differentiating the investigation of "objective mat-

> **Watch Out**
>
> There are many ways in which cultural normative relativism is problematic. I will look at the issue further in chapter 10. For now, suffice it to observe:
>
> a) It is one thing to say that different things are *called* good in different cultures. It is another to say that different things *are* good in different cultures. If "child sacrifice was good for the Maya" means that the Maya valued it, OK. But if it means that it was good for the Maya to value it, the consequences of that practice make it anything but obvious.
>
> b) It is one thing to say that our values are *influenced* by the culture in which we are socialized. It is another to say that they are *determined* by that culture. If these claims were equivalent, internal social critique and reform would be impossible. But critique and reform occur, and nothing that occurs is impossible. So the two claims are not equivalent.

ters of fact" (science) and "subjective matters of taste" (ethics and esthetics). Today, the cultural relativists' umbrella has expanded to include even what used to be called "objective matters of fact." *When in Rome, think as the Romans think.*

B. Institutional facts. Certain truths about matters of fact describe states of affairs that are conventionally or institutionally constructed. "Institutional facts" represent states of affairs that depend on the conventions of the culture where they occur.

> *Example.* A society may be organized so that its members may trade in grain futures. Another society, lacking appropriate conventions, provides no such market. So it can be said only of some societies that "fortunes may be made by trading in grain futures." That is a local truth that presupposes an institutional fact (the existence of a futures market) about social organization.

One way to bolster cultural epistemic relativism would be to say that *all* facts are (or presuppose) institutional facts. But this is not true of all facts. Consider the fact that tigers are carnivorous. Further, even for those facts that are institutional, we must note that they cannot be created with a free hand. A society could not establish a market in grain futures were there no grain, or woman's suffrage were there no women. Nevertheless, the notion that facts themselves are free social creations feeds the postmodern conviction that all *knowledge* is culturally determined.

C. The sociology of knowledge. In the early decades of the twentieth century, social scientists began seriously to entertain the notion that all knowledge is influenced, if not determined, by socialization (see Karl Mannheim's *Ideology and Utopia*). Anthropologists had long recognized that members of different cultures described the world differently, but with a certain tendency toward condescension in their reports: *The aborigines of Australia say that human pregnancy is caused by the stick ritual* [nudge, wink]. The new wave said that each culture's cosmology, polity, medicine, and religion were "true for them," just as their morals were "right for them."

Though it is difficult to make a case that Australia's First People were in *any* sense right about the etiology of pregnancy, most academics came to agree that the "sociology of knowledge" was, nevertheless, *generally* the case. Remorse over the impact of European imperialism on the rest of the world made the sociology of knowledge more easily convincing. A growing mistrust of "Western" science made a contribution, too. And vested interests in various local world-views also encouraged the notion that (collective) believing somehow makes things (locally) so. After all, if knowledge is a function of culture, then no outsider can say that our worldview is mistaken. The good news is that this discourages meddling in other cultures' innocent affairs. The bad news is that it equally discourages doing anything about the destructive affairs of a culture—our own or "alien."

D. Language games. According to the later Wittgenstein, modern philosophy had too narrow a view of the uses of language. Its uses, he said, are countless, and their number not fixed. In his *Philosophical Investigations* (¶23), he listed the following examples:

> Giving orders, and obeying them—Describing the appearance of an object, or giving its measurements—Constructing an object from a description (a drawing) —Reporting an event—Speculating about an event—Forming and testing an hypothesis—Presenting the results of an experiment in tables and diagrams —Making up a story; and reading it—Play-acting—Singing catches—Guessing riddles—Making a joke; telling it—Solving a problem in practical arithmetic— Translating from one language into another—Asking, thanking, cursing, greeting, praying.

He called such enterprises *language games* to emphasize that language-using activities, like games, follow *many* rules and that *different* distinctions must be drawn between what works, and what does not, in each. *Creativity*, for example, is a mark of effective storytelling, but not of doing sums; and *referential accuracy* is a mark of effective airline timetable construction, but not of writing sonnets.

Appraising the play of any game by the rules of another is a category mistake; and thinking that the rules of a game should obey *themselves* is another. So too, for language games:

- The lines of a sonnet no more need to be true than the moves in a chess game need to follow suit.
- "Be accurate" is a rule for describing, as "follow suit" is a rule for bridge; but "be accurate" is no more accurate or inaccurate than "follow suit" follows or fails to follow suit.

Consequently, while a "move" in the descriptive language game may be true or false, the rules of the game are not true or false themselves. They are not descriptions but *directions for describing*.

This is not to say they cannot be appraised. They can, but only on external grounds such as *do they make it possible to achieve the game's goals?* The answer to that depends on both the nature of the rules and the goals of the game. So for instance, since the goals of description games include things like helping ourselves and others anticipate experience, and creating a record so as to save our own and others' time and energy, their key rules should be aimed at things like reliability and efficiency. So "always lie" would be a poor convention for them, and "double check your data" would be a good one. But "always lie" and "double check your data" are still neither true nor false, for they are not, themselves, descriptions.

An utterance can only work or fail to work (be felicitous or not) in some game or other. Since what counts for felicity is a function of the game being played, absent *all* contexts an utterance has no felicity conditions at all and, consequently, no meaning at all.

According to the logical positivists, an attempt at description that lacks *truth* conditions is *cognitively* meaningless. The present point is similar, but more sweeping: an utterance that has *no* felicity conditions (truth conditions, sincerity conditions, whatever) is meaningless *across the board*. A meaningful utterance must have some standard for success and failure. Only language that has a use has a meaning. Its meaning *is* its use and is game dependent.

Different language games have different points:

- Expressive: to show and elicit feelings
- Verdictive: to pass moral, esthetic, or legal judgment
- Explicative: to elucidate understanding and share it
- Performative: to create institutional facts
- Fabulative: to entertain, reinforce, or encourage
- Imperative: to get someone to do something

Each game will have felicity conditions appropriate to its point; and those conditions can be complex. Consequently a move in a language game can fail in more than one way. For instance, consider *performative* language. This is the language that we use to create (not describe) certain institutional facts: *I promise to be there; I forgive your rudeness; I pronounce you husband and wife;* and so forth. There are many felicity conditions for such locutions, according to J. L. Austin's "Performative Utterances" and John Searle's *Speech Acts*. Here are four. Note *truth's* absence:

- The convention that is invoked in the performance must exist and be accepted by all parties. If not (as with the "purchase" of Manhattan Island where there was no convention of private ownership in place), the performance is *void*.
- The circumstances in which we invoke the convention must be appropriate, and the procedure must be carried out correctly and completely. If not (as with "promising" something that is not in our power), the performance *misfires*.
- We must not use a formula without the requisite thoughts, feelings, and intentions. If we do (as in "promising" with mental reservations), the convention has been *abused*.
- The convention must be invoked without coercion. If not (as when we force a "promise" on a child), the performance is *not responsible*.

So for instance, a promise can work even though it is not true, because promises, on this analysis, are neither true nor false. Thinking that they *must* be true or false radically misconstrues the promising game.

Since different language games can even be played at the same time, it is possible for the same discourse, simultaneously, to work and fail. For example, a given philosophy lecture might be either true or false, creative or trite, and riveting or boring.

This does not mean that the same discourse could both work and fail in the same game. If the game is description, then the discourse will be either true or false, not both and not neither. But if different cultures categorize what is to be described in radically different ways, then it might be possible for different descriptions to be true in different cultures. If this is the case, and if cultures alone determine the categorical structure of the games played in them, then the way is clear for cultural epistemic relativism to flourish.

E. Paradigms. Thomas Kuhn, working in the "Unity of Science" tradition, but calling it into question, contended that its dogma of scientific objectivity was mistaken. Even science, he said, is perspectival. Scientific claims are only true relative to the "paradigm" under which they are formulated; and paradigms are conventional functions of time, place, and circumstance that replace one another over time.

The positivists' model of science did not *describe* scientific practice. It was a rational reconstruction of what science *ought* to be, according to empirical dogma. Kuhn, in contrast, based his analysis on an examination of what scientists actually do. However, if all inquiry is paradigm driven, so was Kuhn's: a *different* paradigm from the orthodox positivists', to be sure, but a paradigm nonetheless.

If we examine the actual history of science, we will see that it is not the linear progressive play out of one continuous game. It is, rather, a succession of distinctly different games—related in that they share the goal of describing and explaining the external world, but disparate in that each one is driven by its own conception of what questions to ask, what counts as evidence, and consequently what we can "know" on its terms.

So we do not find universal truths in science across time. Not sharing the same conceptual equipment, for instance, pre- and post-Copernican astronomers did not see the world the same way. What one affirmed, the other apparently denied:

> ### The Unity of Science
>
> The "Unity of Science Movement" is another name for Logical Positivism and Logical Empiricism. Thomas Kuhn's book, *The Structure of Scientific Revolutions*, was published as a monograph in the movement's *International Encyclopedia of Unified Science*. So his own revolution was just that—it came from within.

The sun revolves around the earth, said the former.
No, the earth revolves around the sun, said the latter.

This, however, is not a real case of "P and ~P." If truth and falsehood are paradigm dependent, so is meaning. The senses expressed by "the sun revolves around the earth," under pre- and post-Copernican paradigms, are not the same. Indeed, insofar as two paradigms are genuinely conceptually different, a claim articulated in one cannot even be expressed in the other. Claims in the two systems are "incommensurable" and mutually "untranslatable." This is because, paraphrasing Wittgenstein's *Tractatus* 5.6 and 5.641, the limits of our paradigm are the limits of our world, and our world is *the* world.

If this is right, the traditional dogma of a sharp subjective/objective distinction has collapsed. The benchmark against which subjective opinion used to be weighed and found wanting has turned out to be subjective itself. If so all that remained necessary to establish cultural epistemic relativism was proof that paradigms are exclusively *cultural* products. This is unlikely, of course. It is far more likely that paradigms are the products of culture *and* the biological capacities of the human organism *and* specific contingent events.

F. Antipositivism. Another factor that encouraged the acceptance of cultural epistemic relativism since mid-century was widespread disaffection with logical positivism. The positivists' exclusion of speculative metaphysics from the realm of cognition was not well received by a wide variety of philosophers, historians, social scientists, and litterateurs who chafed at the assertion that their claims were "strictly nonsense."

But if various utterances are moves in distinctly different games and can be weighed only on their own game's rules (Wittgenstein), or paradigm bound and subject to no paradigmatically external tests (Kuhn), then the positivists' empirical verification doctrine does not apply to (much less constrain) the pursuits of those who do not share their framework or play their game. Consequently, advocates of Marxism, dialectical idealism, transcendental theology, Freudian psychoanalysis, ecofeminism, parapsychology, and other anything-but-empirical ideologies can ply their trades without concern that they are epistemologically second-class citizens.

2. Characteristics of Cultural Epistemic Relativism

Many postmoderns—teethed on cultural normative relativism; armed with the notions of institutional facts, the sociology of knowledge, language games, and paradigms; and mistrusting the Enlightenment, empiricism, linear science, and so-called progress—fix reality, not in the eye of the individual (epistemic free enterprise), but in that of society. Whatever anyone knows is a culturally determined social construct.

Furthermore, in this view, what counts as evidence is as culturally determined as everything else. So whatever evidential criteria are indigenous to a particular culture are valid for it and its members. Standards like consistency, testability, and public confirmation need not have universal priority. What has local priority depends on what cognition model is established in a particular culture's ethos. If, as in the Enlightenment, precise observation and measurement are the cognition model, inquirers will run experiments, crunch numbers, and be ready for adversarial confrontations. But if, say, literary interpretation is a culture's cognition model, inquirers will ask whether a particular gloss is interesting, deep, persuasive, and empathetic. Every paradigm (game) has its own procedures (rules).

So for consistent cultural epistemic relativists, power is knowledge. Contra appearances, this is *not* an extension of Thracymachus's "good is what is in the interest of the stronger" into epistemology. In this view, knowledge is an ad hoc function of power, and power is an ad hoc product of culture. So knowledge is a twice ad hoc function of *whatever a culture happens to be.* So saying "power is knowledge" is not saying that powerful individuals or groups conspire to decide what will be true; but that the mere occurrence of a society generates power and, in the practice of that power, truth and knowledge *happen.* As Michel Foucault sees things in *Power/Knowledge,* this is how cultures, necessarily, define the known and knowable within them.

3. Problems with Cultural Epistemic Relativism

According to postmodern cultural relativism, neither a culture's epistemic paradigm nor the institutions it generates arise out of individuals' intentions. The intentions that lie behind them are the *culture's* own. So responsibility goes *there.*

Of course, if there are no such things as cultural intentions, then *nothing* would be responsible for a culture's epistemic paradigm and institutions. They would either be strictly causal products, or just "come down." Either alternative is problematic. If they are strictly causal, then the possibilities of human action and choice are attenuated. Worse, where "things come down" is the paradigmatic explanation, the possibility of human action and choice is erased. Where a culture's epistemic paradigm just comes down, there is neither history (or learning from it) nor science (or controlling the present or planning the future in terms of it)—only inchoate "happenings."

So *can* a culture intend, or is this just palpably false anthropomorphism? Either way, there are problems:

- Since a culture's epistemic paradigm determines its members' experience, belief, and knowledge, then there is no basis on which they could question it or question the propositions and behaviors that express it. So on this account, *no internal culture critique is possible (much less legitimate).*
- Since different epistemic paradigms, and the claims made under them, are mutually incommensurate and untranslatable, there is no basis on which an outsider could intelligibly question one, or the propositions and behaviors that express it. So seen, *no intelligible external critique is possible.*
- If epistemic paradigms are self-validating, then each one that occurs, along with the propositions and behaviors that express it, is valid on its own turf. So seen, *extracultural interference is always improper.*

A. Is internal culture critique impossible?

Internal culture critique (cognitive subversion) does occur. But, in the theory at hand, we can know only what our culture provides for. So deviant claims cannot constitute knowledge. Indeed, unless a deviant claim occurred in a culture whose paradigm admits inconsistencies to be true, a single case of deviant *knowledge* would show that the paradigm-generated claims that it contradicts are, in fact, false and unknown. So deviant claims must amount to no more than *beliefs*. But, in the theory at hand, we can *believe* only what our culture provides for. So even deviant *beliefs* are counterexamples to it, and many such counterexamples exist: the intellectual desertion of their priests by the Mayan peasants, the gradual erosion in Europe of the concept of the divine rights of kings, the extension of suffrage to women, and the abolition of slavery in the United States, for starters. More subversions are in process today; and, unless we are perpetually willing to say that the marginalizing of women, homosexuals, Third World peoples, children, and edible livestock are sacrosanct, the notion that knowledge is wholly determined by culture and beyond internal critique is at best simplistic and misguided, at worst disingenuous and immoral.

B. Is external culture critique unintelligible? External culture critique (alien protest) does occur. But, in the theory at hand, claims made under one epistemic paradigm are incommensurate with, and cannot be translated into, claims made under another. So such protests are unintelligible to the members of the culture whose ideas are under critique. Indeed, the ideas being critiqued are also unintelligible to those who think they are protesting them. So a single example of alien protest that is intelligible to the natives, or of a domestic practice that is intelligible to outsiders, will show that the theory is faulty.

Numerous examples exist, for instance, the condemnations of Eurocultural racism by members of African and Asian cultures. If those condemnations were not intelligible to Eurocultural chauvinists, they could not have been the occasion of all the rationalization, histrionics, and bad faith that have marked Western political and economic colonialism and exploitation over the last millennium. The alien victims of that exploitation were perfectly capable of understanding the ideology behind it, and of demonstrating its flaws in terms that their exploiters, in turn, understood equally well.

C. Is universal paradigm respect possible? Many cultures have held their own belief system to be superior to that of others and have taken upon themselves the noble task of straightening out the beliefs and practices of their epistemically challenged neighbors. Upon confronting this phenomenon (e.g., in the imposition of Christianity on the Western Hemisphere's indigenous peoples), cultural relativists are likely to deemphasize their untenable claim that external *critique* is always *unintelligible* and emphasize instead the somewhat more plausible claim that external *interference* is always *wrong*.

The notion that every paradigm is valid for the culture that embodies it and that, consequently, all cultures and paradigms should be respected by outsiders sounds like a reasonable way to affirm the virtue of being a cross-cultural good neighbor and to encourage multiculturalism. Unfortunately, as the example that follows shows, it does not work.

> *Example.* Consider two cultures, A and B. A might be inclined to meddle, disinclined to meddle, or indifferent about meddling with B. B might favor being meddled with, object to being meddled with, or be indifferent about being meddled with by A.
>
> On the principle that every culture's paradigmatic views are valid for it and should be respected, what would be the propriety of A actually meddling with B in each of the nine possible combinations? The following table shows the answers.

In seven of the nine situations, the principle can be consistently applied. The results of applying it in those seven settings, however, are hardly startling. There are, however, two conflicted cases: where B wants what A

Culture A's Paradigmatic Bent on Meddling	Culture B's Paradigmatic Bent on Being Meddled With	Propriety of A Actually Meddling with B
POSITIVE	POSITIVE	OK
POSITIVE	NEGATIVE	CONFLICTED
POSITIVE	INDIFFERENT	OK
NEGATIVE	POSITIVE	CONFLICTED
NEGATIVE	NEGATIVE	NOT OK
NEGATIVE	INDIFFERENT	NOT OK
INDIFFERENT	POSITIVE	OK
INDIFFERENT	NEGATIVE	NOT OK
INDIFFERENT	INDIFFERENT	FLIP A COIN

declines to offer, and where A pushes what B declines to accept. *Whatever* A does in those settings will deny the principle that every culture's paradigmatic beliefs are valid for it.

- If meddling with B is A's paradigmatic bent and B paradigmatically eschews such meddling:

    P1 *If it is legitimate for A to interfere with B, then B's paradigm is not valid for B.*

    P2 *If it is illegitimate for A to interfere with B, then A's paradigm is not valid for A.*

    P3 *Either it is legitimate or illegitimate for A to interfere with B.*

    ∴C *Either B's paradigm is not valid for B or A's paradigm is not valid for A.*

- If being meddled with by A is B's paradigmatic bent, but A paradigmatically eschews doing so:

  P1 If it is legitimate for A to interfere with B, then A's paradigm is not valid for A.

  P2 If it is illegitimate for A to interfere with B, then B's paradigm is not valid for B.

  P3 Either it is legitimate or illegitimate for A to interfere with B.

  ∴C Either A's paradigm is not valid for A or B's paradigm is not valid for B.

More concretely, given the historical *ethos* of the United States, we deny the principle of universal paradigm respect when we say that the United States has no business meddling in the affairs of other nations. To say that affirms that while other cultures' paradigms are valid for them and should be respected, the U.S. paradigm is not valid for it and should be challenged.

On grounds of "culture respect," the Unites States has been enjoined to refrain from proselytizing in various societies on behalf of pollution abatement, fishery restrictions, literacy, zero population growth, democracy, religious tolerance, the rights of children, women and ethnic minorities, free trade, and industrialization, and to refrain from exporting to Third World shores the products of Western science and technology such as medicines, synthetic fertilizers, bioengineered cereals, movies, and television.

For the United States to take a strict "hands off" posture would deny its own paradigmatic bent toward meddling; but allowing "hands on" would violate the cultural integrity of its target cultures. "Hands on or hands off," however, is a clear case of $P \ v \sim P$. So denying both alternatives yields $\sim(P \ v \sim P)$ is a patent self-contradiction. So since the principle of universal paradigm respect cannot be consistently maintained in all cases, it is not a coherent vehicle for barring cross-cultural meddling.

There are ethical principles that would bar some cross-cultural meddling. "Do no harm," for instance, would discourage a society from

Culture Respect

Urging the West to honor and learn from other cultures, but forbidding it to evangelize its own, is unfair, of course. To be sure, the West does have much to learn from others. For example, considering the U.S. penchant for armed violence, domestic instability, homophobia, ecological wantonness, and material greed, virtually any input would be helpful. But it also works the other way. Its governmental magnanimity (e.g., the Marshall Plan) and its private benevolences (e.g., CARE and AFSC) manifest its paradigmatic commitment to the notion of universal human welfare. And that is a notion that some of the world's other cultures might usefully honor and incorporate.

removing a defenseless people from its land in order to use it for nuclear testing. Other ethical principles, however, *endorse* some cross-cultural meddling.
"Avert harm," for instance, would encourage a society to airlift food, medicine, and relief workers to a locale devastated by monsoon floods, even if—
in the indigenous paradigm—such events were seen as manifestations of divine will that should be passively accepted. And, unfortunately, moral
deliberation cannot say which principle to follow unless it is allowed to bring
cultures themselves under review, thus denying cultural normative relativism
and cultural epistemic relativism alike.

D. Is universal paradigm respect wise? Even in the seven of nine cases
where universal paradigm respect can be consistently followed, it is not clear
that doing so is wise.

1) Universal paradigm respect would require noninterference with cultural
activities and circumstances such as:

- female circumcision in western Africa,
- bipartisan genocide in the Balkans,
- famine in the sub-Sahara that is locally ignored,
- religious warfare in Ulster and the Middle East, and
- pandemic parasite infestations in any society that favors exorcism over
  medical treatment and insect abatement.

Further, depending on our definition of "culture," it could require noninterference with the claims and institutions of a variety of ideologically driven
groups, giving tacit endorsement to notions such as:

- "African-Americans can't learn management skills."
  At one time, the corporate culture of Texaco, Inc.
- "Snakes never bite the faithful."
  The culture of Appalachian charismatics.
- "Federal tax law is null and void."
  The culture of Common Law and Posse Comitatus.
- "Using a common cup is not dangerous."
  Some Eucharistic cultures.

2) Universal paradigm respect provides no criteria for assessing the alleged
wisdom, or deciding whether to adopt the practices of, various outside cultures or internal subcultures. In the area of health care, for instance, it provides no basis for honoring and incorporating acupuncture and herbalism
from various Asian and indigenous North American cultures while rejecting
crystal power from Wycca or chiropractic, homeopathy, naturopathy, psychic
surgery, and laetril and aroma therapies from the assorted other subcultures
around the globe that practice them.

3) Not every culture is so substantial that its epistemic paradigm deserves universal respect. Cultures that are spontaneous, vigorously long-lived, widely distributed, open to external events, and composed of generally quick-witted and well-informed people are more likely to have an epistemic paradigm that deserves respect than those that are contrived, brand-new or old and torpid, local, closed to external events, and composed of generally slow-witted or uninformed people. The former will have had ample opportunities for paradigm stress and to make adjustments to deal with it. The latter are comparatively untested.

a) Spontaneity. A society that has come together as a result of the general interests of an ad hoc membership is less likely to be agenda driven than one cobbled together for a purpose. It is consequently more likely to be adaptable, and to enjoy a long and vigorous life.

> *Examples.* Virtually any indigenous regional society can stand as an example of a spontaneous culture. The Amana, Oneida, and Heaven's Gate societies exemplify contrived ones.

b) Longevity and vigor. The passage of years brings fortune's slings and arrows to challenge a culture's "take" on the world. So one that endures (without hibernating) is more likely to have met and adapted to challenge than an upstart. However, the "cake of culture" can numb a society's responsiveness, so that some aging ones fail to adapt, and slowly die.

> *Examples.* China is an ancient and robust culture. Early-eighteenth century France was an ancient but log-jammed one. During its not-brief-enough career, the apartheid culture of the Republic of South Africa was the very model of the *parvenu.*

c) Distribution. Wide geographic distribution presents a culture with a variety of events and circumstances to challenge its "take" on the world. So one that is widely distributed is more likely to have met and adapted to challenge than a strictly local one.

> *Examples.* The societies that collectively constitute Indian culture, Chinese culture, and Euroculture survive robustly in an extraordinarily wide variety of environments. The society of the Maya, on the other hand, was local to one area.

d) External contact. Cultures that are open to contact with the outside world confront a wider variety of phenomena than those that are closed. Consequently, they are more likely to have been challenged, and to have had a chance to show their paradigm's mettle.

> *Examples.* The cultures of the Inca, of the indigenous peoples of Amazonas, and of some pockets of Appalachia exemplify isolation. They may be contrasted to

any of the historic trading cultures such as Britain, India, and ancient Egypt (which was trading beyond the Black Sea by 2500 B.C.).

e) General intelligence. A culture can display more or less general intelligence among its members as a function of historic events or conscious policy. One way to increase it is to discourage close inbreeding. A second is to adopt school and childcare policies that provide cognitive stimulation. A third is to put a premium on importing and retaining gifted individuals. Reverse policies work the other way.

Cultures with lots of smart people, for whatever reason, are more likely to have reputable epistemic paradigms than those whose general population is comparatively dim.

Examples. James Oglethorpe's colony was noted for its vigorous importation of talent. So is Canada, today. Examples on the other end of the scale are numerous, but hard to make inoffensive. I will limit myself to one. It is possible that the reason why tidewater Virginia was on the forefront of political and intellectual affairs in the eighteenth century, but has had very little to contribute to them in more recent times, has something to do with who left (and who stayed home) as the challenge of the frontier moved westward.

f) Access to information. A culture in which information is widely and freely exchanged is more likely to have an epistemic paradigm that deserves respect than one in which the information bazaar is stifled or closed. Its status will vary with the presence, availability, and freedom of the media, the encouragement of literacy, the level of schooling standards, and the accessibility of education to the general population.

Examples. The Soviet Union, Nazi Germany, and Virginia-until-after-the-Civil-War (when it made its first provision for public education) all stand in ready contrast to societies like contemporary Japan, Iceland, and Sweden.

None of these criteria will do by itself. Nor are any of them absolute. Furthermore, in making an assessment of a culture, we must carefully control for the presence of manipulation, pathology, and dysfunction in the way it operates. Manipulation can cause false readings, and pathology and dysfunction suggest that a culture is on a dead-end street, even if it has not yet reached its terminus.

4) The proof of a paradigm is in its fruit. A respectable paradigm will underwrite a culture that is viable for its members. But if a respectable paradigm is a *sufficient* condition for a viable culture, then a viable culture is a *necessary* condition for a respectable paradigm. So a collapsing culture says bad things about its own fundamental ways of knowing.

On the other hand, a respectable epistemic paradigm is not a necessary condition of social prosperity. Consequently, the fact that a culture is thriving does not guarantee that its fundamental ways of knowing are reliable. Its success might be entirely accidental.

> *Example*. A local environment may be so easy that it doesn't matter what the people who live there think they know. The fish just jump into the skillet, the fruit trees bear year-round, there are no local diseases or parasites, and no European adventurers have yet arrived.

This is why we need to look at whether a society is adaptable to alternate environments, or what happens when plagues (or human invaders) blow in on the wind. An adequate epistemic paradigm for paradise may prove inadequate to provide a workable theory of disease and reliable medicines, or to prepare an isolated community for external aggression.

5) The occurrence of dysfunctional epistemic practices in a culture is prima facie evidence that its paradigm is inadequate.

a) Paradigms frame experience in much the same way that theories frame scientific observation. Consequently, paradigms that lack the characteristics that mark viable theories are highly suspect.

- Viable paradigms, like viable theories, anticipate events and grow and adjust to accommodate novel ones.
- Viable paradigms, like viable theories, are fertile. They generate inquiry that expands their horizons and range of application. A viable epistemic paradigm must be capable of growth. It will at least have room to accommodate any experiences that are possible (on its terms) but have not yet occurred, so that—when they do occur—we can make sense of them. A viable paradigm does not have a closed door to the future.
- Viable paradigms, like viable theories are experientially connected. Otherwise they could not deal with events. Further, they must be adaptable lest events burst their seams. This not only includes being adaptable to novel events on the local scene but also to the events that arise when the culture is exported to a new area of inquiry, a different physical environment, or another day and time. Within the limits of adaptation that are open to paradigms, a more adaptable one is a more viable one. This shows historically in cultural expansions and contractions, when more viable paradigms take over in new places and circumstances, and less viable ones give way.

   It is important to note that the viability of a paradigm and the armament of a conquering culture (including brainwashing) are very different matters. A more viable paradigm shows itself by working better *without* relying on invasions, pogroms, and mental health clinics.
- Viable paradigms, like viable theories, adhere to reliable epistemic standards, that is, criteria for differentiating what is known from what is not. Absent reliable standards for ordering and ranking beliefs, people could

neither learn nor plan. Then, unable to avoid adversity, they could survive only by chance. Absent reliable epistemic standards, the human limb would have fallen from the evolutionary tree long ago.

b) For theories, and perhaps for paradigms as well, the need for reliable epistemic standards has both an inferential and an observational side. On the inferential side, a viable theory is coherent: all the truths voiced under it must be consistent with each other. On the observational side, a viable theory responds to experience: it provides a clear notion of what sorts of experiences "count" and standards of "due process" for handling them as they occur.

(i) Incoherent theories are useless because they allow the inference of anything at all. But is it possible that coherence is not a suitable standard for paradigms? Might it be that favoring coherence is a case of prejudicially imposing one piece of the Western paradigm (logic) on other cultures that constitute their own forms of life?

But logic is *not* a local sport in the world's intellectual flora. It is indigenous everywhere. Nor is the idea that coherence is essential to reliable inference a Western cultivar. Distinguishing between reliable and unreliable inferences in terms of coherence is an essential part of *any* cognition game.

While cognition games are not the only games there are, there is a radical difference between games played under a nonepistemic paradigm, ones played under an alternate epistemic paradigm, and ones played under a flawed epistemic paradigm.

Nonepistemic enterprises are legion, and whether they are worthy of respect depends on what each one amounts to and on what constitutes felicity for it. The standards will vary of course. Consider the grounds for admiring a comedian, a novelist, and a shortstop.

Regrettably, what may sometimes be called "alternate epistemologies" too often turn out to be merely flawed ones.

> *Example.* Soccer is neither good nor bad baseball, and certainly not "alternate baseball." It would be silly to say, "Baggio played brilliantly on Italy's alternate-baseball team." He earned respect for playing soccer *well*, not for playing baseball *differently*.

> *Example.* A personnel office hires Zorka to cast the horoscopes of job applicants. While horoscopes are not good psychometric devices (they are incoherent and unreliable), they aren't bad ones, either. They aren't psychometric devices *at all*. Horoscopes are, well, *horoscopes*. So it would be very silly to say, "Zorka is a brilliant alternate-psychometrician."

If the point of a game is epistemic, but no notion of coherence is in its paradigm, it is fatally flawed. An epistemic paradigm that does not demand coherence cannot identify reliable inferences. So except for cultures where inferences don't occur, coherence is an essential component of every viable epistemic paradigm. But there are no cultures where inferences don't occur. Indeed, absent inference, *culture* does not occur.

(ii) If a theory did not respond to experience at all, it would not account for observed events—a necessity for its own survival.

> *Example.* The theory that everything that occurs is under the control of an all-powerful, all-knowing, and benevolent God must accommodate the phenomena of child abuse, political torture, and screw-fly worms to survive. Theologians, consequently, spend considerable time constructing theodicies, that is, arguments to reconcile such phenomena with theistic belief. Absent some theodicy or other, theism would disappear.

Further, if we tried to use a theory with no clear notion of what sorts of experiences are relevant to its status, or of how to weigh and test those that are, then we could not differentiate between events that demand theoretical accommodations and those that don't.

> *Example.* Astrologers theorize that astronomical juxtapositions at the time of individuals' births influence their destiny, using a correlation of the calendar and celestial deployment that is said to have been first mapped in antiquity. We must assume that those correlations were revised on the several occasions that the calendar has been changed. Otherwise a modern Leo would not be a true Leo, horoscope casting would be arbitrary and capricious, and astrological theory could only survive in a culture of intellectual sloth.

Viable epistemic paradigms, too, must have a clear sense of what sort of experience counts, and of how to process and appraise particular bits within their domain. For reasons already seen, that processing and appraisal must minimally take into account whether the observations on which epistemic claims are based are appropriately relevant to the claim based on them, repeatable, public or cross-checkable, free of equivocation, and controlled for limiting conditions.

If such concerns don't show up in an epistemic paradigm's arena, the word "evidence" cannot function reliably there. And, if that is so there is no reason to think that the word "know" functions reliably there either. So there is a double reason to refrain from saying that a culture working with such a paradigm *knows* things that others don't—unless we are willing to accept fatal equivocation.

There are, then, many reasons why it would be unwise to practice "universal paradigm respect," even if it were possible. All of this, however, presumes that human discourse is universally driven by culturally determined epistemic paradigms—a far from safe presumption, given that the very notion of a paradigm is beset by many problems. Those problems are the topic of the next chapter.

8

Problems with Paradigms

Have postmoderns gone overboard with the notion of epistemic paradigms? However important such paradigms may be, they do not drive all epistemic disputes, very few bona fide ones actually exist, and those that do exist are not solely determined by culture. So the idea that all knowledge is culturally determined is fundamentally unsound.

1. Not All Epistemic Disputes Are Paradigm Driven

When we say P and someone else says not-P, it is tempting to claim that we know P in our own paradigm and that those who deny it don't share that paradigm or understand what we are saying. If every game is played by its own rules, and everyone plays a private game, no one ever risks being caught out. But that is not what is going on every time people's claims don't jibe. People can disagree within a single paradigm or in the overlap of two. Only rarely does a disparity between two knowledge claims find its roots in bona fide paradigm disparities.

A. People using the same paradigm often disagree but usually have a clear route to closure.

Example. Sam and Paul disagree about the capital of Illinois.

Paul: It's Peoria.

Sam: It's Springfield; here, look at the map.

Paul: Gee, I guess you're right.

Even if Peoria is the capital of alternate Illinois, Paul is wise to give in when he sees the little star on the map. Maps and their conventions fall solidly within a common epistemic arena of testable evidence. Since we could go to

Springfield and see, cartographers who make mistakes about such things are quickly out of business.

B. People using different paradigms sometimes disagree within the *overlap* of their models. When they do, closure is still possible.

> *Example.* Sometimes adolescents act in ways that suggest they live in a world that is surrounded by a sufficiently unbridgeable moat to separate it paradigmatically from the adult world.
>
> Father: Glue sniffers destroy their brains and die.
>
> Son: I can sniff glue and live forever.

Adult and adolescent "takes" do overlap; and the issue at stake here is in the common zone. Unless one of them is very dysfunctional, both the father and the son share the principle of cause and effect. The glue sniffer—in refusing to apply in the immediate case a principle that he ordinarily relies on—is in denial; and denial is a sign of pathology, not "alternate knowledge." It may require therapy to reach closure; but it can be reached.

C. Not all apparent paradigm disparities are real; but when a real one is behind an epistemic dispute, closure is unlikely.

1) Not every apparent paradigm disparity is genuine, even in situations that are the standard models of paradigm conflict.

> *Example.* While there may be a paradigmatic discontinuity between pre- and post-Copernican astronomers, as is often claimed, it is not obvious. Pre- and post-Copernicans shared the same understanding of "goes around." They just disagreed about what goes around what (and why). The old school thought it was a matter of anthropocentric cosmic importance, a notion now rejected in favor of relative mass. But the problem with their account is not that it is now unintelligible or intractably alien. It is that it presumed facts not in evidence, didn't encourage discovery, and required *rococo* orbits to "save the appearances."
>
> While the old "take" had a few extras that are now discarded, it was hardly discontinuous with what followed. The heliocentric view was a breakthrough; but it didn't change (or replace) a thing about the circulation of the blood, the nature and seat of the intellect, the inheritability of acquired characteristics, or the transmutation of base elements. Most inquiry rolled on unchanged. It has now rolled far enough that people with weak imaginations can ask, "How could the ancients have believed that?" But with the slightest effort we can understand both what they believed and why they believed it.

The problem with most ancient cosmology is not that it is so alien as to be incomprehensible, or even that it is epistemically empty. It is that it is demonstrably false—the product of people with a limited sense of evidence and no interest in experimentation. We understand what it means and that no shred of evidence to support it is on offer. We reject it *because* we understand it.

2) However rare, genuinely disparate paradigms (i.e., mutually incommensurate and untranslatable conceptual frameworks) do occur.

Example. Jesus, confronting Pilate, declined the opportunity to plea bargain. We can imagine the following dialogue:

Peter: Tell him it's all a mistake. You know this "King of the Jews" business is treason. If you keep it up they will kill you. Then where will you be?

Jesus: Except a man die, he cannot live.

Peter: Don't play games with me. I know that we all die, that death is part of life, that if we didn't face death, we wouldn't be alive. But you don't have to go looking for it. Don't you want to live?

Jesus: Listen. I don't mean that mortality is a necessary condition of living. If it were, eternal life would be impossible. What I do mean is that what you call death is the portal to life: "death" is birth. I do want to live; but I must die to get there. Got it?

Peter: No, I don't. What you are saying is incoherent. Have you considered analysis? Do you mind if I talk to Pilate about an insanity plea?

Jesus and Peter are genuinely at cross-purposes here. They are not disagreeing about facts in a common arena. If Jesus agrees to common standards of evidence, then Peter could argue that his friend is simply mistaken or confused. But if Jesus insists that inconsistencies can be true, then he and Peter really are in "alternate worlds" with radically disparate paradigms and have nothing to discuss.

2. Few Bona Fide Epistemic Paradigms Exist

People need not worry about paradigms if the very idea of a conceptual framework is incoherent, or if frameworks of sufficient scope and distinction to qualify for bona fide paradigm duty can't be found.

A. Unless self-reference is barred, the claim "a claim can only be true in its own paradigm" is only true in *its* own paradigm. That would be the paradigm of those communities for which "paradigms" is a working conceptual category—which would exclude the majority of communities, past and present. So absent a hierarchy of paradigm types (including metaparadigms to govern the discourse employed when we describe ordinary ones), "a claim can only be true in its own paradigm" will be unintelligible to, and will be ignored by, any community that does not share the fancy. (For additional reasons why the notion of an epistemic paradigm might be a nonstarter, see Donald Davidson's "On the Very Idea of a Conceptual Scheme.")

B. It is unlikely that many alternative epistemic paradigms exist:

- people communicate across alleged paradigm gaps;
- reconceptualizations can occur without revolutions;

- the ways in which epistemic paradigms can differ are limited; and
- multiple natural languages can be learned and translated.

Nevertheless, at least three possible bona fide ones do occur.

1) People of various conceptual stripes communicate without the "incommensurability" which strong paradigm talk implies, suggesting that their allegedly disparate paradigms share at least some common elements.

> *Example*. Psychiatrists and priests can discuss their work with only modest effort. That talk may amount to disagreement; but disagreeing is a very important way of discussing things. They already talk to each other about other things, basing their talk on the common core of human experience; and they can build on that.
>
> What a psychiatrist may see as depression and treat with drugs, a priest may see as demon possession and treat with exorcism. But, while their conceptualizings differ, they are dealing with the same phenomena. People who go to priests and people who go to psychiatrists are all people, sharing the standard human repertoire of functions, malfunctions, and dysfunctions.
>
> So caregivers in both camps will have little trouble comparing notes—once they take into account the common behavior of "depressed" and "possessed" people, and the fact that "my depression is under control" and "my demon is gone" cash out the same in the common life arena that all humans share.

While there are too many common elements in the conceptual arrays of most "paradigms" for their rivalries to be more than *partial*, this is not to say that the disparities that do occur are necessarily *peripheral*. The essence of a culture may reside in the bits of its outlook that are unique, so that understanding *them* may be essential to understanding it at all.

On the other hand, understanding those bits is not impossible, given the larger context in which they occur. Even exorcising demons is part of a larger array of beliefs and institutions (supernatural religion) that touches the common world at many points.

> *Example*. The medievals lived in the same arena we do: Earth. But their practice was shaped by their construal of everything in it as supernaturally connected. Anyone who ignores that, or finds it unfathomable, doesn't have a grip on what their culture amounted to.

But we need not ignore it or find it unfathomable. It is open to anyone who cares to study it or try it on. Cultural and historical anthropologists do that all the time. We can even assess its viability and conclude that while this "spin" may have provided a functional approach to mental health in olden days, it is not functional to rely on self-flagellation and exorcism today—given that Prozac and psychotherapy are now available. In this way, we can come to understand not only "where they were back then" but also how the human community has subsequently moved on.

2) Individuals can reconceptualize without psychological trauma, and cultures without riots or pogroms. We know they can because they do. This suggests that conceptual frameworks are more open to adjustment—less intractably "all or nothing"—than paradigm talk suggests.

a) Individuals adjust their conceptualizations upon seeing more of the world or being exposed to other perspectives on it, upon encountering events that "don't compute," or simply upon "growing up."

Example. Jimmy, who was born and raised in a small Georgia town, left his home state for the first time at sixteen to participate in an "I Speak for America" contest in New York City. He saw many things there he had never seen before and talked to many people who didn't see things the way that he and his people did. On coming home, he saw even familiar things "in a new light." His perception of African Americans, in particular, had been dramatically altered.

b) The standard conceptualizations of a society may be adjusted in at least four sorts of circumstances.

Warning: "The standard conceptualizations" of a society are those that are most common or dominant in it. Societies themselves have no conceptualizations, since they don't conceptualize. They are made up of people; and people are the ones who conceptualize. We should try to avoid the fallacy of composition.

- Reacting to data that the received worldview can't handle

  Example. Once a careful computation of the age, constituents, and mass of the sun became possible, it was no longer credible that heat can be generated only by friction and combustion, forcing a revision of the doctrine of elemental immutability—a doctrine that, except for alchemists, was axiomatic until recent times; and at the center, not at the fringe, of the paradigm.

- Reacting to discoveries that make parts of the received worldview unnecessary

  Example. The discovery that plague is spread by fleas and can be contained by programs of rodent control, rendered redundant the notion of the plague as divine retribution, and all of the appeasement behaviors predicated on it.

- By the spread, from "inside," of a new or altered perspective—whether by osmosis and example from an internal subculture, by legislative or judicial reform, or by sheer rebellion

  Example. The use of psychotropic drugs by several subcultures of the United States has diffused into the mainstream, changing not only the moral paradigm for much of its population but also challenging their conceptualization of the mind itself. (It is difficult to maintain mind/body dualism in the face of direct evidence that "consciousness" is chemically alterable.)

Example. Brown v. Board of Education initiated a major revision of the common U.S. conceptualization of race. The civil rights movement that followed it gradually overcame massive resistance—sometimes by force (as at Little Rock), but not always. Eventually, the U.S. culture's take on humans may become genuinely color blind, though it hasn't happened yet.

• By the adoption, from "outside," of a new or altered perspective—whether by spontaneous or legislated emulation or by direct external imposition

Examples. The spread of Eastern religions in the undergraduate community exemplifies the spontaneous emulation of an external culture's "take" on reality; the adoption of democracy by the former Soviet states exemplifies legislated emulation of an alien framework; and the armed imposition of democracy on Japan in 1945 and Iraq in 2003 exemplify external force at work (with varied success).

So individual and collective conceptualizations do change, even without revolutions. But conceptualizations that are not intractably resistant to change don't constitute *paradigms* in the requisite sense.

3) The ways in which epistemic paradigms can differ from each other are very limited. Conceptual schemes, like natural languages, can differ in the list of event constituents that are recognized (in a natural language this is called *vocabulary*), the rules for constructing events out of those constituents (in a natural language this is called *syntax*), and in the variety of "games" to which they are amenable. None of these differences, however, entail unbridgeable gulfs between conceptual schemes. But if the gulf between schemes is bridgeable, they aren't *paradigms* in the requisite sense.

a) "Vocabulary" differences between conceptual schemes are common; but this apparent gap can usually be bridged.

Example. Sam is a Cartesian parapsychologist whose list of recognizable events includes telepathy (which he defines as "direct contact between minds"). Sally is a behavioral empiricist who says she finds the terms "telepathy" and "minds" completely unintelligible. But if Sam can show Sally an example (under controlled conditions), she can make room. That is how people learn new stuff. And, if he can't, then he should reconsider his scheme. That is how people learn to abandon sterile interpretations of what is going on.

b) "Syntactical" differences between conceptual schemes are somewhat less common. Where they do occur, they are likely to depend on syntactical differences between the natural languages that are in use. They are also somewhat more difficult to deal with. But analogs can usually be found to make what is going on intelligible.

> *Example.* Since the roots of most ancient Hebrew words are verbs, the world described by the patriarchal writers has a flavor more of *events* than of *states of affairs* when compared to narratives couched in noun-based Greek. The world accounts of Moses and John, consequently, have rather different spins. But "different" ≠ "mutually unintelligible." Moses and John could have understood each other, and any contemporary scholar who works at it can understand both.

c) If a game is played in one framework but not in another, some of the things going on in the culture that occupies the first framework may be initially obscure to outsiders who occupy the second framework. But if Yanks can learn to appreciate (and even play) cricket, small children can learn to appreciate (and even keep) promises, and diplomats can learn to negotiate (and even solve) intercultural legal disputes, then there is no strong reason to think that culture-specific games are necessarily and incurably opaque to all nonnatives. The fact that differences in vocabulary, syntax, and what-games-are-provided-for do not necessarily generate unbridgeable gaps between conceptual schemes shows that that they do not always constitute *paradigms* in the requisite sense.

> ### What Game Are We Playing?
>
> However many games may be possible in a paradigm or a language, a scheme of conventions is usually established to indicate which one is in play and to remind us of the rules in effect. Many such game-enabling conventions, such as "Once upon a time" and "Do you solemnly swear or affirm," can function within a single general framework. This is how a player knows what to expect and how to react.

4) One set of conceptual frameworks that might be taken as paradigms in the requisite sense is the array of the world's natural languages—each one (or each natural language family) following its own rules and shaping its own reality.

> *Caution.* This might appear to be a Wittgensteinian construal of Kuhn. But, in fact, it does not capture Wittgenstein's notion of a language game at all. Most language games can be played in most natural languages. Chinese tell jokes, Ethiopians make promises, and Inuit give and follow orders; and all three succeed, from time to time, in talking to each other.

There are, however, three reasons why the notion that natural languages constitute paradigms won't fly: natural languages change constantly and gradually, are not mutually untranslatable, and don't determine reality.

a) Natural languages change constantly and gradually. The progressive disappearance of the subjunctive and the erosion of tensing in common spoken

English illustrate the gradual (no-revolution-required) changes that constantly occur in all natural languages on the syntactical side. On the semantic side, a quick perusal of an historical dictionary will illustrate the same phenomenon. But evolutionary changes that can be mapped and understood by anyone who tries are not paradigm shifts in the requisite sense.

The consequent loss of potential for subtlety imposes limits on what is conceptually recognizable to contemporary English speakers. Few, today, would recognize a subjunctive, even were they to see one in print. Fewer still will have had enough exposure to classical grammar by the time they graduate from high school to use a future perfect correctly. But all can be taught to recognize such things, incrementally enriching the world that they can get at. One way to do that is to teach them classical Greek or Latin (both of which are much more syntactically complex than English). Note, by the way, that English speakers can learn Latin and Greek and that, in so doing, they can enrich their English use. This speaks to the "translatability" issue. The obvious benefits of learning more than one language illustrate the linguistic contribution to what we can conceive, understand, know, and describe. This speaks to the "determination" issue.

b) Natural languages are not mutually untranslatable. The vocabulary and syntactical differences between Latin and English are significant, but not unbridgeable. Otherwise, there would be no point in studying Latin. Indeed, if there are semantic or syntactic differences between any language and English that make them mutually untranslatable, no one could say (in either language) what they are. But that would not prevent an Anglophone from learning that other language on its own terms and continuing to use English as well. Many people are multilingual, shifting from one language to another with enough difficulty to make their achievement admirable, but enough ease to demonstrate that these languages are not paradigms in the requisite sense.

c) Natural languages don't determine reality. Natural languages are social phenomena, occurring only where there is more than one individual and functioning according to necessarily social conventions. But this is only one side of the loop. Social conventions are the institutionalizations of frequent individual usage; and that is the product, at least in part, of the users' neural wiring and actual experience, as well as of their language. But neural wiring and actual experiences are neither cultural nor linguistic products. They are biological and event-circumstantial products. So the language that we are given influences the shape of our world, but it does not determine it.

5) Cutting across the world's assorted languages and cultures, three "takes" on the world do show some promise of being bona fide paradigms:

- the "intentional" take,
- the "cause and effect" take, and
- the "things come down" take.

a) The "intentional" take begins in our internal awareness of our own intentions, extrapolating that intentionality to the world in general.

The word "intentional" has numerous uses. In the immediate case, intentional activities are simply ones that are intended—that is, the ones that are not accidental, random, or just the inevitable outcome of antecedent events. Intentional activities need not be deliberate, rational, well thought out, or effective. We can intend recklessly, arbitrarily, confusedly, ineffectually, and so forth. Indeed, according to some, we can even intend unconsciously. The various things that people "decide" or "choose" to do are models of intentional activities in this sense.

Reading all things and events as products of intention is a common phenomenon across human history. In the form of "animism," for instance, it was indigenous to ancient cultures worldwide. It is also a major component of all but the most theologically attenuated forms of contemporary theism—Christian, Jewish, and Muslim.

In the intentionalist view, all of the attributes that go with an event being intended (such as *meaning* and *purpose*) can be extrapolated to events in general. To those who see the world this way, it *always* makes sense to ask what something is "for" or what it "means."

> *Example*. Bill sees cows and dogs as the purposeful expression of a wise creator's desire to meet the human need for food and companionship. So since both were "put here" for a specific use, he has no qualms about using them "appropriately."
>
> (Of course, knowing *what* intentions cows and dogs embody and what use, consequently, is appropriate, is highly problematic—as is evidenced by the fact that some intentionalists don't eat cows and some do eat dogs.)

Not everyone sees the world the way intentionalists do. Most naturalists, for instance, discern intentions only when they examine human actions and artifacts. To naturalists, the inclination to see cows and dogs (and, for that matter, tornadoes and earthquakes) as intentional seems unjustified—almost "alien." "Why in the world," they might ask, "would anyone think that Hurricane Isabel *meant* something?"

One way to describe the difference between those who see intentions everywhere and those who see them only in the behavior of complex organisms is to say that they conceptualize the world differently. For example, "cows were put here for people to eat" could be true for *some* people but false or unintelligible for *others* if they have different paradigms. That will work, however, only if the intentionalists' "paradigm" is coherent enough to underwrite a working notion of truth. If it does not support a testable distinction between what is true and what is false, then "cows, etc." is not true in their framework. It is, instead, a muddle. It presumes facts not in evidence.

But, however muddled, intentionalists are not using a category with which naturalists are unfamiliar or that they cannot understand. A naturalist can understand with perfect clarity what a person means who says that a hurricane was sent by God as a wake-up call to the wicked. Indeed, it is only because they do understand it that they are able to assert with such force that it is a muddle.

b) Most people, most of the time, East and West, take events as causally connected. The notion that "nothing just happens," when formalized, is the first principle of scientific inquiry, the "principle of sufficient reason." And it is not limited to science. The most important practical necessity for everyday "coping" is realizing that what we do has consequences. People who don't make that connection have problems.

The causal "take" has problems of its own, of course: about how tight the causal network is, about whether it has exceptions, and about its implications for human intentions, creativity, free choice, and responsibility. We will examine many of those issues in chapter 11.

Of course, people often have erroneous ideas about what causes what. But such errors are open to correction as long as we maintain the conviction that causal connections are always there to be found and remain committed to the principles of inventive theory construction, controlled experimentation, and public confirmation. On the other hand, if we do not know what causes what and have no interest in trying to find out, we are for all intents and purposes operating in a "things come down" arena. This is so disabling, however, that it reinforces the conviction for the rest of us that causal connections *are* there to be found and urges us to find them as soon as we can.

c) The "things come down" take on events is either an extrapolation from those situations in which we simply do not know what the causal connections are (so that there might as well not be any), or a fundamentally different way of viewing reality in which causal connections play no part. In the former case, it is little more than a temporizing way of handling (by tabling) phenomena that are not-yet-understood. In the latter case—what I call the "Manson" worldview—it is catastrophically dysfunctional.

Those who see the world as a disjointed panorama of happenings come as close to having a genuinely alternate epistemic paradigm as anyone I can think of. While I think I know what their world looks like to them, I am not sure of it; and I am confident that they do not know what my world looks like to me. Even so translation does not break down completely (or, at any rate, not both ways). While I am using a conceptual category (causation) that they find unintelligible, I can see the gaps that its absence leaves in their worldview, as well as the dysfunctions that attend those gaps. So even "Things Come Down" is not so much a functioning alternate epistemic paradigm as a truncated and dysfunctional piece of the usual one.

Most people take the world, at one time or another, from all three of these perspectives: in terms of *intentionality* with regard to the behaviors of people and other complex animals, in terms of *causality* with regard to the aspects of the physical world that have been explained so far, and in terms of *things come down* to temporize over the areas, pockets, and overlaps that we do not yet understand. It is when we try to extend any one of these perspectives to cover everything that "conceptual cramps" are most likely to occur. When they do, philosophical elucidation is called for, including an examination and appraisal of the "paradigms" themselves:

- Does the causal view apply to human actions?
- Does the intentional view apply to the weather?

This is most important. Even if a claim must be judged for felicity within the rules of its own game, the mere fact that a game occurs does not make it playable, much less worth playing.

3. "Paradigms" Are Not Solely Determined by Culture

"Paradigms," where they occur, are shaped not only by the cultures in which they appear but also by the organisms that use them and the events that happen to those organisms. So paradigms are not the product of culture alone. If they were, no one could have a new idea, notice a novel event, or in any other way appraise and rework the conceptual status quo.

I am not denying the contribution that culture makes to the way people take things. Although fads such as Ebonics and Whole Math may exaggerate the way our culture shapes how we see, describe, and enumerate events, it is obvious that it does.

- People who are acculturated in an animistic society do see trees as having malevolent and benevolent intentions.
- People who have been fed the mother's milk of fundamentalism do see gays as anathema and fair targets for bashing.
- The Maya did read the harvest as a function of ritual propriety, not agricultural practice.
- Some recently commissioned academics do see reality as a text open to free interpretation.

We cannot ignore such things and hope to get a handle on the world. Culture does shape perception—even if it is usually more a matter of emphasis, interpretation, and appraisal than of constituting mutually untranslatable and incommensurate alternate realities, and even if the results are sometimes wrongheaded and sterile.

But we also cannot afford to deny the contributions that the organism itself and factual circumstances make. Our culturally influenced conceptual framework may filter what we see, taste, smell, feel, and hear; but if we did not have such antennae (or if there were no signals to pick up) there would be nothing to filter. But we do, and there are. So given that eyes, ears, palates, noses, skin, and membranes are antennae with which people are equipped, and given that events do intrude, we can successfully cope only if we have a paradigm that incorporates these sense modes and accommodates the particular stimuli that occur from day to day.

That means not only that culture alone cannot be responsible for the framework that a functioning organism has in play but also that a limited number of such frameworks are possible. Conceptualizing, unlike employment in a purely capitalist economy, is not "at will."

> *Example.* Construing the world is not like solving a seven-piece jigsaw puzzle that will go together only one way. But neither is it like working a ten-thousand-piece horror that has only ten piece-shapes and random designs on both sides, much less like attempting one with infinitely many pieces that are all identically shaped and patterned.
>
> If all the pieces were cut the same way, we could "take" the world in whatever way we liked. If each piece is unique, then at most one arrangement will work. Reality, however, occupies the middle ground. There may not be only one way to put it together; but there are not infinitely many.

In solving a jigsaw, we may be helped by the fact that there is a picture on the box—a resource not given to people trying to figure out the world. On the other hand, just as a jigsaw can be solved without peeking, the world can be at least partially sorted out by noting the way in which particular pieces either fit or fail to fit, and the way in which a coherent pattern begins to emerge. The historical notion of hermeneutics is useful here: a piece only makes sense in terms of the whole; but the whole is only understandable in terms of all its pieces. This makes a gradual, even progressive, "solution loop" possible.

This assumes, of course, that the world is not incoherent and unintelligible. But that is not an unreasonable assumption. If the world were incoherent and unintelligible, human inquiry would be futile and its outcome unreliable, and one arbitrary "solution" would be as good as another. The fact that such inquiry has been profitable, enabling humans to survive as long as they have, strongly supports the coherence assumption. It does not, however, *prove* it. Human survival *could* be the result of good luck—a "gift of the gods." Anyone who wishes to rely on such things is free to do so; but ignoring evidence, and betting that your luck will hold and the gods will continue to smile, is cognitively reckless and irresponsible.

Many of the people talking about paradigms these days are trying to maintain the notion that every belief is true for those who hold it, and the notion that every paradigm is viable for those who use it, because of an ideology-driven concern to validate people and cultures that have been marginalized by the West. But if racism and sexism are denied status as autonomous self-validating paradigms, then multiculturalism should be too. The proof of a paradigm is not in the political correctness, or even the virtue, of its advocates, but in the useful work that it expedites. Consequently, deciding which epistemic "paradigm" to have, use, or affirm is a matter of vital importance.

R. M. Hare noted in "Theology and Falsification" that it is crucial to have the right paradigm (he called them "blicks"), but that there was no way to determine which one that is. There is, though: take them into the field and try them out, and then ride with one that works. If the one that the local culture supplies turns out to be flawed, amend it or replace it. And, while we're at it, we might as well reform the culture too.

4. Conclusions

When a healthy organism with keen epistemic equipment and a functional conceptual apparatus attentively confronts reality, reliable beliefs about matters of fact result. Upon being repeatedly tested in the open arena of public discourse, those beliefs gradually gain the status of knowledge. They will, however, remain subject to revision. This is because gaining knowledge about matters of fact is not a matter of discovering fixed and necessary truths. Factual knowledge is contingent, differing from true belief only in the level of publicly available evidence that it demands. Achieving it is a matter of closing in on a limit—not arriving at a destination—in much the same way that a graphed curve may infinitely approach intersection with the axis of

> ### Will I Like What I Find?
>
> Working in a functional paradigm does not guarantee our happiness with reality as we find it. When appraising an interpretive package, the question to ask is, "Does it help me come to grips with reality?" If we are happy with the results, that is pure lagniappe. Preoccupation with how we feel about the reality we find can lead us down the garden path to disaster.

its graph. We may never "arrive," but we do get ever closer and, pragmatically speaking, close enough to *work* is close *enough*.

Cultural epistemic relativism is true enough if all it means is that our experiences are filtered through our epistemic equipment and that this equipment includes a conceptual framework that is influenced by our culture. But if it means that our reality is exclusively determined by that framework, it is demonstrably false.

- Reality is not in the eye of the beholder. It may be *filtered* through the eye of the beholder, but it retains an intractable *content*. Hard heavy objects break bones and cause pain, *think what we will*. The real world can leave marks on a person only if there *is* one; and it is known that it *can* leave marks on a person because it *does*.
- Reality is not in the paradigm of the beholder either. Good conceptual equipment will assist in coming to terms with the real world; but our culture is only one source of that equipment. Our physical and rational re-

sources, including our ingenuity, also contribute. If the culture provides a sterile or misleading apparatus, then it should be reformed and that apparatus replaced. Fortunately, history shows that this is possible.

So one epistemic claim is not as good as another. Deliberately formulated belief claims are better than capricious, arbitrary ones. Publicly tested and confirmed ones are better yet. Eventually we arrive at convincing claims that are well construed, coherent, and confirmable within the rules of a viable conceptual framework. They are best of all.

Individual wish fulfillment and cultural agenda satisfaction have nothing to do with what turns out to be best. The quality of our evidence and the viability of the framework within which we construe it are the only things that count.

9

Knowledge and Values

There are good reasons to doubt particular knowledge claims about matters of fact, but none for thinking no one knows anything at all. Knowledge of values, especially moral values, may be less secure.

While most people think such knowledge is possible (and that they have some), others disagree and point to a variety of roadblocks.

- Those who do think moral knowledge is possible disagree about what it amounts to. Ethical egoists, utilitarians, and divine command theists, for example, all say we can find out if something is good by looking for evidence in the right place; but they disagree about what "is good" means ("in our interest," "maximizes happiness," and "pleases God," respectively) and look for evidence in different places. So they don't reach the same verdicts. There is no consensus about what is good the way there is about what is acidic.

- While we would think that a true claim would be true for everyone, moral claims seem to be individual-, group-, or culture-specific. But if the truth of moral claims is relative in that way, then what is known to be good by one person could be known to be bad by another. There is no consistency about what is good the way there is about what is soluble.

- Evidence for moral knowledge is so scarce and ambiguous, and evidential standards for it so lacking, that every moral claim is inconclusive. Modest moral *beliefs* may be possible, but to claim moral *knowledge* is an affront to caution. There is no confidence about what is good the way there is about what is organic.

- Moral utterances do not specify any characteristics of the things they are "about." Lacking *descriptive* content, they are neither true nor false (though they may express a speaker's attitudes and a desire to evoke similar ones in others). Things are not good or bad the way they are rough or smooth.

- Certain conceptions of human nature or of nature itself block the path to moral knowledge by denying the rationality of making moral judgments. Psychological egoists and causal determinists cite universal selfishness and the universal applicability of causal explanations, respectively, to deny the possibility of action alternatives and, consequently, of legitimate moral appraisals.

In this chapter I will examine how ordinary value claims generate such problems and how many of them can be averted. In chapters 10 and 11, I will examine several choice-denying conceptions of human nature, and of nature itself, and show why they are misleading. This will at least leave the door open for moral knowledge.

For it to actually occur, however, some moral beliefs must be justified beyond reasonable doubt. And, for that to be so there must be some reliable evidence for them. So in chapters 12–15 I will examine some places people look for such evidence and show where it can be found.

1. Value Talk's Characteristics

A. Value talk *looks* descriptive.

Normative claims occur in a wide variety of settings, including appraisals of food, drink, art, music, literature, and human conduct. Although they occasion a great deal of argument, people make them without blinking and appear to know what they are doing—describing states of affairs as good or bad.

Descriptions attribute properties to things. Evaluations seem to do the same. "Stayman apples are red" and "All the dogs that played Lassie were male" attribute *redness* and *maleness* to their targets. Grammatically, at any rate, the following sentences all seem to attribute *goodness* to theirs:

- Being true to yourself is good.
- Andrew Wyeth's *Anna Christina* is good.
- Boar's Head pastrami is good.
- James Rachels's refutation of ethical egoism is good.
- Mother Teresa is good.
- Constitutional democracy is good.

Such claims come in negative and comparative forms, too: McPherson's "99 Bottles of Beer on the Wall," synthetic mayonnaise, the ontological argument, Osama bin Laden, tyranny, and being a *poseur* are *bad*; and while Heller's, Gordon's, and kindness are *good* fugues, gins, and policies, Bach's, Quintessential, and honesty are *better* ones.

B. Goodness is not a first-order property. If these sample statements are true, then goodness looks like a property. But it is not a first-order property like "redness" or "sweetness" because no one can identify the sense that discerns it. Redness is discerned by sight and sweetness by taste; but qualitative discernment is not so localized. It appears to be a function of the whole organism, in response to various sensation combinations in equally various circumstances.

Second-order properties are combinations of first-order properties. A good Stayman apple is not red, sweet, crisp, fresh, *and* good. It is red, sweet, crisp, and fresh, *hence* good. For Stayman apples, "good" means red, sweet, crisp, and fresh. "Red," "sweet," and so forth, are first-order properties. For Stayman apples, "good" is the second-order property of having this particular set of first-order ones. It should also be noted that "good" also functions as an excluder, marking the *absence* of some concrete defect rather than the *presence* of some positive attributes. Good Stayman apples, for example, are notably *not rotten*.

C. "Good" is not a univocal term. "Good" does not always invoke or rule out the same property or property set. It variously marks the absence of capriciousness, carelessness, cruelty, excess, futility, ineptitude, staleness, and vapidity, and the presence of empathy, fairness, health, probity, proficiency, attentiveness, restraint, and wholeness—*and this is just a sampling*. Which properties it invokes or rules out depend on its target and on the context. Good bananas and good watermelons have little in common; and what constitutes a good weapon depends on what we are trying to kill. Indeed, a good fugue, a good linebacker, a good night's sleep, a good person, and good weapons for killing doves and cockroaches may not share even *one* clear-cut property in common.

When "good" is used, an implicit reference is made to *some* standard set of first-order properties, but *which* set is highly variable. The claim that X is good simply asserts that X has the combination of properties that are specified by whatever standard is in use. So correctly saying that X is good involves locating the appropriate standard as well as accurately finding that X has the properties that are enumerated in it. Judgment comes into play only in the selection of the standard. The rest is just observation and reporting, albeit at a somewhat complex and abstract level.

D. Abstraction, ambiguity, and description. The abstract link between "good" and its targets, and its variable reference to different sets of first-order properties, does not make evaluations less descriptive than "fact" claims. To be sure, second-order properties are less directly connected to their targets than first-order ones. Further, we have no idea what is being predicated by a variable term unless we understand the context. But "fact" descriptions use second-order and variable predicates too.

Fact descriptions are not limited to simple predications such as *this apple is green*. They also include second-order predications, such as *apples (but not pineapples) are drupes*, and *oranges (but not gooseberries) are berries*. (That the botanical concepts of *drupes* and *berries* are complicated is one reason why the two samples sentences, though true, are not obvious.)

Furthermore, since "green" is a label not only for an arc of the spectrum but also for unripe fruit, not every predication is as simple as it may appear to be. (Unless we know which definition is in use, we might believe that *ripe Granny Smith apples are green* is self-contradictory even though, in fact, it is not). Second-order predication and variable standards of application are endemic to discourse across the board. However, the examination of some sample evaluations, and the standards they invoke, makes it obvious that few fact descriptions are as indirect and variable as run-of-the-mill evaluations are. This is especially clear in the case of *comparative* evaluations.

- Beethoven's *Eroica* is better than *The Farmer in the Dell*, and *Legally Blonde* is better than its sequel.

  The standards involved in comparing musical scores or films include the complexity and originality of the works under review. Complex and original works bear a great deal more repetition than simplistic or derivative ones.

- Norman Rockwell's paintings are simplistic and trite, compared to those of Hieronymus Bosch, but are still a better choice for decorating the rooms of a hotel.

  Complexity and originality are standards for paintings as well as music; but not the only ones. For representational paintings, subject matter is often a relevant consideration. The same painting could be a drawing card at the Louvre, but a business-killing disaster at the Sheraton.

Shooting Yourself in the Foot

While the force of "better" and "worse" varies, the idea that whatever is *better* (in *some* sense) is preferable to whatever is *worse* (in the *same* sense), is common. However, "preferable" is ambiguous. It can mean either that something is preferred or that it *ought to be* preferred; and not everything that ought to be preferred *is*. Even with a simple judgment of effectiveness, it is not always safe to assume that everyone prefers means that will achieve their goals. For some, effectiveness seems to be the thing least desired.

- Mozzarella and sausage are better on pizza than mayo and mandarin oranges; backfin crab cakes are better than sea leg croquettes; and wines from the Rhone are, on the whole, better than those from the shores of Lake Erie.

One important standard for comparing foods and wines is whether an item is true to the cuisine it represents. (Chez Twee may be trendy, but it's a bad place for Italian food.) Another has to do with the complexity and subtlety of their flavors. (That is why we serve Châteauneuf du Pape at room temperature but Niagara Nites ice cold.)

- It is better for students to write their own essays than to download something from the web.

The "work" of a student who cheats does not reveal what he or she has, in fact, learned. So cheating on papers defeats the purpose for assigning them, erodes the credibility of grades, and turns hiring qualified employees into a crapshoot.

There is nothing about this variability, however, that makes value knowledge impossible. The truth of all of these examples, in fact, is far more obvious and easily known than the truth of most modern physics.

E. Four types of evaluations. Reflection on the variety of settings in which something may be called good or bad shows that evaluations fall into four main types. All of them occur commonly in esthetic, moral, and practical venues; and although they are distinctly different they are easily confused. Equivocation, consequently, is possible and troublesome.

- Token evaluations. Some evaluations assert that an entity, process, or condition is a good (or bad) token of its type, without regard to the quality of the type it represents.

Harry Truman was a good machine politician.
Nelson Rockefeller was a bad Republican.

Here, "good" means *exemplary*, and "bad" means *atypical*.
- Appraisals of means. Some evaluations assert that an entity, process, or condition is good (or bad) for some use, or as a means to some end, without appraising the use or end in view.

"Gettin' 'em drunk" is a good way to score.
Acquiring a tapeworm is a bad weight loss regimen.

In such contexts, "good" means *effective,* and "bad" means either *futile* or *dysfunctional*.
- Judgments of intrinsic value. Some evaluations seem to assert that a thing, process, or condition is good (or bad) in itself and should, consequently, be pursued (or avoided), or that certain acts ought (or ought not) to be engaged in, for their own sake.

Honesty is the best policy (no matter what).
Cruelty is evil (whoever does it, for whatever reason).

Follow your star (wherever it leads you).
Pleasure is better than pain (any way you slice it).

There are several interpretations of what "good," "bad," and their cognates mean in these contexts; and there is intense argument over which interpretation to follow. This is where the main philosophical action is.

- Mixed judgments of value. Some evaluations combine the appraisal of means and of ends to assert that an entity, process, or condition is good (or bad) for some use, or as a means to some end, *and* that the use or end in view is good (or bad) in itself and ought (or ought not) to be encouraged or pursued for its own sake. Such evaluations are often stated as imperatives.

An Army recruitment slogan: Be all that you can be!
The motto of the Scottish Munros: Dread God!

Such locutions appear to claim that we ought to do what they enjoin us to do—implying that what is enjoined is a good means to a worthwhile end.

1) A type standard is always implicit in token evaluations (where we say that an item "exemplifies" some type standard in use). The type standards, of course, are conventional and can change, but whether they are satisfied is a matter for public argument and empirical settlement.

Carefully stated, token evaluations are conditionals: *If you want an exemplar of type P, see token K.* But people are not always careful. Instead of saying, "If you want an exemplar of ATVs, see the Crusher," they are likely to say, "Crushers are good ATVs." So it is unclear whether they mean Crushers exemplify the typical characteristics of ATVs, or that they are ATVs of higher than ordinary quality, or even that Crusher ATVs are *good things*. Opportunities for confusion are rife when we cite a good exemplar of a bad thing—for instance: *The pigeon drop is a good con.*

It is clear, however, that merely to say something is an exemplar of some type is not to make a moral claim. So even though we can know that Huey Long was a good populist and that Mussolini was a bad Catholic (in that one did, and the other did not, exemplify the type indicated), there is no venue here for moral knowledge.

2) Some goal or other is always implicit in means appraisals. These locutions say how effective an item (or kind of item) is for achieving a goal, whatever it may be.

Carefully stated, means appraisals are conditionals: *If you want to achieve goal G, then use means M.* But people are not always careful. Instead of saying, "If you want to receive a liberal arts education, then enroll at Washington and Lee," they are likely to say, "Washington and Lee is a good liberal arts college." So it is unclear whether they are claiming that Washington and Lee is an effective place to get a liberal arts education (whatever such an education may be worth), or that liberal arts education in general (and Washington and Lee as an exemplar of it) are *good things*. Opportunities for confusion are rife when we cite a highly effective means to a lamentable end—for instance, *Cobalt bombs are a good way to exterminate all life*.

How problematic evaluating means is varies with the degree of consensus there is on describing the means' point. Many English speakers disagree about what we go to concerts for, hang paintings for, buy food for, or go to college for. Consequently, they also disagree about what constitutes good means for those engaged in such enterprises.

- If we go to concerts or films only to hear or see what is familiar and easy, then a nursery rhyme ditty may be a better bet than Beethoven, and *Red, White, and Blonde* than its precursor.
- If we want to scare the hell out of people, Bosch may be a better choice than Rockwell for decorating our hotel.
- If we want novelty when dining, Pizza Mandarin at *Chez Twee* may be the best choice; and, if economy is our overriding concern, sea legs qualify.
- If we think that the purpose of going to college is to delay our need for employment as long as possible, or that the purpose of building them is to warehouse unruly teenagers until their hormones subside, then letting others do our work may make sense while there.

But there is *some* consensus about the main purposes of most common human enterprises. Life is open ended, but not infinitely so.

In addition, it is usually easy enough to see that a nonstandard standard is in play and respond accordingly:

Example. A student says, "I'm in school to party as long as I can. So if it takes cheating to avoid flunking out and having to go to work, then cheating's the thing for me."

It is clear, when we are careful, that merely to say some procedure or other is an effective way to achieve some goal or other is not to make a moral claim. So even though we can know that cyanide in Kool-Aid is a good way to kill ourselves and that counting sunspots is a bad way to predict the market (in that one is, and one is not, an effective way to achieve the goal indicated), there is no venue here for moral knowledge.

3) Judgments of instrumental value are a combination of means evaluations (just examined) and goal evaluations (next). Most moral claims fall into this mixed category. Their essentially moral dimension is in their identification of some goals as inherently worth pursuing, not in their specification of behaviors and attitudes that will get us there.

Most people recognize only a few, or even only one goal: doing what we want, pleasing God, maximizing happiness, whatever. The merits of such choices will be examined in later chapters. Of course if we choose a bad goal, there is little to be said for using good means to reach it. We might hope that those with bad goals would choose poor means.

Once people agree on what ends to favor, the means arguments can be settled at the experiential and public level.

> *Example.* Steve and Jane favor sexual fidelity in marriage, while Rip and Lola favor availing themselves of erotic opportunities whenever and wherever they occur. The former believe that maximizing human happiness is intrinsically good and argue that consideration for others as well as oneself, especially our spouses and children, requires fidelity. The latter believe that only our own pleasure is good in itself and argue that as long as we avoid disease and injury, there is no reason to refrain from any sexual opportunity that presents itself.

The means evaluations are a snap for both couples. Each is secure in its fidelity or inconstancy, provided only that:

- their actions actually achieve their intended goal;
- the result is, in fact, worth pursuing for its own sake; and
- no additional results cloud the picture.

Caution is required, of course. A technique can achieve its intentions and, at the same time, achieve a great many other things as well. Agent Orange defoliated trees effectively but also injured the people who were exposed to it. Ends alone do not justify means. Only actual results can do that, as we shall see in chapter 14.

Here, finally, a genuine *moral* question arises:

What goals, if any, are worth pursuing for themselves?

4) Judgments of intrinsic value. People stridently disagree about what (if anything) is worth pursuing for its own sake ("good in itself"). Consensus, however, is neither necessary nor sufficient for demonstrably true fact descriptions. So why should it be thought necessary or sufficient for demonstrably accurate appraisals?

- People can agree and still get things wrong.

  > For years everyone believed the corners of the earth to be supported by four elephants. So consensus is not sufficient for descriptive accuracy.

- People can disagree, even when proof is in hand.

Some people still reject the notion that plague is caused by germs. But those who have it, even those who think it is caused by weakness of faith, have streptococci in their bodies and can be cured with a shot that kills the bugs. So consensus is not necessary for descriptive accuracy either.

All that fact descriptions require for epistemic legitimacy is truth conditions that open them up to public test and confirmation.

The same thing is crucial to the epistemic legitimacy of intrinsic evaluations. They need truth conditions, too. But what that amounts to depends on what "X is good in itself" *means*.

a) Many think that "X is good in itself" attributes a testable property to X, so that moral cognition is possible, but disagree about what kind of property it is—natural, supernatural, nonnatural, or formal.

(1) Ethical naturalism is the view that goodness is a natural property, or a second-order property that invokes a set of natural properties. A natural property is one that can be sensorily accessed. So ethical naturalists think that "X is good in itself" attributes such a property to X. They have six different notions of what that amounts to:

(a) X affirms and fulfills our own interests.

In *Atlas Shrugged,* Ayn Rand identifies the good with the pursuit of our own interests. Nathaniel Branden, in *The Virtue of Selfishness,* espouses the same "ethical egoism."

(b) X affirms and fulfills essential human potentials.

In his *Nichomachean Ethics,* Aristotle identifies the good with what he sees as essential human capacities (e.g., understanding) and the virtues that bespeak their fulfillment (such as wisdom). In *After Virtue,* Alasdair MacIntyre espouses the same sort of "virtue ethics" in modern dress.

(c) X is prized by all normal people.

In *An Introduction to the Principles of Morals and Legislation,* Jeremy Bentham endorses maximizing pleasure (as opposed to pain), citing its universal human appeal. In *Utilitarianism,* John Stuart Mill advocates the same sort of "consequentialism" but focuses on the higher pleasures (which, at least, all could *learn* to favor).

(d) X is obedient to, or in conformity with, nature itself.

"Naturalists" and "romantics" (including a variety of contemporary eco-moralists from Wyccans to Greenies) resonate with Nietzsche's *Beyond Good and Evil* or Rousseau's *Discourse on the Sciences and Arts* in identifying the good with nature or natural laws (the content, of course, depending on what conception of nature stirs them).

(e) X is orthodox.

Many members of the general population (including the editors of the Richmond *Times Dispatch*) essentially urge us not to rock the boat. Though they may identify the customary with God's will, nature's way, or the wisdom of the Founding Fathers, their real allegiance is to the status quo, whatever it may be.

(f) X preserves the interests of the establishment.

In Plato's *Republic,* Thracymachus claims that while moral talk is ostensibly a map of the virtues, divine will, or human happiness, and so forth, it is actually a program to protect the existing power structure's interests. Harry Browne, in "The Morality Trap," makes the same point: conventional morality is a device of social control.

(2) Ethical supernaturalists believe that "X is good in itself" attributes a property to X that can only be discerned supernaturally (typically by revelation). So the claim is usually said to mean:
  (g) X is obedient to, or in conformity with, God's will.

This group includes a variety of religionists from Moses, Jesus, and Mohammed to Doh. The principles that they espouse depend on which God they follow, of course.

(3) Ethical nonnaturalists hold that goodness is a sui generis property that cannot be reduced to natural (or supernatural) properties. To them, "X is good in itself" simply means:
  (h) X is good in itself.

In *Principia Ethica,* G. E. Moore said that any translation and reduction of an evaluation into a sensorily based description is fallacious and involves a significant loss of meaning. For instance, after a hedonist determines that something is pleasurable, we can still intelligibly ask if it is *good*. In this view, goodness is observed directly by the moral sense—not by sight, taste, smell, touch, or hearing (or revelation).

(4) Ethical formalists hold that "X is good in itself" attributes a *logical* property to X—one that can be rationally (rather than empirically) discerned. For instance:
  (i) X is consistently universally generalizable.

This is the view of Immanuel Kant's *Grounding for the Metaphysics of Morals.* It is, essentially, the coherence theory of truth applied to morals; and it carries with it the problems indigenous to that theory—the possibility of rival coherencies and experiential sterility. Kant claimed that obedience to duty for its own sake and treating people as ends in themselves rather than as means are instances of the good, but both injunctions have coherent rivals and neither offers any concrete guidance.

For any of these nine analyses of moral evaluation, there must be testable moral truths that are universal in their application, and each has its own notion of what those truths are, how they are discerned, and how they may be verified.

2. Problems with Universal Moral Cognitions

There are two main objections to the notion that there are testable moral truths that are universal in their application:

- Moral claims are individually or group-specifically relative. They are descriptive; but what they describe is either the attitudes of the individual who utters them or the prevailing attitudes of the culture in which they occur.
- Moral claims have no testable content of any kind. They do not describe *anything*.

A. Autobiographical relativism. Even if we reject the notion that "X is good in itself" attributes a real property to X, we need not say that it attributes no property to anything at all. That view simply misidentifies the attribution target. "X is good in itself" is about the *speaker*.

> *Example.* Those, like Moore, who say that human companionship is good in itself are not attributing any property to it but asserting that they prize it unconditionally. Similarly, those who say that child abuse is bad in itself are not attributing any property to it but asserting that they are against it in all circumstances.

Such self-descriptions attribute properties whose presence or absence can be empirically discovered. Do we have the attitudes we claim? If we speak truly (or, for that matter, lie, misremember, or fail to know our own minds), our behavior will show it.

This analysis has an odd effect, however. While Brigham may reply to Henry's "I favor (serial) monogamy" with "I don't," that does not negate what Henry said. No one can do that without addressing *Henry's* attitudes. The only negation of Henry's "I favor (serial) monogamy" is "No, you don't." So unless a person is lying, misremembering, or doesn't know his own mind, no one can ever say his value claims are false.

> *Example.* Suppose that Brown goes to a hanging, applauds when the trap springs, and remarks, "Hangings are a good thing." Suppose also that Green, another observer, weeps inconsolably and retorts, "No, they aren't; they're evil." As long as Brown is genuinely applauding and Green is genuinely weeping (if the autobiographical account of evaluations is correct), both speak the truth.

In this analysis, the content of an evaluative utterance is indexed to its utterer. So its applicability cannot go beyond her. "I favor X," said by one person, and "I'm against it," said by another, can both be true, even though the claims they "translate" ("X is good" and "No, it's bad") look contradictory.

"X is good" and "No, it's bad" do, undeniably, reveal an attitude conflict. It is just that they seem to do a great deal more than that. If they don't do more than that, then the commonsense understanding of moral discourse is a serious misconstrual, and a very large part of what people say does not mean what they think it means. As common as value talk is, however, anyone would think that time in the arena would have excised so blatant a confusion by now.

In other accounts of moral talk, straightforward disputes do occur, whether the disputants are "same school" or not:

> *Examples.* Suppose Brown says, "Doing X is good," and Green says, "No, it isn't." If both are utilitarians, Brown is saying that doing X will produce the most happiness for the most people in the long run, and Green is saying that it won't. If both are "natural lawyers," Brown is saying that X is a natural act, and Green that it is an unnatural one. If Brown and Green are not of the same school, then Green's denial of Brown's claim may be a rejection of the criterion in use, or a claim that it is not actually met. Thus, if Brown is a utilitarian and says, "Doing X is good," and Green is a natural lawyer and replies "No, it isn't," Green may be saying Brown's criterion is screwed up ("doing X may produce happiness for everyone, but it is still an unnatural act"), or that Brown is wrong on his own grounds ("doing X will have bad consequences"), or both.

In every case, Green says Brown is mistaken; so they cannot both be correct. To achieve that in the autobiographical account, Green's reply would have to mean one of three things:

- I know you think you favor X, but that's a mistake. You're actually against it.

  Although psychiatrists often make such a claim to their clients, ordinary folk are rarely in a position to do so.

- I know you favor X, but your grounds for that are poor.

  But if Green means *that*, then Brown must mean "I favor X *on good grounds*;" which is close enough to "there are good reasons to favor X" to return us to the notion that value claims are actually about their ostensible targets.

- I know you favor X, but it is immoral to do so.

  In this view, Green means, "I am against your favoring X." Brown, then, can be against Green's being against his stance, and so forth. The depth of their conflict, then, is a function of how many reflections are nested in the mirror.

We may reject the autobiographical account as well as the nine traditional object-oriented accounts. If so we might opt for *cultural* moral relativism or conclude that evaluations have no testable content at all.

B. Cultural relativism. The opinion that moral values are culturally determined is very widely held. One currently popular way to package this conception of moral subjectivity is in terms of "cultural normative paradigms." This nicely parallels the postmodern construal of epistemic relativism in terms of cultural epistemic paradigms. This view is seductively plausible, but impossible to defend. Cultural moral paradigms have the same limitations that were seen to mark their epistemic counterparts. They may *shape* the way in which people appraise what occurs, but they do not *determine* it; and the way in which they shape it may be wrongheaded.

While it is obvious that the behaviors and characteristics that humans prize vary from one culture to the next, it is not at all obvious that these variations are determined by culture alone. Nor is it obvious that they are as fundamental as they may seem. Furthermore, what is morally endorsed in a given culture may be only what is *mistakenly* deemed to be good there. If "moral" simply meant what a culture endorsed, then its endorsements could not be morally evaluated themselves. But various cultures' endorsements are frequently evaluated, even by "insiders." As long as one person, anywhere, can intelligibly say, "My culture's endorsements are morally corrupt," "moral" cannot mean what a culture endorses. But it is known that people can do that because they *do*.

1) Evaluations are functions of many factors. Evaluative variations between people and groups of people are not determined by culture alone. The human behaviors and characteristics that people prize vary not only as a function of the cultural traditions that are locally established but also as a function of:

- the physical environment,
- the presence or absence of abstract reflection,
- the influence of religions and political ideologies,
- the influence of "opinion leaders,"
- the contingencies of natural and political history, and
- the idiosyncratic contributions of whatever prophets, sages, and philosophers grace the local scene.

For instance, moral considerations surround the protection and conservation of anything that is essential to life and hard to come by. What is essential to human life is fairly standard (shelter, food, water), and is biologically determined. And what is hard to come by is a function of the physical environment and historical circumstances.

Example. Desert dwellers have more to say about the value of water and the immorality of wasting it than Amazonians do—as well they should—and culture has nothing to do with it.

So it is a mistake to say that values are determined by culture.

2) Some moral variations are only apparent. Moral variations between cultures are not always fundamental or irreducible.

a) The same value can be expressed in different ways in different circumstances. Where water is scarce, a populous and growing community might choose to establish communal wells and regulations for rationing and turn taking. A thinly populated and stable community, on the other hand, might allow private possession but provide rules for benevolence toward travelers and strangers in the land. Behind the details of various societies' ways of distributing scarce essentials, however, a common concern for human need is obvious. It may be embellished by tradition; but its ultimate sources are the human organism, its needs, and its natural environment, not the culture it inhabits. Indeed, the ultimate sources of the culture itself are also the human organism, its needs, and its natural environment. The plow shapes the furrow, not vice versa.

This is true of much more complex behavior patterns, too. Traditional Inuits, for instance, did not put their elderly in senior care. They encouraged them to go out and die. Even here, however, the motivation is common across most cultural borders: to maintain the family by marginalizing its unproductive members. The means chosen may seem extreme, but they were chosen in a harsh environment where food was scarce and a nomadic life necessary. And they were effective.

b) Apparent value differences can be the expression of the same value in the context of different beliefs about what the facts are. In a society in which belief in an afterlife is widespread, benevolence may take a very different form than it takes in one where the belief that *this life is all you get* is common. But benevolence, in terms of the facts as they are perceived, is prized across most cultures, for all the variations in its implementation.

Example. Some North American First People dispatched their parents in healthy midlife to assure their well-being in the next world. They may have acted on scant evidence, but they were not malevolent. Their deeds were acts of kindness.

For that matter, altruism as a motivation for homicide is not unheard of in North America *today*—not so much to speed its targets' arrival in paradise, or to assure their health and fitness there, as to terminate suffering, despair, and mental incapacity.

3) "Moral" does not mean what a culture endorses. Some practices that some cultures endorse are morally abhorrent. Here are five that have even

been recognized as such by members of cultures where they were commonly practiced. The mere occurrence of such internal disclaimers is all that it takes to show that culture alone does not determine morality:

- enslaving captives,
- sacrificing humans,
- burning heretics at the stake,
- mutilating infants, and
- burning widows (suttee).

If culture alone did determine what is moral and what is not, then no culturally endorsed practice would be subject to review, no rejection of a culture's "paradigm" defensible, and no moral growth possible for any society.

The real issue of morals is whether human behavior should be tailored to meet human needs as they occur or be bent to the demands of the gods, of nature's "laws," of our political masters, or of local orthodoxy. The answer can be discovered through careful reflection and detailed attention to the facts and circumstances of people's lives. Culture doesn't say. So cultural moral relativism can be set aside.

C. Moral skepticism. Without evidence connections, an utterance carries no knowable freight at all. As noted previously, even beliefs presuppose testable evidence connections; and what moves us from belief to knowledge is more of the same. Otherwise, there is no content to be believed, much less known. Many people, however, are convinced that moral evaluations, however analyzed, are not testable. In their view, the answer to "How do we verify moral claims?" is, "We don't."

The Logical Empiricists, for instance, claimed that unless moral talk can be reduced to sensory language (or can be shown to denote perceivable sui generis properties), it is untestable and "cognitively empty." In this view, furthermore, G. E. Moore's argument that reductionism is fallacious was sound; but his notion that nonnatural goodness can be discerned by the moral sense was groundless. Consequently, for those such as A. J. Ayer (in *Language Truth and Logic*) who accept this conception of empiricism, moral evaluations aren't descriptions, moral goodness is not a property of any kind, and moral cognitions never occur.

The claim that "X is good" is cognitively empty can be read two ways:

- Moral utterances are useful, but their use is not aimed at cognition. They don't *assert* anything, but they can *show* our affections and the disposition of our will.

The emotivist theories laid out in Charles Stevenson's *Facts and Values* and R. M. Hare's *The Language of Morals* belong here. In the simplest form of this account, "X is good in itself" means approximately: "Hurrah for X!"

- Moral utterances have no use whatever. "X is good" is *vacuous*—"full of sound and fury, signifying nothing."

This is where you're left if you think that all of the cognitive analyses of value talk are buncombe and you find no merit in emotivism. Such nihilism is common.

1) Emotivism. Emotivism is committed to two principles that deny the ostensible descriptive character of moral utterances:

- Finding something good begins with prizing it.

No one can examine anything and say, "I can see with my eyes that it is red, hear with my ears that it is loud, and discern with my moral thingamabob that it is good." People don't find things good in the way they find ripe bananas yellow and American footballs oblong. Value is a function of valuing. Valuing is primitive; value is derived.

- An evaluation is an expression of its speaker's attitudes, showing them to others and evincing like ones in them.

If Mother Teresa said, "Political killing is evil," and a 9/11 pilot replied, "No, it is virtuous," they would not be describing political killing, describing themselves, or even describing their attitudes. They would be *ventilating* and *acting out* their attitudes and trying to influence each other. An inelegant emotivist might translate their exchange this way—with a strong overtone of "Come on, see it my way!" in both.

Teresa: "Political killing: Yuck!"

Pilot: "Political killing: Wow!"

Teresa no more describes herself as having a negative attitude toward political killing than fans who yell, "Boo Irish" at a football game describe themselves as having a negative attitude toward Notre Dame. If Richmond loyalist Geoff Goddu shouts, "Boo Irish," no Notre Dame fan would ever shout back, "That's false!"

We can describe our attitudes. If his therapist said, "Describe your attitude toward political killing," the 9/11 pilot would likely say neither "Political killing is virtuous" nor "Political killing: Wow!" He would merely say, "My attitude toward political killing is very positive."

If moral utterances simply express and evince attitudes, how we construe moral *dispute* is completely transformed. What might have been construed as argument in the sense of comparing and offering claims, counterclaims, and evidence, can only be construed as argument in the sense of chest pounding.

Although that is quite a different sense of *argument*, it still involves attempts to change people's minds. If we shout, "Political killing is evil" long and loudly enough, we may successfully evince a negative attitude toward it in our hearers. But that will be a matter of their being moved or persuaded, not of their being convinced.

There are disputes where outbursts are the entire story—sandbox iterations of "Nanny Nanny boo-boo," for instance. Moral arguments, in contrast, seem more complicated. In them, the conclusions that people reach are traditionally alleged to be open to evidential review and reasoned assessment. In the sandbox, there is nothing to review or assess.

No analysis of moral argument that fails to make room for review and assessment of *any* kind is viable. However, there is nothing, in principle, to prevent an emotivist from making room for review and assessment of *some* kind (though it cannot, on this view, be evidential). All that is required is a working set of alternative felicity conditions for the appraising game; and there are several possible sets available.

> *Example.* After hearing all the pros and cons, a war crimes judge concluded that making lampshades from the skin of gassed Jews, Gypsies, and homosexuals was horrible and that those who did it deserved public exposure and lengthy imprisonment. Since her conclusion was not a description, it was neither true nor false. But it was not senseless because it can be assessed—as a ruling or verdict—not for its truth but for whether it is fitting.

If "fitting" will work as a felicity condition, we could acknowledge the expressive character of moral utterances *and* keep them open to review on objective grounds. Will such "objective emotivism" work?

2) Objective Emotivism. There are many significant utterances that must be weighed on grounds other than truth or falsehood. This does not relegate them to the realm of test-free blather, however. Used-car sellers would be happy if the language game of puffery were free of all review, but people have protection even in areas where truth is not at stake.

a) "X is good" may show its speaker's attitude to a state of affairs, rather than describing it, and still be open to objective assessment in terms of whether it is *apt* or *fitting*. People have a strong sense of what responses are fitting (or not), in the arenas of etiquette and practical judgment, and in the moral arena as well.

> *Examples.*
> At the funeral of a clergyman, the widow jumped on her pew in the middle of the eulogy, shook her fist skyward, and shouted, "Goddamn you, God!"
> At a wedding, incredulous laughter was heard from an ex-spouse as the officiant said to the groom, "Forsaking all others, cleave only unto her until death do you part."
> A school principal suspended a six-year-old boy for sexual harassment when he kissed a girl classmate's cheek during recess.
> A college president dismissed a young instructor for cheering the student side at the annual student/staff bowling tournament.

A college's trustees demanded its president's resignation for altering grades in return for sex but recommended him to another college where, upon being hired, he did the same thing.

A high ranking cleric rationalized a church official's theft of money from its charity fund to build a home swimming pool, saying that fiduciary responsibility is very stressful.

The problem is to spell out noncircular grounds for differentiating responses that are fitting from those that aren't. If that is as hard as finding grounds for directly differentiating behaviors as good or bad, then transplanting the issue from whether a predication of goodness is true to whether an expression of approval is fitting would be a waste of time.

b) One basis for calling an attitude fitting would be its consonance with the attitudes of normal humans in similar situations.

Making any use of this, of course, presupposes having a map of the attitudes normal humans have in situations of various kinds, a map that does not depend on any question-begging determination of whether a person is normal in terms of whether her responses are fitting.

Empirical psychology could provide such a map only if human attitude/situation correlations are uniform. They are, in fact, fairly uniform in spite of the fact that individuals who say, "Ooh! Do that again," when we drop a bowling ball on their toes, occasionally crop up. Such attitude deviations are not only rare; they also may be linked to neurological and developmental pathologies that we can "control for." Taking that into account, then, an attitude is fitting if it is consonant with those of clinically normal humans when confronted by similar states of affairs.

c) There are problems with this:

- It encourages us to see virtually any attitude deviation as a sign of covert pathology.
- It generates a deadly dilemma relative to cultural deviations from "species normal."
- It makes what is fitting a matter of historical accidents and contingencies.
- It masks other distinctions between attitudes that people are quite capable of drawing.

(1) If we see moral mavericks as displaying deviant attitudes rather than as asserting corrupt beliefs, we are more likely to respond to them with treatment than with arguments and evidence.

Example. During 'Nam an activist student was busted for smoking pot, expelled, and immediately drafted. When the dean who expelled him was informed that he had been called up, he danced a jig, and said, "It serves the little pinko right." The provost did not argue with the dean, or label his beliefs mean-spirited, mistaken, or corrupt. She just insisted that he see a therapist and relieved him of his duties pending a "cure."

This shift—from challenging beliefs with arguments to modifying attitudes with therapy—is common. It sent Soviet dissidents to the gulag in Stalinist times, and Chinese intellectuals to the farm in Maoist times, all for their "mental health."

(2) In this analysis of "fitting," we can either allow that the attitudes that are standard in each culture are fitting (there) or that every attitude deviation from "species normal" is unfitting, even if culturally generated. This is not a comfortable dilemma.

(a) We can easily imagine one society where political killing is a commonly prized method of assuring national ideological purity, and another where that practice is commonly shunned. In the first society, a person who says, "Political killing is evil" is an attitude deviate; as is a person in the second society who says, "Political killing is virtuous." In the first, an attitude is common, hence fitting, which is uncommon, hence unfitting, in the second, and vice versa.

In this analysis, we can appraise attitude deviance only within a culture. No culturally common attitude is "unfit," no matter how isolated or dysfunctional its milieu. But, in fact, some culturally common attitudes are quite inappropriate, humanly speaking.

> *Example.* (This is from the "B" feature of a Saturday matinee at the McLean Theater in southern Illinois at about the same time as *Man Made Monster.* I wish I could remember the title.)
> Little Tulu was fed to Mogu at the vernal equinox, having been caught early in her performance of the Dance of the Awakening for a British sailor. Having been stopped in time, giving her to Mogu met the need for a virgin for the planting sacrifice as well as the need for a deterrent to others who might reveal sacred mysteries to outsiders. Tulu herself was the only one to express a deviant attitude, as the people gathered and cheered her plunge into the lava. But we could argue that her scream expressed a more appropriate human response than the crowd's cheers—no matter that the latter were entirely consonant with the local culture's conception of what is clinically normal.

(b) This problem could be averted by defining "clinically normal human attitudes" as the ones people would have, absent any unusual acculturation. With a map of the affective proclivities of healthy human beings in "standard" cultural conditions, we could specify fitting and unfitting attitudes across all cultures, including the odd ones.

But suppose that, as a matter of contingent fact, everyone in every community on earth believed that harvests depend on pleasing the gods and that they take great pleasure in the painful death of those who would reveal a sacred mystery to an outsider. On that supposition, no lament for Little Tulu's demise could be fitting (although various cultures might perform the sacrifice in different ways, depending on local geology).

(c) This problem could be averted by defining "clinically normal human attitudes" as the ones people would have, absent all acculturation. With a map of the affective proclivities of healthy human beings, as such, we could specify fitting and unfitting attitudes across all cultures, including "standard" ones.

In this analysis, then, if humans in an unacculturated state happened, universally, to prize eating one another, that would be more fitting than the loathing for cannibalism that is common to almost all societies.

(3) This analysis of "fitting" relies on contingent circumstances. If there is such a thing as human nature, its shape is accidental and could be different. So the features of humans that are generally prized (such as caring for their young instead of eating them as guppies do) are contingent, too; and there is no objective ground for preferring them to what might have been or might yet be. It is *fitting* to prize whatever *is* prized.

But if what attitudes are fitting is a function of every alteration that occurs in human dispositions and attitudes over time, nothing protects people the way they are. This is especially pressing, given the fact that tampering with humans is so easy. "Normal humans" are, in effect, whatever the local Ministry of Love has the stomach to make them. We cannot abhor this without being an attitude deviant, unless we can find a more-or-less fixed notion of human nature and hold it constant.

(4) Those who identify what is fitting and unfitting with what is common and uncommon are not in a position to find beneficial prizings and shunnings appropriate and harmful prizings and shunnings inappropriate, when such sentiments run against the tide. Furthermore, they are unable to differentiate between "trivial" and "morally significant" deviance.

> *Example.* Igor prizes several things that other people disdain—the Macarena, the taste of castor oil, and shooting pizza deliverers.

There is a difference between saying that Igor's third affinity is *unusual* and saying that it is *wrong*. The problem with it is not that it is unusual. It is that it is *harmful*. Prizing what is harmful is the very model of an unfitting attitude, even in a nation of brutes. Such prizing is not unfitting because the local society, or most members of the human race, *happen* to decline to share it. Indeed, it is likely that the local society, and most members of the human race, decline to share it because it is unfitting. The horse belongs in front of the cart.

Consequently, emotivism, even objective emotivism, is so problematic that no one who finds it at all plausible that moral appraisals get at something substantial is likely to turn to it.

3) Moral Nihilism. Finding a basis for objective moral evaluation is so notoriously difficult that many twentieth-century philosophers rejected the idea altogether, finding moral talk truly vacuous.

If it is, then there is no objective basis for any appraisals beyond token and means assessments. We can still say things like "Buicks are good [i.e., good examples of] Detroit Iron," or "Saturation bombing is a good [i.e., effective] way to demoralize civilian populations." But claims like "the recognition of human dignity enhances the quality of life," and "integrity is an essential human virtue," are linked to nothing more substantial than an individual's or a culture's inclinations. There is no arguing about taste, so there is no arguing about the quality of a society, its laws and customs, its lifestyle, the intentions that fund it, and the consequences that it generates.

Few, however, will put such nihilism in practice when they find themselves the target of exploitation and harm. There is nothing like being on the receiving end of malice to make the notion of objective morality sprout up like wild onions after rain.

Examples.

An ethics teacher who downgrades students whose essays disagree with his own positions gives Sam a very low mark even though his paper refutes the instructor's position with great clarity and force.

Local juries consistently convict Latinos and acquit Anglos charged with robbery; and Juan and Bruce are convicted and acquitted, respectively, for a holdup they committed together.

A corporation offers Susan 15 percent less than it offers a male applicant for an identical job though she is equally qualified.

Sam, Juan, and Susan's opinion that their treatment is unfair is a justified true belief. So they *know* their treatment is unfair. If it can be shown that unfair treatment is wrong, then they are in a position to know that their treatment is wrong. But if they can know that, artful talk about moral nihilism is entirely disingenuous.

There are several different ways to show that treating people unfairly is wrong and that, consequently, we ought not to do it. But there are also some additional systematic objections to the moral appraisal of human behavior that have not yet been dealt with. If, as some allege, certain features of human nature and of nature itself make it unreasonable to bring human actions under judgment *at all*, then we need not worry about whether this or that *particular* evaluation is justified.

So in the next two chapters, I will explore human nature—what people *can* and *cannot* do. Then, in chapters 12–15, I will return to human conduct —what people *ought* to do.

III

HUMAN NATURE

10

Human Nature: God, Society, and Nature

Self-exploration has been carried to narcissistic lengths recently, but "know thyself" is not a new maxim. Today's self-searching is only the current token of an age-old quest to discover what life is about, its *point* or *meaning*. Seriously pursued, that leads to questions about human life in general. Individual self-scrutiny is sharpened in the context of a broader search. So people also ask, "What is the meaning of human life? What is its point?" But, "What is the point of X?" has a complicated subtext:

- Looking for the point of any X presumes that it *has* one;
- Things that have a point are *intentional*; and
- Things that are intentional are *intended*.

The natural habitat for "What is the meaning of X?" is figuring out what speakers mean by what they say. That ordinarily involves discovering the intentions behind their speech acts, the information they want to convey, and what their purpose is in speaking. (These are not the same. Even though conveying information is a common purpose for speech, it is not the only one. See John Searle's *Speech Acts*.) Further, it may also involve what information can be gleaned from (or read into) X whether it is, strictly speaking, intended or not. (This is how people read "meaning" into sudden weight loss as "Mother Nature telling you to slow down.")

1. The Meaning of Human Life

With appropriate adjustments, this section can be construed as dealing with the meaning of *life*, the meaning of *a* life, the meaning of *human* life, and the meaning of *a* human life.

It is difficult to construe "the meaning of human life" as information that can be gleaned from it except for a certain amount of biology, which is obviously not what those who ask, "What is the meaning of human life?" are after. The question, "What is the meaning of human life?" is usually aimed at identifying its *purpose.*

But we cannot sensibly seek the *purpose* of human life without presuming that it has one. And, given that purposes are exclusively intentional, we cannot sensibly presume that human life has one without presuming either that it provides its own or that there is some "intention provider" or other behind it. Consequently, unless we can reasonably identify who (or what) has purposely produced human life, the most straightforward answer to the question, "What is the meaning of human life?" is "There is no strong reason to think that there is one" or "Your question is ill formed and unanswerable."

Many still ask the question, however, and offer answers in terms of different ideas about where its "meaning" might come from. Possible sources, such as religion, nature, culture, or the efforts of individual humans themselves, suggest intentions such as the glorification of God, the perpetuation of the gene pool, or the preservation and propagation of culture, or deliver the warning that we must *make* a meaning for life rather than *find* one.

Only the first and last of these themes plausibly address the issue of where the requisite intentions come from. It is not at all clear that gene pools and cultures have the capacity to intend anything. Furthermore, while any god would be capable of intending, we need a reason to think that there *is* one in order to go that route. So if we must call the human quest for self-understanding a search for "the meaning of human life," the fourth theme looks like a hands-down winner.

But the human quest for self-understanding need not be described as a search for "the meaning of human life." It may be described, instead, as a search for insight into how we tick, that is, into our inclinations, capacities, and limits, and how they work. Talk about the intention, meaning, and purpose of human life can be replaced with talk how human life functions. Evolutionary biologists, for example, claiming that effective organization need not presuppose deliberation, have replaced talk about the *purpose* of giraffes' long necks with talk about their *functions.*

Articulating the quest for self-understanding in functional rather than intentional terms sidesteps the possibly unanswerable issues of whether human life has a purpose, where that might come from, and how we might know. So instead of saying, "I want to know the meaning of human life," we can say, "I want to understand human beings and how they work;" and if we want our own lives to have a meaning, follow the existentialist injunction and do something to give them one ourselves.

2. On What It Is to Be Human

In exploring people's general inclinations, capacities, and limits, and how they work, I will follow two cautionary principles:

- We should examine the "nature of human nature" from more than one perspective. No individual perspective can provide more than a caricature; but there may be enough illumination in several to facilitate a useful mosaic.
- We should carefully control for bias. Humans generally focus on what is of interest to *us*; and furthermore each individual's capacities, equipment, vocabulary, experiences, and personal interests influence what data will strike home. So while it may be impossible to eliminate such bents, it is important to be alert to them, control for them, and keep them in check.

With these cautions in mind, consider the following questions about what humans "amount to":

- Are humans "separate creations" (perhaps in the "image of God"), or are they "part of nature"?
- What is the relationship between human individuals and human groups? Do individuals create cultures and their webs of meaning, or is the process the other way around?
- If humans are part of nature, are they entirely "complex physical things," or do they have "nonphysical" aspects?
- If humans are entirely physical, does mechanical "cause and effect" govern all their activities? And, if so are all of those activities strictly "determined and predictable"?
- If all human activities are strictly "determined and predictable," are any of them ever sufficiently "our own" for people to be considered "free and responsible"?

A. Humans, creation, and the *imago dei*. Can the key to what is distinctively human be found in a connection to God? A number of different connections have been suggested: being a part of God, being an emanation of God, being nascent gods ourselves, and (of greatest local interest) being specially created by God and fashioned in the divine image. My concern here is not with whether such claims are true, but with what they contribute to understanding human nature.

1) The claim that people are specially created by God contributes very little to a map of human nature in that it does not rule out anything. For example, it does not rule out the possibility that people are continuous with nature. Continuous or discontinuous, they are what they are. The notion that they came from God by a special act would only be informative if we had (noncircular) knowledge of what God's intentions were at the time. Absent such knowledge of what God "wanted people to be," saying that they were specially created tells us nothing about what they are; and it is very difficult to

know what God "wants people to be," even presuming that there is a God that has "wants." It is far simpler just to examine people directly and *see* what they are like.

In fact, being told that people are created by God, specially or otherwise, says nothing about what they are like unless we already know what things created by God are like—in exactly the same way that being told that people are from Germany says nothing about what they are like unless we already know what things from Germany are like. So asking, "Were people (specially) created by God?" is no handle for finding out what they are like. If we already know what they are like, the question is unnecessary; and if we do not already know that, then the statement that they were specially created by God is uninformative.

2) The notion that people bear God's image also contributes little to a map of human nature. Unless we already know God's nature, the claim that humans bear God's image throws no light on theirs—just as remarking to people who are unfamiliar with a local hotel that it looks like the Taj Mahal says nothing to them unless they already know how the Taj Mahal looks. If we already know what people are like, imago talk might throw some light on *God's* nature—just as an appearance comparison might illuminate an unseen Taj Mahal for those who are already familiar with the local hotel. But that is backward. Imago talk, in this context, should tell us something about people, not something about God.

Further, those who claim to know God's nature (and who, if they did, might informatively say "humans bear the image of God") disagree about what the divine nature amounts to and typically appeal to less-than-secure evidence to back up their various perspectives on the matter.

Other troublesome questions also arise when we try to illuminate human nature with references to the *imago dei*:

- Which God's image does humanity bear?
  There are many peoples and many conceptions of God(s). Can we presume that whatever God the local folk worship is the one whose image all humans bear?
- Is being in the image of God a matter of people and God having the *same* attributes, or *similar* ones?
  It is unlikely that humans and God could have the same attributes. Humans seem underqualified; and such talk of God seems impious at the very least.
- If humans do share some of God's attributes in some sense, which of their thousands of attributes are the shared ones?
  Are they ones having to do with human capacities and dispositions? Human mortality? Human appearance? If (as folklore has it) it is the latter, then does this work for insides as well as outsides and for both genders' plumbing?

- If human attributes are only *like* God's—but "His ways are not our ways"—how reliable are the analogies, absent any and all knowledge of one side of the analogy?
  What could it possibly mean for transcendentalists to say that human love and God's love are "analogous," absent any and all knowledge about one side of the analogy?

We must also ask what grounds exist for answering such questions. Without such grounds, the questions are unanswerable; and if that is the case there is little point in asking them. This is a solid (if pedestrian) reminder why it is unwise to plunge into theological swamps when seeking clarity about this present world.

However, short-circuiting any number of things that would be interesting (if unprofitable) to pursue at length, I will assume that the deity imaged by humans is the common denominator of the Jewish-Christian-Muslim traditions, of whom people in the United States have *some* general notion—that is, the God of Moses, Isaiah, Paul, Malcolm X, Mary Baker Eddy, Jerry Falwell, Hillary Rodham Clinton, the pope, and Sweet Daddy Grace. I will also assume that human characteristics such as reflective thought, intention, judgment formation, choice, and action are the ones that reflect the divine. While there is no reason to think these assumptions are true, they do constitute a "most charitable interpretation" of *imago dei* talk for local use. Without such charity, the gambit is hopeless.

Unfortunately, there are reasons to think that it remains hopeless, even when so charitably interpreted:

- If "bearing the image" means *more* than "people engage in reflective thought," and so forth, perhaps something about their origin or destiny, it is difficult if not impossible to provide evidence to back the extras up. But, absent evidence, is there any reason to think the extras are true?
- If "bearing the image" means *only* that "people engage in reflective thought," and so forth, there is no reason to call it "bearing the image of God" unless we have access to the divine and can see that it *is* manifested in these human dispositions. But who has such access?

So since the net effect of *imago dei* talk is either to offer an uninformative re-description of ordinary facts or to voice words that lack any testable content, it would be more straightforward simply to say that people are distinct because they "engage in reflective thought," and so forth, and leave it at that, omitting the *imago dei* talk altogether.

There is, however, an *extrinsic* function that imago talk can serve in religious discourse. The stories that it funds about people reinforce their pursuit of life goals. Perhaps the difference between people who describe humans simply as goal-directed agents, and so forth, and those who cast their account in theological terms, is that the latter have an apparatus in play to encourage people to follow through. This spares imago talk from charges of comprising false or uninformative descriptions by allowing that its primary function is motivational, not descriptive. (See R. B. Braithwaite's classic book *An Empiricist's View of the Nature of Religious Belief* and my video series *Philosophy of Religion.*)

If we construe imago talk this way, however, we are construing it in a way that is unacceptable to many serious theists. To the conservatives among them, at any rate, this is a shallow parody of what is really going on. But to theists who are seriously concerned to make their conception of mankind useful, this account may be the most effective way for imago talk to evade the harsh dilemma of noninformation and probable falsehood. But it leaves one with a no less harsh trilemma of extrinsic motivation, noninformation, and falsehood. And that sums up why the notion that humans were specially created in the image of God contributes so little to a useful map of human nature.

B. Humans, society, and the *imago culturae.* While much of Western humanism since the enlightenment has placed the essence of humanity in individuals, that notion has generated back pressure that has helped solidify more "collective" political and economic views. Individualism is so central to the Yankee way of knowing, however, that it may seem "alien" to conceive of persons in primarily collective terms. But, as a matter of fact, there have always been cultures (and individuals in them) that see a person's meaning and value only in the context of some social fabric.

Hegel espoused such a view in his *Phenomenology of Spirit,* focusing on the notion of collective identity on at least two levels:

- an *ethnic/historical* identity that links each organism to a culture of time and place, and—more abstractly—
- a *metaphysical* identity that sees each individual as a constituent piece of a possibly global Mind or Soul.

Friedrich Schleiermacher made an analogous point in his *On Religion,* claiming that when we try to grasp a particular by abstracting it from its context, we lose our grip on it and inevitably misconstrue its nature. The metaphor he used noted the difference between a bird in flight and one that has been killed and nailed to a dissection board. Things can properly be understood, he said, only "in place."

The notion that human nature must be mapped in terms of the primacy of groups over individuals is even more problematic than the notions of cultural epistemic and moral relativism, to which it is so obviously linked. Surely the capacities and functions involved in self-awareness and choice belong to individuals and not to groups. So it is far more straightforward to see groups as derived from their members than the other way around. Furthermore, the notion of a collective "geist" is certainly less intelligible than the notion of an individual's. Terms like "group consciousness" are useful, but only when they are seen as constructions out of the activities (some singular, others collaborative) of the individuals who constitute the group.

Such group identity conceptions have practical consequences. Those who think that the importance of the individual derives from its connections don't pursue the same policies as those who believe that the importance of groups derives from their constituents. They may urge us to subordinate our private interests to those of our group, and to alter our decisions and actions so as to promote group survival and well-being in ways that vary as a function of the groups we have in mind. Few are driven by a notion of anything as grand as a "world soul," but everyone has family, class, interest group, racial, and national links with which they can identify. Which one of them we identify with is a function of circumstance. Advantaged minorities are likely to favor class over more inclusive sets, and exploited minorities to favor humanity over economic status. Compare *Atlas Shrugged* to *Roots*.

Occasions do arise where people subordinate their individual interests, desires, and benefit to the good of their nation, race, or cause. For instance, expecting conscripts to be happy while doing national service is a common occasion of groupism. Parents also impose it on their children —"That isn't the way *we* do things"—stressing the notion of solidarity with familial, racial, religious, or other identities. This reinforces resolve, validates behavior, and confirms shared beliefs; but it does not necessarily achieve truth. It is an interesting fact about people, however, that they often prefer the security of shared belief, true or not, to the angst that goes with pursuing truth on their own.

The fact that we are uncomfortable with the notion of group identity may itself be a product of groupthink: the social environment that has conditioned us to favor individualism. The notion that even individualism, when it occurs, is group generated and group reinforced ironically exemplifies Karl Mannheim's theory of the "sociology of knowledge," that *all* our beliefs, values, goals, and dispositions are determined by the social fabric in which we are born and conditioned.

There are some problems of consistency and applicability with such theories, however. First, if the theory of the sociology of knowledge is correct, then it must itself be the belief product of social conditioning. That seems to undercut its "objectivity." Further, even if large parts of our dispositions, interests, values, and so forth, start out as projections of our social context, people do seem able to take a step back and become critically aware of them. And when they do, it is likely that at least some of the positions they subsequently take will be "for reasons" rather than "due to causes." Indeed, once anyone recognizes the difference between "taking a position for a reason" and "holding a position as a product of cause and effect," they are likely to change at least some of their positions. That is how new adults are able to reject the ideologies of their parents.

However, the fact that people sometimes change some of their positions "for reasons" may *itself* be caused by the social fabric in which they work. A certain amount of education, for example, encourages it. Indeed, a certain amount of both education and experience may be necessary conditions of achieving a reflective state. But that does not alter the fact that once we get there—however we do it—we can make judgments, not because they reflect the group's values and beliefs, but because they have the best evidence to support them.

Nevertheless, the group identity perspective throws a fair amount of light on how people operate. We may hesitate to say that people are merely cogs in the social machine, avatars of the collective soul, or reflections of groups that are themselves only reflections of larger and older groups, but the fact remains that a large part of what people believe, prize, and aspire to *is* deeply rooted in their group connections.

> *Example.* A sociologist offered to identify the politics of his students by asking their age, hometown, whether their parents went to college, and how much income the family had. He got me, making me suspect that things I thought I believed on mature reflection and judicious choice were, in fact, caused by the circumstances into which I happened to have been dropped—which was, of course, his point.
>
> I was born in the Depression, grew up in the city, and had twelve years of postsecondary education. My mother, father, and three out of four grandparents were college graduates, small-town middle-class professionals. My great-grandparents were agrarian populists. And my ultimate progenitors on these shores were mostly indentured servants, with an occasional Native American or traveling tinker thrown in for leavening. Money was scare, and we knew it was hard to come by.
>
> Was my destiny sealed before I was born?

Realizing the power of social influences can jolt us out of positions into which we have unconsciously drifted with the group tide. Realizing it myself, then, should I have veered to some theocratic or vegan alternative? Not necessarily. The fact that we are doing X as a result of causes does not mean that X cannot be done for good reasons. Many of the association-determined notions that we hold are things that we ought first to think through and then *go on holding.*

The notions that individuals are the products of their culture, gain their beliefs and values from it, and have lives invested with meaning because they are parts of it contribute a great deal to a map of human nature even if collective identity theory is wrong in many of its claims. It makes no room for individual critiques of culture, rebellions, or reforms. It skates close to the abyss of untestable speculation with allusions to a collective "soul." It provides too easy a foundation for skeptical relativism about every facet of knowledge and valuation. But, while we should not accept it in toto, it would be as foolish to deny the way in which groups *shape* (not *determine*) their members as it would be to ignore the contributions of our physical and biological constitution and of our specific, reflective, and willful individuality.

Rejecting the formative role of culture altogether and affirming it to the exclusion of all other factors are both wrong because they both ignore salient facts. We need not swallow the foolish ideology of the "self-made man" in order to see the fact of individuality. Nor need we swallow the notion that we are nothing more than an indistinguishable manifestation of some Whole (whether the Proletariat, Race, World Soul, or Whatever) in order to admit that our selfhoods depend solidly on our links with our kinds.

The interplay of self and culture makes it impossible to say that either exclusively explains the other. People make cultures, and cultures shape people. The relationship is reciprocal, and understanding it calls for a genuine hermeneutic. The reciprocity of self and society, however, are not the only factors that contribute to the way people tick. Behind them both there is nature itself.

C. People and "nature." Many "naturalists" say that humanity is completely at home in the natural order—*of* the world as well as *in* it. To them, explaining and understanding people is methodologically continuous with explaining and understanding all "natural phenomena." The study of nature is thus said to throw considerable light on what people are.

1) Biological continuity.

When naturalists say that people are *of* the world as well as *in* it, they usually intend to convey that people and all other life forms are kin: close kin in some cases, more distant kin in others, but all part of the same encompassing life fabric.

This view, widely shared by secular and nonfundamentalist religious thinkers alike, provides a rationale for the obvious fact that humans share characteristics and capacities with other living things and encourages us to find out things about ourselves by examining our relatives (in the way, for example, Robert Ardrey did in *The Territorial Imperative*).

People share most of the life functions of plants (barring photosynthesis), to which they add mobility, intelligence, and purposive behavior, which they share with animals. While they lack some useful organic adaptations, such as venom and protective coloration, they compensate with an extraordinary combination of intelligence and physiology to underwrite complex intentions, linguistic communication, and the utilization of contrived tools. Perhaps the most important operational difference between people and other forms of life, so far as is known, is that people are capable of a sense of self—past, present, and future. But, as James Rachels shows in *Created from Animals*, even these characteristics can be seen as elaborations of what can be found across the biosphere. This facet of naturalism thus adds a great deal to a map of human nature.

2) Physicalism.

Many naturalists also say that if "people are *of* the world as well as *in* it" then they are entirely physical. (Note, however, that physical ≠ material. Naturalism has room for matter *and* energy.) This view, called "physicalism," has at least five components:

- Physical objects are the only objects there are. Note, however, that "objects" do not include abstractions, linguistic constructions, numbers, and so forth. The issue at stake here is whether there are nonphysical *objects*.
- All of an object's components are objects themselves.
- Even the most complex objects are nothing more than physical *systems* (i.e., physical objects functionally combined).
- The properties of any physical system are functions of its structure and of the properties of it component parts.
- Every object has a temporal beginning and end, changes over time, is (at any one moment) in a particular location in space, and interacts with other objects in strictly regular ways.

Such notions are derived from everyday experience. The objects that everyone can see, taste, smell, feel, and hear work under the constraints of impermanence, change, temporal and spatial confinement, and causal regularity. A thousand clichés commemorate them:

- Impermanence: Nothing lasts forever.
- Change: You can't go home again.
- Temporal confinement: The moving finger writes; and, having writ, moves on.
- Spatial confinement: Everybody has to be somewhere.
- Causal regularity: What goes around comes around.

Most contemporary philosophers agree that the *ordinary* objects of the world are entirely physical. However, the notion that *people* are entirely physical too, with all that that entails, is less widely shared. But there is little reason to think that dogs, rocks, and trees are not entirely physical if people *are*; and if people are *not*, then physicalism is wrong, regardless of the status of dogs, rocks, and trees.

Those who reject the application of physicalism to people usually do so either in terms of the *substance(s)* of which people are said to be made or of the *processes* of which they are said to be capable:

- Some argue that people are, or are in part, "souls."
- Others argue that people are, or are in part, "minds."
- Still others argue that physical processes are all mechanical but that many human processes are not.

But, whether appealing to souls, minds, or nonmechanical processes, their argument is that certain alleged human characteristics and abilities are exceptions to impermanence, change, temporal and spatial confinement, and causal regularity, and that (consequently) physicalism is not true of people across the board. Thus:

- In spite of the fact that people appear to die (like all other living things), it is often claimed that they are actually immortal in some sense. If so they escape impermanence.

   In precisely what sense, of course, varies according to who is talking. There are many notions of immortality, even within the confines of mainstream monotheism. Compare what D. Z. Phillips has to say in his *Death and Immortality* to what can be heard early any Sunday morning on TV when the broadcast industry is meeting its "public service" commitment.

- Ideas, it is said, are timeless, true ideas are unchanging, and people can, in thought, "leave" the present to visit the past and the future. So some human phenomena escape impermanence and change, and humans themselves (along with their ideas) escape the time trap.
- Out-of-body experiences, communication with ghosts, and going in dreams and reveries to distant places are all said to occur and to show that consciousness is not a bodily function (or is not bound to any particular body anyway).
- While only a few humans display creative genius, any novel use of language is somewhat "creative." Such linguistic creativity is common and shows that human activity is not limited by the constraints of regular causation.

   Human creativity is not confined to language. There are creative and hackneyed painters, composers, and architects, too. I cite linguistic creativity because Noam Chomsky's influential neodualism is based on it. (See his *Cartesian Linguistics* and Randy Allen Harris's *The Linguistic Wars*.)

But if people can evade the constraints of time, space, and regular causation in these ways, and anything that is entirely physical can't, there must be something "nonphysical" about them to account for it.

a) Substance. Perhaps people could evade the limitations of physical objects if they were, at least in part, made of "different stuff."

Few would argue that humans are *entirely* nonphysical. There are too many things about us that don't escape the constraint list to make such a view plausible. Our bodies do expire, for instance. So even though implausibility did not restrain Berkeley, the orthodox posture of philosophical antiphysicalism is that people are part physical and part "non," as Descartes argues in his *Meditations.*

There is a crucial assumption at work here: that the characteristics of things vary only as a function of what they are made of. On that assumption, both the limitations of things and the nonlimitations of people must be due to the stuff of which they are made. Things are made exclusively of physical stuff (matter and energy). So people must be, at least in part, made of nonphysical stuff (whatever that might be).

Historically, two different nonphysical stuffs have been suggested: soul stuff and mind stuff. People, then, are said to be "not entirely physical" because they are made of soul stuff and mind stuff as well as of physical stuff. The short way to say that is to say they have souls and minds as well as bodies. Thus we might argue:

- Nothing made exclusively of physical stuff can evade impermanence, but people, in their immortality, do evade it. So people must be—in part—nonphysical. The immortal part of people is that nonphysical part: the soul.
- Nothing made exclusively of physical stuff is independent of time and space, but thought is. So that which thinks cannot be exclusively physical. So since people do think, they must be—in part—nonphysical. The thinking part of people is that nonphysical part: the mind.

However, as Gilbert Ryle clearly demonstrated in *The Concept of Mind,* a half century ago, it is a category mistake to think that different functions must be explained in terms of different substances.

1) It is not just physical stuff that has the properties that physicalists attribute to objects, but particular *arrangements* of it. While it may be the case, contingently, that no ordinary arrangement of physical stuff is permanent, the stuff that is arranged—now this way, now that—is as permanent as permanent can be. So if we believe that people are immortal, all that is needed to explain it is for the stuff they are made of to be arranged in some remarkably enduring way. The stuff *itself* is fine as it stands. Matter/energy is indestructible.

2) There is very little reason to think that any coherent property cannot be accounted for in terms of an appropriate arrangement of the stuff things are made of. Common experience suggests thousands of examples of altering form to achieve different functions, from the simple to the incredibly complex. Clay can be fashioned into vases or bricks; bricks can be thrown or laid; laid bricks can make roads or walls; and walls can be used for anything from

windbreaks to war memorials. Similarly, sand can be used in a litter box or as a source for silicon; silicon can be fashioned into a heat insulator or a rectifier; rectifiers can be simple AC/DC converters for television sets or complex memory chips; memory chips can go into Christmas cards that play "Rudolph" or computers; and computers can be used for anything from playing solitaire to writing philosophy.

Indeed, the whole point of physical science is that all things have the same constituents—so many compounds of so many elements made of so many particles, wave packets,

> ## Souls or Living, Breathing Things?
>
> We can question whether there is any reason to think people are immortal in the first place. The issue here, however, is only to make it clear that immortality does not entail *nonphysical substance*—a point strongly supported by people who believe in it in terms of "resurrection bodies." Historically, the soul is a philosophical accretion to religion. Genesis says that Adam became a living, breathing thing when God breathed on him. It says zip about a "soul."

and so forth. Even if we don't have all of the details right yet, we *know* that incredible diversity can be achieved by arranging the same building blocks in different ways. Think of Legos. But, in fact, we are getting ever closer to having the details right. Contemporary neuroscience provides an increasingly detailed picture of the way that even the most obscure bits and pieces go together, and work together, for people to do what they do. For an overview, see Steven Pinker's *How the Mind Works*.

3) Caution is in order, however. Some functions are notoriously difficult to arrange for; but are they impossible?

- While it is notoriously difficult to nail Jell-O to the wall, a standard blob of Jell-O is only one arrangement of that product. If it won't hold a nail in this configuration, we can arrange it into another in which it will—frozen.
- Inconsistent arrangements, however, are always nonstarters. Even clever engineers can't design tires with great traction but no rolling resistance. If life is a process and all processes are entropic, can we arrange something to live but not run down? Perhaps not. So perhaps immortality is not in the cards.

Nevertheless, there is no reason to think we must leap to "substantial" differences to explain difficult and perplexing attribute differences. With a little ingenuity, a "structural" answer may well serve.

4) In any case, multiple substance explanations have a fatal flaw—the difficulty, or even impossibility, of "methexis," or interaction between substances. Substances that are radically different from each other may not be able to interact with each other.

Example. If God is wholly other to humans and (as would follow) humans wholly other to God, then their interaction is blocked. Humans could not reach up to God, nor God reach down to them. ("Up" and "down" are figures of speech here. If they were literal, it would not necessarily be a matter of God and humans being mutually "wholly other." It might just be a matter of both having unfortunately short arms.) If they speak different languages and have no shared environment in which to compare nonlinguistic notes, they can't communicate by swapping undefined markers or use a messenger, demiurge, or intercessor. Here, the languages *are* incommensurate and untranslatable!

But substantial mind/body dualism makes minds and bodies sufficiently different from each other to have this effect, which conflicts with the fact that people's minds and bodies do interact all the time.

Consider one aspect of the alleged mind/body difference: that bodies are located in space but minds are not. So how do messages get back and forth between the two? A mind that can reach the body is (in the reaching) in space and not truly mental. A body that can reach the mind is (in the reaching) out of space and not truly physical. So necessarily, if people's minds and bodies are truly mental and truly physical, respectively, *they do not interact*. If P implies Q, then ~Q implies ~P.

That is all well and good, save for the fact that your state of mind affects your physical performance, and your physical well-being affects your mental acuity.

Example. Sleeping with a high fever (a model of a physical condition), I have a bizarre dream (a model of mental activity). Awaking from an unsatisfactory encounter with Cynthia Nixon (who, as it turned out, is a pod-person), I take two aspirin and return to sleep and (I hope) less fevered dreams.

So people's minds and bodies *do* interact. Since everyone knows that, everyone also knows that substantial mind/body dualism is false (since what it implies is experientially known to be false).

Because it is beset with such an irremediable difficulty, and because it makes no essential contribution to explaining how people evade their physical limits (if they do), there is no good reason to pursue the notion of nonphysical *substance* any further. However, I must still address the question, "Do human functions display any sort of nonphysical *process*?" One colorful way to put that question is, "Are people anything more than cause and effect machines?" The core issue here is "regular causation."

Pineal Interaction?

Nominating the pineal gland as the mind/body demiurge is an exercise in futility. That gland may be remarkable in that, unlike some other brain parts, it is unitary. Furthermore, we may not know exactly everything it does. But we know one thing it does not do: it does not broker messages between space and nonspace. If it could, then there would be no need for a mind/body distinction in the first place.

b) Process. Perhaps what enables people to evade the limitations of things is that they, in part, don't work the way things work. Ordinary things are not only physical, they work mechanically. Perhaps people, even if physically composed, have some parts that work nonmechanically. Then, even if physicalism is right about the stuff people are made of, it would be wrong about their operations. For, while it does not claim that they are as simple as copiers and freight elevators, it does seem to say that their operations are of the same *sort*.

1) Although many people reject universal mechanism, everyone admits that recent technology has produced machines that emulate a wide variety of human behaviors. This suggests, on the surface at least, that human operations and machine operations are not totally dissimilar.

Indeed, it is increasingly difficult to draw a clear line between the two because of the successful efforts of the artificial intelligence industry to build devices that emulate the higher human faculties, and of behavioral and cognitive psychologists to explain even complex human activities in terms of physiology, conditioning, and biochemistry. These successes suggest that the answer to "Could a machine act creatively?" and "Can human activities be completely programmed and controlled?" might be "Yes."

The possibilities that machines could act creatively and people could be programmed make many people anxious and resentful because, on the surface, they seem to deny the image that they hold of themselves as "free and autonomous beings" (which they fear is legitimate only if they occupy some nonmechanical niche in the scheme of things). Mechanism is perceived as entailing the reduction of humans to the status of puppets, prisoners, pawns, or worse.

> ### Bugbears
>
> Dan Dennett's *Elbow Room* and *Brainstorms* both speak to the anxieties that erode our self-image upon confronting wasps, clever machines, and the like. His exposition of the ways in which the free will problem presents itself is brilliant.

Neither the anxiety and resentment nor the thinking behind them are new. They were clear as early as the seventeenth century, when René Descartes argued in his *Meditations* that, although human minds are *not* automata, human bodies and all other animals *are*, in every regard; and Julien Offray de La Mettrie, agreeing that animals are automata in every regard, insisted in his *Man a Machine* that people are too.

People today tend to dismiss (and be amused by) industrial conceptions of Machine People. Gears and wheels that are noisy and leave puddles of oil on the floor seem quaint. The contemporary bogey consists of black-box gadgetry instead. But, whether cast in terms of gears and wheels, valves and tanks, or switches and semiconductors, Machine People stories all evince the same essential issue: "Can the nature and character of humans be fully understood in terms of straight input (design capacity plus programming) and output (behavior)?"

The notion that they can be was originally based on the success of New-tonian science at explaining the rest of the world's occurrences that way. Un-der that regime, unprecedented progress was made in every area of scientific inquiry from astronomy to agriculture. So someone like La Mettrie was in-evitably motivated to attempt the same kind of analysis of human events. The subsequent history of human biology and psychology suggests that the at-tempt was not ridiculous, for those disciplines have effectively and simply il-luminated many facets of the human organism and its operations using just this model. So the application of mechanistic explanation to human activity is not implausible on its face, even though its *perceived* implications for human "freedom and dignity" are off-putting.

2) A mechanistic explanation of event E in system S at time T (*S's output at T*) amounts to:

- a state description of S at T (S's functional capacity plus its dynamic his-tory up to T),
- an account of all forces bearing on S at T (S's input at T), and
- the rules of mechanics (the operating system in use).

Further, not only will this model explain S's doing E at T, it will also predict what S will do later (at T + n) and retrodict what S has done before (at T − n). The rules of mechanics are finite, closed, regular, and descriptive (i.e., they do not legislate, they simply report what occurs). They consist not only of very basic rules such as inertia and gravitational acceleration but also of very particular (and local) ones such as the rule for dominant and recessive genes. Imperfect explanations (present, predictive, or retrodictive) are solely the product of incomplete state descriptions, unknown input, or incompletely understood rules. It is all, in fact, a detailed formalization of the principle of sufficient reason.

3) If mechanism can be successfully applied to humans, it should enable a careful observer to give causal explanations of what individuals have done and are doing and predict what they will do in specified circumstances. It would achieve this by replacing the vague notion of understanding human action, which has no specific decision procedures, with the much more pre-cise notion of describing the genetically determined functional capacity, en-vironmentally provided inputs and reinforcements, and the relevant causal rules that collectively account for all behavior—which has all the decision procedures that are inherent in any empirical/experimental inquiry. As with ordinary events, any gaps in our account of human behavior would be solely the product of incomplete state descriptions, unknown input, or incompletely understood rules.

Example. Classical behaviorism, a twentieth-century application of physicalism to psychology, became the stalking horse for any physicalistic approach to the human sciences—a target for invective because of the perception that it denied that people have minds and that they are free and responsible.

According to some behaviorists, with sufficient information about humans and their behavior in the past, their conduct cannot only be described, causally explained, and predicted but also can be as easily controlled as that of any other closed causal system. This is the conceptual foundation for much twentieth-century talk about human engineering, planned economies, and utopian social organization. (See B. F. Skinner's *Beyond Freedom and Dignity*, Aldous Huxley's *Brave New World*, and George Orwell's *Nineteen Eighty-Four*.) All we need to add to make the picture complete is a little genetic manipulation; and that has become easy enough.

The first charge doesn't stick because it incorrectly reads behaviorism in particular (and psychology in general) as being necessarily committed to articulating its theories in terms of metaphysical substances while, in fact, they can be thoroughly "operationalized." The second charge, however, is more complicated, as we shall see.

3) Operationalism. Behaviorism, cognitive psychology, empirical anthropology, economics, and so forth, for all their denial of immaterial *substance*, need not be taken to deny that people have minds and put them to good use. All we need to do is "operationalize" the use of terms such as "mind" and "mental." This would amount to cashing out mind talk in terms of "operations" (such as planning, making judgments, getting angry, etc.) in which people observably engage, without any commitments or even concern about the kind of stuff it takes to do so. This, of course, is just what many natural scientists have long since done with labels such as "gravity," "mass," "kinetic energy," and the like. You don't need "gravity stuff" in order for physical systems to accelerate toward each other, and you don't need "mind stuff" in order for people to engage in all the regular enterprises of human life, from playing chess to making wishes.

a) The operationalization of natural science did not happen immediately, nor is it universal even today. In spite of the fact that the Newtonian approach heavily emphasized observation, it still made constant reference to a hypothesized (or inferred) substratum of physical objects causally connected with each other in objective space and time "behind" the appearances. Physical realism was implicit in every description and explanation.

Since that time, natural science's continent has drifted away from talk about the "substances" that may underwrite the appearances, and toward the operations themselves—which need not be inferred, hypothesized, or taken on faith because they are there to be seen.

Scientists still try, of course, to string observed events together in terms of theories. But even the theories (since they must be testable) are best seen as not about ineffable forces and ultimate stuff, but about operationally defined laws and principles that can be translated into (or imply) confirmable hypotheses about observable phenomena.

The scientific community has not altogether abandoned talk about unobservables. But, by and large, it accepts them into the system only as far as their explanatory use generates testable output and defines them *in terms of that output*. So it has not had to abandon its traditional vocabulary. Its literature is still replete with words like "force," "particle," and "wave," but it has redefined them. "Gravity," for instance, is simply a term for the predictable regularity of observable accelerations. So while some say the point of science is to "understand basic reality" (which sounds like substance talk), what that amounts to is best understood as simply anticipating and controlling observable events. "Understanding" in working dress *is* knowing what is likely to happen next; and confining attention to the description and explanation of what we can observe (and curtailing speculation about what may or may not be irremediably concealed "behind" it) has the salutary effect of actually increasing predictive efficiency.

b) The practical motivation behind operationalizing *human* science is a desire to get it on the same efficient footing. The supposition is that if we discuss *people* in terms of what is observable (rather than in terms of ineffable substances, powers, and faculties), we will sharply increase foresight and understanding about *them*.

So even as "gravity" is just a word for observable accelerations (understood in terms of mathematical and mechanical laws), so "anger" may be just a word for observable animal behaviors and dispositions (understood in terms of biological and chemical processes). In just this way, cognitive psychology may yet do for linguistic phenomena what physics has long since done for astronomical ones. It seems to be on its way, as is evident in such works as Steven Pinker's *The Language Instinct*, but some, such as Noam Chomsky, demur. (See his *Knowledge of Language: Its Nature, Origin, and Use*.)

"Operational" views are committed to the following principles:

- The only things that count in describing and explaining human events are things that are observable and testable.
- Words, notions, or ideas that don't carry observational freight are unacceptable in explanations and descriptions.
- All acceptable accounts are generalized from, constructed out of, or confirmable in terms of observations.

A hard-liner might conclude that operationalizing mental language is impossible and that, consequently, the traditional vocabulary should be abandoned altogether. George Lundberg, a classic hard-liner, epitomized in his *Foundations of Sociology* what most alarms traditionalists, claiming that there is no difference (other than complexity) between a leaf being blown by the wind and a person fleeing a lynch mob.

To abandon the old vocabulary, according to its proponents, would have the salutary effect of weeding out much of the undergrowth that has historically interfered with systematic attempts at understanding how people tick. Jettisoning talk about agencies, powers, faculties, minds, and souls would clear the path for human science and permanently shelve the never-were-science projects of Descartes, Wundt, and Freud.

Slightly more lenient theorists, while granting that such translations are difficult and still incomplete, remain confident that the exchange can be made. They allow the traditional vocabulary of words such as "self-consciousness," "motives," and "mind"—as long as we remember what the words mean, operationally, and avoid slipping back into their traditional (substantial) interpretation.

In this view, words such as "mind," "intention," "decision," and "reflection" are not at risk unless they cannot be operationally defined in terms of observable behaviors, behavior patterns, and dispositions. Operationally seen, mind talk is not about an inaccessible aspatial appendage inexplicably linked to our spatially located organs. It is about behaviors in which humans engage, dispositions or propensities that they display, and the complex organic system that supports such activities.

So this perspective does not "eliminate the mind." It only reanalyzes what the word "mind" means. It does not say that people have no minds, only that talk about having (or not having) a mind is misleading. Minds are not things (or even parathings) to have *or* to lack. People are organisms that can think, intend, and decide, and the like, regardless of what they are "made of."

Thus, although operationalists eliminate empty references to covert substances, they still leave room for a full narrative about what can be observed. It must be noted, however, that what can be observed in Lundberg's lynch mob fugitive includes fear; something that is never observed in leaves. There are innumerable differences in what can be observed in these two cases. Both can be described in empirical terms, but not necessarily the same ones. Both can be mapped, predicted, controlled, and understood without any talk of mysterious and inaccessible inner stuff; but the fugitive story will involve references to behavior patterns and dispositions that are completely alien to leaves.

Many, however, feel that such translations are illegitimate because they cannot be made without severe loss to what needs to be said about people. To them, efforts to operationalize words like "choose" demean and lessen human status. They feel that such accounts remove the notions of autonomy, responsibility, and integrity from the map of human nature by categorically denying human freedom and choice.

4) Are freedom and dignity passé? Since operationalism, even if it is truly "ontology free," remains committed to mechanical causation, can we go this route without precluding human creativity, choice, autonomy, and dignity? Does it not reduce human beings to automata, caught up in events not of their making and beyond their control? If so then isn't it a distorted, truncated, and sterile view of the organism?

To establish that, we would have to show that mechanical causation *is* "strictly determined" and that "strict determinism" *does* preclude human creativity, freedom, autonomy, and dignity. If both of those allegations were true, then operational psychology might undercut some crucial conceptual foundations of the present culture, necessitating both theoretical and practical alterations to our conception of human nature, social order, education, family, law, and morality.

So the implications of mechanical causation are crucial. Mechanical causation, it is said, explains away or ignores precisely those human dimensions that most essentially define humans—it denies people's freedom and dignity, their responsibility for what they do, their creativity, and even their capacity for linguistic innovation. It reduces individuals to puppets or automata, and society to a well-ordered anthill; and those reductions, it is said, are too high a price to pay merely to expand the theoretical unity of scientific explanation.

On the other hand, while it is easy to see why we might object to mechanism (assuming that it does have these implications), the clinical and experimental use of cause and effect analyses of human activities has thrown immense light on how people function and (hence) on how they can be anticipated, understood, altered, and controlled.

- In the same way that we can use a state description of a physical system to predict its output under specified conditions, we can use a state description of a human to predict its output as varying stimuli are brought to bear on it.
- In the same way that the results of experimental animal psychology show the profit to be gained by considering humans as animals, the results of modern psychiatry (especially by way of drugs) show the profit that can be gained by considering humans as physical input/output systems.

So human activities *are* predictable and controllable, and no model that ignores genetically determined capacities and environmentally determined reinforcements can possibly render that prediction and control intelligible.

Thus, I think that it would be as wrong to give a blanket "No" to "Are humans mechanisms?" as it would be to give a blanket "No" to "Are humans animals?" It would be folly to dismiss *any* illumination and understanding of the species, however uncomfortable we may feel as we confront the model that provides it, and however great our ego involvement in the specie's threatened "status."

Nevertheless, a mechanistic view of human nature does seem to threaten human freedom and everything that is alleged to ride with it. Is that threat real? Does mechanism entail strict determinism? Does determinism actually rule out all notions of choice and responsibility?

In the next chapter, I will grant that mechanism does entail strict determinism but will argue that the status of people as free, responsible, and autonomous can still be maintained in behavioral terms. Indeed, I will argue that strict causation is a necessary condition of human "freedom and dignity"—that these phenomena are impossible in any other account of how people tick.

11

Causation, Freedom, and Human Responsibility

So far, a little light has been shed on human nature: On the one hand, people are social animals, at home in the natural order and subject to its vicissitudes. They are the children not only of their parents but of their culture; and they are players—along with every other thing—in the arena of events. They may be more mobile than parsnips, smarter than 'possums, and more adaptable than either; but they are born, live out their lives driven by appetites and confined by circumstances, and they die. On the other hand, three characteristics are usually thought to set them apart from everything else: they use language not only to communicate but also to record and retain what they learn from one generation to the next; they are self-aware; and they function as free agents, responsible for what they do. There is a problem with this emerging map of human nature, however. The notion that humans—like everything else in the world—operate under the strict rule of cause and effect seems to conflict with the notion that they are free and responsible.

D. Human agency and causation. The idea of human agency amounts to the notion that people sometimes engage in *action* as opposed to mere behavior. Actions are things they *choose* to do in ways that make them *responsible* for outcomes and open to praise or blame. Agency, then, is a crucial underwriting concept for such human institutions as morality, social ethics, law, and education.

1) We often impute positive credit (praise) or negative credit (blame) to people for their conduct.

> *Examples.* The text of a scheduled test vanished from my office, so I wrote a new one (similar but not quite the same) and gave it on test day. Most of the students did a fair job on the questions asked. A few did very well or very badly on the questions asked. One student, however, did a superb job—but on the questions on the *original* test rather than the one I gave.

The Boys' Club was on an outing at the beach, and the kids were playing in the surf when a thunderstorm blew up suddenly. Lightning was crackling just a few hundred yards offshore. The lifeguard blew her whistle to clear the beach, but one boy ignored her. So she bravely plunged in and removed him from harm's way.

2) We must be careful to impute responsibility only where it belongs. For instance, it is unreasonable to blame or praise A for something B did. But attributing responsibility to the wrong party is only one way to misplace it. An act may not be A's responsibility without being anyone else's. It may not be *anybody's* responsibility, or A may be responsible only in a diminished way. Many conditions and circumstances cancel or diminish an individual's responsibility; and whatever the reason, when that is canceled or diminished, so is the reasonableness of rewards and penalties.

Examples. A student with clinically verifiable image-flipping dyslexia confuses *modus ponens* with affirming the consequent and *modus tollens* with denying the antecedent. So he makes mistakes constructing proofs and cannot pass Symbolic Logic—a degree requirement. Is it reasonable to block his graduation?

Salley was caught rifling the drink machine where he worked but said it was because Cabot had threatened to kneecap him with a tire iron if he refused. Who is it reasonable to fire?

Crystal, thirteen, is frightened when she hears the Voice. When she was little, it said she was good. Now it says she should burn forever because she's having orgasms when Daddy takes her. But, it says, she can avoid hellfire by burning herself now. Her legs covered with cigarette burns, she has started having thoughts about Daddy: "He likes it even more than me. Maybe I need to spare him from hell, too." If she torches him, who's to blame?

Bruce lay dead on the green in front of the Commons with his throat cut, and Ted stood over his body with a bloody knife when the police arrived. When asked why he did it, Ted said, "I didn't do anything. Don't blame me! Look at me!" They did, and found slender strings attached to his wrists, ankles, and so forth, that ran up into the sky. "Good Lord," they said, "he's just a puppet, dancing on strings!" (This story is less plausible than the others; but, if it *were* true, no one would blame Ted. He didn't kill Bruce, the string puller did. But what if the "strings" went back in time rather than up in space? That possibility will be examined.)

It is more common to recognize diminished responsibility for bad output than to recognize diminished responsibility for good output. We tend to praise people for good output whether they deserve it or not. But good deeds that people cannot avoid are a shaky foundation for praise and medals. Credit, like blame, presumes choice.

Examples. Joel, who could do square roots in his head at age six, couldn't understand why his college friend, Cheryl, had trouble with differential equations. "They're so obvious," he said. He knew that her parents sent her $100 every time she made B or better on a math test and wondered why his didn't do the same. "After all," he reflected, "I deserve it more than she does."

From early childhood, Marjoe memorized Bible passages by repetition and reinforcement. On really long ones, his mother would hold his head under water in the bathtub until he got them right. By his teens, he could recite any verse from the Gospels on demand. Making a bundle on the tent revival circuit as a boy preacher, he took it as God's reward for devotion to His word.

The next day, Craig was to be featured in the local paper as philanthropist of the year. He sent big checks to many charities. Indeed, he gave away half of his income every year, even though he despised what he thought of as "parasites" and resented every cent he gave away. Recalling that "it is harder for a rich man to enter the Kingdom of Heaven than for a camel to pass through the eye of a needle," and shuddering at the image of a particular Hieronymus Bosch painting that leaped into his mind, he said to himself, "I sure hope God reads tomorrow's paper."

3) The responsibility/mechanism cramp. According to many, the notion that humans are sometimes responsible for what they do is contradicted by the fact that everything a person does can be fully explained in terms of cause and effect. In this view, people never *act*. They only *behave*. If so they are never responsible for what they do and never deserve praise or blame. No one may actually be a puppet on strings like poor Ted, but everyone dances at the command of prior events.

a) The causal/mechanistic conception of people is an extension of the classical Newtonian view that the physical world is an arena of matter

> ### Determinism, Predestination, and Fatalism
>
> Causal determinism should not be conflated with the theological doctrine of predestination. It says nothing about intentions. So "Who cast the dice?" is not the question on the table.
>
> Nor should it be conflated with fatalism. It restricts every event, not just final outcomes. So "Will any road I take go to the same place?" is not the question on the table either.
>
> The question on the table is, "Can human behavior be completely described, explained, and predicted in terms of strict causation?"

in motion. In that view, we can fully understand, explain, and predict events by looking only at their constituents, the cause and effect relationships in which those constituents stand, and the uniform rules of mechanics. This view is called "strict causal determinism."

b) Strict causal determinism rules out the possibility of spontaneously generated events.

Example. If, while sorting rubble at Tel el Amarna, an archeologist found a bronze hammer, she would presume that it was put there or left there at some time in the past. She wouldn't even entertain "spontaneous generation" as an explanation. If hammers just appeared, doing archeology would be pointless. And besides, that has been ruled out, experimentally. (One experiment involved putting gauze over a container of fresh meat on a windowsill to see if maggots would appear on the meat. They didn't, because the flies couldn't get to it. The maggots appeared on the gauze.)

Strict causal determinism also insists that where the same cause occurs, the same effect is forthcoming. Irregularity is out, too.

Example. Typing away at my computer on a still, dry winter day in Charlottesville, I do not worry that Orchard House will suddenly collapse. But if it did, the authorities would not only assume that *something* caused it. They would also have a good idea of *what* caused it and would know how to go about pinning the cause down.

Their search for an explanation would start with a review of similar events with known causes. Buildings regularly collapse because of war, sabotage, explosions, shoddy construction, earthquakes, windstorms, and mudslides. If Orchard House (which is not on a gas main) did collapse on a peaceful, ordinary, dry, still, earthquake-free day, the authorities might look for traces of portable explosives. If they found none, they would call in engineers to examine the rubble for signs of material or design flaws. Careful observation and the process of elimination would bring them to a probable account. But, if causation were not regular, investigation would be pointless.

c) Nonspontaneity and regularity have a number of salutary effects. One is that "practice makes perfect."

Example. Those who enter pool tournaments practice first. But the point of practice is regular causation. If a ball's path were not uniformly set by the way we hit it, why practice?

d) Strict determinism is the foundation of modern science. We could not gain control over events unless they are predictable; and, barring occult methods of prediction, they are not predictable if they "just happen" or happen irregularly. Under those circumstances, we could only "go with the flow" wherever it might wander—which is precisely what people did in prescientific times.

e) It is one thing to talk in such terms about planets, comets, avalanches, tides, and the like. But it seems quite another to talk in such terms about humans and everything they do. Is human activity determined in this way: never spontaneous and never irregular?

Some factors that diminish or eliminate responsibility are obvious: organic deficiencies, accidents, posthypnotic suggestions, threats, torture, physical manipulation, and so forth. Genetic predisposition and ordinary environmental events take their toll as well. But who can escape them? Heredity and environment make us what we are. Indeed, if the causal assumption does apply to people as it does to billiard balls and tidal waves, then humans are never in a position to do anything other than what they in fact do. If physical events are the necessary consequences of natural history, then they are inevitable; and if people always do just what they (causally) have to, then they are all riding through Marrakech with Doris Day on the back seat of that bus singing "*Que Sera, Sera.*"

(1) In fact, explanations of people's activities *are* often cast in deterministic terms. For instance, we can predict behavior in particular circumstances, anticipate regular behavior from individuals, and make a profit selling insurance. The anticipation and prediction is usually statistical, not individual, of course: "A male teen is unlikely to have a heart attack, but very likely to have a collision." The statistics, however, are very precise.

This is not to claim that anyone can always exactly predict what humans will do. No one can do that today. But this present inability may not be the product of some mysterious, dark, and inherently opaque side of human nature. It might be only because no one has enough of the requisite data in hand. But that is a contingent (changeable) state of affairs, as any strict determinist would certainly note.

There are many reasons why no one has enough data. It is easier to put a rat through its paces in a controlled environment than a human. Much human experimentation is frowned on by society at large. So a great deal of data that we would need to run really good predictions of human behavior is missing.

(2) But if people are strictly "in" the causal network, they *never* have options. They can *never* do other than what they do, no matter what that is. And everything that they do is thoroughly predictable, in principle.

> *Example.* Consider Ted and Bruce again:
> If what we do today is the product of what we are today and the causal network now in play; and if what we are today is the product of what we were yesterday and the causal network then in play; and if a state description that captures yesterday is entailed by the state description of day-before-yesterday, and so forth, then Ted's attack on Bruce today was inevitable.
> Consequently, that event was predictable yesterday, a year ago, or even a thousand years before Ted's or Bruce's birth. In principle, we could have said at the Battle of Hastings that "Ted will attack Bruce in 2005." The only thing missing at that early date was sufficient information to provide the initial state description on which causal predictions depend. (God, having all the data in hand, of course, could have said it at any of those times—or even on October 22, 4004 B.C., right after saying, "Let there be Light.")

But if we could never do anything except what we *do* do, it would never make sense to praise or blame anyone for anything.

> *Caution.* Note that this is not because what we *do* do is predictable. It is because the sufficient conditions of what we *do* do *have already occurred*. Predictability is a *result* of causal determination, not what it amounts to. Predictability might obtain even if causal determination did not. Indeed, predictability is incorporated into numerous fatalistic or occult theories about history that do not affirm universal uniform causation at all.

f) The fact that people go right on praising and blaming is inevitable, too. And so is the fact that reasonable people will realize that such praise and blame is footless. It is rather like a snake swallowing its tail. *Everything* that happens is inevitable.

Not everything that happens is reasonable, however. It may be that I am causally obliged to say to a student who cheats, "Shame on you!" and to have nothing to do with him. But it is quite unreasonable for me to react this way. The cheating was not his doing. The dice have been thrown. Blame talk and praise talk are "sound and fury, signifying nothing."

It is not surprising, consequently, that many people believe that the application of strict determinism to humans simply puts paid to the possibility of moral and legal judgment, and to enterprises like education and social ethics as well.

> *Examples.* Teachers may assume that helping people learn to internalize alternatives, think about reasons, and weigh evidence is better than simply manipulating them. But why waste weeks trying to get Jody to *understand* division? All we need to get correct responses is a little amorbarbitol and scopolamine and a strong stomach.
>
> Similarly, if people are going to have to work in the uranium mine, why try to *convince* them that it is nice to work on their hands and knees in a hole in the ground at a temperature of 116°? *Convincing* is much too hard. It is easier to start them on behavior modification at eleven weeks. It is easier still to start with proper additives to the blood surrogate mix before decanting. By Ford, it ought to work!

"Brainwashing, propagandizing, and indoctrination" may be less appealing than "informing, teaching, and convincing;" but differentiating such labels presumes a genuine and discernible difference between "objects in the causal network" and "responsible autonomous agents who have *reasons* for what they do." If that difference is spurious, then the only difference between (say) brainwashing and informing is the difference between efficiency and inefficiency, plus a little bit of emotive freight.

4) Something has gone dreadfully awry. The concepts of mechanism and responsibility both look like useful tools for analyzing human events, but they are "obviously" incompatible. Consequently, we can only hold on to mechanism and abandon responsibility or hold on to responsibility and abandon mechanism, unless we can show—not just assert—a way to maintain both coherently.

That is so difficult, however, that those who want to preserve the reasonable use of "responsible" usually deny that people and their activities are determined this way. They argue:

> P1. if causal determinism applies to people, then responsible action is impossible; but

P2. causal determinism doesn't apply to people; so

∴ C. responsible action is possible.

That is not enough, however. Denying the antecedent is invalid.

> *Example*. If someone told me, "Taking cyanide now is incompatible with your living until tomorrow," and I decided, "O.K. I won't take cyanide now," that does not guarantee that I will live until tomorrow. I might be run down by a truck on my way to lunch.

On the other hand, if causal determinism is, in fact, incompatible with responsibility, and if humans are, in fact, responsible, then of course they are not causally determined (*modus tollens* still works.) But that line of argument is unprofitable because it is question begging, if the issue at stake is whether people are, in fact, responsible.

Further, for any account of human nature to be illuminating, it needs to explain how people do operate, not just how they don't, and show that the actual mode of operation (whatever it is) does not undercut responsibility just as badly as mechanism allegedly does.

Nevertheless, if we assume that strict causation rules out responsibility (an assumption which I will not yet question), the defense of responsibility must start with a refutation of strict causation.

Once that refutation has been achieved (if it can be), we could move on to ask how human activities do work. Two hypotheses have been offered. One is that they are *random*. The other is that they are *de novo*. Unfortunately, as will be seen, it is more difficult to maintain human responsibility for random events than for strictly determined ones. And, although a number of alleged examples of de novo phenomena have been suggested, there has been little explanation of how they work or how their processes (unlike mechanical ones) support responsibility.

5) Claiming that everything else in the world is caused, but people aren't—"That's that, and there's nothing more to say"—is far too ad hoc. It is more plausible to argue that strict causation does not *generally* hold, even in places and situations far removed from human affairs. If strict causation has numerous gaps and holes, then why not have a convenient one in the human neighborhood?

Consequently, many who were less concerned about physics than about freedom and dignity welcomed Werner Heisenberg's indeterminacy theory, thinking its apparently noncausal view of the world's fabric was applicable to human activity without strain. (Indeed, he said so himself in *Physics and Philosophy*.) I will examine his contribution under three headings:

- What does Indeterminism amount to?
- Is it true of human affairs?
- Does it salvage human responsibility?

a) Recall that in Newton's view, events are ordered by causal laws, such that if we understand the laws and have a thorough state description of the world (or a closed part of it) at a particular time, we can produce accurate state descriptions of the world (or the same part of it) at any other time.

In the twentieth century, however, many researchers noted phenomena that do not seem to fit this picture. These phenomena do not have to do with human conduct. They are in the world of physics—the behavior of particles and waves—the very things that, in Newton's view, *should* strictly follow causal laws. There are, for instance, experiments with light propagation —where light is projected through slots in a screen—where, in Newton's view, we should be able to predict what light will go through which slot, but can't.

Committed determinists have two lines of reply.

(1) "We just don't know all the causal laws yet. There may be many more to uncover. So we will keep looking." Preserving regularity by writing off "gaps" as the result of contingent ignorance is the way anomalies are usually handled. This is usually adequate.

(2) "It is impossible to get an initial state description here. Every Newtonian prediction is based on a complete state description plus causal laws, so where state descriptions are not available Newtonian predictions can't be run. This has nothing to do with causal laws breaking down." To get a state description of a system that is adequate for prediction, we must find the location and vector of every item in it. But the items in some systems are so small, relative to the only signals available, that locating them alters their dynamics and measuring their dynamics dislocates them. So on this account, the fact that the input needed for predicting them is always incomplete is a contingent function of the available instrumentation, not an inherent feature of the world.

Analogy: We want to identify the location and vector of one hundred Ping-Pong balls rolling around on the floor of an otherwise empty room, but the only available instrument is a bowling ball fitted with suitable telemetry. (We roll it through the room in a systematic fashion, and whenever it hits a Ping-Pong ball it sends a signal giving the coordinates of the point of impact, etc.) This generates a map that shows where each Ping-Pong ball was when it was run over by the bowling ball, and a floor covered with flat (and stationary) former Ping-Pong balls.

That is the situation we are in when trying to map little particles. There is no signal we can bounce off of one (to find out where it is and how it is going) without either displacing it or altering its vector. So no complete state description is available, and no Newtonian predictions or retrodictions can be run.

Heisenberg, however, contended that such excuses are not the reason why Newtonian predictions fail at the subatomic level. He thought that their failure, in fact, is an inevitable part of the way things are, not just an accident of relatively gross instrumentation, bad luck, or lack of ingenuity at finding laws. No matter how refined our instruments might be, and no matter how minute our signals, there would still be indeterminateness there. It is *built in.*

His contention is supported by additional phenomena that, while they can be predicted statistically, cannot be predicted individually.

> *Example.* Radioactive elements have an identifiable half-life, that is, the amount of time it takes for half of a sample of a particular element to shift down a step in its distinctive pattern of "decay."
>
> Instructron, for instance, has a half-life of fifteen years. In that time, half of any sample of instructron atoms will (each emitting an integrity particle accompanied by an ambition wave) become administron atoms. So if we know the size of an instructron sample, we can predict the number of integrity particles that will be ejected over any fixed period. This is because we know just how many instructron atoms will shift down in that time.
>
> But we cannot predict which of the atoms will degenerate. Suppose that we could line them up and assign them names, Sam, Myra, et al. There is no way to say that Sam will go next April 29, but Myra will wait until July. There is not even any way to say that when the prescribed time has elapsed that these five hundred will be gone and these five hundred will not. The only thing that we can say is that half of however many there are will go each time the half-life period rolls by. We don't know which ones, and we can't find out which ones.
>
> That is disturbing. If this one rather than that one decays, there should be a cause; and if there is a cause the results should be predictable.

Heisenberg's theory, however, explains why not. All physical events are indeterminate to a degree, but the degree is inversely proportional to mass, according to a precise formula. So if we know the mass of a thing, we also know just how indeterminate its behavior will be. The indeterminateness will be discernible only for items that have very low mass. By the time we reach items with the heft of a hydrogen atom (which is not terribly big as things go), the indeterminacy has dropped off to an extremely minute level, and strict Newtonian prediction and retrodiction are possible.

So *discernible* indeterminateness is confined to extremely minute particles, wave packets and the like, and classical mechanics holds at the observable level as a special case of indeterminism reaching the vanishing point as a function of increasing mass. But as mass decreases, the indeterminateness increases until events appear to be absolutely random.

That has provoked argument; but the argument is not about whether the phenomena occur. It is about what to say about them *when* they occur. Most physicists ride with the Heisenbergian view: indeterminateness is part of the system in principle, and not a product of either circumstance or instrumentation. Some others argue that it is a product of instrumentation or inadequate theory, and that all physical systems are determinate even where they are not, circumstantially, predictable. But everyone now grants that (for whatever reasons, contingent or necessary) there are events that simply cannot be mapped and forecast in the way that Newton suggested everything could be.

This view seems to describe how things work sufficiently well that it has been incorporated as a standard pattern of contemporary physics. I will assume, consequently, for argument's sake, that it is correct. The question for me is, "What implications does any of this have for understanding people and their behaviors and actions?"

b) Does built-in indeterminism apply to people and how they operate? It obviously doesn't if we are talking about people as *things*. Human beings are moderately large and fairly dense. Such hefty objects are well above the line, and safely in the determinate domain.

But this is beside the point. Granted, if people were folded up and rolled around the floor, their interactions would be determinate in the Newtonian way. But the issue is human *conduct*—what people "think," "intend," "decide," "will," and "choose" to do. These phenomena are not like rolling two-hundred-pound objects across the floor. They are, rather, deeply internal to the organism, somewhere in the inner workings of the central nervous system. They begin in transactions at the subcellular level that may amount to the discharge of a single neuron, or the deflection of such a discharge by a chemical tag constituting a memory trace.

> ### How Indeterminate Is Indeterminism?
>
> We might keep the notion that the world is determinate but revise our account of how its determination works. Perhaps the flaw in Newton's system is the notion that vectors can be mapped with four-dimensional coordinates. Replace that with an account of wave functions, and we can continue predicting future states (even at the sub-sublevel). But the prediction will be stated in terms of wave functions, too. This keeps the world determinate but changes the mathematics of "mapping" it and the meaning of "state description."

So when we track a human organism's internal causal network back to the neural roots of deciding, intending, willing, and so forth, we arrive at phenomena of sufficiently low mass that Heisenberg's principle *does* come into effect. So ultimately, human actions *are* indeterminate.

While such a view is not totally implausible on its face, it does depend on three arguable assumptions:

P1. Human actions and behaviors can be traced back to processes in the central nervous system.

P2. Those processes can be reduced to physical and chemical transactions within and between nerve cells.

P3. The vehicles of those transactions are sufficiently low mass to be covered by Heisenberg's principle.

From these three assumptions, it would be valid to infer:

∴ C1. Human actions and behaviors begin with unpredictable transactions.

On the other hand, if one (or more) of these three assumptions is (are) false, the argument is unsound, even though it is valid, and Heisenberg's principle would not have been shown to apply to human conduct.

Indeed, even if they are all true, it takes a fourth premise to reach the conclusion that human actions and behaviors are not just unpredictable but uncaused as well:

P4. Heisenberg's own interpretation of the indeterminacy principle is correct.

∴ C2. The beginnings of human conduct slip the causal net.

If this added premise is *not* true, the application of the indeterminacy principle to human conduct has no clear implications for responsibility one way or the other. What is at stake is whether the unpredictability is merely *de facto* or is *per principium*. If it is the former (due, say, to ignorance), causal necessity could still be in play.

> *Demonstration.* Let C = *caused*, PP = *predictable in principle* and PF = *predictable in fact*. Then, even if $(x)[\sim PPx \supset \sim Cx]$, it would not follow that $(x)[\sim PFx \supset \sim Cx]$; given that the transposition of the former, $(x)[Cx \supset PPx]$, is possibly true, and the transposition of the latter, $(x)[Cx \supset PFx]$, is known to be false. QED.

If all four premises *are* true, however, then human actions are, at root, *random*. Consequently, no mechanistic roadblock of an individual's responsibility for his own actions would come into play.

We might think that this theory—by providing an "out" from lockstep mechanism—will save the day for morality, law, education, and the like. That would work, however, only if a lack of inevitability due to randomness is enough, by itself, to assure responsibility; and, as will be seen, responsibility can be blocked in more than one way.

c) People who apply Heisenberg's principle to human action do so because they want to salvage choice, responsibility, and the moral enterprise. They do not do it because experimental data shows that decisions actually begin in neural transactions. They *assume* they do, because they think that assumption provides a way to rescue freedom from causal bondage. In fact, however, if decisions begin in neural transactions and those neural transactions are *random*, then "free choice" (so seen) is a mockery, and while responsibility has been saved from the alleged troll under universal causation's bridge, it has been delivered into the hands of a more fearsome ogre.

Revised Example. Bruce's throat is cut, and Ted is standing there. When an officer arrives, the following dialogue ensues:

O: What happened here?

T: I just cut his throat.

O: I can see that, he's still warm. Did you have a seizure?

T: I don't have seizures. And I didn't say that I *recently* cut his throat. I said I *just* cut it.

O: Why did you do that, for God's sake?

T: No reason, man. Don't you listen? I *just did it*.

O: Were you mad at him?

T: Not at all. We're friends. Hello?

O: Did you plan it out? Wait for him? Hide the knife at first?

T: Not that I recall.

O: Did you hear voices telling you what to do?

T: Heavens, no.

O: Do you do this sort of thing often?

T: I don't really think that I'm the killer *type*, if that is what you mean. Look. When I said I *just* cut his throat, I meant *merely*. That's it, the whole story. I *just did it*.

O: What do you mean, you "just" cut his throat merely? People don't "just do things."

T: Sure they do; and this is one. Nothing *made* me do it. It wasn't anything like a spasm or twitch; I don't have compulsions or hear voices, and I'm not wired to somebody in the sky. Intentions, purposes, and goals had nothing to do with it. I had no reason or grounds, and it certainly had nothing to do with my character and disposition. It wasn't something that I was born to do or brought up to do. It was, in fact, just something to do. I could just as easily have done something else. The last time I saw him, I bought him a coffee. This time, cutting his throat just popped into my head like, you know, *at random*.

O: Cool. I understand now. I took philosophy once, and we talked about stuff like that. Once in a while things happen that can't be traced back to *anything at all*. They're not the result of *any* sufficient condition being met. They just *come down*. Awesome. Now lie face down on the grass and put your hands behind your back while I cuff you and read you your rights. That's what comes down next.

If Ted's story is sincere (and he isn't just bobbing and weaving to *evade* responsibility), he is certainly not to blame for Bruce's death. He may be an appropriate target for therapy and seclusion, but not for moral appraisal. He (like Manson) is a walking paradigm of diminished responsibility. Furthermore, sincere or not, if his story is *true*, he is off the "responsibility hook" altogether, along with the rest of us. *No* one is responsible when causation "takes a holiday."

If we want to talk about Ted being responsible for cutting Bruce's throat, the first thing we must establish (not sever) is a set of connections between the kind of person Ted is, the kinds of things he generally tries to do, the kinds of motives that he has, and the particular thing that he has done this time. To say that the event is the unpredictable result of random discharges is the very antithesis of such a program. We would find no use whatever for words such as "praiseworthy" and "blameworthy" in the context of any such "Things Come Down" analysis of human deeds.

Ordinarily, we assume that (normal) adults are responsible for most of what they do. So if Ted did do this (i.e., if it was not done by someone else, now hiding in the bushes), we will assume his responsibility and start looking for motives, and so forth—unless there are clear mitigating factors (in his character and capacities, or in the concrete situation) to show that his responsibility is "diminished." Diminished responsibility is narrowly defined and case bound.

But the "mitigation" on the table here is neither narrow nor case bound. On the indeterminists' account, it applies to every human activity that involves neural functions; and on any physicalistic account, that is all of them. That is why "No one is responsible when causation 'takes a holiday.'" So any claim that people are genuinely responsible for what they choose to do (because choosing involves neural functions and is, hence, random and indeterminate) is just a howler.

There is a great deal more at stake here than the absurdity of blaming people for randomly generated deaths.

> *Example.* Professor Erb believes that no music student deserves credit for having a good ear. It is just a "gift of the gods." (That is an old fashioned way of saying it "comes down.") But every music major is required to take Solfeggio, which the chair has assigned to Erb this year. So Erb gets an algorithm from the electronic composition professor and has his computer assign the grades randomly.
>
> If Erb is right in thinking that having a good ear is a random event, his grading method is not unreasonable. But Professor Myers, who hears about Erb's plan, is a student of Heisenberg and believes that every human decision begins in random neural events—even the decision to study for an exam rather than blow it off. So he borrows the same algorithm and gives random grades to all of the students in his premed chemistry class. "People," he says, "who can work lab problems because they chanced to study, and people who can't because they chanced not to, will all be graded by chance." However consistent, Myers's scheme has scary implications.

This story has a perfectly general point. To undergird responsibility, we need to be able to trace actions back to phenomena over which the organism has reliable control. But no one has reliable control of random events, inside her head or elsewhere. So no one is responsible for such things. Random zaps in the neighborhood, or even in our innards, are not to our credit or blame. While it may be that strict determinism links our acts too tightly to events over which we have no control, that is not remedied by severing all of those acts' causal connections. It is the tight links between our character and dispositions and our acts that make us accountable for them; and in a world of random events those links are gone. Whether or not automata can make responsible choices, dice can't.

6) A hard dilemma.

> P1. If human acts are the inevitable product of prior events, then the notion that people are ever responsible for their acts is untenable. We cannot be responsible for events that were cast in stone before our birth.
>
> P2. If human acts are random, then the notion that people are ever responsible for their acts is untenable. We cannot be responsible for events that just come down.
>
> P3. So if determinism is true or if indeterminism is true, people are not responsible for what they do.
>
> P4. But, necessarily, either determinism or indeterminism is true.
>
> ∴ C. People are not responsible for what they do.

We can formalize this argument as follows, calling determinism D, indeterminism ~D, and responsibility R,

1. $D \supset {\sim}R$
2. ${\sim}D \supset {\sim}R$
3. $D \vee {\sim}D$ ∴ ${\sim}R$
4. $(D \supset {\sim}R) \cdot ({\sim}D \supset {\sim}R)$ 1, 2   Conjunction
5. ${\sim}R \vee {\sim}R$ 4, 3   Constructive Dilemma
6. ${\sim}R$ 5   Tautology

So if we are inclined to say, as I think all human intuitions suggest and all social systems assume, that people *are* sometimes responsible for their actions, we must show that this valid argument is unsound.

If a valid argument is not sound, then at least one of its premises must be false. To deny this particular conclusion, then, we must find either determinism or indeterminism to be compatible with responsibility, or show that they are not complementary notions and, hence, constitute a false dilemma. Since I see no hope whatever of holding people responsible for random events, unless one of the two other alternatives works, the elimination of responsibility is complete.

7) So to escape this rout, we must show either that determinism and indeterminism are not complementary, and that, consequently, it is possible for human actions to escape both categories, or that responsibility *is* compatible with strict causation, appearances to the contrary. I shall briefly explore and reject the first option and then offer an analysis of actions and agents that fulfills the second.

a) Not all pairs of apparently complementary terms are truly complementary. If two terms look complementary but aren't, then what looks like a real dilemma may be a false one. When confronted with a false dilemma, we need not choose a horn on which to impale ourselves. We can "leap between the horns."

> **What Is Complementarity?**
>
> The complement of a set is everything that is not a member of it. So the sum of a set and its complement is everything. It is common to name a complement by attaching a prefix like "non" or "im" to the base class's name. Most "opposites," however, are not complementary. Heroes plus cowards does not exhaust the universe (even the universe of persons). The most common mistake with complementarity is to take two classes as complementary that are not collectively exhaustive: to reason, for instance, that anything that is not male must be female (or vice versa).

Attempting such a leap, Stephen Cahn suggested, in his *Philosophical Explorations: Freedom, God, and Goodness,* that while the causal network does not include every event, not all of the events that it excludes are random. Some events have causal connections; so we cannot be responsible for them. Some are random; so we cannot be responsible for them, either. So if there are any acts for which people *are* responsible, those acts must be neither determined nor indetermined. The third option consists of acts that *originate* in an agent's goals, intentions, purposes, and motives. Such acts are neither caused nor random. They are *purposed*; and because they are, charge tickets can be sent. Responsibility for them is blocked by neither mechanism nor a lack of "connections."

Though it is well intended, I am not convinced by Cahn's move because I see no reason to exclude goal-directed, purposive, or intentional acts from the causal network. In any empirical account, an individual's "purposings" are just as causally determinate (by their character and upbringing) as the rest of their features, attributes, and activities—a point well made by John Hospers many years ago in his "What Means This Freedom." So Cahn's gambit doesn't succeed at breaking out of the causal network. If, as Cahn argues, causation really is incompatible with responsible freedom, then "purposed" acts are no more free and responsible than ones that are caused in other ways.

Doing X for a purpose is quite different from being manipulated into doing it; but the difference is due to the *kind* of causes in play, not to any lack of them. That we have certain purposes in mind (when we do) is part of what causes us to act the way we do. A purpose, as such, may not be a cause itself, but the having of a purpose is. Similarly, temperament and experience cause us to adopt certain goals and to reject others; but temperament and experience don't randomly materialize out of the void. Genes and conditioning are back in play. Since all of this is firmly within the causal net, Cahn's libertarian ploy fails to escape the dilemma. If we are never responsible for caused events, responsibility is still in trouble.

b) Is Compatibility possible? Can we accept a deterministic account of human conduct and reject the "hard" interpretation of what that account entails? That would amount to saying that human behavior is determined, but its determination is compatible with the agent's responsibility for it. To say this without absurdity demands a plausible account of how it is that the causal determination of an event and an agent's genuine responsibility for it are possible.

In the next section, I will spell out one account of how that works.

> ### "Soft" or "Hard"?
>
> The terms "hard" and "soft" determinism, though popular, are too easy to misconstrue as labels for those who believe that everything is caused and those who believe that some things are not caused.
>
> But "hard" and "soft" determinists do not disagree about the universality of causation. Both say everything is caused. They disagree about whether that universal causation rules out free choice. Hard determinists say that it does. Soft determinists disagree, insisting that it does not.

8) Here is a three-part argument to show that the determinists' horn of dilemma can be occupied:

- First, I will show that causation and freedom are not necessarily incompatible. I shall do this by way of an analysis of "free" as an "excluder," and by showing that what "X is free" excludes is rarely, if ever, causation.
- Second, I will argue that freedom, not the lack of causal connections, is the true prerequisite of responsibility.
- Third, I will show that, at least on occasion, the sort of causation to which human conduct is subject is not of the "freedom-incompatible" sort and that (consequently) it is not of the "responsibility-incompatible" sort either.

a) If we say that a paint chip is *cerise*, we attribute a fairly specific property to it. But as Roland Hall (following Wittgenstein and Austin) showed in his essay "Excluders," many adjectives do not so much attribute properties as exclude them. "Real" is such a word, as are "true" and "free." Saying "X is real" does not attribute any specific property to X. It excludes one, and the one it excludes depends on the setting. Saying—at Crab Orchard Lake in November while pointing to a floating object—"That is a real duck" does not say that the object is suffused with the essence of realhood but that it is not a decoy. Saying—to a young customer at Saks just before Mother's Day—"The lace on this handkerchief is real" does not say that it displays the distillation of realdom (or that it is not a decoy!) but that it is not machine made. Indeed, depending on circumstances, "real" can mean:

- Not artificial.
  In the case of leather, *not synthetic*.
  In the case of lace, *not machine made*.
- Not imaginary or otherwise subjective.
  In the case of playmates, *not pretended*.
  In the case of images, *not hallucinatory, drug-induced, and so forth*.
- Not spurious, below par, or unworthy of the name.
  In the case of money, *not counterfeit*.
  In the case of silver, *not adulterated*.
- Free of affectation and pretense.
  In the case of promises, *sincere, without ulterior motives*.
  In the case of a backache, *not feigned or malingering*.
- Not of small worth or to be taken lightly.
  In the case of criticisms, *not casual*.
  In the case of alibis, *not dismissible*.
- Not idealistic or impractical.
  In the case of plans, *not pie in the sky*.
- Not other than what it seems.
  In the case of an oasis, *not a mirage*.
- Not intangible or movable.
  In the case of property, *not cars, cash, and the like*.

To treat "real" as though it always attributes one specific property leads to asking, "What is Realness?"—which is unanswerable.

"True" is another excluder. When used about descriptions or assertions, that is, on its home turf, it can mean that a statement is:

- Not a lie.
  The jury must decide if the defendant's alibi is true.
- Not a mistake (honest or otherwise).
  The lineup didn't provide a true identification.
- Not misconstrued.
  The child's account of the divorce was not the true story.

Elsewhere, what "X is true" excludes is more varied. It could mean any of the following:

- X is not general, vague, or gappy.
  Is Russell's History of Philosophy *true history?*
- X is not fake.
  The Charlottesville Anastasia was not the true heir.
- X is not misleading.
  Ignore the compass. Where is true north?
- X is not peripheral.
  Epistemology is true philosophy compared to esthetics.
- X is not a hybrid.
  A mule is not a true horse.
- X is not a sport, mutation, or throwback.
  White marigolds are unlikely to breed true.
- X is not artful, considered, or contrived.
  True love never counts the cost.
- X is not distorted or truncated from a rule or standard.
  That window hangs true.

To treat "true" as though it always attributes one specific property leads to asking, "What is Truth?"—which is also unanswerable.

Finally, "free" is an excluder, too. When we say, "X is free," we rule out one or another property from a long list. Often but not always, what is excluded is a constraint of some sort. But there are many different sorts of constraints. Consequently, there are many different ways for X to be free. Indeed, it is possible for X to be free in one sense, but not free in another:

- An orbiting satellite's trajectory is close to free fall.
  It is not subject to forces other than inertia and gravity.
- Free padding and labor until January 15!!
  You pay no more than the advertised price of the rug.
- Lift the cruise control lever for free wheeling.
  Do this to disengage the wheels from the engine.
- Lincoln freed the Southern slaves.
  —voided the enforceable application of property law to—
- The warden had the pardoned embezzler set free.
  He released her from custody.
- The guard freed the imprisoned killer to use the head.
  He took the leg shackles and handcuffs off.
- Is that rusty hinge free yet?
  Is it movable?
- Are you free tonight?
  Are you without other engagements?
- I can't play poker Friday. I'm not a free man any more.
  I would love to play; but I dread the consequences.

- Multiple choice tests stifle my freedom.
  I can think of alternatives that aren't on the list.
- Can I make a free choice from the menu?
  May I take two items from A, or one each from A and B?

To treat "free" as though it always attributes one specific property leads to asking, "What is Freedom?"—which is also unanswerable.

b) To the extent that our freedom is impaired (i.e., to the extent that constraints of one sort or another restrict our conduct), there is some reason to think that our responsibility for what we do is diminished. That is why people ask, when they want to know whether to hold us responsible for Y, "Was Y a free act?"

The presence or absence of constraints is crucial when we are trying to determine the responsibility of an ostensibly competent adult. The diminished responsibility of incompetents and minors is itself largely due to the fact that they are encumbered by constraints ordinarily absent from competent adults. But ostensible competence can be subtly eroded.

> *Example.* Suppose the Congressional speaker of the house took $100,000 contributed to a tax-free educational foundation he controlled and spent it to defray his own reelection costs. In inquiring whether this was a *free act*, the House Ethics Committee is trying to find out whether any conditions were present to diminish his responsibility for this improper diversion of funds.
>
> There is more than one concrete way to diminish an individual's responsibility. So there is more than one concrete property that "was diverting the funds a free act?" is aimed at excluding. Only if they *all* are excluded is his act (completely) free and the speaker (entirely) responsible:
>
> - Was there a gun at the speaker's head when he signed the check? Were his children being held hostage?
> - Had he so internalized the ethics of his peers that he sincerely believed that getting caught is the only sin?
> - Was he lacking in any fundamental physical equipment, like connections to his frontal lobes?
> - Was he lacking in any functional cognitive capacities, like the ability to foresee the consequences of his acts?
> - Was he lacking in any conceptual equipment, like the distinction between "mine" and "thine"?
>
> The committee will also ask a great many more questions. They will not, however, ask if, at the time of the taking, the speaker was not subject to forces other than inertia and gravity, was available without any add-on to the advertised price, had his wheels disengaged from his engine, could not have property law enforceably applied to him, had been released from custody, had had his leg shackles and handcuffs removed, was movable, had no other engagements, and

so forth. The only limits that need to be excluded are the ones that are responsibility diminishing, relevant, and likely.

If the answers to any of the relevant questions were "yes," then it would be clear that the speaker did not engage in the taking *freely* (or *completely* freely, at any rate). If so he would not be (fully) responsible for his deed. If, on the other hand, his action was unimpaired by any such constraints, then it was free and he should be held responsible for it.

It may be noted that *causal connections* is not on my list of factors that diminish responsibility. Indeed, I cannot think of a single real-world case in which the word "free" functions to exclude causal connections as such. This is because causation, as such, is not constraining. What "free" does exclude is causal connections of certain specific sorts—coercions first and foremost.

If we did use "free" to mean *absent all causal connections*, we would have some difficulty being understood. That just isn't the way the word is used. Further, if we insisted on using "free" in such a novel way, not a day would pass before a new word would have to be coined to do the job "free" has always done. "Scree" might do. Then, "free" being coopted to mean *acausal*, "Was X *freely* done?" would drop out of use and "Was X *screely* done?" would serve in its place. But there is no point in such circumlocution. People don't need a new word to assess responsibility. They already have a perfectly good one for excluding responsibility-diminishing constraints: "free."

c) So a free agent is not one whose acts have no causal connections, but one whose acts are free; and a "free act" is one that *is our own*, in the sense that it has not been alienated by one or another kind of responsibility-diminishing constraints.

Here is a model of how free agents perform free acts:

(1) Visualize a screen on which there are dots and clusters of dots variously scattered, some close together and some far apart. Visualize, further, one-direction arrows, connecting dots within a cluster, dots in different clusters, clusters and dots, and clusters themselves. A connecting arrow can be either direct or mediated. A cluster can function like a dot in its own right and be connected to other dots or clusters of any size or complexity.

Parts of the screen may be virtually opaque because of the density and frequency of the dots, clusters, and connecting arrows. Between clusters, varying amounts of clear space appear, as a function of the diminished density and frequency of the connections.

The screen represents "space-time." The dots (and clusters, functioning as dots) represent "things" and "systems" that may be simple or complex, both in composition and structure.

The arrows represent "causal connections."

Variations in the strength of different causal connections are marked by the thickness of the arrows, and by attenuation over distance.

Dot-and-arrow clusters (i.e., things, systems, and their causal connections) represent "states of affairs."

Some highly complex clusters represent "persons."

A person (usually a human organism) is a packet or nucleus of particular kinds of connected behavior. Individuals are distinguishable from each other in terms of their spatial and temporal locations and the specific behaviors that go on in those locations.

(2) With such an operationalized conception of persons (as organisms with mapable capacities, dispositions, and interests), we can trace out the causes that produce the particular behavior that an organism issues and label that behavior free or not, depending on where the thick, frequent, and short arrows come from.

To say that a particular system (or activity of a system) is free (i.e., is a person's own responsibility) is not to say that it has no arrows coming in, but to say that its connections lie predominately within the cluster itself, and its external links are relatively few and thin.

If the arrows to a system's activity come primarily from outside, or if those that do come from outside are much stronger than the internal ones, then the activity is not the system's "own."

Some causal connections (represented by very thick arrows) are preemptive, assigning responsibility solely to their particular system of origin. As the arrow patterns vary, the degree of responsibility varies, too: from full responsibility to diminished responsibility to no responsibility at all.

(3) Systems (including organisms in general, and persons in particular) are themselves caused, of course. A system always has some arrows coming in. Otherwise, it would not be there. But once it is there, what is of interest is what behavior *it* issues—what *it* is causing or doing now, not the impenetrable thicket of ancient history.

Responsibility tickets do not go back forever. They go back only to the point where the incoming arrows start to become thin, long, and tenuous. Our genes and our early environment are given. What we do with them (or about them) is not.

d) Problems and objections. In affirming the universal causal structure of events, but drawing a distinction between connections that block responsibility and ones that don't, this model has four problems:

- It presupposes an adequate operational definition of "person;" and fleshing that out is a very difficult task. Consequently, we might object to it, saying:
  Operational definitions are useful only where they are possible. No one has ever given an adequate operational definition of "person;" and until someone does, this kind of analysis of responsibility is just smoke and mirrors.

- It allows that persons, like everything else, are caused themselves. The causal connections that culminate in any particular activity ultimately come, sooner or later, from "outside" the acting system itself. So in this account, a person-system has no *ultimate* control over the constituents, capacities, and dispositions that make it up. Consequently, we might object to it, saying:

  If the causal system that operationally constitutes me is itself externally caused, then I am not ultimately responsible for the things that I do. But unless I am ultimately responsible for an act, I am not responsible for it at all.

- It locates personal responsibility with a "relative" or "floating" cut-off point. Consequently, we might object to it, saying:

  This is too imprecise and vague to be of any use at all.

- It makes no ontologically substantial provision for the occurrence of the de novo activities of which people are capable (and which make them what they are). Consequently, we might object to it, saying:

  People can do things that cannot be explained in mechanistic terms, no matter how fancy the operationalizing. This model offers no substantial Selves to choose our goals, chart our lives, or revise our characters. The very things that make people free and responsible are left out.

e) Replies. These are significant objections; but they misconstrue and over-react to the model at several points:

- First, no one can deny the difficulty of articulating an adequate operational definition of "person." However, I see no reason to fall back on homunculus talk because of that, or because some attempts at operational psychology have been crude, shallow, or stalking horses for unattractive ideologies.

  We can fight the temptation to revert to untestable mysticism without buying an account as simplistic as (say) Skinner's. (It is fairly evident that people are self-aware in ways that chickens never dream of. So we should not reduce human self-awareness to the ability to differentiate oneself from others in a mirror.) With time and hard work, I see no more reason to think that empirical psychology is a dead-end street than empirical medicine. Both have gaps; but if the currently incomplete account of Alzheimer's syndrome does not drive us back to witchcraft, then neither should the currently incomplete account of decision making drive us back to Ghostly Selves.

  Since the alternatives are all one or another version of substantial dualism (which cannot work), I take this difficulty as motivation for hard work, not for reverting to the occult. This may be a "leap," but it is *practical* one.

- Second, the claim that people are not responsible for their acts unless they are ultimately responsible for their own existence and character seeks an impossible causal purity. Looking for such "absolute" responsibility is as misguided as looking for logical certainty about matters of fact. All we need for knowledge about matters of fact, as has been seen, is evidence beyond reasonable doubt; and all we need for an agent's responsibility for an act is for the preponderant number of the act's strong causal connections to arise within the system that constitutes the agent.

   This is so even in the arena of "natural facts." It may be the case that we could not be bitten by a snake had not a meteorite struck the Yucatan long ago, killing all the dinosaurs, and allowing other life forms (like people and copperheads) to evolve. But we are still more concerned about snakes when we go hiking than about meteorites.

- Third, the charge of "relativism" is harmless. Responsibility *is* a relative matter. Most of what we do is partly in our hands and partly not. The fact that the cut-off point "floats" is annoying but not impossible to live with. People have had lots of practice, in both morals and law, at getting it (approximately) "fixed."

- Fourth, those who reject this approach may have too simple a conception of what can be operationally handled. It is obvious, for example, that one of the things that marks humans as different from other organisms (and is an important part of what makes it possible for them to be responsible) is that they can reflect on their dispositions, goals, motives, and so forth, and, through that exercise of reflection and reason, *change* them and, thus, change themselves (as Harry Frankfurt nicely shows in *The Importance of What We Care About*). The question is not *whether* people do such things, but *how*.

Appealing to faculties, homunculi, and ghostly drivers is one way to affirm and explain human uniqueness. But it is a flawed way (because of the *methexis* problem, and because it is untestable); and it is not the only way. Why shouldn't a complex system have the capacity to self-adjust? Thermostats do; and people are much more complex than thermostats. People can, for instance: favor cogent arguments over specious ones, commit themselves to a goal or principle, and alter their plans in terms of their projections of the future.

All those processes involve highly complex interplays of memory, anticipation, comparison, and choice from among available options. *How* can they do such things? Well—

- How can a word processor "find and replace"?
   Must it engage in transcendental interplay with the alphabetic forms, or can it just use a complex algorithm and lots of RAM?

- And how can a Mercedes roadster be so "spirited"?
  Must it have fiery little horses under its hood, or just a well-made internal combustion engine?
- And how can a kaleidoscope amuse us?
  Must there be a little comedian waiting inside to perform on demand, or will a complex array of gravel and mirrors suffice?

All these things do the things they do because of the way they are put together. People, too.

8) Conclusions. In this chapter, I have examined what is involved in construing people as free agents in a causal environment. I have argued that people are highly complex organisms that, although completely at home in a universally causal environment, are able to choose among the behavior options that circumstances present. Not only are people themselves sometimes free (in one or another of the many senses of that excluder), their acts are also sometimes free (in the sense that they are their own and not someone else's).

An organism's own free act is an act that is the causal product of factors lying predominately within the acting organism itself: its own desires, intentions, hopes, plans, values, recollections, and so forth Because its acts are its own, having been chosen according to what it elects to pursue from the options that circumstances provide, an organism is *responsible* for them and for their consequences.

In this analysis, even organisms of considerably less complexity than people can act with some freedom. People, however, are especially free because their intelligence enables them to see many more options, weigh much subtler alternatives, and construct far more complicated routes to achieve their ends than organisms with more limited capacities. Their freedom is increased (i.e., their acts are doubly their own) when they scrutinize their own desires, intentions, hopes, plans, values, and so forth, critically revise them, and reflectively commit themselves to them. The sense of our systemic continuity moving in time (out of a past, through a present, and into a future that we can influence and shape), and the sense of having significant control over our route along the way, play major roles in making people the remarkable organisms that they are. None of these things, however, necessitates conceptualizing them as anything more than complex organisms. Consequently, this analysis is compatible with the notion of achieving a high level of knowledge about people by way of scientific inquiry.

The notion of responsibility for our acts has special implications for the foundations of morality—the topic of the next chapters:

- If we are responsible for what we do, then the door to moral evaluation, praise, and blame is open—including reflective moral appraisal of oneself by oneself.

- If we are responsible, we should *accept* that responsibility. This amounts, in part, to coming to terms with the consequences of our acts, biting the bullet, and accepting them as our own.
- Then we can begin to *act* responsibly, by taking the probable consequences of our acts into account and adjusting what we do accordingly.
- Sometimes, we are held responsible for things that are not truly within our control. Living, as they do, in structured societies, people have areas of responsibility assigned to them by birth and circumstance that actually constrain the opportunities and alternatives open to them.
- Finally, even when we feel most at the mercy of circumstance, we can *seize* responsibility for who we are and what we do and "take charge" of our lives. Value often must be made rather than found.

What has been said about people in this chapter should be read in the context of what was said about them in chapter 10. There, the basic *pros* and *cons* were laid out for conceptualizing humans as:

- special creations "in the image of God,"
- inseparable constituents and products of society, and
- at home in, and biologically and physically continuous, in both substance and process, with Nature itself.

Humans are best understood as highly intelligent, adaptable, free, responsible, causally connected, living physical systems that are inextricably interlocked with each other and with all the other things that share the Earth.

This is an empowering account. There are no "meres" in it, anywhere. People are not "mere mindless automata," and so forth. But if people can recognize that they have a great deal in common with animals, plants, and other physical causal systems, that they are rooted in social fabrics of various kinds (families, clubs, political parties, religions, nations, whatever), that a large part of their essential character amounts to being directed and governed by internalized goals and interests, and that they have the capacity and the opportunity to reflect on (and even change) those goals and interests, they can begin to get a real grip on just how neat it is to live a human life, indeed, how neat it is to be a *person*.

Serious attention to the boundaries of the concept of a person alters the boundaries of the concept of moral obligation. So as people continue to work on the map of what it is to be a person, they are likely to conclude that *personhood* and *peoplehood* are not coextensive, but only overlap. We find many clear cases of persons among people. But we also find some borderline cases elsewhere (porpoises, chimps, etc.) and should be ready for "close encounters" if and when they occur. Furthermore, we also find some severely truncated cases among people (flatliners, fetal encephalopaths, etc.). If we take such findings to heart, they will change the scope of our moral outlook—with concrete implications for such matters as animal rights, some cases of induced abortion and euthanasia, and the etiquette of space exploration. Persons in the form of human beings, however, are my immediate concern.

So with a handle on what it is possible for people to do, and what it is reasonable to hold them responsible for, I will now return to the question left hanging at the end of chapter 9: *What is the best way to live a human life?* That is the topic of the next four chapters.

IV

HUMAN CONDUCT

12

Self-Fulfillment and Following Nature

Morality has to do with the "rights and wrongs" and "goods and bads" of human conduct and character. People have different ideas about it, from total skepticism to detailed accounts of alleged moral truths. All such views are rooted in one or another of four action-guiding directives that arise at different human developmental stages. (Lawrence Kohlberg's *The Philosophy of Moral Development: Moral Stages and the Idea of Justice* is a good treatment of this genealogy.)

Do what you're told. While children begin life as savages, they learn at (or over) a parent's knee to do what they are told. The moral enterprise is simple and enforced by giants. We are spanked, isolated, and deprived for disobedience; and hugged, praised, and given treats for "being good." Since the survival of a young child is impossible without adult support, most learn to accept parental rule (at least until puberty).

While many people grow out of this stage to establish at least modest autonomy, most never escape it altogether—allowing society's rules, or God's, to continue the moral quid pro quo that began in the nursery. This should not be surprising. Good citizens are admired, respected, and rewarded; and rebels face ostracism, imprisonment, and even death—and, according to some, hell itself.

Do whatever you want. By thirteen or so most humans adopt the mantra, "I can't wait until I'm big and can do whatever I want." In fact, most have learned by then that—with only modest cunning—they can disobey most rules with impunity. Having successfully filched gum money from the penny jar, lied about dental hygiene, and absorbed hours of violent trash on MTV while allegedly watching *Mr. Rogers' Neighborhood*, they progress smoothly to hiding bongs, ditching school, and, according to Benoit Denizet-Lewis's *New York Times Magazine* article, "Friends, Friends with Benefits, and the Benefits of the Local Mall," hooking up at random.

Wise parents hope that their young teens have an internalized sense of self-protection already in place; know when to interfere and when to look away; and realize that the quest for freedom is developmentally crucial, even when it is poorly conceived and dysfunctionally practiced. *Their* mantra becomes, "This, too, shall pass." For some, however, it doesn't. Many nominal adults still feel that doing whatever they want is what life is about. However, even grown-ups have some rules to deal with, and the sanctions for adult disobedience can be dreadful. So they hone their skills at keeping up appearances with lies and evasions. One rule learned at home seems to stick: "Don't get caught."

Be all you can be. With astute parenting and some luck, something starts in the midteens that may eventually supplant both docile obedience and reckless willfulness. If self-esteem and a sense of cause and effect are in place, they can nudge us onto a path toward long-term self-fulfillment. This can involve stifling immediate desires, cultivating tastes we do not yet have, and looking beyond the expectations of the establishment and our peers.

Some get stuck here, too. And without further development, the entire population is at risk to whatever self-image happens to be driving each individual. Whenever a Genghis Kahn is being all he can be, the rest of us are in jeopardy.

Play fair. If one's own fulfillment is worth pursuing, it is reasonable to think that other peoples' are too. Even young children can be aware of, and committed to, fair play—though more easily when it is to their own benefit rather than that of others. My own learned to say, "that's not fair," by three. In consistent minds, self-respect sparks respect for others.

After all of these stages have occurred, there is a good chance that we are in the moral arena, however we articulate it. The pros and cons of several particular ways to articulate it occupy this and the next three chapters. I will examine two accounts that focus on human fulfillment, two based on obedience, and finally the role of consequences and the provision that can be made for fair play in terms of them.

1. Follow Your Star

However sliced, egoism has something to do with pursuing our own interests. It is, however, ambiguous at three distinct levels; so it can be sliced any number of ways.

First, "our own interests" is ambiguous. It can mean either interests that we have, or self-interests. These are obviously not the same thing; but it is easy to equivocate between them. Any interest that we have is our own rather than someone else's. Even an interest in others is our own interest, not theirs.

Second, "self-interest" is ambiguous. It can mean interest in ourselves, what we are interested in, or what is in our interest. These are obviously not the same thing either; but it is easy to equivocate among all three. We can be consumingly *interested in* things that are not *in our interest* at all, for example, a relationship with a person who is abusive, or a life-threatening habit. We can also *have no interest in* things that are very much *in our interest*, for example, completing our education, or saving some money for a rainy day. And, of course, we can, ourselves, be *interested in things other than ourselves* (such as baseball, stamp collecting, or famine relief), some of which might even be *in our interest*—or, like Narcissus, we may stand perpetually before the mirror, *interested in ourselves alone.*

In this context of layered ambiguity, two views are common:

- Psychological Egoism is the view that everyone is an egoist, whatever that amounts to. It asserts that human behavior is solely motivated by each individual's interests (whatever that amounts to)—that no other forces ever move people to action. This is not a claim about how people should behave. True or false, it simply says that this is the way people do behave.
- Ethical Egoism asserts that human behavior is not always motivated by each individual's interests (whatever that amounts to) but should be. True or false, this *prescriptive* view asserts that people who pursue interests other than their own (whatever that amounts to) are *wrong.*

Egoism, in psychological and ethical dress, is widely accepted. But, due to all the ambiguities, it is sometimes difficult to discern exactly what its advocates are claiming. An ethical egoist might be endorsing one or another of several notions—that people should, variously:

- be motivated by their own motives rather than anyone else's;
- do only what they are interested in doing;
- do what is beneficial to them even if it is harmful to others; or
- not do what is harmful to them even if it is beneficial to others.

Psychological egoists might be asserting the descriptive counterpart of any of these. And careless thinkers can slide around both sets of four.

If psychological egoism (under some interpretation) is true, and if "ought implies can," then every proposal about what people ought to do is in jeopardy. It makes little sense to urge people either to do what they cannot do, or to do what they can't help doing. So if psychological egoism is true, both ethical altruism and ethical egoism appear pointless: the first because it seems to futilely encourage the impossible, the second because it seems to redundantly encourages the inevitable. As always, however, the real world is more complicated than it seems to be.

- Ethical egoism is not always made redundant by psychological egoism. Since we can take interest in things that are not in our interest, and fail to have interest in things that are in our interest, it is possible for ethical egoism to have a point, even if psychological egoism is true. If the latter amounts only to the claim that we do only what we have an interest in doing, and the former to the claim that we should do only what is in our interest (i.e., beneficial to us), then ethical egoism could amount to encouraging people to take interest in things that are beneficial to them—an often useful enterprise in a world where people often take interest in unfortunate things. To succeed at this enterprise, of course, we would have to identify the things that are self-beneficial; and that is a normative identification that presupposes criteria for "beneficial" that have nothing to do with egoism. So when ethical egoism is not redundant, it no longer relies on purely egoistic principles.

- Ethical altruism is not made impossible by psychological egoism either. Even if it is true that we cannot be motivated by anything other than a desire for our own benefit, it is possible to make a place for a nonegoistic ethic. It is possible to manipulate social sanctions to alter the consequences of human behavior and, as a result, the behavior itself. We who are in a position of power can see to it that people generally behave in socially beneficial ways by making the results of socially harmful behavior so horrid as to chill the interest anyone might have in them. In just this way, in his *Introduction to the Principles of Morals and Legislation*, Jeremy Bentham laid out a scheme of social sanctions aimed at enabling people who can only pursue their own pleasure and avoid their own pain to behave in *collectively* beneficial ways. (This also requires specifying some criteria for "beneficial." Bentham's were hedonistic and had nothing to do with egoism. We shall look at such "utilitarianism" in chapters 14 and 15.)

In any case, there is no good reason to think that psychological egoism is true in the first place, as we shall now see.

A. Psychological egoism. The details of any particular brand of psychological egoism are a function of the way in which people's "interests" are conceived. At first glance, if we conflate the multiple ambiguities, all brands of psychological egoism seem obviously false. Anyone can produce stories where people appear to be motivated by anything but "self-interest."

> *Fictional Example.* What about the young Marine private in all those movies that starred John Wayne and Sonny Tufts? He saw the hand grenade drop into the middle of his squad and thought, "I can't let my buddies die." So he threw himself on it and was blown to bits—sacrificing himself for the good of the group.
> *Real World Example.* What about those on whose exploits such movies are based, or the medical researchers who risk death to find the etiology of scourges like malaria and AIDS, or the altogether too many contemporary terrorists? In every case, they offer to sacrifice themselves for a cause (and sometimes succeed).

Such acts are dismissed by psychological egoists with the claim that self-interest is always present, behind even the most stirring cases of apparent self-sacrifice. They are obliged, of course, to provide a *plausible* account that shows that ego feeding is at work in the case at hand. Sometimes, that is very easy to show.

Example. I gave money to my school's UGF drive. I could have spent it on piz-zas, saved it for a vacation, or invested it; but I didn't.
- I gave it away out of pure selfless concern for my fellow humans.
- I know the administration keeps records of who gives and who doesn't, and I am concerned about reprisals.
- I knew that I would be writing about egoism soon and would need an ex-ample of altruistic behavior.
- I wanted to impress my colleagues with what a socially concerned fellow I am by wearing the "I gave" pin.
- I was driven by conditioned guilt avoidance (i.e., I knew I would feel bad if I didn't do my "fair share").

Is an ulterior self-serving motive always present? For psychological egoism to be true, the answer must be "yes," even in hard cases like real grenade smotherers (of whom there have been many) or the New York firefighters on 9/11. (It is irrelevant if such accounts offend our sensibilities. The fact that we may be upset to think that Gandhi's eye might have been on his own politi-cal future at every point in his campaign to free India from British rule, is be-side the point. The truth or falsehood of explanations cannot be settled by enumerating the sensibilities they offend or curry. What counts is evidence, not how we feel.)

An account for such a case might run like this:
  People (especially soldiers) are socially conditioned into accepting a notion of duty; and a Marine has had not only duty, but honor and glory as well, ham-mered into him.
  So a Marine identifies his own ego with the group, eventually seeing the squad as an extension of himself.
  Thus, because of a demonstrable distortion of his own self-concept, he can only serve himself by serving the group.
  Further, if he had not had the guts to step up when the demand arose and had let his buddies die (with the whole platoon watching), he knew that he would be despised by the Corps.

So even a grenade smotherer's self-interest is not hard to find; and if that sort of case can be so easily handled, can we think of any human behavior that couldn't be explained in a similar way? Suggesting ever more stirring cases in the hope that the psychological egoists will run out of steam won't work.

They haven't yet, and there is little reason to think they ever will. So why does their universalization of such explanations break down?

It breaks down because, as they offer ever-more-complex rationales for ever-more-difficult cases, they equivocate over the slippery ambiguities of "self-interest" and "our own interest" noted above. When they say, "All behavior is motivated by self-interest," they do not always mean the same thing; and while one thing that they mean is clearly correct, the other things that they mean are, at least sometimes, clearly mistaken.

> *Example.* Two students graduated from a Christian denominational college with good grades and married each other. The young man was the son of a middle-class family with a house in Connecticut, a condo in Florida, and a thriving retail business. The young woman's Southern family had run a manufacturing firm for generations. Challenging and well-paid jobs were ready for the young couple. Their parents, no doubt, visualized a scenario of unending yuppie success.
>
> Instead, they volunteered for the Peace Corps, were accepted, and were assigned to Sri Lanka (then Ceylon). The first step was California, to learn to raise chickens, speak Tamil, and build outhouses. Finally came Kandy, and hard labor. Asked why they did all this, their answer was simple: "Those people needed help that we could give. So we gave." Who will say that this was self-interest?

The psychological egoists will, of course; and their case may appear both plausible and substantial:

> The young volunteers obviously had a religiously warped self-image of "duty" and "heavenly rewards." In trying to live up to it, they were obviously self-serving. Like other people who do things that help others, they did it as a product of conditioning that made such "service" the only way that they could see to help themselves. So some of the *effects* may have been on other people but the *motivations* were entirely (if unconsciously) self-directed.

Such a rebuttal would be plausible in some cases. I have certainly known people who, had they ever gone to work on such a project, would certainly have done it as the calculated price of heavenly rewards.

On the other hand, these two people:

- were not particularly religious,
- did not worry about an afterlife of punishment and reward, and
- were not strong advocates of "duty."

Apparently, they just thought helping was *worth doing.* They claimed they did it, remember, because "those people needed help that we could give."

For cases like this one, then, psychological egoists have to turn to more recondite varieties of self-interest than hopes for heaven or self-conscious devotion to duty—perhaps to unconscious anticipations of long-term payoffs in this world, perhaps to the insidious aftereffects of early superego cultivation by ideology-driven (but subtle) parents. I, in turn, would try to show that their more subtle hypotheses simply don't apply to the case in hand. The dialogue would go back and forth many times; but, eventually, as I say, "They weren't like *that* either" for the *n*th time, the psychological egoists will play trumps with a statement something like this:

> The truth of our analysis of human behavior does not hinge on the specific attributes of particular individual behaviors. Psychological egoism is an inclusive principle that explains all human behavior. People do many different things, but whatever they do is done only because they have an interest in doing it. They do it in order to gain or achieve something that *they* want to gain or achieve.

So stated, the psychological egoists' counterrationale is simply that:

- *People are motivated only by their own motives.*
- *People do only what they want to do.*
- *No one does anything they have no interest in doing.*

While, barring cases of coercion, I see no way *this* account could be false, it falls far short of *People always pursue their own benefit*, which is where things started. When psychological egoists say that people do only what they have an interest in doing, they are correct, but have shifted ground in a major way. They started out saying that everyone operates out of self-interest, that is, looks out for number one. They wound up saying that everyone operates out of self-interest, that is, is moved by their own motives.

The latter claim, though true, has no teeth. When Attila the Hun raped, murdered, and pillaged, what moved him? His interest in rape, murder, and pillage, of course. When Albert Schweitzer practiced medicine in the African jungle, what moved him? His interest in seeing the locals enjoy better health, of course. Each was moved by his own interests, not someone else's; but those interests were very different. Indeed, the variety of interests in the satisfaction of which people find gratification is enormous; and, while some of them are selfish, others are clearly other-directed. Even though they are *their* interests, they are not interests in *themselves*.

In rebuttal, psychological egoists are likely again to claim that deep down, when we really probe, everybody is out for number one. Then, when we resume reciting counterexamples, they will re-revert to "these people wouldn't do those things if they weren't interested in doing them. It is obvious that only their own interests are at work." And so the equivocation goes on between the meanings of their original ambiguous claim.

That original claim has no fixed truth value. It can only be assessed under each of its alternative meanings. When it means that everyone is looking out for number one, it is exciting but false. When it means that everyone is moved by only his own motives, it is true, but toothless.

Such "explanations" do not contribute to getting a better understanding of what moves people to act. Their net effect is to cloud the issues and lose sight of distinctions that need to be drawn.

> *Example.* Del spends her afternoons teaching in an adult literacy program. I, on the other hand, spend my afternoons making crack in my basement, which I sell to my advisees. Del says she does her thing because she is moved by the plight of immigrant women who can't read and wants to help empower them. I say that I do my thing because I am moved by the thought of what I can buy with the money I get: fast cars, vintage wines, and foxy ladies.

The egoists advise us to describe both of these behavior patterns as "self-interest" (with more than a hint of "selfish"). We can follow that advice if we want to, but blurring distinctions does not enhance communication.

There is an important difference between being motivated by a desire to empower adult illiterates by teaching them to read and being motivated by a desire to make money to gratify our lusts by selling crack on campus. Calling both motivations self-interested does not obliterate the difference. It just confuses the understanding. Indeed, if we followed the advice to call them both self-interested, we would shortly be obliged to invent new words to perform the job that "self-interested" and "other-regarding" (or "selfish" and "altruistic") used to perform.

We then might say that some people are *selfish* (driven by their own *self-regarding* motives), and others are *melfish* (driven by their own *other-regarding* motives). Though it seems much simpler to go on saying that some people are selfish and some aren't, it certainly isn't necessary. Using newly coined terms, we could still encourage people to show one kind of "self-interest" and shun the other. The moral enterprise would not be stymied. However we choose to talk, the difference between people who are self-focused and those who are other-focused is plainly visible in their actual conduct. Anyone can see the difference between the Mafia's interests and the Y's in their dealings with preteen female illegals in Trenton; and linguistic practice should *underscore* that, not *obscure* it.

In a truncated sense of "the same," we might say, "The Y only does what it does because it has an interest in doing it. So it is no different from, and no better than, the Mafia. Their interests have different goals; but each one does what it wants to do so their motives are the same." But the Mafia's motives for trafficking in child prostitution don't even resemble those that so manifestly drive the Y. The only link is the negligible fact that all those motives belong to the persons who have them. Calling them "the same" clouds rather than illuminates human motivation. It is, consequently, dysfunctional.

Further, following the psychological egoists' linguistic advice also interferes with reacting appropriately to people's conduct. Appropriate reactions are, in part, a function of what kind of motivation is at work. If, for example, we discovered that a heretofore admired individual works with adult illiterates only because she believes that this is a way to escape eternity in the fiery pit, our esteem for her would appropriately diminish.

When we discover that the only thing that drives someone is self-interest *in the hard sense*, we withhold praise. But we need not discover that, because it need not be the case. Some people, with or without reflection, think it is delightful to help others. Their motives are still "their own," of course; but they are constructive ones that people can reasonably admire, endorse, and praise.

So summing up, psychological egoism equivocates between:

- attributing selfish motives to all people at all times, and
- urging a linguistic convention to underscore the fact that only our own motives move us.

But the first is frequently false, the second conceals the interesting differences between the actual motives people have, and the equivocation between the two is deplorably misleading.

There is no profit in adopting a view that is sometimes false, sometimes truth-concealing, and always misleading. Instead, we need to examine the full variety of motives that are people's own. Only then can we encourage those that are functional and discourage the rest. For instance, it is possible that people *ought* to follow their own *selfish* motives and lay their own *benevolent* ones aside. That is the advice of *ethical* egoism, coming up next. But to follow (or reject) that advice, we need to be able to identify all our own motives, whether selfish, benevolent, or mixed.

B. Ethical egoism. Ethical egoists, such as Harry Browne (in "The Morality Trap") admit that we can be moved by an interest in or concern for others but insist that we should not allow that to occur. They say that we ought to be moved only by our interest in and concern for ourselves:

- *Pursue your own interest.*
- *Look out for number one.*
- *Do your own thing.*
- *Be selfish.*

Such imperatives are easily misconstrued to suggest an outlook that would bring most people up short if their neighbors practiced it.

1) Misconceptions. To begin with, pursuing what we have an interest in, pursuing what we take to be in our interest, and pursuing what actually is in our interest are all different.

- We may be interested in X whether or not we *think* it is in our interest.
- We may be interested in X whether or not it is in our interest.
- What we *think* is in our interest may or may not be so.

So ethical egoists do not merely exhort us always to do what we are interested in doing. That would trivialize their position, ultimately reducing it to an injunction to be moved only by our own motives (which is redundant because it is inevitable.) Worse, "pursue whatever you think is in your interest" opens the gate to self-destruction. So the ethical egoists' injunction "pursue your own interest" must mean "always do what is actually in your interest," that is, what will actually benefit you.

That still has problems, as will be seen, but it puts an effective damper on exercises in self-indulgence that we know to be self-destructive—either immediately or in the long run.

While it should be clear by now that no ethical egoist is likely to endorse the behavior of Crystal's daddy, however much *he* might enjoy it, we need to be clear about why they refrain from such endorsements. It has nothing to do with the considerations that others might cite:

- Contra legalists, it is not based on any law.
- Contra religionists, it is not based on a notion of divine will.
- Contra utilitarians, it is not based on concern for general human happiness.
- Contra humanists, it is not based on any concern for Crystal's well-being.

All such concerns and respects are beside the point. The only consideration that comes into play is whether bedding Crystal is really in her daddy's interest, given the social fabric in which he finds himself.

Given the common social fabric in most of the United States, such behavior is not in an individual's own interest. First, because sanctions are likely to follow. Second, because such behavior can divert us from other, more self-benefiting, endeavors. And third, at the very least, it tends to make an individual one-sided, dull, and uninteresting to the rest of the adult community. But if it *were* in Daddy's interest, would it then be OK? Is the only thing that stands in the way a set of contingent facts about what will and what will not benefit him in the given circumstances?

Contingent facts change, of course. How much change would it take to make bedding his daughter OK? That is why the phrase "given the social fabric" is so important in deciding what is morally acceptable for incestuous pedophiles (or anyone else, for that matter) on egoistic grounds.

Ethical egoism repudiates most conventionally imagined barbaric behaviors, given the social fabric; but it *could* endorse them in the right sort of world. So while ethical egoism need not alarm our conventional moral sense as much as first appears, it clearly reminds us of the necessity for self-protecting vigilance as the world turns.

2) Ayn Rand's ethical egoism. There have been many ethical egoists; and they offer many arguments in support of their prescriptive ideas. Ayn Rand was an articulate and widely read champion of the cause. Her position is summarized in Nathaniel Branden's *The Virtue of Selfishness* and appears in more literary form in her *Atlas Shrugged, Anthem*, and so forth. (For a presentation of this point of view written with greater care and less attitude, see Adam Smith's *The Wealth of Nations*.)

Rand's case for ethical egoism amounts largely to arguing that its only alternative, "altruism," is inconsistent and life denying, predicated on the assumption that if altruism is out, egoism wins by default.

First of all, she defines altruism as *always subordinating our own interests to others* and treats it (so defined) as the strict complement of her own variety of egoism. Presenting them as mutually exclusive, the choice between them appears to be all or nothing.

Having set up altruism the way she does, it is no wonder she abhors it. But the set up is a parody of altruism, and the choice between it and her own egoism is a false dilemma. To abandon egoism we need not avow "others at all costs." We can value human interests *wherever* they reside (I, thou, whoever) and encourage their *general* maximal satisfaction.

That is utilitarianism, more or less; and it is neither "egoistic" nor "altruistic" as Rand uses the terms. If, for instance, we ate a little less meat and a little more soy, we could free up cereal supplies for famine relief. Observing periodic meatless days for this reason would take *everyone's* interests into account (including our own). So it is neither "egoistic" nor "altruistic" as Rand uses the terms. Her "dilemma" is all straw.

In any case, according to Rand, to deny our own interests or subvert them to those of others is to deny the fulfillment of our own capacities—the dynamic and potential of our own lives. So to undercut ourselves is so pragmatically self-defeating that it is self-contradictory and absurd. But if altruism is self-defeating, then some sort of egoism is the only possible alternative. Therefore, it is only reasonable always to pursue your own interests, without regard to their cost to others.

We might think that, in practice, this would generate horrendous conflict and that, if everyone followed it, society would rapidly degenerate into a state of nature where, as Hobbes describes it in *Leviathan,* human life is solitary, poor, nasty, brutish, and short. Rand denies the implied conflict and squalor, asserting that if everyone pursues what is in his own interest, everything will turn out smoothly in the long run. This is not to say that the things people are interested in do not generate conflicts. They do, but what people are *interested in* is not the same as what is *in their interest*. So even if what two people are interested in generates conflicts, what is actually and finally in their interest need not.

If this generalization of Adam Smith's "invisible hand" is so, each individual can go his own way, confident that everything will work out acceptably, without worrying about the qualms that plague traditional morality's "concern for others." On the other hand, if this is not so—if, so to speak, the invisible hand "slips"—then the conflicts that occur will require a social apparatus for their adjudication and reconciliation. That apparatus is what the traditional institutions of morality and law provide. Rand's egoism, however, provides nothing but the invisible hand itself.

The reliability of the invisible hand is an inverse function of the complexity of the society in play. As useful as Adam Smith's theories may be for simple economic models, they are not adequate for the twenty-first century's economic complexities. In the same way, Rand's notions might work in a village of people who share a bartering mentality; but they fall far short of what is needed to effectively reorganize the detritus of the Soviet Union, or adjudicate the disputes that have consumed Iraq.

3) Rational egoism. Thoughtful egoists reply to such alleged difficulties along the following line:

> While impetuously pursuing what we *take* to be in our interest may generate conflicts, reflecting on the potential consequences of alternative acts (including any likely reprisals) will show the potential flash points where a certain level of cooperation will be needed. So by looking ahead, rational people find ways to reconcile what they do with what others do.
>
> Thus, anticipating individual reactions as well as the general workings of the social machinery, rational people show a modicum of self-restraint, though still pursuing only their own interests. They restrain themselves, not because aggression hurts *others*, but because, in the long run, it hurts *them*.
>
> This is what makes real interests mesh in the long run in the real world. It is why, for instance, there are many things that rationally self-interested members of U.S. society don't do, even when they want to, given its laws, customs, and sanctions, and the retaliatory instincts of its citizenry.

There are problems with this, however. It assumes that everyone has equal access to and influence over events, or that even egregious cruelty is tolerable if we are strong enough, or clever enough, to get away with it.

a) If some people have better access to the facts, or more influence on how the machinery operates, or are smarter than (and can trick) others, then they can pursue their own well-being in ways that sharply curtail the well-being of those others and get away with it.

That is why, in the real world, it is possible for one segment of a community (say the Protestants in Belfast who have greater leverage on the economic system than their Catholic compatriots) to do things in their own interests that clearly curtail the interests of others. It clears the way for tyrannical individuals, too. "The public be damned." "*L'état, c'est moi.*" Or, in the words of a fairly recently deceased Romanian: "You are only a citizen; I rule."

Further, there is no reason to think that dominant groups or individuals always eventually lose their special leverage. It is naive to believe that the truth will always out. It is naive to believe that every molester needs to worry about reprisals. It is naive to believe that every worm will turn. It is naive to believe that crime doesn't pay. In fact, it handsomely pays those with a little intelligence and skill, some leverage on the media, some means of concealment, and the power to kill opponents.

> *Example.* The late Papa Doc Duvalier ran Haiti for years in the way he thought his own well-being required. His life was full and apparently happy. He died no sooner than, at least as content as, and lots richer than, most. (The same thing, however, could not be said for the bulk of Haiti's population at the time. Indeed, the harms he did still have not been put right.)
>
> He did not succeed because the interests of all the people in Haiti reinforced each other and his own, but because:
> - he bought the loyalty of the military and the ruling class;
> - he had a large personal army of goons with lead-weighted billy clubs who enjoyed splitting heads; and
> - the world community, in those days, did not care enough about the general plight of the Haitians to interfere.

So the blithe assumption of the ultimate compatibility of interests is demonstrably false. The ethical egoists' scheme, even in its most rational, long-term form, is predicated on falsehoods.

b) If killing our children is immoral, even when we get away with it, ethical egoism is just as bankrupt at home as it is in Haiti.

> *Example.* In a notorious case some years ago, a father laced some Pixie Stix with cyanide and slipped them into his little boy's loot bag when he came home from trick or treating on Halloween. When the child died just as daddy planned, most people (even egoists, I'm sure) thought this was a despicable act; but the question is, "Why was it a despicable act?"

Some people would say it was despicable simply because wantonly harming the helpless is *bad*. But that rationale is not available to ethical egoists. Was it despicable, then, simply because the father was so stupid as to buy life insurance on his son just days before, and so careless as to pick an uncommon and memorable variety of candy to dispatch him?

If so, then if he had just been a little more clever, the proper moral appraisal of his act (on rational egoism's criteria) would have to shift from "bad" (i.e., stupid and ineffectual) to "good" (i.e., clever and effective). When hurting people does not generate negative feedback, rational egoism cannot coherently recognize any moral reason for self-restraint. Indeed, absent such feedback, self-restraint would be *immoral*, egoisically speaking, however much it might be in the interest of those who are trampled but have no means of recourse.

4) Another version of egoism. An ethical egoist can take a more aggressive approach, admitting the intractable conflicts of individuals' interests, but dismissing them and their consequences as irrelevant. It might go this way: *The only legitimate moral compunction is self-benefit. If that means shortening the lives of others (or making their existence solitary, poor, nasty, and brutish), so be it. They have the same responsibility that I have: to seek self-benefit. I have succeeded, and they have failed. Too bad for them.* (See Nietzsche's *Beyond Good and Evil.*)

This can be dressed up with rhetoric, if we like: *In this world, we either eat or are eaten. Eagles eat rabbits; but rabbits don't eat eagles. I accept that, and like the eagle, have no sympathy for the rabbitty masses. Any of them who had any gumption could try to turn the tables on me. But they are weak and spineless, so they deserve exactly what they get. Winners never quit. Quitters never win. Eagles Rule!*

Such rhetoric usually plays better with the eagles than with the rabbits; but if we can stand the whining, accept the risks, and keep our powder dry, we can simply dismiss the conflicts that self-interest generates from time to time with a cavalier *"the Devil take the hindmost."*

On the other hand, for the rabbit people, the obvious thing to do is to collaborate with others to control the bullies and make their own lives a little more pleasant. Rugged individualists aren't prone to collaboration, though, and tend to see those who are as craven. But, on grounds of self-interest, why shouldn't the rabbit people collaborate to impose their will on the eagle people instead of quietly taking their lumps?

However, if what is important is life, self-fulfillment, and so forth, then there is something incoherent in singling out any *particular* life as being more important than any other, unless we have independent objective reasons for doing so in the concrete case.

> *Example.* While I can easily conceive of cases where a randomly selected panel of objective people would decide that my interests override (say) my neighbors', it would be fundamentally irrational for me to think that mine always override theirs (or, for that matter, that theirs always override mine).
>
> Suppose that by denying my daily steak craving on Tuesdays, I could reduce the local starvation rate by .01 percent. If my interests always override others', I shall have my daily steak.
>
> Suppose that in order to eat I must turn on the water to boil my rice but know that this will make the pipes knock and annoy the people upstairs. If my interests never override others', I shall go hungry.

It would be more reasonable to say that everyone's interests count and decide which ones should override in a given case in terms of the specific circumstances. Then, in a choice between my going hungry and my neighbors being annoyed by knocking pipes, they get annoyed and I eat. My interests override theirs—not because they are mine but because they are more important in the circumstances. In a choice between having steak every night and reducing the starvation rate, the others' interests override. Not because they are "theirs," but because having *something* to eat is more important than my gustatory monomania.

If what is important is the fulfillment of interests, then it doesn't matter whose they are. This is why, in any adequate moral scheme, some principle of "fairness" will come into play. (Fairness amounts to acting consistently, and dismissing all notions of a priori status priorities, in any situation where the interests of more than one individual are at stake. A scheme that makes no place for it is like a scale that won't reset to zero.)

Furthermore, when deciding which interests we are to override and which are to be overridden, "always our own" vs. "always another's" frequently isn't the issue in play at all:

> *Examples.* Tomorrow is the third football game of the season. As usual, Fred has two free tickets and plans to take one of his two sons to the game with him. The boys drew straws before the first game, to establish a rota. Jon drew first turn and went to game one. But Chris was sick for game two, and Jon went in his place. So Chris has not been to a game yet, and Jon has been twice. Whose turn is it now? Fred has no interests at stake, either way, but must decide which son to take.
>
> Two patients are dying of liver malfunction, but there is only one liver available for transplant. Although the surgeon has no interests at stake, one way or the other, she must decide who will live and who will die.

When second- and third-party interests are at stake for a first-party decision, neither egoism nor altruism is any help at all.

5) Conclusion. The ethical egoists' criterion for moral judgment is clear enough, but clearly inadequate. We can gild it in various ways, claiming that all interests eventually coincide, that vicious behavior will eventually come home to roost, or even that only the weak fail. But none of the gilding is credible, so the criterion itself is not improved. The notion that all that counts in moral evaluation is whose interest is at stake is simplistic, and the notion that *self*-interest always wins is a barbarism.

Ayn Rand characterizes "altruism" in such an extreme way that she makes selfishness appear reasonable in contrast. Her "altruist" is *forever* prostrate and subservient to the whims of others. Even Jesus, hardly a Randian, enjoined his followers to love others *as they loved themselves.* So he was not an altruist, as Rand defined them. But no one is.

But there are alternatives to egoism and to altruism as she portrays it. In one, the satisfaction of interests counts, but without regard to whose interests they are. In another, with no interest in interests at all, morality is formulated strictly in terms of playing by the rules. I shall examine both, but only after marking another dead end.

2. Follow Nature

If "Follow Your Star" is poor moral advice, perhaps "Follow Nature" is a little better. Following nature, however, is difficult.

A. Ambiguity. Although many sages have advised that people should follow nature, it is not always clear what that means. Consider, first of all, four common normative uses of the words "nature" and "natural."

1) Television advertisements say that the shampoo Jojoba is made of natural ingredients and imply that it is, consequently, better than its rivals. This raises two questions: a) "What makes an ingredient 'natural?' and b) "What makes having such ingredients 'better?'"

a) A natural ingredient might be one that occurs

- in nature,
- without human interference or artifice, or
- with only minor human interference or artifice.

The first is a nonstarter. In its most straightforward sense, "nature" is *whatever occurs*. So in that sense, anything that happens, occurs in nature, that is, nothing that happens is unnatural. The second is only slightly more promising, assuming that Jojoba is not a completely unprocessed secretion of some sort.

So what the Jojoba people must mean by "natural ingredients" is that the contents of their product are not *very* manufactured, that is, they occur without *major* human interference. How natural a thing is, then, is a function of the *degree* of human involvement in its production: more artifice = less natural, less artifice = more natural. How natural a product is, in this sense, is not always easy to discern:

> *Example.* Compare Jojoba to four (imaginary) alternatives:
> - *Jojoba* is made, in part, from a tropical tree bean, if labels can be trusted.
> - *Synthese* is a designer compound that is synthesized directly from sedimentary element pellets that are found in the Atlantic.
> - *Tarbaby* is manufactured in Minnesota by the high-temperature distillation of open-pit lignite mine slurry.
> - *Desert Breeze* is a simple hand-stirred emulsion of camel dung, brine, and wind-fallen olives from Saudi Arabia.
> - *Soap* is produced worldwide by adding water that has been filtered through wood ashes to heated animal tallow.

A precise "naturalness" ranking of these five shampoos is difficult. The ingredients of *Synthese* are "found," but the way they come together could not happen absent industrial chemistry. So are the basic ingredients of *Soap,* and its chemistry, though primitive, is still essential. *Desert Breeze* comes closest, since stirring is the only human activity involved. *Tarbaby* is farthest, since it is an industrially produced derivative of a highly mechanized mining operation. And, as far as *Jojoba* is concerned, who knows what is in it *beside* beans? So at best, give it a tie with *Desert Breeze.*

b) Although it is often presumed that *more* natural is better than *less,* there is no particular reason to think that this is true. Are *Desert Breeze* and *Jojoba* better than *Soap?*

The quality of a thing is, in part, a function of how effective it is for achieving some end. For a shampoo, that amounts to how well it cleans hair. Other factors are the absence of undesirable side effects in its production or use, cost-effectiveness, the avoidance of drudgery, and (perhaps) elegance or style. For shampoos:

- Which cleans hair best?
- Which has the least damaging impact in production and use?
- Which is the best buy?
- Which is quick and easy?
- Which is most elegant?

The fact that something occurs with minimal human artifice is irrelevant to all of these issues except, possibly, user safety and environmental impact. But the answer to the question "Are more natural products safer for users and the environment than less natural ones?" is "Not necessarily." Even though the New Age seems besotted with the notion that natural products are better in just this sense. Producing them, unfortunately, often imposes great costs on the ecosystems that are plundered to feed the fad. The only way to find out if something will harm users is by testing it. Its place on some "naturalness" scale is irrelevant.

Some artificial products are relatively harmless, and some natural ones are downright lethal. Anesthetics are nice to have when we are facing surgery, wherever they come from. And, although it is truly "found," quicklime is not a good shampoo.

The only way to find out whether the production or use of a material is ecologically harmful is by testing its production and use. Its place on some "naturalness" scale is irrelevant, too.

Some artificial products are manufactured with great respect for the environment, and some natural ones are harvested or handled with devastating ecological impact. While Dupont moves heaven and earth to reduce the runoff from producing synthetic fibers, the overflow from hog lagoons is killing Pamlico Sound, the Appalachian woodlands are being pillaged in the search for ginseng root, and the rhinoceros is being killed off for better sex.

Indeed, naturalness-as-such is usually neither here nor there, with the result that the way the word "natural" is used these days, is little more than as a *persuasive* trigger, calculated to set off a romanticized nostalgia for an imaginarily remembered pristine and bucolic countryside—when, in fact, most bucolic countrysides are anything but pristine.

> *This is true even for fertilizers, although there is a hidden issue in the fertilizer controversy. Other elements (besides nitrogen, etc.) can be present in manufactured fertilizers. (I will not say "chemical fertilizers." No fertilizer is made up of anything but chemicals.) On the other hand, other elements (besides nitrogen, etc.) can be present in the codfish that we put in the corn hill with the seed. The issue here is purity, and nature is not, in and of itself, pure.*

2) Everyone who reads *Teen* or *Tiger Beat* has run into the profound injunction "Be natural!" peddled as important personal advice. In most contexts, it is roughly synonymous with "Be yourself!" and cashes out in the neighborhood of "Don't put on airs!" or "Avoid pretension!"

But if a modern avatar of Attila the Hun wrote to *Teen*'s advice columnists, should *Teen* advise him (as they have so many other anxious supplicants) to be himself? All things considered, one of the things a lout most needs to do is put on a few airs. How useful is it to advise him to be his own natural self when that is repellent, antisocial, and dysfunctional?

So perhaps, we should restrict such advice to *normal* people. Unfortunately, that doesn't help much, since "normal" and "abnormal" present the same problems as "natural" and "unnatural" all over again. Taking that into account, we could replace "natural" with "normal," remove any and all judgmental force from "normal" (i.e., boil it down to mean "common" or "frequent"), and rescue the injunction "be natural" as an encouragement to avoid deviance: "Don't do anything unusual!" Unfortunately, that leaves us at the mercy of whatever happens to be common at the time (which is frequently unpleasant). So file the advice columns' and the gigolo guides' use of "natural" along with that of the hucksters.

3) Nietzsche took Nature as a serious model for humans and their conduct. People should look to it for their moral paradigm. Being very specific, he said that we should look to the eagle, soaring grandly in the sky (with keen eye and mighty wings). Is this helpful? In fact, while people often admire some things about eagles, there are other eagle traits that they don't admire at all. Indeed, some eagle habits are quite nasty. Further, if we do look to the eagle

as an exemplar of Nature, what about all the other exemplars of Nature to which we could just as easily look? Grub worms for instance, or termites. Granted that they are pale and tend to flee the light, their place in Nature is nevertheless quite solid.

We can extol any model we like. If we want a bold and aggressive society, nature offers lions and eagles. If we want an ordered and disciplined society, nature offers army ants and communal baboons. Nature gives no principle for choosing. People must supply that themselves. Compare Nietzsche's notion of nature's paradigm to those visible in Thoreau, Rousseau, and contemporary Green politics. Nature, like the Bible, can provide a proof text for any axe we want to grind.

Indeed, it is impossible to suggest a life form that does not have a place in nature. Whatever occurs has a place in nature, since nature is the only place where things occur. Consequently, an injunction to take nature as our model is nothing more than an encouragement to do the unavoidable: *Be sure that everything you do is something that happens!*

So obviously, those who ostensibly endorse Nature as a model for humans have something far more specific on their agenda. As did Nietzsche, they select a particular "type" in nature that they find admirable for their own reasons and urge that type and no other as their model. (Nietzsche himself found natural models for both masters and slaves, eagles and camels, but urged people to emulate only one. That model's virtue did not reside in its *naturalness*, but in its strong will and self-assertiveness, which Nietzsche admired for reasons of his own.)

That is fine only as long as we don't fool ourselves into thinking that we are just "following nature"—with our *real* normative principles (whatever they may be) neatly concealed all the while.

4) An alternative approach is to note that everything has a role to play in nature and urge humans to find their own (collectively and individually). But there is either no problem in finding that role, or an insurmountable one, depending on whether "everything has a role to play in nature" means: everything has *some role or other* in nature, or everything has a *proper role that it should play* in nature.

a) On the first line, "Follow nature!" cashes out as *Be sure that what you do is something that at least one human does!*—which people cannot fail to fulfill, whatever they do. This is vacuous and can be set aside.

b) On the second line, we must determine which of the many roles that people play in nature are their *proper* ones. Making that determination is highly problematic for anyone who claims that nature itself is the only paradigm morality requires:

- "Proper" is normative, not descriptive. (For the record "essential" is just as normative as "proper." Whether coyotes are essential or superfluous depends on how much we value jackrabbits.)

- When we make the judgment that a particular role is a proper one, our normative principle cannot be its "naturalness" unless we are willing to argue in circles.
- So the notion of people's proper role cannot be fleshed out in terms of what is *natural* for them, or even in terms of what satisfies *natural law*, without vicious circularity.
- So it will have to be fleshed out in terms of another principle: perhaps self-interest, utility, or rule following.
- So we might as well bag the talk about "proper roles in nature" and go directly to that other principle.

All of the appeals to nature seen so far are blind alleys. I will now turn to an allegedly more promising variation on the theme.

B. Greek naturalism. In his *Nichomachean Ethics,* Aristotle said the virtue of a thing is achieved when it fulfills its essential capacities—those that set its kind apart from all other kinds. So if we want to know what is virtuous for X, we first identify its kind's capacities and then isolate the species-unique ones among them. *Its* virtue resides in *their* fulfillment. (Plato had used a political model in his *Republic*, not the biological one Aristotle favored. But, though the latter is more obviously "natural," both men were working truly common ground.)

1) The application of this principle to humans makes clear their continuity with the rest of nature but also their unique place in the way of things. Following Aristotle, it worked like this:

- All life forms possess one soul—the *nutritive* one—in common. Even plants share it, along with every animal and human.
- Humans, along with every species of animal life, possess an *active* soul in addition to the nutritive one. This sets them apart from plants (which lack it). People and animals do not placidly occupy space, metabolize, and reproduce. They respond, interact, move about, and adapt. Thus, people share *two* aspects of their being with animals: their biological processes, and the intentional activity that the will makes possible. These two souls exhaust the psyche inventory of the lower orders.
- Humans alone possess a third psyche: the *rational* soul or the *mind*. Because they have minds, they not only carry out life processes and respond actively to their surroundings but also make their surroundings respond to them. These three souls are the source of the traditional notions of human *affective, conative,* and *cognitive* powers.
- There is a particular virtue associated with the exercise of each of the three souls: Temperance for the first, Courage for the second, and Wisdom for the third.

- People achieve their *unique* virtue (Justice), and flourish, only when they exercise their minds in reflection and exercise their wills and appetites under its constraint.

2) Many moderns consider this conception of humanity wholesome. It recognizes human kinship to the whole living economy but demands that people keep their diverse powers under the discipline of their intelligence. It provides a coherent and intelligible model of what a human being is, and a road map of sorts to virtuous self-fulfillment and human flourishing. (With a little Christian vermiculite, this is the soil in which more recent "virtue ethics" took root. See William Bennett's *The Book of Virtues* and Alasdair MacIntyre's *After Virtue*.)

3) However, either all and only uniquely human capacities have attendant human virtues, or there are some that don't.

a) If the former is the case, two problems ensue.

First, rationality is neither uniquely nor universally human. Other life forms are capable of rational thought. Some monkeys, for instance, respond with reflective empathy to the plight of others, going hungry when they see that taking food from a hopper subjects their peers to pain. Rather than watch their lab mates writhe, they simply stop eating. This has some clearly affective dimensions, but it also relies on understanding causal connections. If that is not cognitive enough, consider dolphins' communication. That is *clearly* rational, and they're not even primates.

Also some humans (the vegetative comatose, trauma victims, and one-second zygotes) lack rational capacities. But we who recognize the rationality of some nonhuman primates and cetaceans must, on a "capacities" account of morality, welcome them into the moral arena. And we who recognize the nonrationality of flatliners and the like can, on the same account of morality, excuse them from it.

Second, even if rationality were uniquely human, it would not be the only capacity that was. This means that there is a possibility of additional human "virtues" whose practice may not, in any obvious way, contribute to human flourishing. To see this, keep two principles in mind: *What human virtues amount to depends on what capacities turn out to be uniquely human;* and *Whether people will "flourish" by practicing their virtues depends on what those virtues are.*

Many capacities are uniquely human, but not edifying: unique capacities that real people actually have, as evidenced by behavior unique to the species. For instance, humans are the only ones able to paint portraits, but also the only ones able to appreciate pornography; the sole ecologically aware species, but also the only one with the capacity for vandalism; the only species with the capacity to indulge in religion, but also the only one with the potential for practicing ritual child sacrifice; and so forth. It could, of course, be argued on various grounds that these capacities are not sufficiently basic to generate virtues of their own. We shall see.

It should be obvious that cultivating virtues that might allegedly accrue to the uniquely human capacities for appreciating pornography, engaging in vandalism, and practicing witchcraft are dubious routes to human flourishing. Consequently, we are likely to decide that only *some* uniquely human capacities have attendant virtues.

b) But if that is the case, this approach to morality turns out to be arbitrary, circular, or untestable. There must be grounds, after all, for figuring out (or deciding) which uniquely human capacities have attendant virtues and which don't; and there are relatively few on offer.

(1) Just because. These do. Those don't. That's that. *This might even be true; but it sure is arbitrary.*

(2) In terms of whether the capacities in question are good ones or bad ones. *But the plan was to identify the goods and bads of human morality in terms of the virtues unique human capacities generate. If we must morally evaluate the capacities themselves, this approach is incurably circular.*

(3) In terms of what we can discover by revelation or intuition. God might say, or we might "just know." *But revelation and intuition, lacking decision procedures, are not viable channels of cognition. Appeals to them are irretrievably untestable.*

(4) In terms of whether a capacity is "basic" (on the notion that only basic ones have attendant virtues). *This is much more promising, but to make it work, what "basic" means must be specified concretely, and reasons given for the notion that only all basic capacities have attendant virtues.*

(a) What does "basic" mean in this context? The word "basic" has many uses. Some ("lacking in silica" and "nonacidic," for instance) are irrelevant. Its more relevant uses fall into three chief families:

- Regarding the simplicity (irreducibility) of a thing: *The simple is basic; the complex not.* But the idea that the mind is *irreducibly simple* is far from obvious. That is, in fact, one focus of the argument between those who see it as a substance and those who see it as a functional complex.
- Regarding the essence of a thing: *The essential is basic; the accidental is not.* This looks more promising, but is the mind "essentially" human? Insofar as there are people who do not have any rational capacity, and nonpeople who do, it is difficult to claim that the possession of rational capacity is "of the essence" in the way that it needs to be.
- Regarding the root (source) of a thing: *The root is basic; the branch not.* While we could argue that rationality is the root of human *personhood*, it is not the root or source of the organism. It begins simultaneously with the organism and continues to develop with it over time.

On the other hand, perhaps the rational capacity is the root of those troublesome other human capacities—pornography, vandalism, witchcraft—rather than vice versa. It seems obvious, for instance, that the capacity to appreciate pornography is derived from the capacity to imagine; and, perhaps, the capacity to imagine is one part of the rational capacity. (If so, of course, then the rational capacity is not partless.)

If this line of argument is plausible and generalizable, then the only question that remains is why basic capacities (in this sense) get virtues and non-basic (i.e., derivative) ones don't.

(b) Why do only basic capacities have attendant virtues? The only apparent reason is that if derivative capacities had attendant virtues, then there would be immoral virtues (absent a question-begging direct prohibition of immoral virtues). But that is circularity once removed.

The notion of an immoral virtue sounds self-contradictory; but that is only because we are accustomed to defining virtues in terms of values. *This* system is supposed to define values in terms of virtues (and virtues in terms of uniquely human capacities, whatever they may be), and it cannot do that without begging its own question.

So in spite of the fact that Greek Naturalism, as stated previously, "recognizes human kinship to the whole living economy, but demands that people govern their diverse powers under the discipline of their intelligence," it is shaky in formulation and arbitrary, circular, or untestable in practice. It ignores the fact that many of the noblest human capacities are shared with non-humans and the fact that acting out many of their unique ones produces loathsome behavior. Sadly, we can mend these glitches only by smuggling moral judgments into the specification of which capacities engender virtues, appealing to revelation or intuition or by sheer act of will.

If, as seems likely, there are concealed assumptions (about which human capacities are *good* and which ones are *bad*) behind virtue ethics, then it is not an unbiased mapping of human nature. It is, rather, a selective mapping of those capacities that the mappers appreciate and endorse for normative reasons of their own. It has nothing to do with following nature *as such*. Like the reasons for Nietzsche's preference for eagles over camels, the true "moral principle" is concealed beneath the rhetoric. The classic notions that morality amounts to "living virtuously" and that living virtuously amounts to "fulfilling the capacities that are uniquely human" sound helpful. To flourish, however, we must fulfill our good capacities and stifle our bad ones; and to do that, we have to know which are which.

Since nature doesn't say which are which, we must turn elsewhere to find out. Many people turn to God or Society for an answer; but, in so doing, they lay down "Follow Nature!" for another banner.

13

Obeying Rules

Since self-interest and nature cannot determine good conduct and character, many people turn to *rules* instead, defining right conduct as behavior that conforms to proper rules, and good people as those who act rightly. Such moral systems are alleged to identify which human capacities are worth fulfilling and which parts of nature are good, as well as to ameliorate rampant selfishness. They are also said to simplify moral decision making and reinforce the stability of society.

While everyone makes *some* use of rules in the moral enterprise, the connection between rules and conduct can be seen in two ways.

- The value of rules depends on whether they endorse good acts. Proper rules *reflect* good acts.
  Seen this way, rules are *less* basic to morality than acts.
- The value of acts depends on whether they comply with proper rules. Proper rules *define* good acts.
  Seen this way, rules are *more* basic to morality than acts.

People who think that rules are more basic to morality than acts are called deontologists.

While deontologists all agree that morality amounts to obeying proper rules, they disagree about what makes a rule proper. There are at least four views about that.

- A rule is proper if it comes from the *highest authority.*
  When the "highest authority" is identified as God, proper rules amount to *divine commands* or *the laws of God.*
- A rule is proper if it is established (by formal acts, tradition or precedent) and operative in the community.

Here, proper rules amount to a combination of *positive laws*, *common laws*, and *traditional mores and folkways*.
- A rule is proper if it reflects natural values.
  Here, proper rules amount to *natural laws*.
- A rule is proper if it is consistently universalizable.
  Here, proper rules amount to *applied rationality*.

With such diverse perspectives on what makes rules proper, it is no surprise that deontologists don't all have the same set of rules. Nor is it surprising that their assorted sets are beset by numerous problems.

In this chapter, I will first look at some of the special difficulties that are involved in the notion of following God's rules. Then I will look at the *pros* and *cons* of deontological morality in general.

3. Obeying God's Rules

The literature on theistic morality is huge. In its Judeo-Christian subset, which is also huge, we could do worse than look at the works of Richard Niebuhr, Dietrich Bonhoeffer, Rudolph Otto, and Will Herberg. Some theistic moralities are individual, mystical, and subjective. Others are highly institutionalized and authoritarian. All, however, are predicated on the existence of a God that:

- is external to oneself and one's group,
- has established standards against which people and their conduct are to be judged, and
- lets (some) people know what those standards are.

A. Given the *correct* set of standards, one could put it to work. But the correct set isn't *given*. One has to *find* it, and there is more than one place to look. Christians, Muslims, neo-Mithraists, and hundreds of other groups all have their own idea of which standards (as well as which of the alleged gods that are said to provide them) are *the real thing*. Consequently, one needs some sort of justification for saying that any particular set of rules is truly God-given, and that alternative and incompatible sets are not.

Many individuals, through provincialism, ignorance, sloth, or zeal, will not admit that they need to justify their belief that the rules embodied in (say) the New Testament, the Koran, or the Code of Cloven Bull Foot are the real thing. But as long as alternative rule sets (from alternative gods) are out there, we do need good reasons for choosing one set of rules over the others, whether we admit it or not.

1) Several different lines of justification are used; but they all begin with the notion that if a set of rules is from God, then it is *necessarily* morally correct and should be obeyed. If that notion were true, we could proceed directly to "How can we know that a particular rule set is, in fact, from God?" But its truth needs showing.

People who defend the notion that "If a set of rules is from God, then it is *necessarily* morally correct and should be obeyed," will make one or the other of two claims.

- Nothing worthy of worship promulgates immoral rules.
  God's goodness guarantees the propriety of God's Will. God only wills things because they are good.
- God is, by definition, the final moral authority.
  God's authority guarantees the propriety of God's Will. Whatever God wills is good just because God wills it.

Neither of these claims, however, will carry the needed freight.

a) The first claim makes acts morally prior to rules. While that may be correct, it is no way to defend the notion that rules define good acts. Furthermore, it underscores the fact that to decide that a being is God (i.e., deserves worship) is to make a moral judgment. We cannot decide whether worship is deserved unless our values are already in place. Consequently, the pronouncements of God *cannot* tell us what is valuable. We have to know what is valuable in order to know which "god" to listen to.

b) The second claim can be read two ways. (Recall that the word "authority" has two senses.) Neither will do the job.

(1) Not even an authority in the first sense ("one with relevant expertise") is certain to issue proper rules. Even experts make occasional mistakes. However, even if we soften the claim to make it, "God's expertise provides a reasonable assurance of the propriety of God's will," a problem remains: knowing that a rule set comes from an *expert ruler* requires showing either:

- that the rules themselves are good ones, so that we can infer that the one who promulgated them is an expert; or
- that the one who promulgated the rules is reliable enough in tested cases to be trusted in untested ones.

The first directly presumes that a standard for good rules is already in place. The second is a safe practice only as long as it continues to be reconfirmed in use; but that *also* presumes that a standard for good rules is already in place. Either way, appeals to God's expertise involve an independent value judgment that God *is* an expert. Consequently, for those who cite God's expertise, the claim that the rules come from God is no longer morally basic.

(2) On the other hand, the notion that an authority in the other sense ("one who is in control") is sure to issue proper rules ignores the fact that, within human experience, those in control are often morally corrupt.

To be sure, The One in Final Control may not have some of the traits that make human power players so untrustworthy. But how can we *know* that? The only way we could would be to know that It is *good*; which means, once again, that validating the source of a set of rules can only occur when our moral values are already in place.

So it is *not* clear that a set of rules said to be from God is necessarily morally correct and should be obeyed. Furthermore, even if it were clear, when we proceed to ask, "How can we know that a particular rule set is, in fact, from God?" more troubles quickly arise.

2) The answer to, "How can we know that a particular rule set is, in fact, from God?" will involve an appeal to self-evidence, intuition, inertia, or revelation. None of these appeals will work.

- It is self evident that this set comes from God.
  Self-evident means one of two things: "obvious to me" or "necessarily (i.e., formally) true." Only the latter is the real thing. (Appeals to the "obvious" are actually appeals to intuition or inertia.) Unfortunately, however, formal truths are still vacuous.
- It is intuitively clear that this set comes from God.
  Intuition won't work because, among other reasons, there are too many rival intuitions—and no internal grounds for choosing between them. Further, all that appeals to intuition usually mean is "it seems obvious," and what seems obvious is a function of inertia, not truth.
- Everybody in my culture thinks this set comes from God.
  "Go with the flow" is too circumstantial to verify life commitments. "Jesus is God in Texas" is too easily matched with "Allah is God in Sudan." The fact that someone was born in Texas rather than Sudan makes his or her familiarity with Jesus more likely than familiarity with Allah; but familiarity is not evidence of truth.

  Riding the inertia wave does not *necessarily* prevent us from landing on the right beach. We *can* "get lucky." But, while trusting to luck may be harmless when picking a $1 lotto number, it is inadequate for choosing a way of life.
- God has revealed that this set is proprietary.
  There are many alternative "revelations," and the choice between them must be made on good grounds. Claiming that it is revealed that a particular set of allegedly revealed rules are really revealed is blatantly circular. So is claiming that it is revealed that the rule revealer is really God. And, besides, how do we know that these revelations are true? Are they revealed too? Thus, appealing to revelation only moves the demand for good reasons back a few (or infinitely many) steps. It does not meet it.

So, claiming that a rule articulates God's will does not validate it. We must first determine that there is a God who wills in the first place, which of the numerous alleged gods is the Real One, whether that "real God" did, in fact, will this rule, and whether the rule in question has been accurately received and recorded. But all of those moves presume that we have the values in place that are necessary to make such judgments. Deciding which allegedly God-given code to follow involves making a moral appraisal. Consequently, as is lucidly explained in Kai Nielsen's *Ethics without God*, God-given rules cannot define morality; morality has to define them.

B. As difficult as it may be to locate God's moral rules, many people think that they have them in hand. But the possession of allegedly God-given moral rules encourages fanaticism and alienates responsibility.

1) God-given moral rules cultivate fanaticism by telling their practitioners that their practices are divinely guaranteed, not open to question, and exclusively true. Secure in the impossibility of being mistaken, it is much too easy to justify appallingly destructive treatment of infidels. This phenomenon is neither trivial nor rare. Consider the status of religious minorities in Ulster, Bosnia, Afghanistan, Sudan, and Alabama.

It also works as a facade for interests that are, at root, political or economic rather than religious per se. That phenomenon is also neither trivial nor rare. Consider the imperialism and/or colonialism of England, the United States, Germany, France, Spain, Belgium, and Portugal.

2) If God tells us what to do, then our responsibility to figure out what to do, our responsibility for what we do, and our responsibility for the consequences of what we do are all alienated to God. But these three responsibilities are essential parts of what it is to participate in the moral enterprise at all. An individual with no responsibility to figure out what to do, no responsibility for what he or she does, and no responsibility for its output, is out of the moral arena altogether. The notion of a moral puppet is an oxymoron.

C. So if there is a way to be a responsible moral agent, it is not to be found in "Obeying God's Rules" any more than it is to be found in "Following Nature" or "Following Your Star." Not every rule-based conception of morality involves an appeal to God, however. In the next section, setting deontology's contingent theistic dimension aside, I will examine the *pros* and *cons* of rule-based morality as such.

4. Obeying Rules as Such

Whether articulated in terms of divine law, natural law, positive law, tradition and precedent or applied rationality, rule-based moralities have certain features, and certain problems, in common.

A. Ambiguity. The words "rule" and "law" are both ambiguous. Both have a "descriptive" and a "prescriptive" use.

Descriptive rules are reports of what happens "as a rule." They are true or false, depending on whether they accurately report what actually happens. They can be homely and mundane or abstract and formal. Very basic ones (for example, *"what goes around comes around"* and *"for every action there is an equal and opposite reaction"* are called "laws of nature.")

Since rules of this kind do not endorse or prohibit anything, people can neither obey nor break them. When *exceptions* to a descriptive rule occur, we revise the rule rather than trying to "punish the perpetrator."

Prescriptive rules, however, are imperatives designed to channel events, not indicatives designed describe them. They can be neither true nor false; but can be coherent or not, enforceable or not, constitutional or not, well conceived or not, etc. They can be positive, negative, or procedural: *"You may turn right on red after you stop"; "One may not buy, possess, or sell heroin in Virginia"; "To claim your prize, submit two proofs of purchase."* Some are intentional edicts or legislations. Others are expressions of accumulated precedents and conventions. Both legislations and conventions deal with behaviors that range from the fairly trivial (the rules of Australian football, books of proper table manners) to the crucially important (the U.S. Tax Code, Common Law).

Ordinarily, when *violations* of normative rules occur, the perpetrators are punished and the law stands. (There are exceptions. Widespread and uncontrollable disobedience may eventually result in legal revision. Consider the Volstead Act and the Eighteenth and Twenty-first Amendments to the Constitution.) Punishment, when it occurs, is measured out in a system of sanctions that, themselves, can either be legislated (ranging from a few minutes in the penalty box to a lethal injection) or conventional (ranging from a parental scolding to being socially ostracized).

> **Crimes against Nature?**
>
> Equivocation between prescriptive and descriptive senses of the word "law" is the main source of "natural law" ethics and of the notorious prohibitions of "crimes against nature" and/or "unnatural acts" that grace various bodies of positive law. People should know better. The occurrence of *descriptive* natural laws is obvious. Equivocation makes the occurrence of *prescriptive* ones seem obvious, too, even though that would involve the occurrence of such things as imperatives, conventions, precedents, edicts, and/or legislations without human artifice. At least "divine law" ethicists have a notion of where their non-humanly-sourced normative laws are supposed to have come from.

Although it is easy to equivocate between the descriptive and prescriptive senses of "rule" and "law," *descriptive* rules and laws are of minimum interest or use in spelling out morality. Morality is about what we *ought* to do; and saying that we *ought to do something* presupposes that we have some choice in the matter. But saying that we obey descriptive laws is only to say that we do things that happen (or do not do things that don't happen). But *whatever* we do is something that happens—there is no choice about *that*. So, to say that we *ought* to obey a descriptive law (i.e., ought to do the inevitable) presupposes two incompatible assumptions. No theory based on inconsistent assumptions is useful. So, no descriptive natural law theory of morals is useful.

Prescriptive rules, on the other hand, have a place in almost every system of morality. Indeed, in some, they are held to be the *basis* of the entire enterprise. After examining whether that notion is correct, I will look at the roles they play in moral systems generally.

B. Are rules the *basis* of morality? There is no doubt that prescriptive rules occur. They are part of the fabric of human society at every level. But, morally speaking, are they *basic* or *derivative?* The ramifications of two issues suggest that, even though they are important, they are not basic.

- Is the justification for obeying them *external* or *internal?*
  "Because the consequences of obedience are preferable to those of disobedience" and "because of where they come from" would be *external* justifications. "Because their truth is immediately knowable" and "because a rule is a rule" would be *internal* justifications.

  If the justification for generally obeying moral rules is external, then the rules themselves are not morally basic.
- Should every moral rule be obeyed every time?
  If any moral rule has exceptions, we must decide when to follow it and when not. Further, if there are rival moral rules or conflicting ones, we must decide which one(s) to follow and which not. But unless those decisions are themselves rule-governed (covered by second-order rules), then rules are not morally basic. On the other hand, if they *are* covered, but the second-order rules themselves have exceptions, rivals, and conflicts, then rules are still not morally basic (absent an infinite regress of rules for rule selection).

  Infinite regresses. If every act must be preceded by a decision to act, and every decision to act is an act itself, then before we act we must decide to act, and before we decide to act we must decide to decide to act, and so forth, ad infinitum. Unfortunately, on such an analysis, there is not enough time for even *one* act (and its necessary predecessors) in a finite lifetime.

  So, too, with rules. If there must be second-order rules for picking first order ones, must there not also be third-order rules for picking second-order ones, etc., ad infinitum? If so, then coming up with the right rule will take a *very* long time.

Nevertheless, there are moral uses for rules, and plausible reasons for obeying them, whether they are morally basic or not.

1) *Reasons for generally obeying moral rules.* I can think of three plausible reasons for generally obeying moral rules: the good consequences that ensue, the rules' authoritative source, and our direct discernment of their truth. The first two are clearly external.

a) Consequences of obeying rules. Moral systems based on rule obedience are alleged to have six useful consequences. They

- expedite deliberation and action by avoiding repetitive make-work,
- reduce the labor and stress of independent decision making,
- discourage "special pleading" and "being arbitrary" in favor of consistent decision making,
- enhance successful human interaction by improving the ability to predict what people will do,
- reinforce social stability by enhancing successful human interaction, and
- enhance the achievement of a society's goals by reinforcing social stability.

I will comment on each of these in turn.

(1) Expediting deliberation and action. Working without any rules would require reinventing the moral wheel each day, and spending so much time deciding what to do that little time would be left for doing. And, without general rules, we would be unequipped to deal with emergencies. We do not have time for deliberation when a Manson stands in the door.

On the other hand, the same "expedition" can be obtained by recalling past ad hoc decisions summarized, perhaps, in prima facie rules, or "rules of thumb." (A prima facie rule is one that explicitly includes the possibility of being overridden. Prima facie rules are very important to utilitarians, as we shall see.)

With secure evidence that some benchmarks are true, all that purported order and efficiency could be attractive. But order and efficiency are not enough to license ignoring *content*. The content of ideologies is important, whether we are talking about theistic, economic, or political ones. It makes a difference whether we are committed to Nazism, Libertarianism, Maoism, or Democracy, or to this or that (or any) religion. One reason it makes a difference is that some political systems (and some religions) are committed to the notion of human dignity, responsibility, and other morally worthwhile things, while some are not. Efficiency in the pursuit of degradation has little to recommend it.

(2) Reducing labor and stress. Citing rules to back up employee dismissals, for instance, is easier than actually evaluating the quality of people's work, and diminishes (or eliminates) anxiety over the consequences of letting them go. With both deliberation and outcome responsibilities set aside, however, a rule follower becomes a nonparticipant in the moral enterprise, becoming (instead) a mere extension of who or whatever made the rules. That can have extraordinarily bad results. Consider all of the people who ever said, "I was just following orders." That is, after all, what "obeying the rules" boils down to.

Furthermore, even though there is an apparent simplification of the moral enterprise that is achieved by shoving all of the responsibility off onto an "external source," it is *only* apparent. It doesn't actually save the labor of evidence collection. It only relocates it.

Example. If we are committed to the Democratic Party Platform, we do not have to figure out a position on farm subsidies. The platform spells it out. That appears to save a lot of time and effort; but on what reasonable grounds (other than the truth of its planks) might we subscribe to that platform to begin with? Consequently, *reasonably* subscribing to the platform saves us no time and effort at all, even though it seems to. We have to weigh all the planks, in order to reasonably subscribe to the whole.

(3) Encouraging consistency. Because the rules themselves are usually in place before any particular individual comes on the scene, obeying them has an aura of objectivity and longevity that discourages deviations and exceptions. This can interfere, however, with empathy, mercy, and other humane adjustments to justice that may be highly valuable.

(4) Enhancing human interaction. It improves the ability to predict what people will do, and consequently enhances successful human interaction. One very nice application of this principle is Jurgen Habermas's notion of the prerequisites of human conversation, as laid out in *The Theory of Communicative Action*. If we cannot expect rule-governed language use, communication becomes impossible.

On the other hand, accurate predictions are not *impossible* without rules. We could make fair predictions in at least some cases by relying on human inertia alone. Regular behavior and rule-governed behavior are not the same thing. Rules can generate regularity; but so can habits.

(5) Reinforcing social stability. If everyone knows the rules (his or her station and its duties) and obeys them, then not only do people know what to expect, but also social relationships become constant. It is only when people get "uppity" that change and disruption begin to set in.

On the other hand, the value of stability per se is an open question. Like the other alleged advantages of obedience, the value of social stability depends on the specific rules that are being obeyed to produce it, and the merits of the social system that is being stabilized.

(6) Enhancing the achievement of social goals. Consider the benefits of following "Roberts's Rules" for conducting the business of a university faculty. Even with them, faculty deliberations have trouble reaching closure. Without them, *nothing* would happen.

However, enhancing the effective achievement of a society's goals is only as good or bad as the goals themselves. Letting a faculty (or a congress) dither in chaos might be a good thing, sometimes. Further, assiduously sticking to the rules can undercut the achievement of social goals by preventing cutting to the chase when that is what is really needed.

Example. A severely retarded young man was convicted (on the alleged victim's testimony) of molesting a young girl. After he had been in prison for some years, she recanted (saying that she made it up). After considerable deliberation, the governor granted the convicted felon a full pardon and released him. The prison doctors said he needed rehabilitation to reenter society, and the local social service agencies put a price tag of $50,000 on the required therapy. A private bill to pay for it was eliminated from the legislatures' deliberations, however, because it was filed five minutes after the deadline for new bills. The severely retarded (no longer young) man is now on the streets, unemployed, untreated, and a prime candidate for eventual lifetime state accommodations.

In spite of the fact that the consequences of following the rules can be a mixed bag, the consequences of obeying *some* rules under *some* circumstances are beneficial enough to encourage compliance. But are there any reasons to obey rules that are not so *utilitarian*?

b) Sources. Perhaps a particular set of rules should always be obeyed because it is from an unimpeachable source. Whether that move is plausible depends on the source we have in mind; and the usual ones on offer—God, tradition, and law (i.e., what *lawyers* cite)—are thorny.

(1) God. If we *know* that the source of the rules is God, obeying them might be justified by an appeal to filial piety and the conviction that a rule giver truly worthy of worship would never issue bad ones.

But knowing that the rules come from God involves knowing that their source deserves to be worshipped, and knowing that presupposes that our basic normative criteria are already in place. Consequently, rules endorsed this way are *not* morally basic.

(2) Tradition. Justifying obeying a set of rules because it is traditional is hopeless, given the variety of traditions that history provides. We would first have to find out which tradition was *right*. Only then could we say that a particular set of rules was the set to obey (now because the *right* tradition confirmed it). But how shall we decide which tradition is right? Local traditions are the most familiar and, usually, the most compelling; but that may be nothing more than provincial chauvinism at work. The only possible criteria are a) the quality of the behavior a tradition calls for (which leads right back into ad hoc consequentialist judgments), b) a "higher" rule set (which only relocates the problem), or c) the discernible truth of the rules at hand.

(3) Law. Justifying obedience to the rules because they are embodied in the law shares all the problems involved in justifying obedience by appealing to tradition. Additionally, it makes morality inconstant (inconsistent over time). The law, after all, changes whenever the sovereign so decides, regardless. How often (and in what way) such changes will occur will vary from one society to another, as a function of many different factors. Law is especially likely to be erratic when the sovereign is an individual (such as a ship's captain or a dictator), is irrational (such as George III or the Virginia legislature on the issue of "crimes against nature"), or is in the thrall of

special interest groups (from the East India Company to Halliburton). When the law can change for erratic reasons, the constancy of practice and consistency of expectations which rule following is supposed to encourage go by the boards.

Further, justifying obeying the rules just because they are embodied in the law can severely endanger human welfare. Consider what people were legally commanded to do in Virginia in 1845, in Germany in 1937, or at Abu Ghraib prison in 2004.

Further still, if our only moral duty is to obey the law, our moral responsibility is completely alienated to another.

Finally, the identification of morality with obedience to the law prevents the possibility of bringing the law itself under moral judgment. Since, under such circumstances, talk of morally good law is redundant and talk of morally bad law is self-contradictory, morally criticizing and improving the law is totally blocked.

In sum, obeying rules because they are said to come from God, are traditional, or are embodied in law, cannot be justified without appealing to the legitimacy of the particular God, tradition, or law invoked; and that is not something that the source itself can establish without circularity.

There are, however, two additional ways in which we might know that we have the right rules: discovering that obeying them brings better consequences than obeying any alternative set (and better than the results of ignoring rules altogether), and direct discernment that they are correct. But, since an appeal to the *consequences* of obedience would be ironically self-defeating for any rule moralist, the only entirely coherent reason to obey a particular set of rules must be the direct discernment that they are correct.

c) Direct discernment. If we could directly discern that a particular rule or set of rules is correct, then we could infer that what it endorses (or enjoins) is good (or bad), and that it should always be obeyed. Claiming that we can directly discern that a particular rule or set of rules is correct looks like an *epistemic* claim. On analysis, however, making such a claim about a particular rule set amounts to saying that it is one or another of three different things, none of which are both informative and epistemically reliable. It may mean that the rule set is *formally* correct, *intuitively* correct, or *obviously* correct.

But formal *truths* are vacuous; and there is no reason to think formally correct rule sets fare any better. Further, *intuited* truths are unreliable; and there is no reason to think intuitively correct rule sets fare any better. And, finally, *obvious* truths can be mistaken; and there's no reason to think obviously correct rule sets fare any better.

So direct discernment does not validate constant obedience under any interpretation. Consequently, since internal justifications for obeying moral rules all depend on direct discernment, there is no internal justification for obeying moral rules. There are still some *external* ones. But if the only justification for obeying moral rules is external, then moral rules are not morally *basic*. They are still an important part of the enterprise, but not as the *source* of values. Proper moral rules are derived from basic values, not *vice versa*.

2) Alternative rules, rule conflicts, and exceptions. Using a rule that has exceptions or rivals means using our *judgment*. But using our judgment about which rule to follow, or whether to make an exception in a particular case, is *not* "just following rules." This is evident when we consider cases. Look at the rules about killing, starting with a classic:

- Thou shalt not kill.
  On its face, this bars killing *any* living thing: plant, animal, or human. For humans to survive, at least plants need to be excepted. But any such exception will be the result of someone making a *judgment* about what is practical and fair. Only with such external decision do we get to:
- Thou shalt not kill humans.
  On its face, this bans capital punishment, all but the mildest wars, and the use of lethal force in self-defense and the protection of the defenseless from abuse, torture, and death. Most people have decided that these are reasonable exceptions. So, exercising judgment again, they have made an external decision to say:
- Thou shalt do no murder.
  But the force of *that* depends entirely on what is judged to constitute murder. Most people decide that murder is something like *wrongful intentional killing with malice and deliberation*. But defining "wrongful" is, once again, an exercise of judgment that is external to the rule itself. So, exercising their judgment in many different directions, various people have articulated a large number of rules about killing people that are allegedly more specific, exceptionless, and/or applicable.

Which killing rule should we pick? More important, why?

- Never prevent a human life.
  Certainly no contraception; possibly no chastity.
- Only kill nonviable potential humans.
  Conservative pro-choice.
- Kill any potential human its bearer chooses.
  Aggressive pro-choice.
- Let nonviable human infants die.
  Standard medical practice for anomalous neonates.
- Kill nonviable human infants.
  Generally illegal, but it has its medical advocates.
- Never let a human being die.
  The rationale for aggressive geriatric care.

- Never kill yourself.
  The law in most states (but not Oregon).
- Never help humans kill themselves.
  Now the topic of active debate.
- Never kill a human being.
  No war, no executions, no abortions, no lethal force.
- Only kill human beings for a good reason.
  Some war, self-defense, protecting the helpless and/or innocent, and a few abortions (at least for rape and incest).
- Only kill a human being if you have a license.
  Killings by executioners, police, bounty hunters, the military, and 007. No private enterprise.
- Only kill bad people.
  Arnie's position in True Lies.
- Kill anyone you would prefer dead.
  The apparent position of a growing number.

And—since killing is not the only moral issue there is—the same rule-selection problem will crop up again and again as we try to work out a complete rule set to cover all contingencies.

Further, even when we have (somehow) chosen a set of rules to cover the full variety of moral issues, three problems still remain.

- First, since any set of rules must be finite, there will be "gaps" where judgment is required.
- Second, whenever two or more rules conflict, we must decide which one to follow. For instance, since many people subscribe to both "never let a human die" and "never kill a human," judgment is called for in many complicated pregnancies—kill the baby, or let the mother die?
- Third, unless the rules are remarkably precise and numerous, there are bound to be exceptions to them.

Finding effective ways to choose between alternative rules, to adjudicate rule conflicts, and to decide when to make exceptions constitutes a three-part problem that no list of rules can solve internally.

Perhaps we can find some second-order rules that will help. However, the following possible Rules for Rule Picking illustrate the difficulties we run into when looking for such help:

- Pick one that is coherent, intelligible, and easy to apply.
  Which of the listed Killing Rules is incoherent, unintelligible, or difficult to apply?

- Pick one that is consistent with a finite, coherent, and intelligible rule set.
  More than one set can be finite, consistent, and intelligible and still include individually atrocious rules.
- Pick one that is consistent with a *good*, finite, coherent, and intelligible rule set.
  But a good *rule set is just one containing* good *rules.*
- Pick a *good* rule.
  Well!

So, once again, it is quite clear that no rule (or rule set) is *basic* to morality. On the other hand, while rules are not basic, they are still important.

C. Though not morally basic, rules are still important. In spite of the troubles that occur when we try to make them morally basic, rules are morally useful as reminders, time savers, and sources of social cohesion, as long as we have the right ones and keep some *caveats* in mind.

The only point of moral rules is to assure good conduct (even, if necessary, for the wrong reasons). To be sure that they achieve their point, we must remember that they:

- sometimes need revision,
- almost always have exceptions,
- can conflict with each other, and
- often will not work without extrinsic reinforcements (positive or negative).

It is also important to remember that moral rules tend to:

- confuse people's ideas about moral motivation, and
- take on a life of their own.

1) Rules sometimes need revision. A frequent weakness of rule morality, as usually practiced, is inflexibility. In contrast to utilitarians, who can adjust their methods of maximizing the good to fit fluid circumstances, Rule Moralists tend to stick with their rules, no matter what. But rules often *need* to change, for several reasons.

a) Because a rule is a social convention, it can "calcify," that is, become so institutionalized that people automatically obey it, without any thought about why it became a rule in the first place. Once calcified, a rule tends to be obeyed even when the reasons why it became a rule no longer obtain. Rules that have thus outrun their usefulness should be changed.

Consider pre-refrigeration dietary laws and conventions. These days, oysters "R" in season year round; but many people still decline them from May through August. Similarly, although the danger of trichinosis can be eliminated by hard-freezing pork for twenty-four hours before cooking it, millions of people refuse pork altogether.

b) Sometimes there are rules that the vast majority of a population refuses to obey, even in the face of draconian sanctions. The fact that they are nearly universally flouted undermines the general respect for rules that any society needs in order to function. Without such general respect, the general "rule of law" breaks down, and a wide variety of atrocious behavior is increasingly likely to occur.

The Depression Era prohibition laws are a good example of this. Some contend that contemporary marijuana laws are, too. A society needs to put its energy into rules that can be enforced. This is not to say that popular behavior should never be banned. (Racial and sexual discrimination are very popular, but need to be controlled.) It is, rather, simply to note the difficulties involved in relying on rules to modify widespread behavior. At the very least, *attitudes* need to be addressed and modified, too, until the rules "make sense" to most people.

c) A rule may not generate the good results for which it was fashioned, or may generate bad results along with them. Societies have rules in order to achieve good results. When one achieves very bad results, or no good ones, it probably needs to be changed. We must look at *all* the consequences of a rule and adjust its formulation accordingly.

It has been argued that the criminalization of abortion in the late nineteenth century led not only to the desired results (fewer abortions) but also to "gynecological bondage" to those women who complied, and to a dreadful mortality rate for those who attempted to have abortions anyway, under medically uncontrolled circumstances. It has also been argued that the decriminalization of abortion in the twentieth century lead not only to the desired results (safer abortions and the increased independence of women), but also to a dreadful increase in careless promiscuity and the use of abortion as a technique of after-the-fact birth control for unwanted pregnancies.

In contrast, prohibition probably did not decrease the per capita consumption of alcohol by as much as an ounce. All it did was to generate the cash flow that made it possible for the mob to expand the scope of its interests.

The gist of the matter is that when new and unforeseen situations arise, we may need to modify or delete an existing rule, and/or add new ones to the set. As far as positive law is concerned, established procedures for doing this are part of the fabric of any society that is adaptable enough to survive. This is why enduring societies tend to have legislators, not just executives and police officers. A judicial branch, armed with precedents and (in some societies) constitutional restraints completes the balancing act, seeing to it that the legislators do not run amok. Thus, we can have laws that are responsive to new situations, and some stability and continuity at the same time. It may not be utopia, but it is a long way ahead of the state of nature and the divine right of kings.

It is far more difficult in the area of morals, however. While no one is likely to believe that (say) the U.S. Code is permanent, universal, and sacrosanct, many people believe that every needed moral rule is already in place and inviolable. This is a mistake, however. New situations can require moral modifications, deletions, and additions as well as legal ones.

> *Example.* From legends handed down over eons, we know that the ancients felt a *moral* impetus to multiply and fill the earth. (In fact, in some sparsely settled areas of the world, that is still so strongly felt that bounties are paid to large families.) In the twentieth century, however, the race came up against a crunch between diminishing natural resources and exponentially growing populations. So many people felt a moral urge to put limits on human procreation.

Until quite recently, inconvenience and "old fashioned" moral scruples seemed to be winning out, but easier methods of contraception, coupled with the realization of what the rest of the world is up to, is gradually turning things around. Even in Ireland.

Other traditions are changing, too.

- Traditionally, women felt a moral impetus to marry and stay married. This impetus was reinforced by law and custom. Independent, single women were ostracized; anything other than the most menial employment was almost impossible to find; divorce was difficult if not impossible; and property laws were chauvinistic beyond contemporary belief. Societies made no provision to support, succor and/or encourage women who had the good sense to walk away from abuse and degradation.
- Traditionally, children felt a moral impetus to take personal care of their parents when they became infirm.
- Traditionally, homosexuals were despised, ridiculed, and punished, even for relationships that were longer-lived and more monogamous that the heterosexual norm.
- Traditionally, *caveat emptor* ruled the marketplace, and no one even dreamed of such things as truth in advertising, consumer protection, product liability, occupational safety, pure foods and drugs, environmental protection, and the like.

Many people, especially those conservative Christians who rally around the flag of "traditional values," see changes in the rules as primary evidence of moral decay. But even while they discourage change in the moral rules in general (perhaps because of their idea that the God who provided their rules "is the same yesterday, today, and tomorrow"), they nevertheless do make provision for changes in particular cases. Why, after all, do those who worship Yahweh no longer practice human sacrifice or go on crusades? It was especially obvious early on, when the new Christian sectarians walked away from traditional Judaism, and Paul had all his arguments about whether followers of Jesus needed to observe the Law. Consequently, even the most conservative contemporary Christians should recognize the possible legitimacy of an old set of moral rules being replaced (they would say *fulfilled*, of course) by a new one.

2) Rules almost always have exceptions. As far as criminal laws are concerned, this is why there are courts, not just police. But it is imperative to realize that this is just as true with moral rules as it is with legal ones. We must be careful about this, however. To note that the rule against (say) stealing has some exceptions is *not* to endorse a lawyer's "borrowing" from her escrow account to bet on the lottery. But exceptions do occur. For instance, of the six clearly moral rules in the Decalogue, only one can be practiced without exceptions. The injunctions against other gods, idolatry, desecrating the Sabbath, and flippant oaths in the divine name may be exceptionless, but it is not at all clear that they are *moral* rules in the first place. Perhaps simply due to poor imagination, I can think of no circumstances in which coveting would be a good thing. But there certainly are exceptions to the commands about killing, stealing, bearing false witness, filial piety, and adultery.

> **Do Rules Prevent Caring?**
>
> In her influential book, *In a Different Voice*, Carol Gilligan insisted that the received notion of a proper society, driven by "justice" and rules, is excessively deductive, linear, and impersonal. A *proper* system, she said, would be less blind to extenuating circumstances, emphasize affection, and focus on relationships and caring, rather than on the "letter of the law."

- *Thou shalt not kill.* Over and above the traditional exceptions of executions, self-defense, protecting the defenseless, warfare, and the like, the survival of every individual living thing depends on taking the life of other living things (vegetables, or their seeds, at least). Even confining our diet to "found" meat or "wind-fall" fruit won't work. The process of digestion itself will kill at least some of the flora that inhabit what we find washed up on the sand or beneath the tree, or what the cat brings home.

- *Thou shalt not steal.* Stealing for its own sake is detrimental to social harmony; but taking a quarter from a newspaper rack to call 911 (to report a fire at the orphanage) would surely be excusable. So would taking an antivenom kit from an unwilling hiking companion (by force, if necessary), if bitten by a rattlesnake fifteen miles from the nearest telephone. It all depends on what we are stealing *for*, and on whether (as in these cases) some other moral consideration is overriding. (One moral consideration can certainly override another. Life, we would think, is more morally basic than property, although there is no rule that says so.)

- *Thou shalt not bear false witness.* Reading this as it is usually read (not as only prohibiting false adverse testimony in court, but as prohibiting lying in general), is it always immoral to say what is false with the intention to deceive? Of course not. Updating Plato, not only should we refuse to return a borrowed handgun to a drunken neighbor who demands it in the middle of a domestic brawl—we can even lie and say, "I don't remember where I put it."

- *Thou shalt honor thy father and thy mother.* Does this entail succumbing to sexual abuse by one's parent, or refusing to report it to avoid shaming him or her? It has taken many individuals years of therapy finally to realize that it does not.

- *Thou shalt not commit adultery.* While the adultery rule is important to the preservation of the personal trust and domestic security to which partners and children have a right, it is not exceptionless. Many of the exceptions involve unlikely scenarios, but that does not defeat the point that exceptions can occur. A man might reasonably consider adultery to be his social duty if he were the only nonsterile male in his community after a nuclear war. So, too, a female might reasonably believe that she was guiltless in yielding to a rapist who is married to another woman. (A recent story from Pakistan, where a woman was condemned to be stoned to death because being raped by her sister's husband constitutes adultery under a strict construction of the law, brings the point home: not that the adultery rule is useless; only that it cannot reasonably be taken as absolute.)

> ### Adultery or Something Else?
>
> Note that the adultery rule only prohibits us from sexual intercourse with someone who is married to another person. Fornication, premarital tomfoolery, and general licentiousness are entirely different affairs, so to speak. I am not addressing them here, not because I think they are morally unobjectionable; only because the Decalogue itself is silent about them.

The fact that ordinary moral rules have exceptions in extraordinary situations might tempt us to "adjust" the way they are formulated until all the exceptions are "built in." Then a "properly formulated" rule would be exceptionless. (This is how the Decalogue came to be glossed out into a few hundred volumes of commentary and interpretation.) But since no one could possibly enumerate every conceivable exception in advance, "properly formulated" moral rules become trivial. For example, "Don't kill" becomes

"Don't kill except in the situations enumerated in Appendix A, or in any other situation where killing is OK."

So, we need to accept the fact that useful moral rules do have exceptions, and be ready to exercise our moral judgment when hard cases arise. Moral judgment is what is needed. Rules can only summarize it, not replace it. (On the other hand, while an exceptionless rule is about as fit for the moral enterprise as a bazooka is for squirrel hunting, it is obvious that a rule with *many* exceptions is no rule at all. A call for judgment ≠ a license to be arbitrary.)

3) Rules can conflict with each other. In the real world, respect for life and respect for property can sharply conflict. Ordinarily, life rules win over property rules; but not always:

> *Examples.* A Virginia apple grower booby-trapped his orchard with dynamite, intending to maim middle school kids who tried to pinch his apples. "No Way," said the courts.

> A Virginia grocer beat a would-be robber nearly to death in defense of his produce. "A Hero," said the media.

In the same way, an agent's general social obligation to tell the truth can conflict with his or her particular obligations of fidelity, loyalty, and obedience to her or his principal. So can our simultaneous obligations to pay our debts on time and keep food on the table for our children. So can the public's right to know and an individual's right to privacy. The news is full of examples of the ways in which people are torn between the demands of multiple rules.

So, once again, we have to exercise judgment. One way to do that is to prioritize the rules in terms of the relative importance of what each one is designed to achieve. That is hard enough. But we also must make judgments about "same-level" conflicts. In neither sort of case, however, are the rules *themselves* enough.

4) Rules often won't work without extrinsic reinforcements (positive or negative). By and large, society might run more smoothly if everyone always obeyed the rules simply because they are the rules. Many people just won't do that, however, even though some may comply with a rule for other reasons (e.g., because it is known generally to have good results, because time is not available for an ad hoc judgment, because we will be rewarded if we obey it, or because we will be punished if we disobey it and get caught). So, a practical concern for people living in groups urges us to comply with the rules when we are inclined not to.

One way to make people comply is to establish a system of rewards and punishments that will make compliance beneficial (and noncompliance harmful) to *them*. Even a committed Rule Moralist could follow this program. In fact, many do.

> *Example.* If a Rule Moralist knows that lying is intrinsically wrong, and is in a position to write the rules, one rule will surely be "Don't lie." Realizing that

many people don't care much about rules, as such, and are inclined to lie when it looks useful, the rule maker can get them to do the right thing by rewarding truth telling and punishing lying. Then even those who feel that there is nothing inherently wrong with lying will think, "If I lie I will suffer," and not lie.

Here, the *justification* for the rule is still simply that it is right (i.e., it captures what is known to be intrinsically proper); but the *motivation* for obeying it (for the masses) is not that it is right, but that it is self-beneficial.

If, as a result of such a system of sanctions, the masses do the right things for the wrong reasons, should this be taken as a defeat of the Rule Moralist's program? I think not. While it is blatantly elitist in that it suggests that the masses are incapable of the true morality that their rulers practice, a distaste for elitism may be no more than a contingent aberration, local to egalitarian cultures. On the other hand, it does raise an interesting question: *If consequentialist sanctions are needed to make Rule Morality work, why not go straight to consequentialism?*

5) Rules can confuse people's ideas about moral motivation. Placing heavy emphasis on rules, as such, can easily encourage people of a certain temperament to treat rules as ends in themselves. Under such circumstances, when they "do the right thing," they may do it "for the wrong reason." For them, *rule compliance for its own sake* may have replaced *good will* as the wellspring of their interactions in the community. Is this a bad thing?

It certainly isn't *unfair*. If using rewards and sanctions to get people with aggressive personalities to behave properly is acceptable, then using rules to get people with dependent personalities to behave properly should be acceptable too. Furthermore, if good behavior is the important thing, why should we care what it takes to produce it?

Unfortunately, however, the nature of our motives and the quality of our deeds are intimately connected. Barbarians revert to barbarism when no one is looking, and Rule Fetishists go right on complying, even when the rules with which they comply are atrocious and destructive.

Furthermore, encouraging compliance for its own sake discourages people's use of their judgment. If that is discouraged long enough, their capacity for using it will atrophy. But everyone needs to keep that capacity in good running order, since (sooner or later) everyone will encounter situations for which there is no rule.

Consequently, we need to be very careful about encouraging rule compliance for its own sake. If immediate output were *all* that mattered, then any motivation that worked would do; but if the nature of our motives shapes everything that we are likely to do in the long run, then we need to cultivate the best motives we can find. Surely there are better ones than rule compliance for its own sake.

6) Rules take on a life of their own. I have already noted that the fact that rules tend to "calcify" is a good reason to deny them *basic* status in the moral

enterprise. It is also a good reason to be reflective when *using* them. Once a rule is in place (perhaps for very good reasons, initially), it is likely to remain in place even if has no continuing use—indeed, even if it has become dysfunctional.

> *Examples.* The law books are full of (often amusing) anachronistic regulations that no one has bothered to revoke. These include bans against taking baths on Sunday and kissing cows, and the requirement that horseless carriages be preceded at all times by a lantern-carrying man on foot. Laws need to be buried when they die. Otherwise, like some proverbial Chicago voters, they can continue to make mischief for generations. This is why some laws are now written with an automatic sunset clause.

There is no "automatic sunset" clause in moral rules, however. So we should check them, from time to time, to see if they are still doing what they were adopted to do in the first place.

D. Conclusions.

1) Moral rules are very useful. It would be difficult to maintain social order and stability without some.

2) Nevertheless, they are not *basic* to the moral enterprise. They are not the source of what is good and bad. They cannot even be articulated unless a notion of what is good and bad is already in place.

3) Consequently, moral rules are neither good nor bad in their own right. That this or that edict is a moral rule is no guarantee of the quality of its *content*. That is a function of the actual behavior it reinforces, and the impact of that behavior on humans and their affairs.

4) Moral rules are usually codified (by legislation and/or cultural inertia) into positive laws, common laws, and traditions. This is useful, too, because many people will not follow them without the external motivation that laws and traditions (and sanctions) provide.

5) However, along with the laws and traditions that embody them, moral rules tend to "calcify" over time, encouraging unreflective compliance with the received notion of "good" and "bad" behavior, *whatever it may be*. This makes reform difficult, even when the received notion of "good" and "bad" behavior is demonstrably dysfunctional.

6) Consequently, along with the laws and traditions that embody them, moral rules should be subject to constant review and kept open to revision or replacement in terms of improved conceptions of what is of value.

14

Considering Consequences

"Follow Your Star" and "Follow Nature" prove to be inadequate distillations of the moral enterprise. "Follow the Rules" fares a little better; but as useful as moral rules are, none are any better than the behavior they endorse, and no behavior is any better than its impact on humans and their affairs. Consequently, many people believe that the key to morality is *weighing the human consequences* of the behavior options that are available in concrete situations. Their banner is "Consider the Consequences."

5. Consequentialism

Traditionally, systems that conceptualize morality this way have been called *teleological* (from the Greek *telos*: "end" or "purpose"). People who hold such views, consequently, are often accused of thinking that "the ends justify the means"; and, strictly speaking, the label does suggest that what we are aiming at is the only thing that morally counts. That is absurd, of course, and it is not what they are up to. They know that many acts don't achieve their goals at all, and that few acts achieve just their goals and nothing else. They believe that an act's *results* are what justify it—that the proof of the pudding is in the eating, not in the cook's fond hopes. So I will call them *consequentialists* rather than *teleologists*.

There are many different formulations of consequentialist moral theory. *Utilitarianism* is the most common. In this chapter, I will examine utilitarianism's general characteristics and some of the difficulties commonly attributed to it. In the next, I will examine the three most important questions about utilitarianism: whether its treatment of rules is consistent, whether its provision for rights and fair play is adequate, and whether its conception of human nature is secure against manipulation.

A. Utilitarianism. In 1789, in his *Introduction to the Principles of Morals and Legislation*, Jeremy Bentham articulated an account of morals intended to emulate the rigor and precision of empirical science. To succeed, it required quantifiable experiential variables in terms of which moral phenomena could be understood.

Bentham identified those variables as *pleasure* and *pain*, and developed around them a calculation procedure (the *hedonic calculus*) for deciding what we should and should not do. According to him, a morally proper act amounts to doing what will, in a concrete situation, maximize pleasure and minimize pain, in the long run, for all those on whom the act has any impact. On this view, the moral enterprise is 1) consequentialist, 2) empirical, 3) hedonistic, 4) situation relative, 5) has a purely quantitative decision procedure, and 6) combines psychological egoism and moral pluralism. Not all these characteristics are shared by every version of utilitarianism, but they are common enough.

B. Utilitarianism's general characteristics and their problems.

1) *Consequentialism.* Utilitarians don't appraise acts in terms of their intrinsic value because, as they see things, acts are inherently value-neutral. The only things that are intrinsically good or bad are certain states or conditions of sentient organisms. So, acts that produce those states or conditions are *extrinsically* good or bad. Acts derive whatever value they have from the states they produce. Believing this is what makes utilitarians *consequentialists.*

Many criticisms of utilitarianism attack its consequentialism—not because consequences are morally unimportant, but because exclusive attention to them may downplay other factors that also matter morally—factors such as agents' intentions, attitudes, and motivations, or the rule compliance and fairness of acting in a particular way. For instance, since there is a difference between appraising acts and appraising agents, a good act might be one that has certain *effects* while a good agent might be one who acts *in a certain way* or *for certain reasons.* If so, utilitarianism could be right in affirming the former and wrong in overlooking the latter. The most common attacks on consequentialism, however, involve the claim that acts, as such, have intrinsic value themselves, regardless of their outcomes.

For example, when Joseph Fletcher, a mid-twentieth century religious consequentialist, said (in his book *Situation Ethics*) that it is not always wrong to engage in unwed sex acts, the clergy at large attacked him as a sensualist and libertine, claiming that unwed sex acts are, as

> ### Intrinsic and Extrinsic
>
> The value of an *intrinsically* valuable act is internal (i.e., resides in the nature of the act itself). The value of an *extrinsically* valuable act is external (i.e., is derived from the act's rule compliance, intentions, motives, goals, or consequences).

such, morally improper. Fletcher, of course, did not say that unwed sex was good as such. He said that it was morally neutral. On his view, maximizing *agape* (that is, selfless or spiritual love) in the world is the only intrinsic good, so unwed sex can only be *derivatively* good or bad as a function of its effect on the world's *agape*-quotient. *Agape* is harder than pleasure to get at, test, quantify, or confirm empirically. But consequentialism itself is the present issue, not the very unorthodox consequences Fletcher favored.

Do consequentialists "miss the point" of moral evaluation by focusing on the consequences of acts, rather than on the nature of acts themselves? Are some acts so wicked, in and of themselves, that there are no circumstances in which doing them would be moral? That's the conflict between consequentialists and their opponents, in a nutshell.

a) That conflict is not quite what it appears to be, however. Those who attack consequentialism tend to claim that some acts are so wicked that there are no circumstances in which they would be morally justified. While that directly denies the claim that there are circumstances under which doing any act would be morally justified, that is not a denial of what consequentialists actually say—that is, *if* the consequences of doing an act maximize the good more than those of not doing it, then doing it is morally justified.

The "if" clause is neither accidental nor unimportant. Because of it, it would take an added premise to get from what the consequentialists *do* say to what their opponents *take them* to say: For any act whatever, there actually *are* circumstances in which the consequences of doing it will maximize the good more than those of not doing it. But consequentialists need make no such claim. It is entirely possible that there are some acts that always have maximally horrific results. Whether that is so or not is a factual matter on which a consequentialist would take no a priori position. One settles facts by looking at cases.

Putting the shoe on the other foot, when the consequentialists' opponents say that some acts are so wicked that there are no circumstances in which they would be justified, they must mean one, not both, of two things: either *Some acts are so wicked that doing them is never morally justified, even if the consequences of doing them would maximize the good (however defined) more effectively than those of not doing them,* or *Some acts are so wicked that circumstances are never such that the consequences of doing them would maximize the good (however defined) more effectively than those of not doing them.* The first directly contradicts what consequentialists say. The second only contradicts a descriptive claim that they do not ordinarily make. So the real conflict *must be* between:

- *For any act, if the consequences of doing it would maximize the good more effectively than those of not doing it, then doing it is morally justified;* and
- *Some acts are so wicked that doing them is never morally justified, even if the consequences of doing them would maximize the good more effectively than those of not doing them.*

That, finally, makes clear what is properly at stake between consequentialists, as such, and their opponents. But it makes it equally clear that anti-consequentialists need to say what, precisely, could make an act so wicked that we should refrain from doing it, even when its consequences would maximize the good more effectively than those of not doing it.

b) Perhaps these *very* wicked acts are (1) ones that offend God, (2) ones that break the rules, (3) ones that ignore individuals, (4) ones that overlook intentions, (5) ones that overlook the fact that one can give offense without doing harm, (6) ones that are unfair, or (7) ones that a decent person couldn't stomach doing.

(1) Refraining from an act in order to avoid offending God presupposes that we know what acts offend God, and that presupposes that we can identify God. That could only be done, however, if we had a clear understanding of what is good and what is bad already in place. How else would we know that a putative God was the real thing? So we cannot *identify* what is good and bad this way. It is question begging.

(2) If we knew ten good acts and ten bad ones, we could keep things straight with a rulebook: do the former, don't do the latter. That would be efficient; but, of course, it presumes that we are able to identify the good and bad acts without using the rules. Otherwise, we could not have formulated those rules in the first place. So we cannot *identify* what is good and what is bad this way. It is question begging, too.

(3) Does consequentialism allow acts which wickedly trade off the interests of individuals against those of society as a whole? While it is a guide for choice between larger and smaller numbers of individuals, I don't think it even addresses the choices that are allegedly sometimes necessary between individuals and *The Whole*.

Were we to say, on consequentialist grounds, that we ought to do something that is very hard on one individual, it would not be because it produced benefit for "society," but because it produced benefit for other individuals (lots of them). This is trading off *one* against *many*, not trading off one against the whole. We cannot make the argument over consequentialism into a squabble between individualism and collectivism unless we blithely confuse the properties of sets with those of set members (the fallacies of composition and division). Efficient individuals do not necessarily constitute an efficient committee. Gigantic machines are not necessarily comprised of gigantic parts. Even in trading one individual for a few thousand, it is still individuals' benefits that consequentialists take into account and maximize, not those of metaphysical constructs.

(4) In spite of the fact that everyone knows where the road paved with good intentions goes, it is odd to omit intentions altogether. Everyone also knows right things can be done for wrong reasons.

Consider a man who, hating his neighbor, plots murder. Hidden in the attic with a high-powered rifle, he draws a bead on his neighbor in the garden, and blasts away. Being an atrocious shot, he misses his target, but hits a copperhead at his enemy's feet. So, fully intending to do murder, this inept assassin saves his neighbor's life instead. Shall he be praised or condemned? It might appear that, on consequentialist grounds, he deserves praise. If that were so, then consequentialism is in trouble.

But it is not so. He may deserve congratulations on his good luck, even as his neighbor deserves congratulations for a double escape from death. But these are not moral verdicts. The only moral verdict due is a negative one for *not* choosing the action alternative calculated to maximize benefits. Since he did *not* choose to kill the snake, there is nothing about that to evaluate on consequentialist grounds. He *did* choose to shoot his neighbor; and, unless substantial argument can show that it would be a good thing for his neighbor to die, the verdict on his choice must be negative. Consequentialists do not ignore intentions; they simply say that the only intention worth having is the intention to maximize benefit.

Furthermore, we always need carefully to differentiate evaluating acts and evaluating actors. An act can be good (because it has good consequences), even if it is done for the wrong reasons. But if it is done for the wrong reasons, the actor gets no credit. We can prize an act but scorn the actor, even as—conversely—Yahweh is said to hate sin, but love sinners.

(5) We *can* give offense without doing harm. Otherwise there could be no "victimless crimes." But can utilitarianism bar offensive (but nonharmful) acts?

Example. Suppose that a male college student is a "peeping Tom." Ensconced in a tall tree with a good pair of night glasses, he regularly spends his evenings peering through one particular window of the women's residence hall. But he only looks. He never attacks his target, either physically or verbally. Nor does he make any attempt at intimidation or blackmail, or tell anyone what he sees. Thus, he never damages the body, mind, or reputation of his target. Indeed, he feels so "protective" and "caring" toward her that he would never dream of any such harmful or damaging behavior. Finally, suppose that he is so clever that no one ever knows that he peeps. But he does. He is always there, watching by himself and for himself, thinking lascivious thoughts.

Most people find such behavior repugnant; and many explain their aversion to it by noting that it involves an invasion of the victim's right to the privacy of her own body, whether or not any tangible harm is done.

We might think that the only utilitarian ground for a right to privacy is that it is a preemptive defense against tangible harm, and—since that has been ruled out by hypothesis in this case—that *this* peeping must be acceptable on utilitarian grounds. So if invading a person's privacy is wicked in itself, then utilitarians are caught condoning wickedness.

But privacy rules protect people from far more than this one remarkably harmless peeper. *He* may be benign, but peepers generally are equipping themselves for lascivious talk at the very least; and may even be working themselves up for rape. So it is useful to ban peeping in general, since we do not ordinarily know in advance which peepers will be benign, and tolerating benign ones is likely to encourage the more aggressive ones.

So utility protects privacy in terms of the *general* consequences of *types* of acts. It involves weighing rules as well as acts. Consequently, if the general protection of privacy fosters human happiness, we can incorporate it into a rule and back it with sanctions—not because every violation would be grief producing, but because a society where that rule is in place is more happiness maximizing than one where it isn't. Judging the rule in terms of *its* utility (in addition to judging individuals' acts in terms of *theirs*) brings all of the cash value of the right to privacy into the system, but keeps it solidly empirical and firmly consequential.

(6) Even if we could conceive of a situation where slavery would maximize pleasure over pain in the long run (taking into account the grief of the slaves as well as the joys of their masters), it certainly would not be *fair* to the slaves. Slaves are treated unfairly, and treating people unfairly is wicked. So, if there are circumstances where consequentialists would condone slavery, then it condones wickedness.

But it misconstrues consequentialism to claim that it must endorse slavery in "pick A or B" circumstances. Consequentialists do not say that from two arbitrarily selected alternatives, we must pick the one that produces better results. Rather, it demands that we assess the choices between *all* available options in a given situation.

> *Example.* The United States did not face a *bona fide* dilemma between civil war and the preservation of slavery in the nineteenth century. If war and slavery had been the only options available, war was certainly preferable; but they weren't. Some changes in farming practice (crop diversification to short circuit the contingent necessity of plantations), some increased industrialization (to diversify the economy, lower the prices of manufactured goods, and bring the region into the economic mainstream), and sufficient taxes to make slave owning economically prohibitive were all worth considering.

The claim that consequentialism is obliged to tolerate unfair behavior is almost always based on false dilemmas. We cannot be a proper utilitarian and only consider truncated alternatives. In fact, an important component of any enlightened consequentialist view of social morality is the principle of fair play. And the reasons for this are *consequentialist* reasons.

(7) In his brilliant essay, "Consequentialism," James Cargile criticized all consequentialist moral schemes on the grounds that there are some output justifiable acts that no decent person could ever stomach doing. For instance, even if

it were the case that the ritual sacrifice of a human child would avert some angry god's wrath (perhaps a major earthquake in a densely populated region), a decent person just couldn't *do* it. (Note that such putative justifications have long been offered for various dreadful practices, and that we cannot skirt Cargile's issue by saying they have all been predicated on false beliefs. On his view, *decent* Mayan priests could not have done what they did, even if their beliefs about crops and gods had been correct.)

In saying this, Cargile is not just another rule lover, willing to sacrifice untold benefits for the sake of a favored precept. He is quite willing to admit that no acts are so bad that they could not be justified by beneficial consequences in truly bizarre circumstances. He just says that some are so repellent that it is impossible for an uncorrupt person to do them.

> *Example*. Several of our captives probably know where and how the terrorists plan next to strike, but we don't know which ones they are and none of them are volunteering any information. Following an ancient tradition, it has been suggested that with the application of *pein fort et dur* they might be more forthcoming. God knows there are thousands of lives at stake, so isn't it time to heat up the pokers?

We might decide, weighing the torture of a few against the possibility of another 9/11 and all the torments its victims would go through, that the benefits of the former *must* outweigh the harms of the latter. But could a morally healthy person actually roll up her sleeves and wade in, however fine the consequences forthcoming?

In saying "no" (as he would), Cargile would be making a point about moral *character*, not about acts or consequences. If his point is well taken, then even if consequentialism were a correct judgment system for acts, it would still fail in practice: no decent person could always use it.

But isn't consequentialism being bludgeoned with a false dilemma here? Are these two options the only ones available? What about sodium pentathol? Could we try bribery? A consequentialist weighs *all* the options, not just some. Sometimes, however, no third option is obvious; indeed, sometimes there simply isn't one.

> *Example*: It has been suggested that Virginia should legislatively define a flat EEG as legal death and waive all restrictions on the use of "dead" humans so understood. Then, with an intact spinal cord and a little help from the doctors, some "dead" people could continue metabolic and respiratory functions and could be utilized as organ donors, grafting tissue farms, hormone and vaccine factories, and experimentation subjects for new medical and surgical techniques. All that is required to achieve these enormous potentials, which cannot now be achieved in any other way, is a few new laws, and some people who could stomach working on "the farm."

While such work may be too gross for fastidious people to stomach, that may be a point about the quality of the actors, not of the acts. Consequentialist principles can still stand, even when decent folk lack the fortitude to act them out. We would simply live in a world where some demonstrably good things never get done because people are too *nice* to do them.

But is the proper notion of what makes a person "decent" a function of *fastidiousness*? Surely not; and even if it were, it would have to be shown in some noncircular way that fastidiousness is a morally good thing (and not just a product of socialization and/or temperament).

So most of the standard objections to consequentialism as such simply misconstrue what it amounts to, portraying it as the practice of antinomian license, in much the same way that hedonism as such is commonly portrayed as untrammeled licentiousness. Both portrayals are caricatures. However, several real challenges to consequentialism as such remain. In the next chapter, I will return to them, examining the place that utilitarians make for rules, rights and fair play, and the dangerous possibilities of manipulating humans to make them happy at lower cost. In the meantime, there are other aspects of utilitarianism to consider.

2) *Empiricism.* Bentham focused on pleasure and pain because he took them to be directly empirically discernible.

- Identifying them is a matter of experience, involving nothing mysterious, occult, or spiritual.
- People sense them directly and openly, in the same way they sense heat, texture, noise, and the like.
- So they are repeatable, testable, and confirmable, according to all of the standard empirical epistemic bench marks.

While this conception of pleasure and pain is essential to the success of Bentham's plan, it is arguable—especially with regard to pleasure, which is much less clearly a "sensation" than pain is. In addition, many people object to empiricism as such, especially when applied to questions of value.

a) The direct empirical discernibility of pain is clear. We feel pain in much the same way that we might feel a draft or a wall. Pains can be located, modulated, and compared; and we can summon one up intentionally as easily as we can arrange to see a sunset or hear a waterfall.

The direct, empirical discernibility of pleasure, on the other hand, is a little more tenuous. This is highlighted by the differences between the ways people speak of pleasure and pain "sensations."

- There are many sensations in which people "take pleasure" or that "feel good." But it would be rather odd to say anything like, "Every time I do X I feel *a pleasure*." This, in spite of the fact that people readily say, "Every time I do Y I feel *a pain*."

- We do not say anything like "I *took* pain in Y," while "I *took* pleasure in X" is absolutely standard.
- It is normal to speak of our "aches and pains." We *have* them, directly. So we might say, "I'm having two pains right now, one in my upper left bicuspid and one in my right big toe." Pleasures, on the other hand, are not so discrete or locatable. So we never say, "I'm having two pleasures right now." Of course, we could have two sensations simultaneously, and find both of them pleasant; but that is not quite the same thing.

The point is that pleasures appear to be somewhat less direct than pains. Pain is a relatively straightforward label for sensations of a certain kind. Pleasure, on the other hand, is a label for a certain kind of reaction to sensations (although the sensations that give rise to the pleasure reaction are fairly uniform).

b) Pleasures and pains are not quite as public, nor quite as well-defined, as standard utilitarians might have us believe; although they are, again, closer on pain than pleasure:

- People can take pleasure in a wide variety of experiences, and disagree about them commonly. Thousands take no pleasure in listening to Snoop Dogg, but thousands do.
- Pain, on the other hand, is more standard across the population. Granted that some people are more, and some less, sensitive to it; it is quite implausible to claim that thousands of people feel pain when having a root canal, but that equally many don't.

For all that, pleasure and pain are *more* empirical than satisfying the will of God or fulfilling one's virtue, since one cannot empirically determine what the will of God or one's virtue might be. So the move to hedonism is a move *toward* moral empiricism, even if it is somewhat loose and imprecise.

c) Of course, those who reject empiricism as such, as a wrong-headed way to find out what's what (perhaps on the ground that it cuts us off from higher things), will certainly not be any more content with it in the moral arena than they are in the fact arena.

Hedonism and Utility

Hedonists are far more numerous than hedonistic *utilitarians*. Many people favor hedonistic egoism: the view that one's own pleasure is all that counts. There may be a few that favor hedonistic *altruism*: a moral scheme, perhaps, for compulsive odalisques or teachers. We could also be a utilitarian without being a hedonist at all. We could say, for instance, that the only thing that is morally worthwhile is the maximum generation and distribution of manual labor ("sweat utilitarianism"), regardless of how people feel about doing any.

But if empiricism is a legitimate epistemic standard for factual inquiry (as I have tried to show in chapters 3 and 4), and if the occurrences of pleasures and pains are factual states of affairs, then it is a legitimate epistemic standard for moral inquiry too.

3) *Hedonism.* Value systems that are based on pleasure are called "hedonistic," from the Greek word for pleasure (*hedone*). Many people decry it, believing that it is where moral rot begins. They apparently conceptualize pleasure along the lines of a Roman orgy: naked people reclining on satin pillows and eating peeled grapes while the city burns. But such narrow conceptions of pleasure reveal more about their authors than they do about hedonism. Not all hedonists are lounge lizards, wallowing in decadence. Some even find pleasure in mathematics.

In any case, the standard utilitarian position is hedonistic—with various amounts of fine-tuning in the articulation.

- Some favor the encouragement of pleasure over pain.
- Some favor the encouragement of pleasure and/or happiness over displeasure and/or unhappiness.
- Some favor the encouragement of a state of perceived well-being (*eudemonia*), of which pleasure and/or happiness, as opposed to displeasure and/or unhappiness, is an important constituent but not the only one.

There are important differences between these views:

- The second and third use positive and negative variables with the same empirical footing. Both pleasure/happiness and displeasure/unhappiness are *systemic* responses to stimuli, not sensations as such. In contrast, the first uses disparate variables: pleasure is systemic, but pain is closer to a sensation.
- The second moves utilitarians away from the first's preoccupation with body functions (the natural habitat of pleasure and pain), to make room for phenomena that arise in more complex parts of the central nervous system and are not associated with any distinct "pleasure zone." In this way, it expands utilitarianism to include the joys of listening to Bach and of solving anagrams and the despairs of bereavement and of anxiety. It also avoids the third's reliance on a possibly nonempirical distinction between proper and improper virtues that frequently rides with the notion of *eudemonia*.

Those who criticize hedonism (regardless of the fine-tuning) usually have some specific not-very-admirable pleasures in mind. But, while it is obvious that people do sometimes take their pleasure in unfortunate ways, utilitarians are not committed to the notion that one pleasure is as good as another across all times and circumstances.

In his *Utilitarianism*, John Stuart Mill went so far as to claim that some pleasures, as such, are qualitatively better than others. That was an aberration, however, because it calls for a value criterion other than pleasure itself. If pleasure is *the* good, then the only way a pleasure can be better is for it to be more pleasurable. As Bentham clearly saw, that means more intense, longer lasting, etc. The "etc." covers a lot of ground, however.

Consider the pleasures associated with sexual promiscuity, for example. From one traditional point of view, sexual promiscuity is bad in itself. So, according to many, utilitarianism must be corrupt because it allegedly allows it on the grounds that it is pleasant. But does it really allow it? Under most circumstances, no; not because sexual promiscuity is intrinsically evil but because it dulls the senses, trivializes human relationships, generates corrosive emotions, encourages conflict, diverts attention from other pleasure sources, and, hence, generally *diminishes* pleasure in the long run.

So any utilitarian who pays close attention to facts will see that licentiousness is discouraged by considerations of moderation and diversification. However, moderation and diversification are not added criteria of intrinsic value. They are simply reasonable means toward maximizing the one good. So, their critics to the contrary, hedonistic utilitarians are not committed to a life of squalid licentiousness. Of course, pursued senselessly, hedonism would be self-defeating. Carelessly seeking *a* pleasure, without regard for *all* the consequences that will follow, is folly. But, since that folly is clearly demonstrable on strictly utilitarian grounds, proper utilitarians don't pursue hedonism senselessly.

4) *Purely quantitative decision procedures.* Utilitarianism's decision procedures have four important aspects: a) the claim that pleasure and pain are precisely quantifiable on several independent scales, b) the notion that these various quantifications are collectively useful in determining moral priorities, c) the notion that who has the pleasure and pain is irrelevant to moral calculations, and d) the notion that only the quantity of pleasure and pain (never the quality) is morally cogent. Each of these four aspects has been the target of criticism.

a) Quantitative precision. Pleasure and pain are said to be precisely quantifiable in several ways, including intensity, duration, purity, and fecundity. The first two are, perhaps, the most obvious.

- The pain associated with passing a kidney stone is more intense than that associated with having a hangnail.
- The pleasure associated with an orgasm is more intense than that associated with a back rub.
- The pain of bone cancer lasts longer than that of a stubbed toe.

- The pleasure of a Lucullan feast lasts longer than that of scarfing a Snickers bar.

But while such loosely quantitative observations about pleasures and pains are obvious enough, actually assigning numbers is far from easy or precise. Physicists are not content to know that X's half-life is shorter than Y's. They want to know *how much shorter*. That is the difference between being loosely quantitative and actually quantifying. But there are problems in actually quantifying pleasures and pains on Bentham's scales; and, unless we can do it precisely, the hedonic calculus is not what he meant it to be.

- Extent is OK. People can be counted.
- Duration is almost OK. Pleasures and pains can be roughly timed, but it is hard to know precisely when they start and stop.
- Intensity is marginal. While we can roughly compare pains as more and less intense, it is difficult to be precise about just *how much* more or less intense X is than Y. For starters, we do not know what scale to use or what, exactly, we are "counting."
- Purity is very tricky. It is easy, perhaps, to distinguish between that which is pure and that which has some adulteration; it is even quantitative in the broad sense that we can say that X has more adulterants (or more of one adulterant) than Y. But can we put a number on that? 99 and $^{44}/_{100}$ percent perhaps?

In any case, the calculations are more straightforward with pains than with pleasures. For instance, the "pleasure quotients" for an orgasm and a back rub can change dramatically as circumstances vary, but a lodged kidney stone always hurts just about the same (and distractions don't help). This is because pains are much more *directly* empirical than pleasures. Systemic reactions take a back seat to sensations.

b) Prioritizing. Pleasures (pains) that are pure, close, and certain are said to override ones that are mixed, distant, and iffy.

- I would not decline an afternoon with President Bush if he appeared on my doorstep and said, "Let me explain the Patriot Act to you," in the hope that by spending that time writing a fan letter to Fabio he might give me a five-minute interview if he ever happened to come to Richmond.
- I would not decline a shot of Demerol on the way to the ER (if I had broken my hip and was writhing in the back of a rescue truck with bad struts) on the grounds that 1 in every 186k people develop a sensitivity to meperidine, which makes them break out in a mild rash if it is ever administered a second time.

But while such loose "calculations" of various possible combinations of proximity, certainty, purity, and the like are obvious enough, generally speaking, actually crunching the numbers in real cases (presuming that we can assign them in the first place) is problematic.

A different sort of problem becomes evident if we try to use the various scales *together* (the whole point of Bentham's apparatus).

- The number scales that we use for each quantifiable feature of pleasures and pains are obviously different; for example, duration is measured in minutes, intensity is *not*.
- Are the scales for each quantifiable feature additive, serial, or related in some other way? While regular Tylenol (5 grains of acetaminophen per pill) is precisely twice as strong as pediatric Tylenol (2.5 grains of acetaminophen per pill), an earthquake that measures 5 on the Richter scale is *not* precisely twice as strong as a 2.5 one. Metric weight is additive; but the Richter scale is not. So, is an intensity 5 pain just *worse* than an intensity 2.5 one—or is the scale additive, so that a 5 is *precisely two times worse* than a 2.5?
- Can one score be significantly added to another—say intensity and propinquity—for a "two feature score," or can averages be meaningfully struck? Is there any reason to think that the unit reasonable for purity is the same (or behaves the same way) as the unit reasonable for fecundity? If not, then adding them together and running an average would be like measuring temperature in degrees, height in inches, and body weight in stones, adding up a total, dividing by three, and assuming that resulting number is a significant measure of agility, charm, or taste.
- Are the several scales of equal weight? If not, how many of *this* does it take to outweigh how many of *that*? This is especially problematic with, but not confined to, comparisons of extent and intensity. Will one euphoric individual outweigh 128 mildly discomfited ones, or one tormented individual outweigh 785 marginally jolly ones? Just how miserable must thirty-seven slaves be to outweigh the pleasures of their master and the consumers of cheap clothing made from the cotton they harvest?

Quantifying Bentham's categories does make *rough* sense, however, as long as we do not press the technicalities: intensity (because people generally like pleasures more intense and pains less), certainty (because people often want to trade off a mild pleasure that is quite certain against a massive pleasure that is rather iffy), propinquity (because the long-term future is rarely as real to people as the immediate), etc. This has important practical implications. For rational people, it isn't enough that it would be fun to go to a party tonight and drink seven martinis. We must also take tomorrow's horrors into account, along with any and all other pleasure-pain factors that may be relevant. Similarly, a reasonable person will not drive a racing car at 165 miles per hour on the highway, since however much fun that would entail, must be weighed against its other, probably painful, consequences. Everyone makes such broadly quantitative hedonic judgments every day; though not, of course, with a pocket euphorolator.

c) Eliminating indexing. Utilitarians assert that since pleasure is good, and more pleasure is better, then pleasure should be maximized without any indexing coming into play. They do not say that I should pursue my pleasure at whatever cost to others. Nor do they say that I should pursue the pleasure of others at whatever cost to me. Rather, they say that if more than one person is affected by my act, then I should determine the pleasures and pains that are likely to attend it for *all* of them, and maximize the net amount of pleasure over pain *regardless of whose it is.* Psychological egoists argue that this is impossible, absent a complex system of social sanctions. Ethical egoists like Rand, moreover, argue that it is immoral.

From a utilitarian point of view, the following statements are all true:

- Value depends solely on the quantity of pleasure and pain, with no regard whatever for whose it is.
- So, only the fact that my pleasure is *pleasure,* not the fact that it is *mine,* makes it worth pursuing.
- So, any person who puts a thumb on the scale to make a special case of him or her self is simply immoral.
- However, on grounds of sheer consistency, one is just as deserving of consideration, *ceteris paribus*, as anyone else is. Everyone counts for one. No one counts for two or more; and no one counts for zero.

In contrast, psychological egoists would argue that only our own interests *can* move us and that no one *can* be interested in the pleasure of others, concluding that prizing unindexed pleasures is *impossible*—while ethical egoists would argue that although it is *possible* for people to take interest in the pleasure of others, it is highly improper for them to do so.

Utilitarianism, however, is not implausible in concrete settings. Consider an instructor who, since he enjoys failing students, decides to maximize his pleasure by failing everyone without regard to the quality of their work. To do so would make a special case of his own pleasure, ignore his students' interests, and decrease the world's net pleasure quotient. Or consider another instructor who relishes student admiration and decides to give every student an A without regard to the quality of his or her work. Then, in the long run, those who received their marks without learning the material may become conduits of grief to others (especially if the class was surgery).

Utility insists that we should weigh every available option and choose the one that, in the long run, will bring the most happiness to the most people.

So the most promising option for instructors is to assign students the grades they *earn*. That would:

- encourage those who have been slothful to work harder,
- encourage those who have done well to take pride in what they have accomplished, and keep it up, and
- encourage the long-term production of better-educated citizens for the whole community.

Output, after all, is the *only* thing that counts.

And, if anyone insists on pursuing his or her own pleasure at all costs, sanctions can be brought into play. Utilitarians are quick to recognize the frequent necessity of legislation and enforcement.

Thus utilitarians can work around psychological egoism, should it be true (as Bentham took it to be). And they simply reject ethical egoism as incoherent. How could it be that *this* pleasure is good and *that* pleasure is bad, simply because this one is mine and that one is yours?

d) Only quantity counts. Utilitarian purists allow no "qualitative" distinctions between various sorts of pleasures. Bentham, for instance, made no qualitative distinction between the pleasures of a pig wallowing in mud and those of an informed listener hearing Mozart at the keyboard.

Many consider this to be degrading to the "better" side of human nature. "Higher" pleasures, they say, should "count more" than "lower" ones. In his *Utilitarianism*, John Stuart Mill noted this and "fixed" things by distinguishing between "high" and "low" pleasure and adding a *qualitative* scale to Bentham's list of purely *quantitative* ones. There is a point to this line, however, only if some pleasures actually are, in themselves, *better* than others (not just more intense or more certain, but *better*). But if that is the case, then pure utilitarianism is off on the wrong foot entirely. Thus it can be argued that Mill's "fix" abandoned Bentham's project altogether.

It is easy to understand why Mill wanted to incorporate a distinction between "higher" and "lower" pleasures into utilitarianism. The view that some pleasures are *qualitatively better* (not just longer, more intense, etc.) than others is widely shared: the pleasure of playing chess, for instance, as compared to that of playing tic-tac-toe.

(1) A wide variety of qualitatively distinct sensations are all pleasures. The word "pleasure" has no single, sense-specific use. Consequently, we must recognize the qualitative distinctions between various sensations (orgasm, say, and smelling baking bread). *This* qualitative distinction is not an evaluative one. It is simply the recognition of the identifying differences between assorted sensations that are, in fact, different. The evaluative move comes when we ask how pure (intense, long-lasting, etc.) the attendant pleasure is, and that is still quantitative.

It should also be noted that while purity, duration, intensity, and extent are measures of a pleasure itself, fecundity, certainty, and propinquity are measures of the characteristics of situations in which pleasures occur. All are important, and all are quantitative.

As will be seen in chapter 15, some issues about some ways of pursuing pleasure, and about their side effects, have normative dimensions: issues of dysfunctionality, of the encouragement of single-pleasure preoccupation or tunnel vision, and the like. But, as will also be seen, none of these necessitate making evaluative distinctions between pleasures as such. They involve, rather, the necessity of recognizing that the short-run maximization of this or that pleasure may interfere with the long-run maximization of *pleasure*.

Even so, anti-utilitarians will still lament to the effect that some people enjoy some pleasures inappropriately. Enjoying may be good, as such, but when we enjoy *the wrong things or* enjoys things in *the wrong way*, we are wicked; and the quantity of enjoyment cannot tell us which things and ways are the *right* things and ways. But, as we shall see, while there are many good reasons to encourage some people to relocate their pleasuring, those can all be articulated on one utilitarian ground or another.

(2) The identification of what is "high" and "low" often reveals little more than the class biases of those who are doing the identifying. Since those who write about such things tend to think of themselves as intellectual, Brahmin, and refined, the "high" list is usually comprised of things such as enjoying deep literature, "long-hair" music, and philosophy. The "low" list, in contrast, is usually comprised of more proletarian enjoyments such as squirting Cheez Whiz, belching and farting, watching "reality" television, reading Harlequin romances, and line dancing.

If discouraging such behaviors (or, at least, discouraging taking pleasure in them) were all that the high/low distinction amounted to, it could be dismissed as condescending elitism. There is sometimes a possibility, however, that more is at work here. We *can* draw apparently nonquantitative distinctions between pleasures in nonelitist ways.

(a) *Simple pleasures and complex ones.* Kicking our shoes off after a day's work is very simple, and very enjoyable. Watching a hockey game after a day's work is very complicated, and very enjoyable. The latter is more complicated than the former, if for no other reason, because it involves keeping track of a great many things going on at the same time. However, it is what we are enjoying (taking pleasure in) that is more or less complicated, not our enjoyment (pleasure). Further, there is nothing about utilitarianism's quantitative bias to discourage us from enjoying simple and complex things both, and no particular reason to think that either is better or worse in itself. Perhaps, however, complexity is connected to something more cogent: *the development of our capacity for enjoyment.* The more we enjoy complex things, the more our capacity for enjoyment will grow. If so, the enjoyment of complex things could be encouraged on quantitative grounds.

(b) *Easy pleasures and difficult ones.* The Roman circuses are a proverbial example of easy pleasures. Perhaps they were popular with the masses *because* they were so undemanding. And, perhaps they were popular with rulers because they distracted the plebs from social criticism, and because they were much cheaper to provide than things like literature, music, and philosophy. Deriving pleasure from a John Cage concert, on the other hand, is notoriously difficult. One reason why easy pleasures might be worse than hard ones is that they may be *so* easy that they short circuit our pursuit of *anything* that takes more effort; and some things that take a lot of effort are, in fact, very enjoyable if given a chance. Only one example is necessary: watching TV as compared to reading books. This might be a reason to discourage easy pleasures: to give the others an opportunity to develop, thus extending the variety (quantitative) and amount (quantitative) of pleasure available to us.

(c) *"Natural" pleasures and "acquired" ones.* There are a great many things that people have to learn to like. This raises the issue of "difficult" vs. "easy," again; but also raises the issue of whether or not utilitarianism provides grounds for teaching people to enjoy things they would never try on their own. Doesn't it allow us to leave people in uncultivated naiveté?

Not at all. If acquiring some tastes will expand the range of pleasures that are available to people, there is every quantitative reason to help them acquire them. (It should be noted that not every acquired taste is, in fact, beneficial in the long run. People may not be born with an appreciation for bran muffins, but they are not born with an appreciation for neat gin, either. But *which* tastes we should cultivate can be answered on utilitarian grounds, too.)

(d) *Dead-end pleasures and open-ended ones.* Watching cartoons may be fun for preschoolers, but it "doesn't go anywhere." Guitar lessons may be only mildly enjoyable for a third grader, but they open the door to considerable pleasure a few years down the road. Utilitarians know about long-term consequences, and that they can be quantified. The specific quantitative scale that is most important here was on Bentham's original list: fecundity. There are good quantitative reasons to explore highways in preference to culs-de-sac.

(e) *Fleshy pleasures and cerebral ones.* Some people are quite sure that, for instance, reading Kant is qualitatively better than having a cuddle. This is not obvious, however. If it is better, it is probably because philosophy is more complex, challenging and open ended than slap and tickle.

Further, there is no reason why we cannot enjoy *both*. The only thing we need to guard against is getting so fixated on *any* pleasure (even that of reading Plato) that the world's happiness quotient falls short of its potential maximum. People with carnal preoccupations (or philosophical ones, for that matter) make poor utilitarians.

(f) *Perverse pleasures and normal ones.* It is said that some pleasures are *sick* and should be discouraged. Can we discourage, say, watching snuff movies, tethering june bugs, eating live monkey brains, and getting it off with corpses on purely quantitative grounds?

As long as "perverse" and "sick" and "normal" are clinically defined in a way that is not question begging, a utilitarian should have no problem with keeping things straight. Perversity and sickness, clinically understood, are demonstrably dysfunctional.

Problems arise, however, because many anti-utilitarians have an agenda-driven notion of which pleasures are perverse or sick. That agenda *may* reflect medical, psychological, or other knowledge; but it may equally well reflect nothing deeper than local custom.

> *Example.* Onanism is perverse according to some interpretations of the Old Testament. Its perversity needs showing, however, and showing it would involve more than merely saying, "it's unnatural." Indeed, it is difficult to imagine how its perversity could be shown, absent any clinical evidence whatever that the lonely vice is in any way harmful if practiced in moderation.

(g) *Dysfunctional pleasures and functional ones.* The problem with things like snorting coke is not that they are "low." They are defeatable on purely *quantitative* grounds. In the long run, they produce more pain than pleasure for everyone except dealers. Problems arise, however, because many antiutilitarians have an agenda-driven notion of what sorts of pleasures are dysfunctional, and there is no strong reason to think that their agenda is correct.

> *Example.* The fact that one who does not approve of nude art *says* that it corrodes a viewer's respect for persons doesn't make it so. If it does, demonstrably (and if corroded respect for persons is harmful, demonstrably), then there is every utilitarian reason to discourage it. But does it? That is a question for physicians and psychologists to answer, not crusaders.

We could try to establish a weighting factor to discount the enjoyment scores that are earned by dysfunctional behavior, and to enhance those earned by others. That would be like the familiar practice of weighting GPAs in terms of the rigor of the schools where they are earned. It would not be easy, however. Are dysfunctional pleasure occasions worth half as much as functional ones, or only 10 percent? But it is not question of whether to use numbers. It is a question of what numbers to use.

5) *Situation relativity.* Utilitarians believe that it is reasonable for the same act to be evaluated differently under different circumstances, since the consequences of an act will vary as a function of the circumstances in which it occurs. If, in a certain situation, act X would maximize pleasure (well-being, happiness, whatever), then, in that context, it is the proper thing to do. If, in a different context, the same act would maximize pain (grief, sorrow, what-

ever), then, in that context, it would be the wrong thing to do. So utilitarians have no fixed list of acts that must always be done or avoided. Such "situation relativity" always draws adverse comment.

Those who criticize utilitarianism commonly point out that it is "relative." It certainly is, as has been seen in the examination of its consequentialism. The question is, "Is that a flaw?" I think that it is not; and I think that those who believe that it is a flaw simply misconstrue the system.

The statement "X is relative" is an incomplete statement—just as incomplete as "X is a function of." For some X to be *relative*, there must be a Y that it is *relative to*. "X is relative to, or varies as a function of, Y" is a complete statement. So to say that morality is relative is to say, "morality is relative to . . ."—and whether that is a corrupt notion depends entirely on how one fills in the blank.

Anyone who says that morality is a function of his or her own preferences is corrupt. So is anyone who says that it is a function of the sovereign's whim. But utilitarians only say is that it is a function of what the facts are, concretely.

Anyone who says that a given behavior always has the same moral value, no matter when, where, or in what circumstances it occurs, is out of touch with how the world works. For instance, there must be a little "give" in any action-guiding system so as to take relevant differences between people into account. This is consistent with, and a part of, basic utilitarianism. Utilitarians are not committed to the identical treatment of every individual, but to the maximum benefit of the maximum number. That commitment may entail equal opportunity. It certainly entails equal consideration of interests. But it is often incompatible with "identical treatment." A utilitarian society would not dream of providing *identical* training to two individuals, one of whom (a wheelchair-bound paraplegic) had the capacity to be a neurosurgeon, and the other of whom (an image-reversing dyslexic) had the capacity to be an Olympic wrestler. The happiness of the two, and the happiness that they can contribute to others, demands that they be trained differently. Note that it is their capacities that are crucial, not their desires. The fact that a person would like to be an opera singer is beside the point if he or she is mute. Identical treatment in such a case may be *liberal*, but it is not *utilitarian*.

This is one of utilitarianism's strengths, not a weakness. While we must guard against the inclination to make a special case of ourself (or others, for that matter) groundlessly, we dare not rule out the possibility of occasional special cases that can be defended on objective and public grounds. There can, after all, be a good reason for thumbing the scales from time to time. This is why any rule that a utilitarian adopts is strictly prima facie—that is, open to revision when the case requires.

Example. Oscar Levant was a rude man. Grocers and barbers as rude to the public as Levant was would soon be out of their jobs and friendless. People do not ordinarily tolerate derisive condescension. But, while Levant had a great deal of "temperament," he also had a great deal of entertaining musical talent. Treating him in the way that would ordinarily maximize pleasure when dealing with rude people would have actually diminished it in this case. So people said, "He sure is an S.O.B., but we can put up with it." Levant still had few friends; but he had (and deserved) many fans.

However, we should only thumb the scales for behavior the bad effects of which are genuinely outweighed by benefits that are bona fide, substantial, and demonstrable.

> *Example.* Suppose that, in response to the general upset about what Hitler did to the Jews and Gypsies, someone said, "The leader had an enormous task: re-organizing German industry and rationalizing the power structure of Europe under proper German leadership. He saw that he could not succeed without a scapegoat to consolidate national self-interest. Anyone with so grand a goal should not be judged by the same rules that constrain ordinary little people."

Rubbish. With such goals in view, people might not have objected to a little rudeness or self-aggrandizement. But "rudeness" is not the word for Hitler's stance, and justifiable self-aggrandizement stops *way* short of more than 6 million homicides.

6) *Combining psychological egoism and moral pluralism.* By refusing to index moral calculations of pleasure and pain, utilitarians make it clear that moral agents should take the interests of others into account along with their own. Given the clear inadequacies of psychological egoism, that would not pose a problem were it not for the fact that many utilitarians are psychological egoists, as was Bentham himself. But if the pleasures and pains of others, as such, can't move us, how can it be that we *ought* to include them in our moral calculations? The answer, as we have seen, is in the construction of a system of social sanctions and reinforcements that will make the pursuit of social benefits self-beneficial. That is not as easy as it looks, however, and it is not foolproof.

Bentham claimed that personal pleasure and pain are the *only* motivations behind human behavior—that people are always motivated only by their own interests (the principle of psychological egoism) *and* that those interests are limited to obtaining pleasure and avoiding pain (the principle of hedonism). But how can anyone who believes this believe that people have moral obligations to others?

a) Although Bentham thought universal psychological hedonism to be true, it isn't. There may be some who always seek only their own pleasure and always avoid only their own pain, but there are others who don't.

- Everyone seeks and avoids other things besides pleasure and pain. While we may take pleasure in obtaining what we seek, that does not mean that pleasure is what we seek. When I shop for food (because I know I will be hungry at supper time and that the pantry is empty), I do not look for pleasure on the market shelves; and while I hope that I will enjoy the meal when I eat it, that is not all that motivates me to prepare it.

- Many people have interests that, while trivially "their own," are focused on targets other than themselves. Psychological egoism is still false or trivial.

- A few people shop for grief. It is an important psychological fact that some people have an interest in self-harm, whether or not it is in their interest to have that interest. We should not trivialize that away with word magic, lest the need for (and the possibility of) therapy become concealed by bad theory.

b) Nevertheless, even though it is false that everyone always seeks pleasure alone, most of the force of Bentham's egoistic hedonism can be carried by the weaker claim that anticipations of pleasures and pains regularly influence—and sometimes determine—people's behavior. People usually prize their own pleasure and disdain their own pain. So, when they know pleasurable and painful consequences are at stake, it is common for them to adjust their behavior to gain as much of the one, and avoid as much of the other, as they can.

Further, human nature being what it is, people regularly "put a thumb on the scales" when weighing their own interests against those of others. With a little skill at rationalization, we can even make self-preference appealing and plausible (to ourself if not to others). So it is obvious that even if psychological hedonistic egoism is not *universally* true, it is true often enough to pose a major problem at the practical level: *how can people who are strongly biased in favor of gaining their own pleasure and avoiding their own pain be expected to take an interest in others?*

c) Utilitarians recognize the necessity of reinforcing the common good with external constraints. With appropriate *rules and sanctions*, even rank egoists can be encouraged to behave decently. Society simply lets them know that if they behave well they will be rewarded, and if they behave badly terrible things will happen to them. On utilitarian grounds, after all, it is better for good things to be done (or bad things left undone) out of manipulated selfishness, than for bad things to be done (or good things left undone) out of uncontrolled selfishness.

Example: Professor Z fantasizes about exploiting first year students and would take advantage of his position as a freshman advisor to maneuver innocent, malleable, and appealing ones into unspeakable acts, except that he knows that if he did (and got caught):

- he would lose his cushy, undemanding academic job and have a hard time getting another;
- he would be arrested, tried, and possibly convicted of molestation and/or statutory rape;
- he could serve hard time in prison and be forced to try sexual practices in which he has no interest;
- he would be ostracized by any conventional people who learned about his activities;
- he would run the risk of being beaten up (or worse) by his victims' irate parents; and
- his wife would leave him, taking custody of their children and most of whatever income he might continue to earn (if he did avoid prison) as a clerk at Shoe-Rama.

So he leaves his students alone. Society has arranged things so that the pleasures and pains that would be the likely results of the behavior he fantasizes will be of no final interest to him as a rational and careful consequentialist. He may not be admirable, since he does not act for the noblest of interests; but he does behave himself.

Of course this does not always work. Some people never get caught. Some do, but hire lawyers. Most important, some either cannot believe that they might get caught, or are incapable of rational self-interest.

If we mistrust the ability of large numbers of people to perform good acts on their own, we *could* excuse the general population from the moral enterprise altogether, give them lots of rules and sanctions, and rely on the utilitarian commitment of the sovereign elite to keep happiness well-maximized. History, however, suggests that this will work only if a complex system of *distributed* power is in place. Those in charge will sometimes put their thumbs on the scale, too. That is why Burke recognized the dangers of absolute power and why eighteenth-century liberals insisted on institutionalized checks and balances.

C. Interim conclusion. Utilitarian consequentialism is regularly criticized on a wide variety of grounds; but, upon examination, it looks coherent and practical enough to be promising. Three main areas of difficulty remain: whether the way in which utilitarians use rules is consistent, whether the provision that they make for justice, rights, and fair play is adequate, and whether their notion of human nature is coherent and not open to dangerous manipulation. These issues are the topics of the next chapter.

15

The Utility of Rules, Rights, and Fair Play

Although they do not consider that they are morally basic, utilitarians make constant use of *rules*. They do this in two distinct ways, justifying them on strictly consequentialist grounds as:

- Summaries of behavior patterns that experience has shown to maximize human happiness "as a rule" and
- Principles of social organization such that societies that have them can better maximize human happiness than ones that don't.

Rules of either sort, for utilitarians, are hierarchized for conflicts, are prima facie, and are supported by a network of conventional and legal sanctions.

Further, because they recognize the importance of such rules, utilitarians recognize *rights* in society, chief among them the right to fair treatment. Like the rules, these rights are justified on strictly consequentialist grounds, hierarchized, prima facie, and supported by sanctions.

In the first two sections of this chapter, I will examine the ways in which utilitarians justify and use rules and rights. Their use of them depends heavily on a contingent, empirical account of "normal" human capacities and interests. Today, this is being challenged by ever-more-effective techniques for altering human capacities and interests. This poses a problem: can utilitarianism protect people from "benevolent" tampering? I will examine that problem in the chapter's third section.

1. Utility and Rules

A. Moral *aides-mémoire*. Utilitarians need not reinvent the moral wheel each day. They keep careful track of what experience has shown to maximize human happiness "as a rule," and establish (and enforce) regulations based on that experience. But they note that those strictly utilitarian regulations are also strictly prima facie.

For instance utilitarians, like most people, follow the rule, *"Don't kill people."* They do so on the grounds that killing them has been found to be a poor way to maximize human happiness. Consequently, they do not have to rehearse the *pros* and *cons* of homicide every day. This saves time, and it also diminishes the opportunities for special pleading. For them, however, this rule can be overridden for strong reasons in extreme circumstances. It is, after all, nothing more (but also nothing less) than an action-guiding summary of human experience *so far*. That is why they can defend themselves, individually and collectively, even with deadly force if need be, without self-contradiction.

There is a clear difference between utilitarian rule users and those who follow rules for their own sake.

- The former, seeing rules as summaries of what people have learned in *ordinary* cases, are always ready to break, override, or amend them in *extraordinary* ones. For them, believing that we can respect rules without ignoring cases and can adjust to cases without ignoring rules, the moral enterprise is participatory—filled with decision making, and charged with responsibility.
- The latter, convinced of the virtue of rule following, as such, cannot allow that one be broken, overridden, or amended. For them, treating every rule as absolute and universal, the moral enterprise is not participatory. There are no moral judgments or decisions for them to make and take responsibility for.

Many people waver uncomfortably between respect for rules and concern for cases. They feel guilty when they break a rule, even for a good reason; but they also feel uncomfortable about applying standard regulations in nonstandard settings.

Examples. Mark Dupree is out of work and out of money, and his children are hungry. Panhandling on a street corner, he asks for spare change to buy a head of cabbage for supper. A kind person rummages in her pocketbook to find him a quarter; and, as she does, a tissue and a five-dollar bill fall at Mark's feet without her notice. Mark and the kids have Spam with their cabbage that night, but his is seasoned with guilt.

Constable Spingarn knows that the city code prohibits business activity in R-1 zones like the block where the Duprees live. He also knows that Olive Dupree has been taking in ironing for cash for several weeks now. Unable to ignore the fact that she is breaking the zoning ordinance, he writes up a citation summoning her to magistrate's court; but he worries how she will pay the fine, and is embarrassed to look her in the eye.

The normal behavior of utilitarians is quite ordinary. For the most part, they play by standard rules and don't lie, cheat, steal, or kill people. All that sets them apart is their commitment to the notion that no rule is more important than people and that some rules are more important than others. This makes them flexible, responsive, and useful to have around.

> *Example.* My house is on fire with me asleep upstairs. My neighbors are out and their house is locked. The paper carrier sees the blaze at 4:30 in the morning and knows that there is a telephone just inside the neighbors' front door.
>
> I hope that she is a good utilitarian, ready to ignore the breaking and entering rule and the local noise abatement ordinance. I want her to break in next door and call the fire department. I also want her to honk her horn like mad until I wake up.
>
> On the other hand, I also want her to be generally respectful of people's interests, as they are supported by the prima facie rules of everyday moral consideration. After all, she knows when I go on vacation, and has seen me get money out of a canister in the pantry every month to pay her. But if she is a good enough utilitarian to break the rules in emergencies, she is probably a good enough one to keep them ordinarily.

So far, I have only noted how utilitarians use moral rules as prima facie guides to conduct based on common experience—summaries of infinitely many ad hoc decisions about individual acts over time. When they use rules this way, they are *act* utilitarians. Their bottom line is finding the act that will maximize the good in the concrete case. *Rule* utilitarians, however, use rules in an additional way.

B. Rule utilitarianism. From this perspective, we must weigh the probable consequences of having this or that rule *itself* in place in order to establish that having it in place will be useful overall, *even if there are possible cases where it would be disadvantageous to obey it.* Here, we follow a rule, even when an act that it commands might be harmful or one that it bars might be beneficial, because the rule *itself* has been deemed useful and "put on the books" accordingly.

> *Example.* If promise keeping is a useful convention as such (i.e., if a society that maintains it, *come what may*, is more beneficial to human well-being than a society that does not), then we should keep our promises even in isolated cases where doing so is not advantageous to the general welfare. Since contracts will be worthless in a society in which promises cannot be relied on, we will see its commerce diminish to the level of face-to-face goods-in-hand barter. So promises should be kept.

It is not always easy to tell an act utilitarian from a rule utilitarian in practice. Both perspectives can generate the same behavior.

> *Example.* I did not throttle the dean today, even though I felt like it when he told me that my request for a summer research grant had been turned down because

of the growing athletics deficit. My self-restraint might be explained in three different utilitarian ways.

- On the spot, I quickly calculated the likely results of the options (for simplicity's sake, kill him and never have to put up with him again, but go to prison and likely take the deep breath; or put up with him one more day, but keep my life and freedom). Easy decision. He lives on act utilitarian grounds.
- I recalled that I (and thousands of others) have contemplated the *pros* and *cons* of particular homicides, and that we have arrived at a prima facie rule to refrain from it except in overwhelmingly extraordinary circumstances. Noting that his behavior today was no more clueless than usual, I bowed to conventional wisdom. He lives—still on act utilitarian grounds, but as summarized in a prima facie rule.
- I remembered that people long ago decided that banning vengeance killing is essential to civilized life, even when the ban protects individuals whose dispatch would have no negative repercussions. So, in spite of knowing four ways to cap him without getting caught, and knowing that he would not be missed, I settled for the continued stability of a society where individuals are not encouraged to make such decisions on their own. This time he lives on rule utilitarian grounds.

For rule utilitarians, whether to comply with *some* of the rules in place does not require decision making, provided, of course, that they were put in place on utilitarian grounds in the first place. But those rules are still ad hoc and prima facie, because people not only had to decide whether to put them in place to begin with (on grounds that were circumstantial and subject to change), but also because the circumstances that made them useful to adopt could change sufficiently to make them useful to revoke.

The difference, then, between act utilitarians and rule utilitarians is *not* that the latter use rules and the former do not. Rather, it is that in a limited number of "socially basic" cases, rule utilitarians replace individual decisions about rule compliance with a collective decision about rule adoption and maintenance. Rule utility is, consequently, less individual, but no less circumstance-dependent than act utility.

C. Rewards and punishments. However utilitarians conceive of the rules they use, they enforce them with rewards and punishments. This started with Bentham, who thought that sanctions were necessary to make people (all psychological egoists, on his view) take the interests of others into account. While not all utilitarians share Bentham's dismal view of human nature, they all do recognize that selfishness (along with stupidity, denial, and general foolishness) is common enough to make sanctions useful for the encouragement of good behavior.

Example. If I thought I could dispatch a dean without society caring enough to do anything about it, I might actually do it. On the other hand, a failing logic student, noting society's indifference to philosophy professors, might do the same for me. So, even though it is an impediment to the satisfaction of my own homicidal desires, I am glad that society does care—enough, in fact, to have harsh antihomicidal sanctions in place.

It is a truism that the sanctions provided by contemporary U.S. society do not always keep everyone's selfish and/or foolish behavior in check. For instance, homicides, in Richmond at any rate, seem to be out of control, for all the sanctions that are in place. This poses a practical problem for utilitarians. Society needs to find sanctions that *will* work.

Example. There was a time when the threat of fire and brimstone worked fairly well. But relatively few people believe in Hell these days, and it is not a very *immediate* threat, even for those who do. Consequently, many people urge that the state build more prisons, tighten up the judicial process, and impose more draconian penalties.

On the other hand, many people urge the increased use of positive reinforcements for good behavior, day care centers, morals education in the schools, and frequent spot ads on television.

All a utilitarian could ask for would be for both sides to look at *results* for a change.

This is an important issue; and it is crucial to realize that it is a *utilitarian* one. Rhetoric aside, what sanctions will work is a question about testable consequences. All we need to do is try different ones and see. It is *most* crucially important, however, to realize that society will not work at all, in the absence of sanctions of some kind. Unless and until everyone is both rational and kindly, Bentham's conviction that people "need to be nudged" will stand.

D. How and why utilitarians break rules. While it is true enough that utilitarians are willing to break (or override) the rules, from time to time, there is no reason to think that they are wicked in doing so. Breaking or overriding a rule that is generally beneficial, but harmful in a specific situation, can be a good thing. We need to remember what rules are for, and that no rule can fit every circumstance. However, even though it is obvious that most rules have exceptions, we must exercise great care to avoid mistaking minor inconveniences for catastrophes, petty benefits for utopia and, above all, making a special case of ourself.

Example. Sharon's college has an honor system. Every student has solemnly promised not to lie, cheat, or steal. She is taking biochemistry and has studied hard to learn the material because she knows that her scholarship and medical school admission are at stake. Sharon opens the mid-term exam confidently; but draws a blank when she reads the questions. Seized with frustration and panic, but knowing that her notes are in her briefcase, Sharon says to herself, *"All the information is in my head, but it is log-jammed. A ten-second glance at my notes is all I need to shake things loose and make the answers fall into place."* But she also thinks, *"I gave my word that I wouldn't cheat."* So, she is in a quandary. There are two rules, "Don't Cheat," and "Keep Your Word," which seem to require her to take her lumps. Or can she let herself "weigh outputs," "adjust to the circumstances" and take a peek?

While a utilitarian would not necessarily say that Sharon should peek, the issue is at least open. Unless the consequences of cheating and promise breaking are *always* bad, there is at least a possibility that some specific circumstances would allow some specific cheating and/or promise breaking. Only concrete cases will tell.

On the other hand, concrete cases fall into patterns. That is why there are no automatic exceptions to rules that reflect common experience. In fact, there are many consequentialist reasons why Sharon should bite the bullet, keep her word, and leave her notes alone. Here are six.

- **The danger of making an exception of oneself.** It is difficult to be objective about what the consequences of an act will be when our own neck is on the chopping block. Caution is strongly called for.
- **The danger of setting a bad example.** Others may see her peek. She has good reasons for peeking; but will they have equally good reason when they follow suit?
- **The slippery slope.** If she cheats today, it will be easier to cheat again. Only those who don't start never have to stop.
- **The availability of other options.** Talk to the instructor and ask for an extension, a hint, or a make-up; take a walk or a Valium; pray.
- **The desire to avoid sanctions.** Expulsion would be worse for her prospects than a bad mid-term grade. And the embarrassment!
- **Remembering what the rule is for.** Schools ban cheating, among other reasons, in order to increase the likelihood that their graduates can function effectively, even under stress. People who crack up during a test may not belong in the operating room, even if cheating would get them there.

In real life, people find it useful to subscribe to rules customarily and to bend or break them occasionally. When they do the latter, they know that there is a significant danger of special pleading. It is easy to talk about what is best for everyone when all we really care about is our own benefit. Human weakness can flaw even the best-intended endeavor. But this is not a rule lover's criticism of utilitarianism. It is a cautious utilitarian criticism of utilitarianism. Utilitarianism may be hard to practice, but at least it does not blinker us with the fantasy that a single pair of shoes will fit all feet.

2. Utility and Rights

The strongly utilitarian flavor of America's laws and customs is obvious. It stems, no doubt, from the strongly utilitarian atmosphere of the century when the foundations of those laws and customs were laid down. There is another obvious flavor in its laws and customs, too: a firm belief in human rights. This was also fashioned in the intellectual atmosphere of the eighteenth century; and is, perhaps, even more obvious than utility in the early documents of this society. But the juxtaposition of utility and rights creates a strain. Can a concept of human rights be defended on utilitarian grounds? Indeed, does utility leave room for such a concept at all, or does it make all talk of rights hollow and disingenuous?

A. Definitions. A right is an individual's entitlement against others, either to require a benefit or to bar an encroachment. So we who have a right are targets of both positive and negative obligations. Those entitlements can be absolute or prima facie, universal or limited, found or conferred, and procedural or substantive; and the status that warrants them can be "natural" or conventional.

Absolute or unqualified rights cannot be legitimately overridden, or ignored. They have no exceptions. If a person had an absolute right to medical care, then those with medical resources would have a no-exceptions obligation to provide it. If a person had an absolute right to pursue happiness, then anyone in a position to interfere with his or her pursuit would be under a no-exceptions obligation to refrain.

Prima facie rights, on the other hand, can be overridden or ignored under specifiable circumstances. If a person has a prima facie right to education, then those with educational resources have only a qualified obligation to provide it. If people have a prima facie right to private property, then the population at large has only a contingent obligation not to interfere with their stuff. When an exception to a prima facie right is claimed, however, the burden of proof is on the claimer.

> *Example.* While the person who owns the only local pharmacy is on holiday with her shop locked, a local child is bitten by a snake. The owner's prima facie right to the integrity of her property (which includes several ampoules of antivenin) is overridden by the child's prima facie right to medical attention and by the circumstances. So the authorities are free to break into her pharmacy, take the medicine, and treat the child. They have no right, however, to break into and loot privately owned shops at will. They *must* "make their case" first.

The scope of a right is limited to those who have the status that warrants it. If the status warranting a right is held by everyone, then that right is *universal*. If not, then it is *limited*. The prima facie/absolute distinction applies to both universal and limited rights.

A *found* right is one that pertains to a certain status independent of any human act of grant. Some say that all humans have the right to pursue happiness, even when those in power have never granted it and refuse to recognize it. In contrast, the right to drive a car, where it occurs, is clearly *conferred* (and can be taken away).

A *procedural* right guarantees a process, where a *substantive* right guarantees a result. However, the actualization of substantive rights is often a function of the process followed. In the United States, for instance, the procedural right to due process guarantees only the form of legal proceedings, not their outcome. But, by insuring such procedural features as *notice of charges, representation by counsel*, and *cross-examination of witnesses*, it provides some assurance that the outcome (whatever it may be) will be well tested and justified.

The status that warrants the occurrence of a right can be either "*natural*" or *conventional*. For example, rights warranted by being human (if there are any) rest on a "natural" status (species), but the right to vote depends on a conventional one (citizenship).

B. Do people have any rights? Many people have conventional, conferred, and limited prima facie rights. Citizens of the United States, for example, enjoy the conventional, conferred, and limited prima facie right to trial by jury. Does anyone have any natural, found, universal, and absolute ones?

1) First of all, there are problems locating any *absolute* ones. In the U.S. Declaration of Independence, the founders enumerated a short list of rights which accrued, they believed, to all "men" independent of conventions and bestowals: life, liberty, and the pursuit of happiness. But even these putatively natural, found, and universal rights were clearly prima facie, not absolute. No one starts a bloody revolution believing in an absolute right to life.

Utilitarians, at any rate, would expect moral rights, like moral rules, to be prima facie. Circumstances, after all, prevail. Exceptionless rights will not work in an ethic that is predicated on situation relativity. But a notion of prima facie rights, with all its attention to the burden of proof, is precisely made to fit such a scheme. Such rights will nicely embody the general rules of conduct that utilitarians have refined in practice.

For instance, people have a prima facie right not to be killed precisely because it is generally wrong to kill them; and it is generally wrong to kill people because, *ceteris paribus*, killing them works against the maximization of human happiness. Affirming that right amounts to saying that there is a heavy burden of proof incumbent on anyone who sets out to kill another person.

2) Second, there are problems locating any *found* ones. There is no problem with conferred ones, of course. If a world government proclaimed that all earth people would henceforth enjoy the right to representation in its councils, there would be at least one natural, conferred, universal, prima facie right. But are there any universal, natural, prima facie human rights that are *found* (or "innate")?

A caveat: This is not a matter of whether any such rights are universally *recognized*. The occurrence of a right does not depend on its recognition. Even the most vigorous champions of innate human rights are quick to point out the need to reform common practice so that it will reflect them.

Opinion is divided, but my own inclinations are positive. Reflecting American liberal humanism, I would start with the suggestion that all people have a prima facie right to life, liberty, and the pursuit of happiness—independent of all acts and conventions, and whether everyone recognizes them or not.

This will not work without fine-tuning, of course. The right to life, for example, suggests that we have a right to be alive. But we all die, and there can be no right which creates an obligation that cannot be met. So the right to life is better understood when it is refined and reformulated as the right not to be killed. The right to liberty also needs heavy qualification in any populous society. The right to the pursuit of happiness invites confusion between what we pursue and how we feel when we get what we pursue. The founders obviously did not enjoy plenary verbal inspiration. Suitably adjusted, however, the list will work.

This list is not just the result of chauvinist bias, either. Worldwide human experience has shown such rights to be essential ingredients of any social structure that has a hope of maximizing human challenge, fulfillment, and well-being. So there is a utilitarian rationale for at least some prima facie human rights: without prima facie rights to life, liberty, and the pursuit of happiness, human well-being cannot be maximized.

There is a fourth necessary human right also, which is just as basic to the maximization of human well-being as life, liberty, and the pursuit of happiness. It is procedural rather than substantive; since being human is the only status required to warrant it, it is natural and universal; and if it is not innate, it should be conferred in every society because it is a working precondition of all other human rights. This is the universal, natural, prima facie, procedural human right to fair treatment. No substantive rights can be effectively implemented in its absence.

C. The right to fair treatment. Recognition of the right to fair treatment is an essential component of any society organized to maximize human happiness, even though anti-utilitarians seem to think otherwise.

1) Utilitarianism is allegedly open to injustice.

Example. Hitler's Nazis sought to restore German industry, rescue its people from economic hardships, and reestablish Germany as the political leader of Europe. Feeling that this task would be impossible without an ideologically and rhetorically powerful handle on national unity, and given that anti-Semitism was already widespread, they chose the Jews as scapegoats for Germany's loss of the Great War and for all the disasters that followed. The "final solution" was, consequently, justified by its projected consequences: German prosperity and hegemony. The suffering and death of six million or so Jews would be outweighed by benefits that would accrue to even larger numbers. But this was clearly discriminatory and unfair. So it was wicked, even though utilitarian reasoning endorsed it. That is precisely what is wrong with utilitarianism.

At least three things are wrong with this example: it does not take all available options into account, it is biased for self-interest, and it assumes that consequences and intentions are the same thing.

The Nazi's options were not limited to genocide and continued economic hardship. Had they been utilitarians (they were not), they would have had to consider all the options they had; and there were many available that were consequentially preferable to genocide. The really best one would probably have been for them to resign from office and reestablish representative government.

No doubt, they preferred staying in office. Perhaps they even enjoyed the killing. But self-preference is not the deciding factor for utility. The Nazi's articulation and pursuit of so-called Aryan supremacy at no point involved rational people objectively weighing the interests of all concerned parties. Instead, it amounted to a group of distorted people weighing a limited set of alternatives in terms of galloping bias. (I am not using "distorted" arbitrarily here. The Nazis were clinically abnormal themselves and propagated their own warped views among the general population by means of propaganda, media control, and painstaking conditioning in clubs, churches, and schools.)

In any case, the actual consequences of Nazi policy bore little or no resemblance to their ostensible ends. So, even if they formulated their policy on utilitarian grounds (they did not), its results clearly demonstrated that their judgment was riddled with nonutilitarian errors. Consequently, Nazi policy was in no way an exercise of utilitarian judgment.

Here, however, is a stronger (if imaginary) case:

Example. Imagine a world populated by only twenty individuals, nineteen of whom are sadists. (Since they are all the people there are, we will have to accept sadism as in some sense "normal.") Further, suppose the nineteen hit on the idea of torturing the twentieth for their own delectation. Wouldn't it be proper, on utilitarian grounds, for them to proceed?

The calculation would start by weighing the nineteen's pleasures against one person's pain; and that looks like no contest. Further, if the immediate choice (between frustration over not torturing number 20 and the fun of getting on with it) does not exhaust the alternatives, even in this pretend-world, we can eliminate one option after another, by hypothesis, until the only ones left are "torture number 20" and "be tormented by frustration." Wouldn't the utilitarian option-of-choice then be to start heating up the pokers?

Perhaps if we were ever in a situation of this highly imaginary kind, we would be obliged to say that torture was the moral order of the day; but, since we do not live in that sort of world, we do not have to choose that way. When we make real decisions in the real world about things like slavery and torture, careful consideration always leads to the rejection of those actions on utilitarian grounds. Utilitarianism works as a basis for rejecting slavery, genocide, and torture in this world, whatever problems it may have in rejecting imaginary behaviors in imaginary worlds. So, if utilitarianism is to be shown to be unfair, its opponents need a case that is realistic.

> *Example*. My city has a serious problem. Its murder rate has increased to the point that many residents are leaving.
>
> The city government needs to reassure the population at large, and also to discourage potential killers. Catching and punishing some would help— perhaps dragging them down Monument Avenue in chains and hanging them in Monroe Park. That would let the bad guys know that Richmond is not willing to put up with their stuff any more, and will encourage the good guys to stop eroding the tax base. But since it is proving very difficult to find and convict the actual miscreants, why shouldn't the authorities arrest a few of the city's deinstitutionalized vagrants, "convict" *them*, and have a public hanging anyway? Several benefits would occur:
>
> • The general population would believe that the government was finally doing something about crime;
> • Actual and potential criminals, vividly seeing what would happen to them if they got caught, would change their ways; and
> • The population (and the tax base) would be stabilized.
>
> All three manifestly benefit 600,000 citizens at a very low collective cost: the death of a few street people who were parasites on public resources anyway. Unfortunately, however, to hang such people in the park as an example to the community for something they didn't do, just isn't *fair*. So it is wicked, even if, in the real world (scapegoating being far more effective than most would like to admit), it would be useful. *It is better to let a dozen evildoers go free than to unjustly punish one innocent person.*

Utilitarianism, however, need not endorse such injustice. In fact, it can and does make a place for fair play *on its own grounds*. In order to show that this is the case, and how it works, I must clarify what fair treatment actually amounts to. Then I can show why fair treatment, properly understood, is an essential part of utilitarianism as such.

2) What does fair treatment amount to? It is not identical treatment across all variations in time and circumstance. The principle of fair treatment is, in fact, a principle of justified discrimination.

a) What is justified discrimination? While all politically correct people are committed to the policy of *nondiscrimination* these days, no rational person could possibly be committed to a policy of *indiscrimination*. While discrimination based on fraudulent or irrelevant distinctions should be avoided, legitimate and relevant distinctions demand appropriately discriminating responses.

> *Examples.* Suppose that the clothing czar in some collectivist state is responsible to distribute gloves to the population at the onset of winter. How many gloves should each citizen get? The answer should not be an automatic "two." It depends, among other things, on many hands each person has. One-handed people are not being treated unfairly if they receive only one glove for their one hand, even while two-handed folk receive two—one for each hand.
>
> Suppose that there is a Licensing Board to determine who will be allowed to perform brain surgery in Virginia. Who will be licensed?

- All applicants?
  Surely not. My neighbor's fourteen-year-old might apply.
- All applying graduates of accredited medical schools?
  Surely not. Neurosurgery is a specialty requiring intensive training, which not all medical students pursue.
- All applying graduates of an accredited medical school with a certified specialization in neurosurgery?
  Probably. But the license will be revocable for cause (for example, if one develops Parkinson's disease and is allergic to L-Dopa).

The definition of justifiable discrimination is implicit in the examples just given. To *fairly* treat individuals differently:

- there must be a real difference between them,
- the difference must be relevant to the treatment in question, and
- the difference in treatment must be commensurate to the difference between those treated.

The difference between having two hands and having one is a real difference. It is also relevant to how many gloves we can usefully wear at one time. "One glove per hand" is a commensurate policy. Similarly, the difference between those who have uncontrollable tremors and those who don't is real. Further, it is relevant to the effective performance of brain surgery. Finally, barring those with uncontrollable tremors is not overcompensating. All reasonable life and practice is predicated on just such discrimination: hiring, promoting and firing, grading, graduating, and expelling. People who are relevantly different are rarely treated "the same," but they can still be treated fairly. "Fairly" does not mean "the same."

b) Why does discrimination have a bad name? Discrimination is far too frequently based on fraudulent distinctions or irrelevant ones, and/or is overdone. Barring people from voting on the basis of "Negro blood" is based on a fraudulent distinction. There is no such thing as "Negro blood." Excluding people from law school because they have black skin is not based on a fraudulent distinction. There is such a thing as black skin. But it is based on an irrelevant distinction, because skin color has no bearing on a person's capacity for legal training. Excluding deaf people from music school is based on a difference that is neither fraudulent nor irrelevant. There is a real difference between being able to hear and not being able to hear; and whether we are able to hear has some bearing on musicianship. But excluding them may be incommensurate to the difference, because being able to hear has a variable bearing on musicianship, and can often be "worked around."

On the other hand, where a difference is real and relevant, and the contemplated response-variation is commensurate to the difference dealt with, fairness not only tolerates discrimination, it demands it. But the burden of proof is on the one who claims that a particular discrimination is fair. If the burden can't be met, then the discriminatory treatment is intolerable.

c) Why is fair discrimination a good thing? Discriminating fairly assures the likelihood that the recipients of a benefit can utilize it productively and without dysfunction. Also, discriminating fairly assures the likelihood that the recipients of a scarce benefit will be those who will utilize it most efficiently for the consequent benefit of the rest of the population. Discriminating fairly includes:

- students who do better work getting higher marks,
- artisans who make more useful products getting more customers,
- politicians who govern more effectively getting more votes, and
- dentists who regularly pull the wrong teeth losing their licenses.

On the other hand, discriminating fairly does *not* include:

- women being discouraged from studying science,
- minority workers being paid less than the going wage,
- mayors' children not being carded, and
- hospitals denying emergency care to the indigent.

Discriminating fairly is a good thing for the same reason that wearing shoes that fit is a good thing. Unfortunately, it is sometimes easier to tell whether shoes fit than whether a particular discrimination is fair.

- Should low scorers on the standard SAT be granted special admission to university under any circumstances?
- Should women of childbearing age be allowed to work with lead compounds in a paint factory?
- Should a veteran or a member of some previously disadvantaged group receive hiring preference?

But no one said the moral life is easy. It is, in fact, an unending round of risk and decision. In it, however, commitment to playing fairly goes a long way toward assuring good results, even if it does not guarantee utopia. At the very least it offers assurance that when life, liberty, and the pursuit of happiness are curtailed, it is for real and relevant reasons that can be defended in the public arena.

3) A special fairness problem. In some cases, *equally maximal* distributions of the good appear to be possible with or without taking fairness into account. The fair way, however, is still preferable.

> *Example.* Suppose there were ten units of obtainable value to be distributed among the five members of a very small society. Since there would be no sum difference between giving two units to each of the five and giving all ten units to one, no obvious utilitarian distinction can be drawn between these two arrangements, one of which is clearly unfair.

This suggests a more general question: How does a utilitarian choose between sum-equal alternatives? Flip a coin? The answer, if the alternatives are genuinely sum-equal, is *of course.* Such situations are not very common, however.

a) This criticism is most clearly cogent when the "good" under discussion is some concrete, discrete, and portable commodity (gold bars, for example). *All things held equal, a five-person society where one member has ten gold bars and four members have none is manifestly less fair than a society where each member has two.*

But pleasure and pain are not concrete, discrete, and portable commodities. They are readily generated *ex nihilo,* and have only a movable "cap." Indeed, a society where one member had ten gold bars, and the other four had none, would see the generation of a vast amount of unhappiness on the part of the four—undoubtedly more than enough to outweigh the glee of the one who copped all the gold. So that society would not only be unfair, it would be immoral. But it would be immoral on the distinctly utilitarian grounds that its unfair commodity distribution generates a much-less-than-maximum balance of pleasure over pain.

b) Utilitarians would argue that this is generally the case: different sum-indistinguishable distributions of things people like (or are averse to) generate different pleasure/pain balances. So they are morally distinguishable. The critic's mistake occurs in misidentifying the distribution that is up for evaluation. Once we recognize that pleasure and pain (joy and grief, whatever) are states generated in the organism by surrounding states of affairs, then we will realize that those states of affairs must be reasonably fair in order for the pleasure/pain balance to be optimized.

c) On the other hand, couldn't that balance be easily maintained in the face of *concealed* disparities? If the one person with all the gold were able to keep it a secret, then perhaps the four without any would not suffer the pangs of deprivation, even if they liked the stuff just as much as Midas. So an unfair distribution of goods, coupled with a little concealment, should be acceptable on utilitarian grounds, even in a society where everyone has the same wants and interests.

In fact, this does not follow at all. In making a utilitarian assessment of people's pleasures and pains, we must consider the absence of possible pleasures as a negative factor, not just the presence of actual pains. The four would be happiest if there was a fair distribution of gold and they knew it. Less happy if there was an unfair distribution of gold and they didn't know it. Least happy if there was an unfair distribution of gold and they did know it. Thinking that utility endorses concealed unfairness only arises because we have failed to consider an obvious option.

d) If those without gold didn't want any in the first place, they would not be unhappy about their "lack," and the uneven gold distribution would not be immoral on utilitarian grounds. But in those circumstances the gold distribution itself would not be unfair, either. There is nothing unfair about having less of something one doesn't want than someone else has (who does). For instance, it does not bother me that Professor Bunting has 142 miniature owls, while I have none. I don't *want* any miniature owls. In fact, I gave the only one I ever had to Professor Bunting because it gave me no pleasure and I knew how much she enjoys them. So the owl distribution between us is not unfair. Nor, for that matter, is it immoral.

e) This raises a very interesting issue, however. If we could manipulate the targets and intensities of people's wants and interests, we could alter what is relevant and commensurate to them and, hence, what is fair.

A group of people who have been sufficiently conditioned to take no joy in possessions would have no objection to uneven commodity distributions. Absent an interest or sense of deprivation on their part, distribution patterns that omit them would be fair, no matter how disparate. And, since the "conditionees" would have no unhappiness to weigh against the possessive joys of those who have been left alone, such patterns would appear to be moral on utilitarian grounds.

Utility does not say that it would be a good thing to manipulate people this way, of course. It only says that *if* this is the way people were (or had become), *then* there would be nothing wrong with leaving them out of commodity distributions. People aren't that way normally, of course; but it is clear that they could be made to be.

But, *would* it be wrong to manipulate people so as to modify the targets and intensities of their wants and/or interests? Here's the rub: while people don't ordinarily take much pleasure in being manipulated, they might actually achieve higher pleasure scores after a little manipulation, especially in situations where "untampered" appetites are high and resources are scarce. That issue will be examined in section 3 below, Utility and "Normal" Human Nature.

Barring questions of manipulating people's wants, however, utility makes a thorough provision for all the fairness that morally counts.

4) Justifying the right to fair play. I have suggested several ways in which fair play contributes to the general well being of people in society. To the extent that it does, institutionalizing procedures that will assure its occurrence is worthwhile on utilitarian grounds. Here is an additional argument to clinch the case: With the exception of three relatively rare types, which will be noted, people will choose a society that is committed to fair play, over one that is not, every time.

Suppose that some individuals are in a position to choose the way in which the society in which they are going to live will be organized. Suppose further that none of them are in a position, at the time the choice is made, to know what "slots" they will occupy in the new society, once it is established. Finally, suppose that they are considering whether or not several concrete institutions will be part of the new order. (These people are in the "original position" and under the "veil of ignorance." See John Rawls's *A Theory of Justice*.)

- Slavery. *It would be great to have slaves to do all my work for me, but it would be terrible to be someone's slave and have to do all their work for them. Since I don't get to pick whether I will be a slave or a slave owner, the risks are too high to allow slavery.*
- Sanction-enforced laws against killing, assault, theft, and the like. *Without such laws and sanctions to back them up, I could take whatever I wanted from anyone who has it and punch out (or even kill) anyone who objects. On the other hand, other people could take my stuff and beat up on me (or even kill me), too. I wonder whether I will be big, quick and strong, or small, clumsy, and weak. With no assurance about my place in the food chain, I had better choose a system that protects life and property.*
- Regulations to assure consumer protection, job safety, and the like. *If I had the capital to own a business, it would be more profitable to run a sweatshop and sell my goods without worrying about lawsuits. But what if I work in someone else's factory, and have to buy whatever goods others choose to market? I wouldn't like working twelve-hour days, without vacations, health care, or retirement. And I certainly don't want a television set that emits x-rays, hazardous tires on my car, or feces-tainted strawberries. Furthermore, there are going to be far more consumers and workers in any society than there are capitalists and entrepreneurs. So, on the odds, I'll go for protective regulation.*
- Judicial procedures guaranteeing due process. *It would be efficient if the authorities could just summarily jail or execute desperadoes without the complications of lawyers, trials, rules of evidence, etc. On the other hand, what if I was in the wrong place at the wrong time, and the po-*

*lice just gunned me down without blinking; or what if they were em-
powered to stop and search anyone any time, or to enter and ransack
people's homes at will?* (Think of the Patriot Act.) *It all depends on which
foot the shoe is on; and the risks are too high to trust to luck. Due process
had better be in—for sure.*

The same process could be carried out for many other social institutions
that are aimed at fairness; and, for most people, the results would be the
same. "Blind" cost/benefit analysis buys fair play to maximize *our own* happiness; and fair play maximizes our own happiness by maximizing *general*
happiness. Utility necessitates it.

Three types of people might disagree, however:

- the bold risk-takers—the "high rollers,"
- those who won't or can't imagine themselves on the bottom of the totem
  pole—the "wishful thinkers," and
- the self-despising—"martyrs looking for lions."

All three types are self-destructive, however, and can be clinically identified
as significantly "deviant" from ordinary human preference patterns. Consequently, as long as it is reasonable to limit utilitarian considerations to the
maximization of happiness for "normal" people, these three exceptions do
not defeat the point: *the right to fair treatment is solidly based on the principle of utility.* On the other hand, it is not transparently obvious that this lim-
itation is reasonable, especially given the techniques for modifying people
that are now available.

3. Utility and "Normal" Human Nature

Throughout this discussion of utilitarianism, I have confined my attention to
the interests of "normal" people. Because people are the way they are, their
pursuit of well-being can be enhanced by consistent reflection on what
makes them happy, as a rule. But if they were different, then the means to
their well-being would be different, too. That fact raises three related issues:

- Is the current conception of normal human needs and interests correct?
- Could human happiness be furthered by raising people to an "enhanced"
  normal?
- If we want people to be happy, but do not like (or cannot afford) what
  it takes to make them happy the way they are, why not change the way
  they are?

a) Whether the current conception of normal human needs and interests is
correct is more complex than it seems. There are at least three senses in

which we might speak of human needs and interests as normal: psychobio-logical, moral, and descriptive.

- In the psychobiological sense, the word "normal" means *functional* or *healthy*.
- In the moral sense, the word "normal" means *proper* or *up to the (moral) norm*.
- In the descriptive sense, the word "normal" means *ordinary, standard-issue*, or *usual*.

For utilitarians, whether a particular human need or interest is *functional or healthy* is a question best answered by psychologists and biologists with enough evidence-based expertise to make their views credible. For an excellent treatment of a developing empirically based conception of standard-issue human capacities, bents, and needs, see Steven Pinker's *The Blank Slate*. Progress is being made.

For utilitarians, whether a particular human need or interest is *proper* is a convoluted issue. Proper *acts* are acts that maximize the pleasure attendant upon satisfaction of interests. Proper *interests* would be what? Perhaps proper interests are ones the occurrence of which enhances their own (or some other interests') satisfaction. In any case, whatever "proper" means when attached to interests, it cannot mean "satisfactory in terms of some nonutilitarian conception of morality."

For utilitarians (or anyone else, for that matter), whether a particular human need or interest is *standard issue* is vexed by the fact that the traditional map of human nature is inaccurate and the rapidly developing new map of human nature is incomplete. Most of what has been said about human nature until quite recently (and much of what is being said now) comes from people driven by preconceived, evaluative conceptions of what it *ought* to be. Systematic, empirical investigations of human needs and interests are relatively recent; also, since empirical accounts are always provisional, they remain open to amendment in the light of further evidence.

So what human needs and interests should a utilitarian encourage? The issue is particularly vexed in areas where people see the phenomena through judgmental filters and equivocate over the three senses of "normal" to make their propriety judgments look like medical diagnoses or value-neutral descriptions.

This does not mean that utilitarians cannot give moral advice. Far from it. Where there is good evidence that a behavior is genuinely extraordinary, they can discourage it on the grounds that people do not yet know what its long-term consequences are likely to be. And, when there is good evidence that a behavior is genuinely dysfunctional for oneself (e.g., glue sniffing) or for others (e.g., child molesting), they can discourage it on the grounds that there are specific demonstrable pleasure-diminishing harms that it causes to one-self (e.g., brain damage) or others (e.g., psychological trauma).

b) Whether human happiness could be enhanced by bringing people up to an "improved" normal state is a matter of little debate. Of course it could. That is why people send their children to school, make them learn to ride bicycles (even when they fall off), and make them take piano lessons or go out for soccer (even though the skills required to enjoy the piano and soccer have to be acquired through hard work and practice). The results of such enhancements are demonstrable. Few people, having learned to read, choose to stop. Few people, having learned to listen to Bartok, willingly return to "The Farmer in the Dell."

There is a rub, however. If it is acceptable to tamper with the organism so as to enhance its pleasure capacities—by subjecting it to schooling, conditioning, and exposing it to increasingly complex and subtle stimuli, what is to prevent the institution of a "brave new world" through outright, invasive manipulation?

- Shall infants be given wine and caviar with their Pabulum to develop their taste and sensibility?
- Shall young teens be encouraged to have sex on the playground to develop their pleasure sensibilities and techniques?
- Shall everyone have a probe inserted into their brain and retire to their cocoons for a *very* happy, albeit rather short, life?

The utilitarians' answer to these (and all similar) questions is, "No." As empiricists, they know that discretion is a function of experiential maturity, and that those exposed to complex stimuli before they are developmentally ready tend to become obsessive/compulsive or worse. So, beneficent utilitarians will temper their enhancement curriculum to things that novices can handle, and give Junior a tricycle (not a Harley) at three, and his own telephone (not a slave girl) at fourteen.

c) Aldous Huxley very effectively captured the practical question of raising human happiness levels by lowering human happiness thresholds. In his novel, *Brave New World*, people were not just the targets of utilitarian benevolence, but also of systematic capacity-manipulating interference, from the moment of their conception. The details of his novel are dated, but the message is not. It is a blueprint for benevolent despotism.

Is this, perhaps, what the institutions of education and acculturation are about in the real world: making the maximization of happiness feasible by manipulating the needs and interests of those to be made happy? Standard middle-school curricula are *not* accidental (and may include dumbing everyone down to the lowest common denominator, but benevolently trying to make it pleasant, all the while).

No ill-will is necessary on the part of the social engineers. It is a matter of making good will *practical*. Only finite resources are available for providing a happiness-inducing human environment; so it may be easier to alter humans than to make them happy the way they are.

> *Example*. Assume there is a society of ten individuals, each of whom has a minimal happiness threshold that requires three units of Soma to trigger. Assume, further, there are only twenty units available before the cost of extraction exceeds the value of the product.
>
> While it would be fair enough for the happiness czar, Compassionata Distributiva, to give each individual two units, no individual's threshold would be met; so all ten would be unhappy.
>
> On the other hand, she could give six of them three units each, four of them none, and bank two for a rainy day. Then six would be happy and four unhappy. This appears to be better, assuming that she uses a fair method to pick the six; but it may still be hard for Compassionata to accept.
>
> So, presume further that for the investment of the cost of only ten Soma units in a program of gene alteration and environmental conditioning, everyone's threshold could be lowered to one unit. But that is exactly the number of units that the society can now afford. So, with adjustments, everyone is happy.

At the gut level, I find this abhorrent. I think this is because it is "normal" people whose happiness concerns me, not that of mutant monstrosities. But that is not a value-neutral judgment. It presumes that there is something *good* about people being the way they are.

On the other hand, it is not a whimsical and arbitrary judgment, either. It is based on the reasonable belief that if people in general were manipulated, I would probably be manipulated, too. That, coupled with a strong affection for myself the way I am, yields personal aversion. That aversion, coupled with a principle of fairness, yields a utilitarian verdict for caution.

If my abhorrence is justified, then a working moral system will obviously need a principle that establishes the prima facie inviolate status of normal humans, plus some clinical, noncircular definition of what being normal amounts to. That, as seen above, is an empirical matter, and waits on painstaking, bias-neutral research.

In any case, utilitarianism is the most effective moral system for working with people the way they are now. Even if they change, it will remain the most effective moral system for working with people the way they come to be, because it will adjust to their needs and interests, whatever they may be. But if any threshold-reducing changes are required to get people from the way they are to the way they will be, they must be sufficiently appealing to people for them to volunteer for the operation.

Time and involuntary manipulation may solve the riddle. In a brave new world where beneficent therapy, eugenic mating, and cloning are readily available, "discount" happiness may be everyone's eventual lot. But if even one untampered soul survives, the rest of Huxley's nightmare will also turn out to be true.

4. How Utility and Rights Work Together

There is no guarantee that everyone can freely pursue happiness without at least some conflict. There is not even a guarantee that one person's pursuit of happiness will never be predicated on another person's bondage (or even death). That is why it is necessary to hierarchize the rights that we recognize, so that (for instance) the right to life always overrides the right to property. (It really does. This is why I can defend my home with lethal force if the lives of my children are endangered by marauders, but cannot booby-trap my pear tree with *plastique* against my neighbors' eight-year-old twins.)

This hierarchization of rights determines which one to honor when conflicts arise. But when people hierarchize rights (just as when they hierarchize rules), they do it on utilitarian grounds.

> *Example.* On what grounds do we decide that an enemy's right to a fair trial overrides our own right to exercise free speech by bearing false witness? Because the allowance of perjured testimony in trials would so undermine the fabric of society as to diminish the general level of well-being.

Furthermore, even while utility is resolving conflicts of rights, rights serve to keep ad hoc utility on track. Established and recognized prima facie rights work as a limit, curtailing the headlong, ill-considered pursuit of benefits that might ignore the lessons of accumulated experience.

Completing the loop, it is utility itself that underwrites these established and recognized rights. Only utility makes sense of them; and only utility can finally bring them to heel when situations are extreme; because utility is what makes them prima facie. The rights (and all the lesser rules) are themselves the output of generations of experimental utility. It is solely because of this that they are open to revision and refinement as human experience and, consequently, human wisdom increases. So utility and rights do not finally conflict. They work together.

5. Conclusions

a) Utilitarians consider the human impact of our acts to be morally basic. Since human pleasure, happiness, and well-being are better than human pain, unhappiness, and grief, utilitarians say that we should act in ways that maximize the former and minimize the latter—as discerned and confirmed in the arena of experience.

b) When the human impact of our acts is held to be morally basic, we can make sense of rules, rights, and justice, good motives and good people, the virtues, and the link between morality and religion.

- Utilitarian rules are prima facie guides to action, based on centuries of collective experience of the human impact of different sorts of behavior. They are completely compatible with the familiar and basic affirmative principle: *Treat people the way you would have them treat you*; and they include such specific prescriptions as: *Don't kill people; Don't lie; Don't exploit the weak and vulnerable; Don't cheat; and Don't steal.*

  All of these are rules because, as a rule, they foster human well-being. Because some are more important than others, they can be hierarchized. And because they are not absolute, they can be overridden *in extremis*.

- Utilitarian rights are prima facie limits on what we can do to others, and prima facie specifications of what we can expect from others. Just like rules (for they are, in fact, very basic rules), they are based on centuries of collective experience of the human impact of different sorts of behavior. They include, among others, the rights to life, liberty, the pursuit of happiness, and fair play. All of them are rights because, as a rule, they foster human well-being in such basic ways that they are prerequisites to the functional operation of any society in which normal people would volunteer to live. Because some are more important than others, they can be hierarchized. Because they are not absolute, all can be overridden *in extremis*.

- While utilitarian good acts are the ones that maximize human well-being, utilitarian good motives are the ones that embody the intent to perform good acts, and good people are those who act out good motives with such deliberate skill that their intended consequences are regularly fulfilled.

  Just as no act is good or bad in itself, neither are motives and agents. Good acts derive their value from their consequences, good motives amount to dispositions to perform good acts, and good people are those who are: 1) disposed to behave well and 2) successful at it.

- Utilitarian virtues are those human attributes that are recognized, on the basis of experience, as dispositional hallmarks of good people. They include things like temperance, courage, fortitude, and charity. But a virtuous act (or person) is not good because it is virtuous; rather it is virtuous because it is good.

- With a working conception of what is morally worthwhile firmly in place, we are in a position to ask whether religious practice is morally justified, rather than whether moral behavior is religiously justified. It is good to have the horse in front of the cart.

c) Ordinarily, the utilitarians' conception of morality does not depart radically from the moral traditions of most functional societies. This should be no surprise. Commonsense considerations of utility are where those traditions came from, by and large.

The three main ways in which the utilitarians' conception of morality *does* differ from other traditions are that:

- It takes consequences, not rules, nature, self-interest or divine will, to be paradigmatic;
- It is always open to revision and refinement in the light of further experience; and
- It puts people in a position of genuine responsibility to make behavior choices and live with their consequences, rather than alienating those responsibilities to the society, nature, or God.

d) The utilitarians' approach to morality does not yield perfection for two reasons:

- People make mistakes; and
- People sometimes act with harmful and malevolent intent.

Nevertheless, for all the possibilities of human error and ill-will, considering consequences yields consistently better results than following your star, following nature or God, or obeying whatever rules happen to be in place. So the more people consider the consequences, the better the world will be for everyone. And, after all is said and done, improvement—not perfection—is what morals are for.

Endnote

Looking Back and Looking Forward

1. Looking Back

In the preface, I argued that philosophical inquiry begins with the logical analysis and clarification of the basic concepts that people use in descriptive, explanatory, and normative enterprises such as science, history, religion, education, politics, and law. In the chapters which followed, I analyzed and clarified four such concepts—ones that are central to a broad range of human concerns and represent the three primary areas of philosophy itself: the concepts of belief and knowledge (representing *epistemology*), the concept of human nature (representing *ontology*), and the concept of moral conduct (representing *value theory*).

A. Belief. In chapters 1 through 4, I explored several problems and confusions that surround the concept of belief, sketched out a map of the epistemic neighborhood, and explored a variety of possible reasons for preferring one belief over another.

- A person's beliefs are his or her experiential expectations—the first step toward knowledge.
- The fact that a belief is familiar, validating, or uplifting—or that an individual, group, or culture believes it—provides no basis for preferring it over others. The one *good* reason for preferring one belief over another is that it is true (reliable).
- Reliable beliefs can be hard to find, given the complex ways in which experiential expectations are generated, and the attendant possibility of faulty perception, misconstrual and misunderstanding, poor inference, and even willful error. But they *can* be found by paying close attention to publicly confirmable evidence and vigorously controlling for limiting conditions.

- The truth of beliefs is a function of what is the case; and that is not under individual or social control, nor a matter of preference, desire, or propriety. The world is what it is; and true beliefs reflect it reliably—for good or ill.

B. Knowledge. In chapters 5 through 9, I explored several problems and confusions that surround the concept of knowledge, sketched out a map of the cognitive neighborhood, and examined the epistemic implications of cultural relativism, including the roles that "paradigms" play in determining what people believe and what they can know.

- Knowledge is, at least, *justified* true belief. It is the limit toward which belief strives.
- There is no impregnable fortress of certainty about matters of fact in the cognitive domain, but there is a more humble domicile for working knowledge—funded by experience, processed by reason, and verified "beyond reasonable doubt" in the arena of public discourse. Consequently, for all its seductive attractions, radical epistemic skepticism is unjustified. Knowledge can be sufficiently approximated for people to function and thrive.
- People are entitled to say that they know a great many things, even though—from time to time—they have to admit to errors in the light of new experiences and reflection on old ones. This discovery and admission of errors, however, does not mark the *demise* of the cognitive enterprise. It is, rather, the chief means of its expansion and a mark of cognitive health.
- While belief and knowledge are influenced by culture, the notion that they are determined by it is untenable. Furthermore, the notion that the history of paradigms is discontinuous and that paradigm changes are always revolutionary, is seriously misleading. What stands as a culture's paradigm for inquiry often undergoes change without loss of continuity and with little trauma—even *improving*, with the passage of time and the accumulation of experience.

C. Human nature. In chapters 10 and 11, I explored several different models of human nature, sketched out a map of what it is to be a person, and examined the possibility of humans acting freely and responsibly.

- The notions that people reflect the image of God, and/or function as they do because they are (wholly or partly) made of special stuff, confuse the question of what it is to be human more than they clarify it.
- The notions that people are continuous with the rest of nature and—like everything else—function as they do because of the way they are put together, are more illuminating.

A close examination of how people actually function raises the issue of whether they ever act freely; and, if free action is impossible for them, whether there is any intelligible use for such words as *responsibility, praise*, and *blame*. Consequently, I explored several different models of human action and causation.

- Causal determinism is the view that all events are the outcome of antecedent sufficient causes operating under the aegis of uniform causal laws, and that they are (consequently) predictable in principle. According to many, the truth of causal determinism would entail that no event can ever constitute a free and responsible act; consequently, that no moral judgments are ever significant.
- Indeterminism is the view that at least some events are not causally determined. But this view is demonstrably just as incompatible with freedom and responsibility as strict determinism is alleged to be, since it breaks the relevant links between agents and their acts.
- So, either the notions of human freedom and responsibility are unreasonable and untenable, or universal causation and human freedom and responsibility are *not* truly incompatible.
- An agent's acts are best assessed for freedom and responsibility in terms of the directness and density of the causal connections between them and both their immediate and remote producers (operationally understood). On this account, an act can be both caused and free, with the result that "responsibility, "praise," and "blame" remain useful terms.

D. Moral Conduct. In chapters 12 through 15, I explored the meaning and force of evaluative judgments and appraisals, looking for the possibility of moral knowledge.

- Although many people look for moral *certainty* or for *necessary* moral truths as the only sure defense against moral skepticism, their quest is ill advised.
- Moral evidence, arguments, and cognitions only need the same footing descriptive evidence, arguments, and cognitions need.
- To have it, one must put moral evaluation on an empirical footing, spell out the kinds of evidence and argument that apply to it, and give a plausible account of "basic human nature."
- On the basis of what reinforces—and what undercuts—untampered human interests, a broadly utilitarian concept of value can be coupled with one general formal principle to yield: *One should maximize happiness over grief, but confine variations in the treatment of individuals to those that can be justified by real, relevant, and commensurate variations in the individuals themselves.*

- This principle of fair play is justifiable on both utilitarian and rational grounds. It contributes to the quality of life that a society can foster, and helps determine whether any particular social arrangement is likely to be chosen "blind."
- This approach provides a working rebuttal to moral whimsy. Common human interests allow people to work toward the articulation of moral beliefs (and, in simple cases, even moral knowledge) in the same way that they work toward descriptive belief and knowledge. *Any* knowledge, moral or descriptive, must be weighable in an arena of argumentation, testable in a network of evidence, and confirmable in the public experience of people who are comparably endowed.
- While the notion that human appraisals are *influenced* by cultural paradigms is important and true, the notion that they are *determined* by them won't fly. We know that various cultures' value systems *can* be appraised and reformed (both from "inside" and from "outside") because we know that they *are*.

2. Looking Forward

Analyzing and clarifying conceptual puzzles—especially ones that have practical implications for how people live their lives—is what basic philosophical inquiry amounts to. And wherever we turn, there are such puzzles at hand. So there are ample opportunities to continue where this book "leaves off." Every time we puzzle out the roots and branches of an everyday belief—or ask, "How does what I think *here* meld with what I think *there*?"—we will be continuing what has been started here.

A person need not be a professional philosopher to do that. Indeed, this kind of reflection is as often found in literature, and in the ruminations of ordinary people struggling with the issues of daily life, as in philosophy books per se. Systematic and dogged engagement, however, may enhance our skill at it.

Those dogged enough to have read this book should have acquired some skill at spotting ambiguity and conceptual slight of hand, and a taste for arguments and reasons over fervor and rhetoric. I hope that they will continue the practice of philosophical midwifery on their own, and—by doing so—enhance their chances of doing "wisely and well" the tasks that unreflective people are ever so likely to screw up.

Those who are both dogged and systematic will pursue, in depth, the analysis and clarification of one or more of the puzzles dealt with here, tackle some new ones, examine what one philosopher has said on a number of such topics or what a number of philosophers have said on the same topic, and begin reading the history of philosophy—both in general and on those particular issues that are most important and/or perplexing to them. That, in turn, can lead to the eventual development of a coherent and inclusive philosophical syntheses of their own systematic "worldviews."

Such an open-ended program may seem daunting; but the quality of our life depends, at least in part, on whether (and how) it is pursued. For starters, here are three puzzles each, in six areas that have not been directly explored here.

A. Religion.

1) *How could a creator that is worthy of worship (i.e., a God) create a world as dysfunctional and full of suffering as this one? Why should we worship anything that is apparently malevolent, careless, ignorant, or weak?*

2) *How could a sovereign that was worthy of worship (i.e., a God) give or withhold favors on the basis of pleading and/or the currying of favor? Can people, with integrity, worship anything that answers prayers or rewards self-serving obedience?*

3) *Can a person justifiably choose the belief and practice of any one religion over any other?*

B. Law.

1) *Could there be any normative "natural laws" without a lawgiver to establish them? If not, unless there are cogent grounds for belief in God, what grounds are there for preferring one set of "positive laws" over another?*

2) *If legality itself is the only standard of right and wrong, can laws themselves be evaluated? If not, then why should anyone who is clever (or lucky) enough to avoid detection obey any law to which they object?*

3) *Would it be morally better for the application of law to be exceptionless, or should it be tempered with mercy?*

C. Society.

1) *Why should democracy be favored over elitism based on talent, intelligence, and other relevant individual merits?*

2) *Why should childless people pay school taxes?*

3) *Are people the product of culture, culture the product of people, or (perhaps) a little of both? Does it matter?*

D. Art.

1) *Can there be art without intention?*

2) *Does it make sense to talk about the "objective meaning" of any artwork?*

3) *Are any artworks better than any others? If so, what standards are in play and where do they come from? If an artwork could be cloned, would the clone be as good as the original?*

E. Education.

1) *How important is understanding? Would there be anything wrong with taking an "information pill," were such a thing available? Is a person who understands set theory better educated than one who can make change and calculate compound interest, but can't define "proper subset"?*
2) *How many kinds of intelligence are there? How many kinds of knowledge? How are intelligence and knowledge related? Can everything and everyone be taught?*
3) *What is most important to good teaching: method, mastery of content, or charisma?*

F. Gender.

1) *Is gender a biological fact, an institutional fact, a cultural fact, or some combination of the three?*
2) *How many human genders are there?*
3) *What, if anything, is the human significance of the gender role differences commonly found in nonhuman animals?*

These eighteen questions in six arenas of everyday concern are only a sample of the puzzles occurring in every area of human thought that call for philosophical analysis and understanding. Of less widespread concern but no less importance, for instance, philosophical puzzles abound throughout the natural, biological, and behavioral sciences and mathematics. Not even the most sophisticated systems of thought are exempt from conceptual cramps and the consequent need for meta-level analysis and clarification. Muddles can turn up where we least expect them, and unexpected muddles are the ones that are most likely to cause trouble. There is, consequently, no shortage of philosophical work to be done. So, *bon appetit!*

Works Mentioned

Ardrey, Robert. *The Territorial Imperative.* New York: Athenaeum, 1966.

Aristotle. *Nichomachean Ethics.* Translated by Terence Brown. Indianapolis: Hackett Publishing Company, 1985.

Asimov, Isaac. *I, Robot.* New York: Gnome Press, 1950.

Austin, J. L. *How to Do Things with Words.* Cambridge: Harvard University Press, 1975.

———. "Performative Utterances." In *Philosophical Papers,* edited by J. O. Urmson and G. J. Warnock. Oxford: Clarendon Press, 1970.

———. *Sense and Sensibilia.* Oxford: Clarendon Press, 1962.

Ayer, A. J. *Language Truth and Logic.* New York: Dover Publications, 1952.

———. *The Problem of Knowledge.* Harmondsworth: Penguin Books, 1955.

Baum, Lyman Frank. *The Wizard of Oz.* Chicago: Reilly & Lee Co., 1961.

Bennett, William J. *The Book of Virtues.* New York: Simon & Schuster, 1993.

Bentham, Jeremy. *An Introduction to the Principles of Morals and Legislation.* Oxford: Clarendon Press, 1996.

Berkeley, George. *Three Dialogues between Hylas and Philonous.* Indianapolis: Hackett Publishing Company, 1979.

Black, Max. *Models and Metaphors.* Ithaca: Cornell University Press, 1962.

Bonhoeffer, Dietrich. *Ethics.* Translated by Neville Horton Smith. London: SCM Press, 1955.

Braithwaite, R. B. *An Empiricist's View of the Nature of Religious Belief.* Cambridge: Cambridge University Press, 1955.

Branden, Nathaniel. *The Virtue of Selfishness.* New York: New American Library, 1964.

Browne, Harry. "The Morality Trap." In *Philosophy—Contemporary Perspectives on Perennial Issues,* edited by E. D. Klemke et al. New York: St. Martin's Press, 1994.

Butler, Joseph. *Fifteen Sermons Preached at the Rolls Chapel,* Preface, §539. London: Society for Promoting Christian Knowledge, 1970.

Cahn, Stephen. *Philosophical Explorations: Freedom, God, and Goodness.* Buffalo: Prometheus Books, 1989.

Cargile, James. "On Consequentialism." *Analysis* vol. 29 (1969).

Castaneda, Carlos. *The Teachings of Don Juan: A Yaqui Way of Knowledge.* Berkeley: University of California Press, 1968.

Chomsky, Noam. *Cartesian Linguistics.* Lanham: University Press of America, 1983.

———. *Knowledge of Language: Its Nature, Origin, and Use.* New York: Praeger, 1986.

Clifford, W. K. "The Ethics of Belief." *Contemporary Review* (January 1987). Reprint, in *The Ethics of Belief and Other Essays.* Buffalo: Prometheus Books, 1999.

Copi, Irving M. "Crucial Experiments." In *The Structure of Scientific Thought,* edited by Edward Madden. Boston: Houghton Mifflin, 1960.

———. *Introduction to Logic.* 11th ed. Upper Saddle River, NJ: Prentice-Hall, 2002.

Davidson, Donald. "On the Very Idea of a Conceptual Scheme." *Proceedings of the American Philosophical Association* vol. 47 (1973–1974).

deMille, Richard. *The Don Juan Papers.* Belmont, CA: Wadsworth, 1990.

Denizet-Lewis, Benoit. "Friends, Friends with Benefits, and the Benefits of the Local Mall," *The New York Times Magazine,* Sunday, May 30, 2004.

Dennett, Daniel Clement. *Brainstorms.* Montgomery, VT: Bradford Books, 1978.

———. *Elbow Room.* Oxford: Clarendon Press, 1984.

Descartes, René. *Meditations on First Philosophy.* Indianapolis: Hackett Publishing Company, 1993.

Fletcher, Joseph. *Situation Ethics: The New Morality.* Philadelphia: Westminster Press, 1966.

Flynn, Tom. *The Trouble with Christmas.* Buffalo: Prometheus Books, 1993.

Foucault, Michel. *Power/Knowledge: Selected Interviews and Other Writings.* New York: Pantheon Books, 1980.

Frankfurt, Harry. *The Importance of What We Care About.* Cambridge: Cambridge University Press, 1988.

Gettier, Edmund L. "Is Justified True Belief Knowledge?" *Analysis* vol. 23 (1962).

Gilligan, Carol. *In a Different Voice.* Cambridge: Harvard University Press, 1982.

Grene, Marjorie Glicksman. *Dreadful Freedom: Introduction to Existentialism.* Chicago: University of Chicago Press, 1959.

Grunbaum, Adolf. *Modern Science and Zeno's Paradoxes.* Middletown: Wesleyan University Press, 1967.

Habermas, Jurgen. *The Theory of Communicative Action.* Boston: Beacon Press, 1983.

Haley, Alex. *Roots.* Burbank: Wolper Productions, Warner Home Video, 1992.

Hall, James. *Knowledge, Belief, and Transcendence.* Boston: Houghton Mifflin, 1975.

———. *Philosophy of Religion.* Chantilly, VA: The Teaching Company, 2003.

Hall, Roland. "Excluders." *Analysis* vol. 20 (1959).

Hare, R. M. *The Language of Morals.* Oxford: Clarendon Press, 1972.

Hare, R. M., et al. "Theology and Falsification." In *New Essays in Philosophical Theology,* edited by A. Flew and A. MacIntyre. London: SCM Press, 1955.

Harris, Randy Allen. *The Linguistic Wars.* New York: Oxford University Press, 1993.

Hegel, G. W. F. *Phenomenology of Spirit.* Translated by A. V. Miller. Oxford: Clarendon Press, 1977.

Heisenberg, Werner. *Physics and Philosophy: The Revolution in Modern Science.* New York: Harper, 1962.

Hempel, Carl Gustav. *Philosophy of Natural Science*. Englewood Cliffs, NJ: Prentice-Hall, 1966.

Herberg, Will. *Protestant, Catholic, Jew*. Revised ed. Garden City: Anchor Books, 1960.

Hines, Terence. *Pseudoscience and the Paranormal*. Buffalo: Prometheus Books, 1988.

Hintika, Jaako. "Cogito Ergo Sum: Inference or Performance?" *The Philosophical Review* vol. 71 (1962).

Hobbes, Thomas. *Leviathan*. Baltimore: Penguin Books, 1968.

Horsburgh, H. J. N. "The Claims of Religious Experience." *The Australasion Journal of Philosophy* vol. 35 (1957).

Hospers, John. "What Means This Freedom?" In *Determinism and Freedom in the Age of Modern Science,* edited by Sidney Hook. New York: New York University Press, 1958.

Hume, David. *An Enquiry concerning Human Understanding*. Indianapolis: Hackett Publishing Company, 1993.

Huxley, Aldous. *Brave New World*. New York: Modern Library, 1956.

James, William. *The Will to Believe*. Cambridge: Harvard University Press, 1979.

Kant, Immanuel. *Critique of Pure Reason*. New York: St. Martin's Press, 1965.

———. *Grounding for the Metaphysics of Morals*. Indianapolis: Hackett Publishing Company, 1993.

Kenny, Anthony. *The Metaphysics of Mind*. Oxford: Oxford University Press, 1989.

Kohlberg, Lawrence. *The Philosophy of Moral Development: Moral Stages and the Idea of Justice*. New York: HarperCollins, 1981.

Kuhn, Thomas S. *The Structure of Scientific Revolutions*. 2nd ed. Vol. 2, no. 2, International Encyclopedia of Unified Science Series. Chicago: The University of Chicago Press, 1970.

La Mettrie, Julien Offray de. *Man A Machine and Man A Plant*. Indianapolis: Hackett Publishing Company, 1994.

Lehrer, Tom. "Lobachevski." *Songs and More Songs by Tom Lehrer*. New York: Rhino Records, 1997.

———. *Too Many Songs by Tom Lehrer*. New York: Pantheon Books, 1981.

Lundberg, George. *Foundations of Sociology*. New York: Macmillan, 1939.

MacIntyre, Alasdair C. *After Virtue: A Study in Moral Theory*. Notre Dame: University of Notre Dame Press, 1981.

Madden, Edward H. *The Structure of Scientific Thought*. Boston: Houghton Mifflin, 1960.

Mannheim, Karl. *Ideology and Utopia*. San Diego: Harcourt Brace Jovanovich, 1985.

Marjoe. Directed by S. Kernochan and H. Smith. Mauser Productions, 1972.

Meiland, Jack, and Michael Krausz. *Relativism: Cognitive and Moral*. South Bend: University of Notre Dame Press, 1982.

Mill, John Stuart. *Utilitarianism*. Edited by George Sher. Indianapolis: Hackett Publishing Company, 1979.

Moore, G. E. *Principia Ethica*. Cambridge: The University Press, 1903.

Morgan, Marabel. *The Total Woman*. Boston: G. K. Hall, 1975.

Nickell, Joe. "Incredible Cremations: Investigating Spontaneous Combustion Deaths." *Skeptical Inquirer* vol. 11, no. 4 (1987).

———. "Investigative Files: Fiery Tales That Spontaneously Destruct." *Skeptical Inquirer* vol. 22, no. 2 (1998).

———. "Investigative Files: Not-So-Spontaneous Human Combustion." *Skeptical Inquirer* vol. 20, no. 6 (1996).

Niebuhr, H. Richard. *Faith on Earth*. Edited by R. R. Niebuhr. New Haven: Yale University Press, 1989.

Nielsen, Kai. *Ethics without God*. Buffalo: Prometheus Books, 1973.

Nietzsche, Friedrich Wilhelm. *Beyond Good and Evil*. London: Penguin Books, 1990.

———. *Thus Spake Zarathustra*. Buffalo: Prometheus Books, 1993.

Orwell, George. *Nineteen Eighty-Four*. New York: Harcourt, Brace, 1949.

Otto, Rudolf. *The Idea of the Holy*. New York: Oxford University Press, 1958.

Phillips, D. Z. *Death and Immortality*. New York: St. Martin's Press, 1970.

Pinker, Steven. *The Blank Slate*. New York: Viking, 2002.

———. *How the Mind Works*. New York: Norton, 1997.

———. *The Language Instinct*. New York: HarperCollins, 1995.

Plantinga, Alvin. *The Nature of Necessity*. Oxford: Clarendon Press, 1974.

———. *The Ontological Argument*. Garden City, N.Y.: Anchor Books, 1965.

Plato. *Meno*. Translated by G. M. A. Grube. Indianapolis: Hackett Publishing Company, 1980.

———. *The Republic*. Translated by G. M. A. Grube, revised by C. D. C. Reeve. Indianapolis: Hackett Publishing Company, 1992.

Popper, Sir Karl Raimund. *The Logic of Scientific Discovery*. 3rd ed. (revised). London: Hutchinson, 1968.

Rachels, James. *Created from Animals*. Oxford: Oxford University Press, 1990.

———. "Egoism and Moral Skepticism." In *A New Introduction to Philosophy,* edited by Steven M. Cahn. New York: Harper and Row, 1971.

Radner, Daisie, and Michael Radner. *Science and Unreason*. Belmont, CA: Wadsworth Press, 1983.

Rand, Ayn. *Anthem*. Caldwell: Caxton Printers, 1953.

———. *Atlas Shrugged*. New York: Random House, 1957.

Randi, James. *Flim-Flam: Psychics, ESP, Unicorns, and other Delusions*. Buffalo: Prometheus Books, 1982.

Rawls, John. *A Theory of Justice*. Cambridge: Harvard University Press, 1971.

Rousseau, Jean-Jacques. "Discourse on the Sciences and Arts." In *The Basic Political Writings*. Indianapolis: Hackett Publishing Company, 1987.

Russell, Bertrand, and Alfred North Whitehead. *Principia Mathematica*. Cambridge: The University Press, 1910.

Ryle, Gilbert. *The Concept of Mind*. London: Hutchinson, 1949.

Schleiermacher, Friedrich. *On Religion*. Richmond, VA: John Knox Press, 1969.

Searle, John R. *Speech Acts*. Cambridge: The University Press, 1969.

Skinner, B. F. *Beyond Freedom and Dignity*. New York: Knopf, 1971.

Smith, Adam. *The Wealth of Nations*. Abridged. Indianapolis: Hackett Publishing Company, 1993.

Stevenson, Charles. *Facts and Values*. New Haven: Yale University Press, 1963.

Teresa of Avila, St. *Interior Castle*. Garden City, NY: Doubleday, 1961.

Turing, A. M. "Computing Machinery and Intelligence." *Mind* vol. 59, no. 236 (1950).

Unger, Peter K. *Ignorance: A Case for Scepticism*. Oxford: Clarendon Press, 1975.

University of California Associates. "The Freedom of the Will." In *Knowledge and Society*. New York: Appleton-Century-Croft, 1938.

Weatherhead, Leslie Dixon. *The Christian Agnostic*. New York: Abingdon Press, 1965.

Wittgenstein, Ludwig. *Philosophical Investigations*. Oxford: Basil Blackwell, 1968.

——. *Tractatus Logico-Philosophicus*. New York: The Humanities Press, 1961.

Index